# SEXUAL ABERRATIONS

## The Phenomena of Fetishism in Relation to Sex

### WILHELM STEKEL, M.D.

AUTHORIZED ENGLISH VERSION FROM
THE FIRST GERMAN EDITION BY
SAMUEL PARKER, M.D.

INTRODUCTION BY
EMIL A. GUTHEIL, M.D.

VOLUME TWO

LIVERIGHT

NEW YORK

Liveright Paperbound Edition 1971
SBN: 87140-049-9
LCC: 71-149628
MANUFACTURED IN UNITED STATES OF AMERICA

# CONTENTS OF VOLUME TWO

# CONTENTS OF VOLUME TWO

CHAPTER XVI

ANALYSIS OF A CASE OF TRANSVESTITISM

CHAPTER XVII

RETROSPECT AND PROSPECT

# SEXUAL ABERRATIONS

SAINT INGLIS.

# SEXUAL ABERRATIONS

## VOLUME TWO

### XII

### THE ANALYSIS OF A CASE OF APRON FETISHISM

Case No. 55. Alfred G., a thirty-year-old clerk, desires to be liberated from his unhappy passion for aprons and his torturing states of anxiety. Up to a few years ago, he was able to accomplish intercourse with his wife only when she would put on a damp and preferably dirty apron. Recently, however, he has noticed that his sexual interest in his wife has begun to cool and he is sliding back to that totally oblivious interest in aprons which constituted his "ideal" in youth. At fourteen he stole a number of aprons, among them one of his mother's, and hid some of them in the cellar and some in the attic. Whenever he would find the time to hide away and put on one of these aprons, he would masturbate, sometimes per manum, sometimes merely by rubbing. At twenty-eight he married a girl he loved and was able to have intercourse during the first few months without the aid of an apron, but soon found that he was impotent without the presence of that article. His wife knows his weakness and always wears aprons in the house, but he becomes very upset and angry whenever she changes them because he likes to see them quite dirty. This is, of course, a difficult matter because his wife becomes unbearably disgusted when the aprons are too filthy.

With the exception of slight signs on the ears and the suggestion of a pointed skull, he is quite normal physically. He developed normally in childhood, manifests a slightly asthenic habitus, but is well adapted and has a good position in a large firm where his exceeding organizing ability and his mathematical capacities make him a desirable and respected employee. He speaks several languages, but is not much interested in the arts and sciences.

His one hobby is aprons. He can stand and watch them in

store windows for hours at a time. A girl in the streets wearing a dirty or soiled apron provokes him and he finds himself following her. In earlier years he used to masturbate before a mirror with an apron tied about him. He would imagine during the onanism that he were one of the girls whom he had followed.

This is the result of the first hour.

In the second hour he was already making changes in his yesterday's information. He relates the following interesting story about the genesis of the apron fetishism which is marked by a curious connection with water.

"I believe my condition to be due to a childhood impression. As a boy of ten,[1] I went fishing in the high waters of the Isar (a river in the Tyrol and Bavaria—Trans.), but we had to roll up our pants in order not to get wet. While fishing once I suddenly stepped into a deep hole and got wet up as high as my abdomen. As I felt the water lapping at my belly, I had a fine, comfortable sensation which I could not at all explain. Subsequently, I strove to regain this extraordinary feeling, and thus came to search for ever deeper holes while fishing in order that I might, despite my rolled-up trousers, get wet again. That, of course, was possible only during the summer, but when the autumn came—o-oh—the water became icy and I didn't dare go in any more. They had begun to wonder at my going fishing in October when the days became cloudy and rainy, and finally I was forbidden to go to the river in such weather. But I wanted to get that fine feeling again and so I came upon the idea of taking a large tub up to the storeroom and filling it with water. But I didn't dare get my clothes wet, otherwise they would find out the meaning of the tricks which I understood already. I therefore undressed and looked for some other clothes up there, and found them: one of mother's old petticoats, some rags which may have been the remnants of an apron, and an old gunny sack. I bound these rags tightly about my body, so that I was well covered, and then sat down in the tub which usually held only as much as my trunk. When the water ran through the clothes and my phallus became wet I had an almost painfully hard erection. I splashed around so that the water could run, or rather tickle, through the cloth and after wetting my genitals a few times I reached the heights of gratification. Then my phallus got soft again and I felt limp (at that time I did not yet get an ejaculation).

"Following such acts, I felt very guilty, became anxious and ashamed and sensed an inexplicable feeling of regret as if I had done something bad. But I didn't stop. On the contrary, I invented new methods of enhancing my pleasures. I would tie the rags more tightly about me, climb with wet limbs and body about the beams of the attic room or slide about the damp floor of the cellar. My purpose was to make myself as dirty as possible. The dust and soot on the beams or the floor would stick to my wet rags and body and then I would add more water and smear it about to make it even more dirty. These climbing and wallowing parties increased my libido to ecstasy. For these purposes I preferred to use either one of my mother's aprons or an old sack which could be tied about the loins like an apron.

"I continued to enjoy myself in this manner until I married. I am really ashamed to have lied to you in the first hour, but I must confess that I continued this form of onanism even after my marriage, but I masturbated less and less frequently as time went on because I continued to struggle against the habit unceasingly. For the past two years I have not masturbated at all. But my wife had to begin wearing the aprons and I want her always to have one on.

"When they would become wet and dirty I would be able to have an orgasm. If the apron were not wet and soiled I would have either a minimal orgasm during coitus or none at all. And now even the apron is insufficient. I am impotent with my wife and for the past two years I have really been living the life of an ascetic.

"When I began to masturbate, I also became very shy and even to-day I find it hard to make friends or even to make acquaintances. This anxiety is particularly noticeable when I am alone, either by day or by night.

"When I am alone in the wood and find my vista cut off by trees or bushes I become fearful. The rustling of the leaves, the noises of insects or animals, the noise of steps far or near, even the falling of the leaves and the call of the birds scare me. I am also restless and anxious if I find myself alone at home or in the office. I simply cannot be alone.

"My anxiety increases at night. The slightest noise makes me quake; the excitement becomes so great that my heart fairly bursts and my limbs tremble. I begin to shake and feel as if I am going to faint. At the same time, I haven't the courage to find out what may have been the actual cause of the noise.

"I might also mention that I have often actually been followed! But of that another time.

"My anxiety manifests itself particularly when I meet strangers, those unknown to me, especially if they are of a higher social class than myself or if I believe that they are better educated than myself; I fear that I might make a fool of myself because they have gone farther in school than I have. I went to business school soon after my second term in high school.

"Under such circumstances, I often lose control of my thoughts or they cease abruptly as soon as I want to speak. Such a sudden lapse of thought also occurs in my daily life otherwise at frequent intervals and I find myself disturbed in my work. I'll be writing a letter and suddenly I forget a word which I have already formed in my mind. I begin to tremble, lose control of the pen, the writing becomes scribbly and infantile; the letter is a mess and I must write it all over again after having planned my thoughts carefully in advance.

"I am also anxious whenever I go into a restaurant. If I don't see a satisfactory place, i.e., a free table, I feel uncomfortable. I could never sit down with strangers. I'd rather run out of the place. The same is true in trains where I feel a desire to find a seat for myself. It is just as painful a business for me to buy anything, to walk into any store. I usually walk past the place about a dozen times before going in. Invariably I repeat the same actions several times. I may have something important to buy, something which I need very much. But I will first look in through the door to see whether there are many people inside or whether I may be alone, what the lay of the land is, whether I will be stared at by many people, etc. I become almost tongue-tied when I have to ask for some article in the presence of other shoppers who might overhear my request. Embarrassment seizes me, I blush to the roots of my hair, begin to perspire; my voice trembles, I even stammer, my heart palpitates, and I feel so uncomfortable that I could rush out of the place.

"It is therefore my striving always to speak only with one person if possible, and if this is not possible I prefer to forego my desires. The result is that I often find myself running from one store to another, always looking in to see whether anyone is inside or not, trying to convince myself that no one will glare at me. Yesterday, for example, I had to buy a toothbrush and some toothpaste, and for that simple purchase I chased from one store to another for two hours or more. When I was nearly exhausted, I decided to step into a little store where I spied only a single saleswoman, but as soon as I discovered the proprietor behind her, I was almost impelled to turn and run out. I mustered sufficient courage to ask for what I wanted, however, bought the first toothbrush she displayed, gave her the money and faded from the view as if I were a criminal who had just committed an evil crime.

"This trait, this fear of strangers, has already caused me plenty of trouble. But each new day brings me new tortures. In my interviews or dealings, I can't suffer the presence of any but my most intimate friends, i.e., those persons to whom I have become somewhat used. Every new member of the firm is another instrument of torture and fright for me.

"I was transferred by the firm from T. to Vienna, and you can't imagine what groans and sighs that cost me. I have not yet been able to force myself to exchange more than formal greetings and absolutely necessary business with my associates in the office and the result has been that I'm looked upon as an inaccessible prig. They don't know that I'd be the happiest of men to be able to associate with them just as any normal man would. I try my best to overcome my inhibitions and hide my nervousness. For example, I'm always inwardly upset during the first few greetings exchanged with a new acquaintance, my voice trembles, but recently I have been able to control myself sufficiently to let no one realize my state.

"My greatest worries are my sleepless nights. I cough, cough, cough the whole night long, but nothing comes up except a little mucus after several hours of irritation. I sigh for air, roll from side to side, prop up my pillow, pull it down again, roll under the covers like a snail, only to throw them off me again. I groan and puff. In a word, it's hell.

"I first noticed trouble in breathing about six years ago during a vacation trip in Salzburg and a few days later in Traunstein. The symptoms were the following: After having slept about three or four hours, I would awaken from a dream which I could no longer remember and feel a pressure in the throat, and an oppressive sensation in the chest. My breathing was not as free as usual. I could not dispel the thoughts of a few harmless occurrences of the day before from my mind. They shadowed me like obsessions. I got to the window, threw it open and gasped for air.

"That was my first attack. The second one occurred a few days later, under the same circumstances and at the same hour of the night. But gradually the attacks increased in length, they got to be a few hours in length, were soon protracted into the morning or the day, and this last May the asthma continued for a period of three weeks. All the medicines I took were of no avail. At first only my palate was dry, but soon I was coughing, and when the asthma became protracted, I began to bring up a muco-purulent sputum which was filled with fine, wavy and pointed threads. Meanwhile, those obsessions reigned in my brain. My whole body perspired, my hands were weak, I finally became very tired, my thoughts were sluggish. It was like a narcosis. But always the attacks began in the same way. After two or three hours of sleep, I would awaken with the above-mentioned difficulties, torture myself until the dawn; until, on the way to the office, the symptoms would begin to subside and disappear completely after about an hour in the office.

"I was the child of poor people and therefore never enjoyed a very good upbringing. During the vacation days, I always had to run errands for my brother-in-law, i.e., for my mother's brother-in-law.[2] He had convinced my parents that it would be good for me to be busy and also earn a little money. That hurt me, particularly when I would be seen by my schoolmates carrying bundles or packages through the town. But I was a good pupil and always brought good report cards home. At an early age, I changed to business school, but that I had to give up, too, because of the lack of money. I then became an apprentice in a business and had to work until 8:30 every evening; so that I had no further opportunity to continue my education.

"No one ever took the trouble to enlighten me sexually. At seventeen I found my way to another country, became independent and worked for myself. But there was no one to lead me, to be my guide in times of need. I battled with myself to overcome my bashfulness and reticence; I tried all kinds of ways. At twenty-one I returned to Munich and soon after joined several clubs and societies in the hope of forcing myself to make some friends and thus overcome my reticence. I even joined a dramatic club and took small parts in some of their plays. I learned to swim in a swimming club, bought books, took a snack from the cupboard of all the arts and sciences, among them, of course, many popular books on medical subjects. These last deepened my hypochondriacal trends. But, for all the trying, I was as bashful as ever.

"It was the severest test for me to dictate my letters to a stenographer. I usually prefer to write them out myself. My memory often fails, but luckily not in business. It is absolutely impossible for me to remember any jokes, stories, songs, verses and the like."

The report of the asthma attacks interested me more than anything else in the last session and I therefore asked the patient what "immaterial" details he had been thinking of obsessionally during the first attack.

He cannot remember the details, but believes it was a conversation with his wife. He then reports a dream, the first in the analysis, and therefore of considerable importance.

"I was in the theatre, but decided I would prefer to see the performance from the stage. I therefore sneaked up onto the stage and found myself an advantageous position behind one of the scenes.

"A prima donna was just at the heights of her rôle when, stepping further backstage, she discovered me behind the scene. She must have been terribly frightened because it seemed as if her voice faltered. But she caught herself immediately and continued her song although the depth of her feeling had been lost.

"I noticed all this and was just about to get off the stage when I saw a stage officer, with a rifle across his back, already coming for me. I excused myself with something like: 'Pardon me, but I think I have made a great mistake. I had an irresistible desire to get behind the scenes once in my life.'

"At that the policeman drew out a pair of handcuffs and said that he had been ordered to manacle me and take me off, but it seemed as if the President had made a mistake. He did not manacle me. I also recall now having got into the cloak room, but whether or not a little bribe helped to set me free and out of the theatre is only a dim recollection."

This dream is interesting from every point of view. From the analytic point of view, first of all, we see that he is the singer who is supposed to observe herself. But he becomes captivated, charmed, and finally flees. That reveals the well-known flight reflex of all fetishists; they can never bring themselves to say a word about the essence of their fictions. The singer loses her voice the moment she feels herself observed, and from that moment on it's all over with her acting. This

fundamental interpretation leads us to expect stubborn resistance from the patient, and indeed, his memory allegedly dried
up the moment he was to talk about his obsessions (the cause
of the asthma). He said he could remember not one definite
or determining detail.

But the connection of this dream with his fetishism and his
paraphilia are still more interesting. Fetish lovers frequently
have dreams of plays and stage performances (as we have
already seen, e.g., in the case of Beta), and, characteristically
enough, such dreams are often the patient's first. They thus
express the theatrical nature of their parapathia.[8] He is playing
a certain rôle and observes himself at the same time. But he
recognizes that he has committed a serious blunder. He catches
himself in time and his moral ego restrains him. Again the
compulsive, constraining character of fetishism is revealed as
in every other case we have examined.

But the most important source of this dream is doubtless the
infantile one. We can recognize in the language of the dream
the fact that in his infancy he had overheard and seen things
which he should not have seen or heard. The result was that he
was severely punished by his father (the president). In order
not to create any suspicions in him or permit him to go off into
a side-path, I asked him who the singer reminded him of.

He promptly answered: "It was Miss R. who has played a
prominent part in my life."

He was requested to continue his associations on Miss R.,
but instead he fell into a fit of coughing, couldn't talk (like the
singer in the dream) and thus passed through the hour.

The following day, he came with his associations all written
out. I reproduce them here in his own words:

"The prima donna in the dream reminds me of that little Hedwig
R. in Munich. I became acquainted with her and her family
through my friend Otto, who has unfortunately since fallen in the
war. He was engaged to her elder sister and wanted very much
to have me as a brother-in-law, so that our friendship would thus
become closer. I would have taken his sweetheart at once, but I
was a little doubtful of Hedwig. She was too flighty, coquettish
and fickle for me. In addition, she suffered from a slight flaw
in her beauty; she had a somewhat red nose. I would neverthe-

less have married her for Otto's sake if only in order always to
be closely attached to him in this manner.⁴ Hedwig, however,
was at that time infatuated with a well-known actor, Lothar M.,
and was always sending him flowers, post-cards, innumerable love
notes and the like. As I heard from others, her infatuation was
in vain. She was always telling me about Lothar, and it naturally
piqued me that I was only playing second fiddle. I wanted to be
the first in her eyes and this attitude of hers humiliated and hurt
me. I wished that actor all the most evil things and always
chuckled with delight whenever I read an adverse criticism of his
acting.

"But I was also afraid of her passions. I had never before had
any success with women and my onanism with my aprons had
been my chief desire. Would I be able to gratify her? She impressed me as exceedingly temperamental, but I was charmed by
her cheerful character, her keen intelligence and her natural humor.
I was never bored by her company, but I did want to humiliate
her, too. I began to find little faults; she would be too forward,
would make too many demands, be a poor housewife, etc.

"And so I vacillated until one day an unexpected experience
nearly made me lose my poise. We had all the while been having
our little erotic pleasures, of course; our feet met under the table,
we sat close to each other on the sofa, etc. But I had never had
an erection when with her. It was simply that a woman without
an apron never animated me.

"But one day we were at a swimming pool together. They gave
us dressing cabinets next to each other, and I tried to get a look
at her undressing through a crack in the boards. I was successful.
I saw that she had lovely, small breasts, and I became a little excited (this is the first contribution to the dream material. He
had seen something forbidden: the prima donna Hedwig. This is
the uppermost dream level). While undressing, Hedwig softly
sang a cheerful song. She had a pleasant voice and I liked to
hear her. The melody possessed a provoking air which seemed
to remind me of intercourse. Outside, we played and chased each
other about, but as long as she was still dry, I wasn't specially inflamed. I joined her more in a spirit of boyish fun than from any
ardent desire for her. But when we went into the water, my
desires rose. I got prompt and even painful erections each time
her smooth, wet body touched my own. I was losing my senses
rapidly. We went off into the bushes and I hotly desired intercourse. That, of course, would have bound me to her forever.

But my passions were so violent that I could no longer control myself. I had an emission and the danger was past. The impression of her wet body near mine was so great that I shall never forget it. Even outside the pool, I was also excited because the wet suit stuck to her body just like a wet apron. I avoided going to a swimming pool with her again because I realized what the experience would mean to me, and soon afterwards I lost track of her because I had to leave Munich. I even communicated with my friend Otto infrequently."

In analyzing this story, we recognize that it was under the influence of a homosexual impulse (love and the friend) that he tried to become intimate with this Hedwig. But his fear of woman caused him to depreciate her and find all manner of faults in her. He felt humiliated because she preferred the attentions of an actor to his own; he thought her flighty and fickle. When he did have an opportunity to gain her, he turned and fled. He felt happy that "the danger was past." Moreover, he accepted a position away from Munich in order to complete his retreat.

He thinks that he nearly committed a serious blunder with this girl. (That explains the sense of having committed a great mistake in the dream.) His inhibitions were to be breached only by the impression of a wet body, but the ejaculatio præcox acted as a protective signal to him.[5] We shall soon see that there were still other motives for his flight from woman.

I emphasize the fact that the dream must also contain a more remote and infantile impression as a basis for the material.

"Had you ever tried to get a look at a naked woman before that?"

After a short pause he says:

"I know that I used to try to catch a glimpse of my mother naked. I think I was about ten when I heard her washing herself in her room one day. I crept into her room without knocking. She was standing naked before the wash basin and when she saw me she seized an old apron and covered herself in front. She became livid with anger and yelled: 'Get out of here! You scamp! Haven't I told you time and again not to come in here without knocking first?' When she was through, both she and her brother-in-law gave me a good beating and then put me in a dark room for having been so bold. Once I peeked through the keyhole and another time I eavesdropped behind a door. The brother-in-law came in and I was whipped by mother as a 'little spy.' "

This is then one experience which might explain his mania for aprons. But, as we shall see in the course of the analysis, this fetishism developed out of a diversity of components. The above-mentioned experience doubtless aided in the fixation of the mania, and we know that the prima donna of the dream represented the mother, the policeman the father, and the brother-in-law (condensation). Meanwhile his associations continue in another direction.

"I am struck by the fact that I gave that policeman a tip or bribe. That point in the dream must have a meaning. My own attitude towards tips and tipping is pathological. I am always afraid that I have left too small a tip and am then ashamed. Not long ago I spent a fortnight at a hotel with my wife. I worried myself to death about how much I should leave. I finally decided to let my wife do the tipping, but I couldn't show my face about the place because I was ashamed of possibly disappointed faces of waiters and maids.

"Nor do I ever know how much I should give the poor or beggars, and invariably pass them by blushing for shame. At the outbreak of the war in Trieste, there was considerable poverty and we were frequently called upon to aid in charitable undertakings for even well-dressed people. Such conditions are most painful to me. I feel like emptying my pocketbook outright. But, since that would be foolish and was not possible, I chose to walk in alleys and streets where I knew I wouldn't be approached by beggars. Whenever I meet with one of them I cannot continue until I have given him something. For that reason I always try to go out of their way, cross the street or act as if I haven't seen them. But I invariably felt impelled to take one look, at least, at them.

"I cannot suffer injustice or coercion. That holds good for others as well as myself. If I see wrong being done to another or myself, I can lose my bashfulness as well as my patience.

"I would like to love all the world and be loved by all the

world. Like a saint, I would like to excel all other men in virtue. In the office, I have to control myself in order not to become too complacent to my own inferiors in the business. I would like to please everybody. On the other hand, I cannot suffer being unrighteously treated or ruled over by anyone. It is in that respect that I am at a disadvantage here in Vienna. In Trieste, I was a departmental head, but here I haven't yet fitted into any special position and feel as if I'm in prison, in chains." (See the handcuff scene with the policeman.)

The following day he begins to speak of his wife. "I derived the greatest pleasures from my wife when she bathed or was in a wet bathing suit. That was often the case in Trieste, where we frequently went swimming together. I would always sneak into her cabin at the beach afterwards and cohabit with her. It was an irresistible impulse and my wife knew that every time we went bathing, one or more embraces were sure to follow."

"Is a wet suit or dress more effective than an apron?"

"Well, I can't say. I often picture women and girls in wet bathing suits. They accent the body's forms so, you know. It's great to feel a naked or tightly clothed body. My attention to the wet clothing was aroused by Hedwig for the first time. Otherwise I always did and still do interest myself in any woman as long as she wears an apron. I am thus specially attracted by cooks, waitresses, housemaids, and other women who regularly wear these articles of clothing. But I invariably insisted that they have their aprons on when they surrendered to my passions because otherwise I was impotent. That was also the reason why I never let myself in for any permanent relationships with any of them. I usually follow such women at night and try to avoid the busier streets. I never had any truly affectionate feelings for them and valued them only for the fact that they wore aprons, preferably dirty aprons, of course. Clean, white aprons leave me cold. I would feel irritated that the aprons could not always be damp or wet, and that led me to seek such company particularly on rainy nights. I would follow the girls until they were thoroughly wet (i.e., if they happened not to be carrying umbrellas), and would then offer them my escort with an umbrella. This usually opened the way for my designs.  Many of the girls would want to take off their wet clothing first, but I would plead lack of time and effect intercourse with them fully dressed in their wet dresses.  That was, of course, the chief pleasure as far as I was concerned."

"Haven't you ever really been in love?"

"That I can't say.  There are two impulses within me.  As regards the apron affairs, there never was any love contained in them.[6]  I have sometimes felt myself in love with other girls, but it was a pale and diluted sort of love, a vague feeling of something pure and elevated.  I have never really been carried off by a genuinely ardent and inflaming affection.  My senses have never been completely overturned.  I have, unfortunately, never experienced such an emotional sensation.  As soon as I had anything to do with the ideal type of girl, the calculating, critical, astute, sharp-dealing man in me prevailed.  And if I noticed that the contact would never be materially advantageous to me, I dropped the girl."

"In other words, you wanted nothing but a rich girl?"

"That's right.  I was the child of poor people, had bitterly learned what that meant, and wanted to climb out of my station.  I desired that I should have an opportunity to make it better for my children."

"You also want money in order to be able to give it away to others?"

"That would be my greatest pleasure.  But there is really something else in that.  I'm afraid that I would be looked upon as a 'filthy' person."

"But your ideal is a filthy apron."

"Well, those are simply the curious antitheses in my breast.  In my life generally, I'm the cleanest of men—also morally.  I can't stand obscene language or suggestive talk, or vulgar jokes, nor would I ever be able to speak ambiguously or in suggestive language with a woman.  I am a puritanical moralist.  I told you that I would have married Hedwig if I had had intercourse with her.  I never even 'diddled' her, as we say in my part of the country."

He remained quiet for a while and then began to speak about his mother.  "When I was in Ala in my seventeenth year, I asked the elder daughter of our landlady for permission to call her mother and to have her call me by my first name, but unfortunately she wouldn't have it."

"Did she resemble your mother at all?"

"Very much. I certainly needed a substitute for my mother, although I was happy to be away from Munich."

Suddenly his associations pass from his mother to the subject of water.

"Water always fascinates me. I'm always attracted by any body of water, and the larger it is the better I like it. For eight years I was a passionate bicyclist and every trip I made ended at some lake or other. I would look for some inn or café facing the lake and was happy to sit by a window or on the terrace lost in contemplation of the water. I would fall into a sort of quiet ecstasy or reverie from which my comrades always had to awaken me. That usually made me the butt of many jibes, too. In Trieste, I always had rooms facing the sea, and I took advantage of every opportunity to take a ride on the water and stare for hours into the waves. Rough water or stormy seas were a source of direct sexual pleasure.

"As a matter of fact, even a tub bath became a downright sexual danger for me because it always ended in masturbation. The temptation was too great. The water was warm, towels were handy which I could wind about my body. I was alone. How could I withstand that? I finally resorted to confining my bathing activities in Munich to public pools because there were always others about. That protected me against my pathological habits.

"That also reminds me that I invariably scrutinize every woman I look at to see if she is pregnant or not. It seems that water and pregnancy are somehow connected in my mind. When I was a child, they used to tell me that the stork brought babies out of the water.

"I'm pretty sharp about whether a woman is pregnant or not. I can almost smell the fact. I can notice it in the brilliance of the woman's eyes, in her complexion, in a certain rounding out of the figure which is apparently hidden from the notice of others. And if I find that the woman in question is pregnant, perhaps only recently so, she becomes a source of tremendous and irresistible attraction for me. I feel as if I could throw myself upon her and embrace her. I can follow such women for hours. I had the happy opportunity once of touching the abdomen of a pregnant woman and I became so instantaneously ecstatic that I had a convulsive orgasm with ejaculation.

"I was also very happy during my wife's pregnancy—especially during the first few months—and was always wanting to touch her abdomen. During that period I had almost daily intercourse with her, much more frequently than I usually desired.

"I'm very much interested, too, in the hinder parts of women. Women in pantalets (my wife included) animate me particularly (homosexual component). At the beaches and in swimming pools, I always look at the women's bellies and if I see a woman who may be pregnant, I can't take my eyes from her. To appear decent, I look aside for a moment, but my eyes wander irresistibly back to her a moment later.

"That reminds me of an experience I had last year. On the way to the office one day, I noticed a woman who impressed me as being pregnant. I saw her thereafter every day and did not have to wait very long to have my suspicions confirmed. The indirect meeting began to be a happy occurrence for me, and I was deeply hurt one day not to see her as usual. I had had the desire to speak to her some time, but whenever I started to do so my whole body began to tremble, my feet shook, and I couldn't bring myself to approach her. I must mention that this lady (perhaps she was a miss?) did not wear an apron, but either a red jacket or a long velvet coat. Moreover, she was blond. My favorite type. Women with light blond, golden yellow or even a little reddish-blond hair have always been my weakness."

He says he feels dissatisfied in Vienna. In Trieste he was a departmental manager and in Vienna he has to take the place of the head bookkeeper who has joined the colors. But the latter hasn't been called yet, and so our patient has no regular position and dislikes to do any of the less important work. He emphasizes the fact that he cannot stand being bossed.

That is probably the reason why he can never come to the office on time. He even comes ten minutes late for each analytical hour as an expression of his independence and obstinacy. He prefers to walk around the block once or twice if he finds that he has come to his office or to my office on time. The desire for punctuality seems to have left him. But if there is anything important on, which demands his punctual appearance (such as a board meeting, an appointment with the director, etc.), he becomes restless, loses control of himself and commits some blunder or other. He likes to leave the office on the dot, however, and drops his work at the moment his working day is over. In Trieste that was not possible because he had to receive the afternoon's mail and sign reports. It always cost him a great effort, however; he became angry and tried his best to arrange things so that he could be through on time. These traits clearly express his limitless tyranny, his exaggerated sensitivity and his pathological lust for power. Like all fetishists who suffer from an infantile fixation, he struggles for independence. The one compulsion is enough for them and they are not sufficiently strong to suffer the imperatives of another person.

He here produced the second dream of the analysis.

I went back to Trieste to bring my family to Vienna. Before the departure from Trieste, my attention was called to the fact that the Italians had advanced meanwhile, and that the grenades and bombs were already falling in the vicinity of or directly into the stations of Nabresina or Opcina (it wasn't very clear), as I was able to confirm.

I looked out the window—it was night—and convinced myself of the truth of the report. The bombs were throwing up terrible curtains of fire which made the night almost as clear as day.

I asked if the train had to pass through Nabresina or Opcina and received an affirmative answer. That made me change my decision to travel and I told my wife that it was impossible for us to leave under such circumstances. But my wife insisted on our leaving, and we left. The rest of the dream was very vague, but I believe that the bombs dropped near our train. I think that one of the cars was struck, but we got through safely.

This dream portrays to us the important matter of his marriage. He appears to have no definite notion as to why he married altogether. He did want to overcome his paraphilia at any price. His wife had a little money, she pleased him, and he did want to have a virgin. The last factor impressed him as the acme of delight. But he seems to be unable to adjust to the marriage. He is too deeply involved with himself, too strongly chained to his phantasies. Any other woman can attract him as long as she fulfills the conditions of his sexual appetite, but the attractiveness of his wife seems to be fading in his heart. Thereupon he proceeds to produce four children, primarily in order to enjoy the figure of his wife during early pregnancy. The obstetrician finally advised them to have no more children and our patient practises coitus interruptus. His potency thereafter decreased and he has lost all his appetite for intercourse. He really doesn't love his children, for he is too much of an egotist to love anyone but himself. He is allegedly incapable of love.

The analysis of this dream reveals the fact that he is harboring death wishes against his family. In this dream, the last chapter of which he has manifestly censored under the influence of a strong moral streak, he permits the destruction of his family. He is again a bachelor.

I ask him since when he has been suffering from fits of coughing and asthma. It appears that these complaints first appeared after he married. His wife was in her fourth month of pregnancy at the time, she was becoming less and less attractive to him and he hated to think of the idea of becoming "just a father of a family." He feared the loss of his freedom. He hated any form of necessity, like all other fetishists who suffer from the compelling force of their violated sexuality. He wanted his independence again, his liberty to travel and go wherever he desired. He also hated the compulsions of military service and was happy that his asthenic constitution made it possible for his firm to have him exempted from every form of army duty.

Just before his first asthmatic attack which he so well described above, he had been in a motion picture theatre. He saw a film in which a man had strangled his wife. This had quite excited him because he had always been secretly interested in choking and strangling and had let his phantasy play with the act. He had even incorporated the act of strangulation in a little novel which he had written as an expression of his literary bent.

The little inconveniences of marriage irk him. He would like to take up the mandolin again, but he can't do so evenings because of the children. Why should he worry about his children? He wants to have his pleasures. He would like to sing, too, and have his wife accompany him on the piano. But she hasn't any time for such diversion. Everything for the children. Those hateful children.

He begins to see that he had really wanted to strangle his wife, and his own choking, coughing, spitting and wheezing had been unconsciously related with his criminal wishes. Just how disturbing any necessity is to him is well illustrated by the following notes he made the very next night. They depict his spiritual condition distinctly enough.

"Two thirty A.M. Last night my wife put the children to bed somewhat later than usual (quarter to ten) and came out of the bedroom with disheveled hair. This gave me a stab through my whole body because it seemed to me to be an indirect suggestion to go to bed.

"I was reading in *Platen* (*Natürliche Heilmethoden*—Nature Cure; a popular German 'doctor book' of the nature cure variety—Trans.). I was only paging through the chapter on 'Air and Light.' Just before, I had been looking up coltsfoot tea which I had lately been drinking as a substitute for beer. I was showing my children the colored plates of the plant before they went to bed, and had advised them also to drink that brew when they grew up. My eldest son, who usually never drank such teas willingly, suddenly took my glass in his hand, had a sip and found the drink to his taste. I felt a curious unpleasantness at the moment.

"At my wife's request to come to bed, I closed the book, although I had intended to read the next chapter: 'How Shall We Arrange the Home?' (I had already read it once before.)

"I must mention that we always went to bed together. But I couldn't fall asleep, and at two o'clock I got up and began to write these lines. Strangely enough, my coughing has been considerably lighter.

"Thousands upon thousands of thoughts and ideas ran through my head like the threads of a shuttle. I wanted to fixate my thoughts in writing, but I thought to myself: you're a poor, conceited fool.

"The thing that cuts me most is the fact that I'm not original. I could die for despair. I strive to appear as original as possible. I won't be an 'average man.' I will not end by being a Philistine."

We see here how he complies with the necessity of going to bed with his wife, instead of continuing to read as he would wish. He doesn't dare to face her in open rebellion. He is an anarchist who keeps his fists in his pockets. But his irritation is so great that he can't find sleep. I begin the hour with the subject of his originality and say to him:

"You have realized your desire for originality in your fetishism. That's why you're so proud of your illness."

He at first denied such a pride, but gradually confessed that he believed himself to be the only one who suffered from such an extraordinary perversion.

He would like to produce something unusual. The World War showed him how essentially evil humans were. He would like to be the prophet of a new religion of love. He would like to wander from place to place and preach love and faith to all. But his family stands in his way. He feels his spiritual rise inhibited since his marriage. Now is the time to cover oneself with glory, to shout for peace, to become a martyr, to die for one's ideas. But he has to live for his family.

From here I pass to the subject of the tea and ask him why he gave his children the coltsfoot tea to drink. He said it was to have them remember the terrors of the war, but he soon recognized that there were more ulterior thoughts behind the act. These thoughts will help clear up the excitement and the symptoms which followed the incident. He had the phantasy of poisoning his children, his family. How easy it would be to mix a poison with that coltsfoot brew, or to mistake a poisonous liquid for the tea. How easy it would be to wipe out a family in this manner. A few days ago he read in the paper of an entire family dying after the ingestion of poisonous mushrooms. How his heart had palpitated when he read the notice.

Thus the two tendencies struggled on in his breast: the religious and the satanic. He wants to become a saint and is in danger of becoming a criminal. His criminal trends were, as a matter of fact, already indicated by his first dream, his guilt consciousness, his shyness and his fear of being alone with anyone.

He does not yet know—or perhaps he does not want to know—why he is so anxious. We expect the analysis to clear up this dark point.

He came with a strange dream.

I find myself in a church. The preacher is talking about love for man and one's duty to die for the Kaiser. I became excited and called out: "The duties to oneself and one's family come first!" Great buzzing and restlessness in the church. I jump up to the pulpit. My bashfulness has evaporated into thin air. I talk with such passion that all the people in the church fall to their knees. They crowd about me, kiss my hands, my feet, the hem of my coat. Some cry out: "A saint! A saint!" One old man laughed cynically. I wanted to fall upon him. He holds a hatchet in his hand and points to an apron. "I've hacked this to pieces and that's how I'll disclose this impostor." The crowd becomes quiet and stares speechlessly at me. I begin to stammer and lose my strength. At that moment a bomb fell into the church. An airplane had dropped it. A piece of the shrapnel flies close to my head. I awaken in fright. . . .

His first association is that it was a Catholic church. He is a Protestant, but shows a great understanding of Catholicism. He would like to have his whole family become Catholic with him, but his wife is against it. He always attends the Catholic church because he prefers the services to the sobriety of Protestant religion.

What he would like above all is to found a new religion which should stand between the two. In his childhood, he had been very devout and had even thought of becoming a monk. He is engrossed in the figure of Christ and reads voluminously in the Christ legends.

On the other hand, it was plain that his sexuality was to a great extent mixed with his beliefs. As a boy he had often asked himself if Christ may have been built like other men, and sometimes tried to look behind the loin cloth which hides the genitals of the Lord in statues. Once he saw a picture of Christ in church: "The Circumcision of Christ." It made a great impression on him and he played with the idea of castrating himself and also becoming a saint.

He desired to become a second Christ; he wanted to introduce the cult of second baptism. The water is for him the symbol of second baptism. The apron is a symbol of the loin cloth which covers the holy pictures of Christ.

From Christ, his thoughts turn to his father, who was also a pious man. His father was given to fits of anger and often came home drunk. He had been mistreated and fearfully beaten by his father.

His father frequently wore a dirty apron while at work. The patient had one day seized an axe and cut the apron into a thousand pieces. But he feared that the pieces would betray the deed, so he collected them and threw them into the Isar (an alpine torrent which runs through Munich—Trans.).

The dream shows us how this sinful act has continued to burden his conscience. In his unconscious, he knows well that this destruction of the apron was a symbolical patricide. And he, the criminal, now wants to preach the word of God! A bomb will destroy him just as he murdered his father. (The Kaiser is a symbol of his father also; the bomb had already appeared in the second dream.)

With considerable resistance he recounts an experience he had at seventeen in Ala. He had gone into the toilet and seen old feces there. He thought: that's the filth of the landlady or one of her daughters. He found an old cloth, rolled the feces in the cloth and ran to the Etsch (an alpine river—Trans.). At a hidden point on the shore, he spread out the cloth and then lay himself on the feces, so that the dampness wet his belly. He rolled in the filth until he got a violent orgasm and ejaculation. Then he threw the cloth into the river and washed himself in the rushing waters. Afterwards he was seized with deep regret and shame (he was reënacting the part of a nursling in diapers). He can't find an explanation for this strange bit of conduct. He acted under the stress of an irresistible impulse. He felt as in a dream.

Then he tells me that he had originally been disgusted by his mother's dirty aprons. Allegedly, his mother's aprons had never been objects of sexual desire for him.

He hated his mother because she was coarse and had often beaten him severely. He thinks that his present condition is ultimately due to the unjust whippings his parents gave him at the slightest provocation.

He had two dreams.

1. In a restaurant, the waiter said to me: "I really like the Italians better than the Slovenes, because they don't dig in so deeply."

2. I was in Nuremberg and was about to take up a new position. I said: with reservations! "My colleague Neuleben told me that the new job was an unpaid one."

The first dream expresses the struggles in his own soul. There was always trouble between the Italians and Slovenes in Trieste. He thinks the Slovenes too false and sympathizes with the Italians. The Italians impress him as being more honest. The Italians here symbolize the Catholic (pious) tendencies in him, while the Slovenes represent the satanic trends. The satanic habits are more deeply engraved (dug in). He doesn't want to dig them up. The second dream expresses the same sort of resistance to a new life (Neuleben is German for new life—Trans.). His reservation is that he will preserve his old position (i.e., attitude). He doesn't want to give up the enjoyment of his old paraphilia (money as a symbol for love and sexuality).

That episode with the feces in Ala is a sufficient indication of the strong infantile tendencies of the patient. In some fashion his mysophilic instincts are connected with his mother, with an infantile phantasy the significance of which we have not yet comprehended.

At this point he comes with a memory which clearly explains to us the origin of his passion for pregnant women. I must digress to mention that I troubled this patient with very few questions in order to influence the course of the analysis as little as possible. I even did not question him about his family history in the hope that he would come upon that matter himself.

On the way to the hour to-day, he saw a girl who reminded him of his four-year-elder sister. When he was thirteen, he noticed that there was something on her mind. For a year she had been having a secret affair with a student and he believed to have discovered signs that she was pregnant. He watched her very closely and became more and more convinced that he was right. There was soon a scandal at home. Father threatened to drive her out of the house, but mother took the girl's part. The student came of a very wealthy family and his father paid a neat sum as hush-money. The family took the daughter's pregnancy as a sort of lucky business stroke after that, but the patient felt deeply hurt because the neighbors and his schoolmates talked about it.

He confessed, however, that he had really looked upon his sister all the while with lecherous eyes and had envied that university student. He would have liked to be in his place. He later recalls that he frequently watched his sister while she was dressing or washing (the singer of the first dream. Condensation).

At this point he also remembers having been present at a very young age (five years) when his parents were once having intercourse. The mother groaned a lot and father said: "It seems to me that the boy isn't asleep," because Alfred had coughed suddenly. Thereupon his mother became abruptly quiet. He didn't understand what it was all about, but guessed that it had to do with forbidden things.

In respect of the Nuremberg dream, he added that while in Nuremberg once he had been very much interested in the notorious medieval torture chamber in the castle. As a youth, the stories of tortures, inquisitions and martyrdom had ignited his fancy. The menials of torture all wore aprons and such bloody aprons appear to play a leading rôle in his parapathia.

Then he said:

"My sister also wore clothes that we called 'apron clothes.' They were these large sizes to cover up the fact that she was pregnant. When such dresses are dirty or damp, they are doubtless of greater effect on me than anything else."

His preference for pregnant women is automatically explained in these communications. No further commentary is necessary.

He is trying hard to recall as much of his early youth as possible and thinks he has recaptured an occurrence from his fifth year. He had been sent to the store and suddenly came upon four elephants which had broken away from the Hagenbeck circus. They were being taken back to the circus in chains.

This appears to be a screen memory. It is of interest to note that the phantasy of binding or chaining which seems to interest fetishists to a great degree, appeared at such an early age. Can the screen memory mean: I have finally conquered my wild impulses?

The memory of having been present at the coitus of his parents came after that and then came a memory from a very slightly later period. Two boys were practising mutual masturbation in a public toilet and he was supposed to join them. He refused.

There follow some more apron memories. A friend of his who was working in a grocery at the time, also wore an apron. Alfred envied him and often asked for the privilege of putting the apron on himself. The other employees also had leather aprons and he often asked to help them out only for the purpose of being able to put one of them on.

The laborers in the oil refinery wore aprons made of sacks. The sacks were wet with oil in front. Great animation. Tried to get hold of one of these aprons.

Ever since he has developed the death wishes against his family, he has also displayed distinct suicidal tendencies. He thought of killing himself and his family if his condition did not improve. He is often dejected and depressed, especially since he has been in Vienna and finds himself a sort of extra in the firm. It begins to appear that he lost his position in

Trieste and that he doesn't want to put it in so many words. I persist in my strategy of awaiting all confessions instead of forcing them out.

He speaks of his pride. Even as a child he refused to say "thank you" to anyone and was often beaten for his obstinacy. They even spanked him in school for this resistance. To-day he will never thank his chief when the latter has promoted him or given him some bonus or other. He would rather die.

His attitude is well illustrated by the following characteristic dream.

Dr. Stekel was puttering around the window, lost his balance and threatened to fall out. Seeing this, I ran to his aid and, extending myself to the utmost and even endangering my own life, I managed to save the doctor from the fall.

I received the medal of bravery and also recall the words "Now we are square" from a conversation which we afterwards had.

This proud patient cannot suffer the notion of my saving him and his being thankful for it. He must square himself by saving my life.

Freud has given us an acute analysis of the meaning of saving dreams. To save someone means to use them sexually. In other words, homosexual feelings of transference are beginning to appear.

He continues:

"When I was in A. (seventeen years old), I took a meal in a restaurant where I saw two pretty girls who wore aprons. I sneaked into some kind of store-room, found an apron which I put on, and masturbated. It was a terrible situation for some-one might have caught me in the act.

"Once I stole an apron from a beer porter, took it home, where I rolled myself in it and tied it tight, made the floor wet, and then rubbed myself on the wet floor until the skin on my belly became wet. Then I got an ejaculation.

"The aprons must be tied very tightly, and the tighter they are tied the greater is my pleasure in them. Those pretty little aprons which don't even come together in the back leave me absolutely cold.

"In A. I went to a brothel with two of my friends. Just before, I had had a great erection, but when we got there I was impotent (homosexual distraction). One of the boys got so excited in there that he afterwards ordered some ice cream in a café and cooled his penis off with it before our eyes."

While living with a friend in A., he used to masturbate with the use of the coverlet. After every onanistic act, he was disgusted and anxious. Before that he would always go into the cellar and get an apron, but he was never fearful. After masturbation, he thinks he sees ghosts and turns on the lights or a candle.

These bits of information make us rightly suspect that his onanistic habits are connected with criminal phantasies. But he claims that he knows nothing of such phantasies. He's altogether too excited at the time to think of anything.

After a short pause, he relates the following astounding facts. "My wife is in the habit of playing with the genitals of both our boys (four and six years old). I asked her why she did that and she answered me that she had seen her foster-mother doing it and her foster-mother was very good to children, having reared many of them. She had always played with the genitals of the foster-children.

"I also recall that my mother once bathed a nephew of mine (seven years old) and thereby played with his penis."

Suddenly he said: "And now I have caught my very first memory. I may have been three or four years old. My mother was playing with my penis. She played with it for some time, too, and I know that I enjoyed it immensely. It seems that I learned it all from her, for when I was about eight, I used to pay a good deal of attention to my nephew. I would carry him to bed, and often slept with him and held his penis in my hand while asleep."

He begins to cough heavingly.

"Do you know what that coughing means?"

"No—but I've just thought of something. I used to put my nephew's penis in my mouth. I think that my mother used to do that to me, too, when I was a baby. I think I can recall her having done that to my nephew, also."

His obstinacy is so marked that he even finds it hard to pray. He trembles and cannot be alone. When he finds himself alone, he becomes more fearful than ever. It is then that he senses the immensity of the divine power that breaks him down and shows him that the bold son of Prometheus is less than a crawling earthworm.

Nevertheless, he is like all the other anarchistic parapathics who would rather recognize God in the form of some roundabout and superstitious ceremony than in the direct manner of faithful prayer. He is the prey of any kind of nonsense which appeals to the mind in the form of superstition. Thus, for example, he had his horoscope taken and believes firmly that everything that was written down will be realized. That horoscope promised him a superior position following upon great labors. It promised him a long life, and he has faith in the mission of his life.

Ever since the beginning of the analysis, his coughing had been improved and for a time had even ceased altogether, but now it is returning. It is always the same when a determination for a symptom has been disclosed by the analysis. The symptom disappears for a time, but inevitably returns again for the simple reason that it is based upon a multitude of determinants. Aside from that, every parapathia, and thus every parapathic symptom, is not of one, but of several dimensions in the human organism.

He produces some new associations on his coughing.

"I was coughing as early as six or eight years of age. My mother had this asthma, too, and so did the brother-in-law" (the mother's brother-in-law, who plays such a leading rôle in his parapathia).

"Then there was also a fellow living in the same house. He was tuberculous and coughed a lot. This fellow (it was at about the same age, i.e., between six and eight) played with my penis, too, and also put his own in my hands. He took me to the anatomical museum and to the picture gallery, where he showed me all the naked women.[8] It was there that he showed me Adam and Eve. Both had fig leaves over their parts which looked like aprons to me. The man said to me: "Sure, you know what's behind those leaves." That man was doubtless either a homosexual or a bisexual.

Now he is disgusted by all homosexuals. He claims he could never touch a man's penis again, let alone put one in his mouth. As a proof of this he relates a tale about an obese innkeeper who wanted to lead him astray, but the "low devil" wasn't successful.

He says that during a coughing seizure, he has an obsessional thought which aids him in overcoming the attack. He must think repeatedly: "They're all forgotten!" Sometimes he even says this magic formula aloud.

In other words, we can see that he struggles against the memories of fellatio and must keep trying to convince himself that "they're all forgotten."

Another remarkable dream.

I saw a man down in a deep well in danger of his life. There was one person, however, who was giving him to eat and drink and thus saving him from hunger. Finally, one day, he was liberated from his living death by being hauled out with a rope. He half helped himself out.

The dream seems to have been interminable. I saw this man suffering, how they fed him and gave him water, and then the saving scene which also lasted very long.

The functional interpretation of the dream is quite clear. There lives in his breast a "better ego" which has never succumbed. It has secretly been kept alive, it is the anagogic ego (Silberer) which will soon be saved. I am to liberate him from the deep well of his parapathia, and he will help along. The deep well is a symbol of his soul.[9]

The man in the deep well reminds him of a laborer in Trieste: Tiberio. He was an ex-athlete with a wonderfully herculean figure. He was very much feared because, although everybody knew that he was a thief, no one could do anything about it. But—his associations halt, as they always do when he begins to talk about theft.

Then he confesses that Tiberio quite attracted him. He had often wondered how big his penis might be. This reveals a second meaning of the dream: the homosexual component of his life will gradually see the light of day. There follow several corroborations of his interest in the bodies of handsome men.

He had a bad night. He coughed so badly that his wife said to him: "I believe you must have the whooping cough." That reminded him of the fact that he had had a severe case of whooping cough when he was six. His mother had been touching and tender with him, got up innumerable times in the night, gave him tea to drink (see the dream about the coltsfoot tea), took him to bed with her, and often soothed him by means of that old and never-failing method: she played with his penis.

His asthma and coughing spells may thus be conceived as the expression of a wish to have his mother repeat those old and pleasant performances.

His mother is still alive, but he seldom writes to her. He is angry with her without, however, knowing precisely what his deeper reasons are. He thinks it is all because she often beat him.

He dreamed:

I am again on the breakwater at Trieste and watch the play of the waves in the sea. It is just before my departure. A funeral passes by. Some persons near by talk as if the King of Greece had succumbed to the grave battles.

The interpretation is not at all difficult. His condition should die and be buried. He cannot stand the grave battles of the analysis very much longer. The word king reminds him of the fact that his name is Constantine and that he uses the word constant or constantly whenever he can possibly fit it in. It is simply because he is constantly thinking of certain infantile scenes.

He also thinks of the time when his elder son was suffering from an angina and he had thought to himself: if he dies, then . . .

He recalls a playmate who died of diphtheria (at eight). He choked because the inflammation stopped up his windpipe. He himself suffers from a fear of choking on a bit of mucus in the throat (fellatio phantasy?). He tells me that a short time ago a prostitute in Vienna was reported to have choked in the act of fellatio.

He had formerly tried always to have intercourse every evening because he believed that that would insure him a comfortable and restful night. But at the moment that his penis began to get soft, his throat would begin to tickle him. This tickling sensation would increase until, late at night, it would break out into a cough. Yesterday was the first time in two years that he tried to have intercourse, and afterwards he again had that unbearable tickling sensation in the throat. (It is unquestionably a fellatio phantasy which appears softly at first only to increase in clarity and boldness in the course of several hours. Perhaps based on criminal impulses against his wife. Strangling? The latter suspicion was naturally not communicated to him, and he himself came upon the first interpretation.)

Unexpectedly, he begins to talk of the time when he was being nursed. He was not weaned from his mother's breast until very late, and claims that he was nursed for two years (he had told me that he often calls for warm milk in the coughing attack because this may stop it promptly). Those old days have never been forgotten. Whenever he sees a woman nursing a child at her breast, he envies the nursling. He had even suckled at the breast of his wife occasionally when she was nursing their children. He got a great deal of pleasure out of doing it. He is an "eternal baby" and his fellatio phantasies are nothing but the substitute for the breast in the male.

His asthmatic attacks first appeared in Salzburg after a sleepless night. He had accidentally seen a woman there who very much resembled his mother. He had also visited the pontifical palace, where they told him tales about the horrible tortures carried out there in the olden days. After that he went to the cinema, as already mentioned. He had harbored death wishes against his family and had thought that if he were free he would live with his mother again in Munich. It is only now that this has become at all clear to him.

He is subject to fits of anger.  He had once fallen upon his sister with a butcher knife and wanted to stab her.

He thinks he has a too narrow œsophagus and that bits of food get stuck occasionally after he swallows them (displacement from below upwards.  He will probably come to speak of anal things soon).  In a restaurant he is always unnerved when any men watch him eat.  He must turn his head to the left (the homosexual side), and then he feels better.  From eating he comes upon cunnilingus.  He frequently practises this, too; prefers sixty-nine, however (cunnilingus combined with fellatio).

To-day he feels as if something is sticking in his throat.

"What can it be?"

"A worm.  As a little boy, I once vomited up a big worm.  I'm terribly afraid of tape-worms.  I once heard that they are several yards long and can be pulled out of the anus like a rope.  Terrible!  Now I remember that last night I had an obsession on the number 1889, and had to keep repeating it over and over."

I ask him about associations on this number and he first reproduces the fact that he was eight or nine years old when that fellow in the house played with his penis.  He states that he slept in bed with him.

He becomes very excited.

"Something must have happened at that time.  Now I've got a frightful itching in the rectum as if I had a worm there.  I think he tried to put his penis into my anus.  I yelped.  I was half asleep.  I recall it only dimly; more as a feeling than as an actual memory. . . ."

His thoughts turn to blood.  He can't look at it.  A bloody butcher's apron disgusts him thoroughly.  He could vomit at the sight of one and has the shivers.  He is nevertheless attracted by the butcher boys, and has often had to put down the temptation to steal their aprons.

"How did you get from that fellow in the house to the butcher's?"

"Well, I left out something which I was ashamed to say.  I mentioned something about cunnilingus, but I was loathe to tell you that I liked to do it especially during the woman's menstrual period. That was what really got me to talking about blood. That man in the house once made an apron bloody after having killed a chicken."

He has no knowledge of the cause of his fits of temper.

He brings me two more dreams:

1. It appears that I wanted to masturbate again, for I find myself in a cellar and was getting things ready; but I couldn't complete my intentions because the wash house across the way was full. The women in there had on pantalets, and they were washing dirty clothes. I looked for the store-room, but it seems that I was in someone's company for I gave orders for seating the company. Then I awoke with a strong erection and an unbearable tickling in the throat which ended in a protracted fit of coughing.

Then I fell asleep again and had the following dream:

2. I went with a company of my friends to a ball and carried a cushion on my arm. Arrived there, we all seated ourselves and I said: "Sorry, but I must get back to my wife and my company." I found them all in the company of my younger brother-in-law whom I greeted curtly and coolly. My wife was sitting on the outside row and my mother with many relatives on the inside row. My mother said to me: "Have you greeted your uncle B. and aunt V.?" I said softly to myself: "Cousin here and auntie there, uncle here and brother-in-law there," and felt uncomfortable in this crowd. I made a few paradoxical remarks and looked for a back seat. After a while I said to my wife: "Come on. Let's get away from this bunch."

This dream if of paramount significance because it will help us to arrive at the specific phantasy behind his onanistic habits. He wants to masturbate, but the women in pantalets disturb him. That already expresses the bisexual nature of his character. We also note that the onanism has something to do with washing. The continuation of the dream in the following section shows that there are connections with his mother who sits in the innermost circle of his heart, whereas his wife gets one of the outside seats. His mother had been devoted to all her relatives and dedicated herself to them as to a cult. He, however, was so fixated upon her that he wanted her for himself alone. He always was cold towards the relatives because of this jealousy, and his attitude frequently brought him beatings which only increased his hatred. His most hated object was his mother's brother-in-law who is here supplanted by his wife's brother-in-law. His mother's brother-in-law had sent him to work when he was a boy, only in order that the patient might not be in the way of the amorous affairs. That was what the boy suspected, at any rate, when he once caught the brother-in-law kissing his mother. He told his father about it and received for these "lies"—more beatings. Ever since then that brother-in-law dislikes the patient and the latter despises him with an indescribable venom.

The cause of his fits of anger was the jealousy of the mother's brother-in-law and all the other relatives. That was also the basis of his hatred of his sister whom he wished to stab to death.

The following day he comes in with some more important dreams.

Mr. B. made some new suggestions which made it possible to continue our Trieste branch throughout the rest of the war without loss. He claimed that he already had considerable orders for transport, and that I could go back.

I looked the orders over and was able to corroborate the fact that there would be much work, but that there could be no talk of our getting any money out of it. The orders were from the chemical and pharmaceutical firm of J. S. in Trieste, and they were well known to have shopped from one agent to another until they had forced the costs down to bed-rock.

In addition to that, the orders were for pharmaceutical preparations, the export of which was forbidden, and the transportation could thus be carried through only under false manifests. Moreover, most of the shipments were destined for Italy (Verona and Milan), i.e., for our enemies in the war. The result would probably be plenty of trouble.

He then related the following:

"After I awoke from that dream, I recalled the following business deal we had last year. There was a middleman in Trieste who had formerly been a profiteer in groceries, and he gave us an order to clear two carloads of farinaceous goods in Italy and bring them to Trieste.

"The carloads of stuff came into Trieste shortly after each other. They were taxed, and then, after a regular procedure of payment of freight, taxes, incidentals, etc., were regularly put on our books. Shortly thereafter, the ministry of the interior sent out a notice to the effect that all wheat, flour and wheat or flour products could be imported free of duty and that the notice was retroactively effective down to a certain date.

"Now, our tariff manager found out that one of those carloads that we had brought in for that middleman could be brought under the new ruling with the result that the tariff could be demanded in rebate. I reported the fact to Mr. B. and he said that would net us a neat piece of business, if the others didn't find out.

"The tariff bill was dug up, sent back to the department of the interior and the money was actually returned to us. But Mr. B. didn't want to return the money to the middleman because the latter had not thought of the matter himself and had also gained a profiteer's price for the goods anyway. Instead, he divided the booty between himself, the tariff manager and me, with the condition that if the money should some day be demanded back, we were to return the spoils.

"I couldn't put this memory out of my mind for about an hour or two. Then I thought again, as I had often done before, of settling in Syria, Beirut, Jaffa, and the pictures I had seen of these cities and places passed before my mind. My mind then went on to the King of Greece, who has been able to keep out of all the treacherous nets laid for him without losing his independence or disturbing the peace of the land.

"Parallels with my own life arose before me and I thought of how I, too, might preserve my independence."

We know already that he was disconsolate at leaving the pretty city of Trieste and the sea. Vienna is too far inland for him. The Danube is too far away from where he lives. This dream affords us an interpretation of the first dream he had in which he was handcuffed.

He is a scrupulously honest man and has nevertheless been a party to a shady deal. Together with his friend B., who is a light-headed "skirt chaser" and gambler, he pocketed the un-deserved tariff rebate. His general mental condition and his shyness have been much more marked since that experience. He is beginning to realize that his transfer from Trieste to Vienna was not so unmotivated as he had thought, especially since B. was dropped from the firm.

He would like best of all to confess to the whole affair, but he is afraid that that would cost him his position. His suicidal ideas are thus objectively founded.

It is even more interesting to learn that he took the money in order to give it away as alms. This is a motive which we observed in the cases of kleptomania. His motive had to do with the enhancement of his egoistic feeling through giving to others (depreciating them); they are then in the position of receivers and must be thankful (a feeling he cannot produce in himself).

In short, our suspicion that there were real criminal factors present is found to be objectively true.

Discussion of this point and his confessions visibly eased him. He said that he would never do such a thing again and intended to send the money back to the other firm anonymously in order to make good the fraud.

His butcher phantasies become more and more noticeable. He dreams:

I was looking for some butter, but got into a butcher shop. There I found a big ball of butter which was half a tub full. My wife thought I had made a mistake, that it was not butter, but margarine. She was leaving me; I gave her ten crowns, but she put her hand in my pocket for more and said: "Let me touch it." I wanted to convince myself whether it were butter or not. I saw the ball lying on the block. It was margarine.

He had kept that occurrence in Trieste a secret from his wife (there seem to have been several such incidents). He is the false one. He is the margarine. But his chief and his wife had believed that he was as pure as butter.

He cannot explain the fact that butter is sold in a butcher

shop. How did he ever get into that meat store? That must have something to do with his aprons.

Suddenly he recalls the fact that he witnessed the so-called butcher's ride in Munich every year. The young butcher's apprentices would come riding on horses up to a big fountain, pull hides over their heads, jump in and then come out all wet (see the fountain dream).

He is full of sadistic phantasies and memories. Once when he was about five or six, he threw a cat from the fourth floor of a house to the earth. She was alive, but he afterwards ran down and continued to torture her frightfully. He lived for days in the books of Karl May and his Indian tales (Karl May is Germany's Wild West author—Trans.). In his dreams, he killed or disposed of all his enemies. In Trieste, he was thrilled whenever scorpions were stuck on needles and burned.

He frequently recalls a fourfold murder and robbery which occurred in Salmdorf. Four women were murdered. He also talks of other murders or robberies which he can remember from the papers.

Up to his tenth year he himself wore an apron.

At twenty-two, he was a witness to the suicide of a mentally disordered person who had thrown himself to the pavement and lay there crushed, stone dead (compare with the dream about Dr. Stekel throwing himself out the window). He ran away from the scene in fright. He can never give aid at a moment when quick action is necessary.

In dreams which I have failed to mention, the word Ariel seemed to dog him obsessionally. The word has relations with his criminal fraud. He had also had sexual relations with a friend named Aurel when he was about twelve or fourteen. His sister-in-law provokes him sexually, and that is also one of the grounds for his jealousy of his brother-in-law. He feels sensually excited whenever she chooses to call him "brother." Recalls baker's helpers (at seven) who were half stripped and wore aprons.

Then he remembers the incidence of his paraphilia. He was twelve. He filled a tub with water, pulled off his pants, got into the tub and made rocking motions. The first time, he only ducked his buttocks, and only after his sister became pregnant did he begin to get his belly wet, too. When he was four, his parents took him along to a vaudeville show where he saw a Hindu belly dancer who made quite an impression on him. Had the desire to become a belly dancer himself.

He liked to watch his sister nurse her child and envied the little one.

Likes to hear of murders and crimes, reads the court room notices and the murder stories in the paper before anything else. He was animated by the story of Jack the Ripper to an unusual degree and likes to read about his escapades even to-day. Once he slit open one of his sister's bathing suits and then masturbated through the slit (with the phantasy of a ripped-open woman). Whenever his aprons were useless, he would gleefully tear them in two; this always gave him an erection.

That may also explain the fascinating effect of the color red upon him. Once saw a palatable-looking cook in the kitchen of a restaurant; she had on a red dress with a white apron and he became sexually excited. Usually, however, white aprons leave him cold.

Dirty aprons do not interest him, but rather repel him if they are worn by elderly women (mother?).

Here he began to cough hackingly, his ideas began to be flighty and he was unable to say anything coherent.

Just before falling asleep, he had a hypnagogic picture: An open mouth and the number ten (teeth). He connects the picture with the phantasy of fellatio (he is in a state of strong transference; he wanted to call me up in the night to have me come to see him because he felt so badly).

In Trieste he had seen pictures of orgies which had provoked him sensually. The naked men with their naked phalluses had particularly claimed his interest. Pictures of naked women usually make no impression on him.

He offers me a résumé of his anxious states. He is afraid that he may fall or that he may drop out of a window. He never goes into the upper balconies of the theatre because he is afraid to look down. He is afraid to walk alone, to go into dark streets or alleys, afraid of burglars (even carries a loaded pistol). He feels uncomfortable when anyone walks behind him. Three times, he has already run for fear of men being behind him. Often hears noises at night, but hasn't the nerve to get up and find out what the cause of the noises may be. He is still a baby in every respect.

He produced the following dream:

I am sitting at table with my family. A cake is served which has a poisonous green color. I say: "That can't be eaten," and my wife replied: "Certainly it can. It's all right." My boy tried it first and changed color. The other children also change color. They've all tasted the cake. Even my wife begins to choke and vomit. I cry to her: "It's not my fault! You brought the cake home!"

He is patently struggling against his own murderous thoughts. He would like to poison his family. He keeps corrosive sublimate (under a death's head seal) at home, and trembles every time he gives his wife or children an aspirin tablet for fear that he may have made a mistake in the tablets.

He is also afraid that the gas might leak out of the kitchen some time, and frequently looks after each of the gas jets on the stove before going to bed (manifest wishes to kill the family by gas).

He begins to recognize the marked vein of homosexuality in him and now confesses that he is really more attracted by men in aprons than by women. His first apron loves were butcher boys in their bloody store aprons.

Suddenly he produces an important bit of information. It was at an uncle of his in S., the birthplace of his parents. From the back of the house, one could see into the courtyard of a butcher's establishment. He would often watch how they slaughtered the hogs and made the sausages (see the dream about all the relatives and about uncle and cousin B). He was about four to six years old at the time. He also recalls that he was about the same age when he saw that cook with the red dress and the white apron. The innkeeper of that restaurant was also a butcher and slaughtered his hogs and calves himself.

When he is on the street, his eyes seem to see only aprons. At the present time, he is primarily attracted by blue ones. He is fleeing from his blood complex. That is why he has now become so sensitive about butcher's bloody aprons. He cannot look at blood, red sausages or rare roast beef. He cannot look at raw, chopped meat because he afterwards loses his appetite.

When he goes to the barber's, he becomes anxious that the razor might cut his throat. He therefore shaves himself. He cannot watch chickens or squabs have their necks wrung. There are times when he cannot touch meat, and has frequently tried to become a vegetarian, but the doctors always advised him to take to meat again for the sake of his weak lungs. As a boy, he had liked to walk in the cemetery, particularly the one near where his uncle lived. Now, however, he cannot bring himself inside the gate of a cemetery nor can he look calmly at a funeral (see the dream about the funeral in Trieste). It would be absolutely impossible for him to look at a cadaver (nekrophilia?). But as a boy, he had liked to run after the funeral processions and would even visit the biers of the deceased whenever he could.

During her pregnancy, he used to press his wife so strongly to his bosom that she would cry out: "Alfred, take care! The child!" He knows that he wanted to kill the child in the womb. It was only a vague feeling during the first pregnancy, but it became quite clear to him during the second one. The second child suffered from an intestinal catarrh and he had "sympathy" with it. He hoped that it would die and be liberated from its suffering. He even harbored the secret thought of strangling it. The tickling in his throat became worse after that.

He is again potent with his wife, and was observing himself during coitus yesterday. He prods with all his might and feels as if he is in a sort of dreamy state. The penis, in other words, becomes a sort of knife or dagger for him. He phantasies that he is slitting his wife's belly open. He now recognizes the criminal nature of many of his thoughts and says: "How shall I free myself from these pathological ideas? Such notions look to me like old mummies."

He was told that mummies frequently crumble as soon as they are brought to the light of day, and this visibly disturbs him.

Yesterday he saw a butcher wagon and had to fight himself to keep from vomiting. He tells me that that was very unpleasant because at the moment he was caressing a very pleasant memory. When he was ten years old, he fell in love with a charming little blonde. The girl wore a lovely little cream-colored apron. He ran after her wherever he could and tried to be friends with her. She was sent to a piano school and he began to make so much noise about it at home that they finally had to send him there, too. It was during that summer that he once went fishing and got his pants wet. He became so sexually excited over this experience that he quite forgot about the girl.

It was, of course, no real infatuation, because he claims that he was in love only once in his life, and that was with his friend Otto, who got him acquainted with Hedwig. Nevertheless, he was quite precocious and had a girl as early as five years to whom he remained faithful until he was seven. As a boy, however, he was interested in the penis of men more than in anything else. At four he would always run to watch the boys urinate in the courtyard behind the house. One of the neighbors with a very large penis caught his eye and he would always run to the window to see whether that man would come again.

He had another dream:

There was another raise in the restaurant and saloon prices. The raise was on lager beer. Just as if a child were being laid upon the doorstep. But one dare not press it too tightly; nothing must happen. . . .

He is afraid of another pregnancy of his wife whom he represents as lager beer. His house is the restaurant and saloon business. Thought of choking the new-born child because he could not satisfactorily keep it.

He confesses to a hitherto hidden paraphilia which derives from his infantilistic character. He has noticed with fright that small children interest him, especially when they are dropping their excrements. He made fun of himself for this interest, but he became annoyed whenever he saw children in such short dresses that he was able to see most of their bodies. "But," he says, "I looked at them despite my moral revulsion." He likes to watch the eight-month-old baby of his sister-in-law. The genitals are what attract him there. A few weeks ago he saw a little youngster defecating in a side street. He stopped and watched the boy with great interest, although he was irritated with himself for having done so.

And now the various expressions of his infantilistic nature begin to appear. The urine and anal sexuality of his children begin to take up his mind, and he also dwells upon these habits in his own childhood. In reality, he has preserved a good deal of his youth up to date. He has begun to watch animals with application: urinating or copulating dogs and cats. He derives sexual excitement from the show. He often feels as if he himself were a dog.

A week passes with nothing but resistances in the air. He presents me with the opinions of opponents of analysis, declares that he is all through with the material, denies that there is any such thing as a transference and tries to make a laughingstock of the whole thing. Although I am very much interested in his analysis, I tell him that the analysis is over for the reason that he insinuates that analysts like to wring as much as they can from their patients (I must advise my analytical colleagues that they should never show their patients that the analysis is of too great moment to them. I recommend that they take on their patients conditionally, i.e., as long as there is a prospect of getting results). In short, I told him that he was free to leave the analysis on the spot if he wished, that further trial was useless in view of his resistances. But only because of his resistance.

The following day he returned full of regret. He knew full well that it was only because he wanted to say nothing about his relation to his mother. He feels altogether upset, states that he wants to remain what he has been and yet wants to get well. It appears that he cannot give up his taste for aprons. He is ruthless and soft-hearted at the same time. Just before the analysis began, he had had a scene with his wife and as he was about to say something nasty to her, he was overcome with sobs and fell into a fit of tears. He may be sadistic, but not at bottom. His mother is the one who made him bad, he says. He was nothing but the servant, the errand boy, at home. He had to run for milk, for beer, for tobacco and cigarettes, run to the store, get this, get that, go to the relatives, tell them this, tell them that, etc., etc. And always the beatings. Once someone's watch showed one of the hands missing. He was to blame, of course. He swore and protested that he had not touched the watch, but it did him no good. He was told that he was a hopeless sinner who would end on the gallows. "I didn't do it," he cried, but he was kicked and trampled under foot and then beaten so mercilessly with the poker that he fell in a faint. They even threw some of the kindling wood after him at times. But the worst of it was that he would always have to beg their pardon after the beatings, otherwise they would torture him all the more. He was forbidden to play with the other children, and often looked yearningly out the window at the others playing in the yard or the street while he had chores to do in the house. His schoolmates used to laugh at him whenever he went by with his market bag. Hardly had he stopped to exchange a word with them, but he would hear the shrill voice of his mother: "Al-fred!" That "Al-fred!" rings in his ears to this day. The boys used to yell it after him in school.

The apron was the sign of his disgrace. He always wore it whenever he went to the store or worked in the house. He was really a housemaid and identifies himself with such a maid. Moreover, mother always had a stick hidden behind her own apron, and that stick would suddenly be whisked forth to belabor him, even when he had done nothing to call down her wrath.

He portrayed some further experiences of his martyrdom, and I must say that they approached the severity of the heart-rending child tortures which only Dickens knew so well how to describe. This patient's upbringing was the richest garden earth for the cultivation of a sadist and criminal. It is a mark of his excellent constitution and character that, instead, he has developed a Christ neurosis.

He dreamed:

I took an automobile ride without telling anyone at home about it. When I got home, my mother yelled at me and threatened me with the stick: "Where have you been." "What do you want, anyhow?" I replied: "I'm an adult already." I then gave her a long sermon.

It is manifest that he is still battling with the ghost of his mother. The auto ride indicates his autoerotism. He masturbates with thoughts of his mother. He has never dared tell her the truth, but in the dream he finds the nerve to preach to her on punishment. Curiously enough, he has never blamed her for anything since he has reached maturity. He had never become conscious of his lamentable childhood until the analysis had plowed up the heartless acts of his mother. He had annulled them all and wanted to forget them. That is why he became resistive in the analysis just before the true picture of his mother was to appear.

The analysis of this dream lasted about a week, but the efforts were richly paid for by the results. We learn that the patient was an enuretic in his childhood and that that was why his mother had beaten him. Wetting the bed was connected with definite feelings of pleasure. He felt fine lying in the warm, wet, steaming sheets; but his mother flew like a fury into this beautiful world of tropical warmth and dreams. She laid him on the cold, hard floor, so that he might not ruin any more sheets, and there he froze pitifully.

His mother also intruded upon his first period of masturbation which now begins to crawl gradually from out of the well of repression. The dream becomes understandable when we know that he used to masturbate in the toilet, and that his mother used to ask him always why he took so long. She forbade him to hold his hands under the quilt. He hated his mother because she deprived him of every form of pleasure without offering him any substitutes.

His paraphilia is also an obstinate attitude towards the mother. Now that he has grown up, he can do what he pleases. Now he'll masturbate all he wants! In many cases, we shall find that the root of the hatred of the patient against the parents is the parents' forbiddance of the onanism.

Our patient never blamed his mother for her sadistic attitude in beating or punishing him. He suffered it all in quiet.
Even as an adult, he had nothing to say against her. He often
wanted to speak of the mistakes she made in his rearing, but
became sympathetic at the thought of her and kept quiet.
Should he really be thankful to her? Did he really receive her
kisses, after all?

In this dream, he finally settles with her. Unfortunately by
morning he had forgotten the contents of that long sermon.
All this analytical work he carried out without my aid. He
feels that he does not want to blame or depreciate his mother
any further.

Dream:

I had a terrible quarrel with my sister because she butted
into my affairs and said something against my wife. I yelled
at her: "Mind your son and leave me alone!"

He awoke with a frightful tickling in the throat and itching
of the glans penis. It is clear that in this dream memories of
his sister announce themselves. She had also played with him
when he was a child, as it seems. She represented his mother
and he was her doll. She always put him on the pot and often
took him to bed.

There follow various memories of his sister which only corroborate his fixation.

He dreams:

I see large letters: S. . . . T. . . . T. N.

In the night he had had the fleeting thought: Stekel—trust—
not.

He resists the communication of the following material. He
offers the opinion that his parapathia is due to some organic
cause. His mother had told him that his birth was a very difficult one. He also fell out of the carriage as a baby and can
show a scar on his head to this day.

When I insisted that his condition was due to psychic causes
he paused for a moment and then said:

"I never mentioned to you that I watched my mother once
very carefully while she was going through a pregnancy. I

was about six years old. She always wore an apron and was constantly looking to see that the apron was tied on straight because we had a roomer who watched her and laughed at her. He kept repeating that one could see the tree growing through the apron. I was very jealous of him."

"Why were you jealous?"

"Because my mother was very nice to him and frequently was alone with him in a room. I suspected that they had something sexual to do in there."

"What happened to that child that was born after you?"

"It died at birth. I never saw it." (Pause.) "I think that my mother must have killed it because she didn't want to have any more children. The whole thing doesn't seem right to me."

He feels considerably relieved and improved. He no longer shows that "go-getter" spirit, nor does he feel impelled to run after aprons and pregnant women. He feels as if he had been liberated from some duress.

He says that the apron appeals to him as something holy, as a relic. An apron can move him to tears. Everything good that he experienced with his mother seems to be expressed in an apron.

Here we see the bipolar attitude towards his mother. I ask him what good he had ever experienced at the hands of his mother.

He is quiet for a moment and then he says: "I had a most curious dream last night."

"I heard a voice saying: 'Mother has it—mother can do it.' Then numbers seemed to appear before me: 408 or 802 or perhaps 208. Mother said to me: 'I can shine your shoes better than you and your wife, for I use a fatty shine polish.'"

His associations on the dream are the numbers 12 (4 plus 8) and 10 (8 plus 2). The association on shoe shining was masturbation.

It was with some resistance that he divulged the phantasy he had had of his mother playing with his penis; once when he was ten and once when he was twelve. He was then lying next to her in bed. He had masturbated lying there and had thought of her. In his attack of whooping cough, he was always soothed by her playing with his genital. The apron is thus the symbolization of the good mother who plays with his penis.

The following day he brought me these notes which I shall reproduce in his own words.

My Love for Aprons and its Explanation.

"I loved my mother eternally, despite her harshness and cruelty towards me, and I suppose that I love her still with undiminished tenderness. I await her letters with great expectation and tremble as I open them. Almost any hour, I can catch myself phantasying that I am speaking with her, or that I am in her company. I count the days before the next letter comes, and I would gladly throw up everything and travel to where she is if she were ill or needed me. The love I bear my mother —to-day—is but a fragment of that tremendous child's love which filled every moment of my former life. Now there is too much hate and bitterness in it.

"My love is not normal, it is disturbed, the stream is diverted. All my love has fled to aprons, they are my ideal; something grand and holy. They have absorbed all the old and ardent love which I gave my mother.

"What with aprons about me, I cannot offer my mother the love which is due her. I feel very near to her, I like to speak with her, but when she touches me I am filled with revulsion and disgust. It is a sort of negative electricity.

"I can explain this transformation of feeling only as follows: I was always the object of beatings, but between eight and twelve years of age I suffered these beatings at the instigation of that brother-in-law of hers. I hated him and he knew it; he knew, too, that I understood the nature of his relationships with my mother. No one took the slightest notice of either my physical or emotional condition.

"There was one beating especially that I can never forget, and not a day goes by, but that I think of it at least once.

"It is through this sort of unjust punishment that my mother tore my love for her from my heart. On the other hand, I was not capable of giving her up so easily and transferring my affections to someone else. And that is how my love for my mother chose the path which led through the medium of the apron. The apron became my fetish, my ideal, my tyrant, the object which so tortures and mortifies me. I am now become the most unhappy and incompetent of men. My bashfulness, inferiority, reticence, all my confused states derive from this one source.

"More. I have proof for this pathological mother love. I always searched for some substitute for my mother. I have already mentioned that inn in Ala. They had two daughters, the younger of whom was lovely, pretty, good-natured, cheerful, friendly; but the elder of them was sour, repulsive, morose and devoid of any charms or virtues. Although, now, the younger one naturally attracted me more than the other, I asked the elder if I might not call her mother. She refused to help me and the result was that I returned again to my confusing habits. There was no other way out for me.

"I should also like to say something more about the apron masturbation. I was not satisfied simply with tying on the whole apron. I wanted something more. What I really desired was to bind and clothe my whole body. I desired to bind myself in such a manner that my arms and legs also would be clamped. That would force me to masturbate by moving and rubbing my belly, like a snake (this is a manifest revival of a nursling phantasy; he is swaddled in diapers and achieves gratification by rocking movements as Henoch first described. It is also a memory of the belly dancer). I was not able to execute this act, however, for I might have been surprised at any moment. In that event, I should not have had time to release myself, whereas it was always possible for me to take off an apron or a sack quickly. Nevertheless, I always tied my knees tightly together. I think that as a baby, they swaddled my knees well, and now I tie myself just as if I were bandaging my knees. It is also possible that my mother was in the habit of touching my bottom, for I have observed her in the care of other children (my nephew, for example), and have noticed that she frequently coddled the child underneath the diapers. She would run her hand over the pubic region, rub its genitals, and that would please the baby greatly. From that I judge that she did the same to me in the crib and when I was in diapers."

Aprons seem to have lost their attraction for him.   He feels
rather shamed, as if he were attached to patently childish habits.

He had another very important dream.

I was in my apartment when the potter or repair man came
and repaired the hearth in the living room.   When he was
through with that, he went into the next room and, with the aid
of some other workmen, dismantled the stove in there, although
it was in good condition and I had not asked that it be repaired.
Without regard for the furniture in the room, they let the parts
fall upon the sofa which was standing near by.   When I protested, they said the landlord demanded that it be done.   The
landlord was also present in the room, although I had not exchanged a word with him.

Later, I discovered that one of the walls in the living room
seemed loose, it looked as if it were slanting, the paper on the
wall hung away and it appeared that the wall might cave in at
any moment.   I also discovered a hole in the carpet.   Despite
all these uncomfortable conditions, however, I did not leave
the apartment, nor did I have the desire to do so.   I even received visitors, although I can remember that part of the dream
only vaguely.

He expresses his dissatisfaction with the analysis in this
dream.   His fetishism is compared with a warm stove.   He
feels that I have overstepped the bounds of my position.   After
all, what he came for was to get rid of his anxiety and regain
his potency.   What a poor repair man I am!   I am destroying
the finest part of his paraphilia (the stove).   I'm paying no
attention to the protests of his inner soul.   But, not only the
stove, the whole house threatens to crash about him.   Is the
whole structure which he so carefully erected to be destroyed?
And then there is that large hole through which he may con-
veniently peer into his own spirit.   And still he refuses to give
up the paraphilia (his home).   He arranges himself as comfortably as he can, new ideas are added (he even receives
visitors).

The next dream leads us even deeper into the riddle of his
parapathia.   This is a so-called key dream.

I was in a theatre at a special performance. They gave "Faust." In the royal box in the corner at the right, almost against the wall, I saw the "queen" with a large, high crown on her head; the crown seemed almost askew or cocked on her head. At the left, in the same box, I saw the "prince regent"; in order to see him well, I had to bend forward in my seat somewhat.

The royal pair were to be given an ovation, and I saw a man in full dress approaching the box. Arrived there, he presented himself dressed in a large white apron, and I thought to myself: how does this baker get in here?

I recognized in the person of this baker, however, the proprietor of a landscape gardening establishment in Trieste. He was a member of a male choir which called itself "German."

Suddenly I also heard Italian being spoken in the gallery. I looked about and noticed two girls who were dressed alike in red checked dresses. They were playing with a young wild beast (lion?), and were constantly pushing it hither and thither.

It seems that I felt the preparations for the ovation were lasting too long, for I went out to get something. As I went out, I noticed that the wild beast ran after me. In order to shake the animal from my heels, I made a wide detour and actually got rid of it.

I passed a bakery shop and noticed a sign in the window advertising a special kind of corn bread.

I went in to buy the bread, but an old woman told me that it was sold out. When I asked for another kind of bread, I also received a negative answer. I then looked about in the shop and noticed a few rolls in one of the glass show cases. Upon my asking whether I could have those, the woman answered yes, and I bought them. Then I saw a piece of coffee cake and bought that, too. When I came to pay, she mentioned the figure 5.237 and I found it too high. I asked for a detailed account and received the following figures: 4.22; .71; .93. When she said 4.22, I asked her how she came by that high figure. She said she had made a mistake and changed it to 2.23. I figured and figured, but couldn't get the right total. I had already scribbled a whole sheet of paper full of numbers before I arrived at the total of 7.11. But even that wasn't correct, and after some more calculation, I got the sum of 5.11 which was the final amount. As I was about to leave the shop, I noticed still another piece of bread lying there; fine, puffy, bread with large holes in it. At that moment, the baker himself walked into the shop and I told him my wishes and the negative result. The baker also saw the piece of bread lying there and wanted to hide it as quickly as he could. I noticed his intention and said: "Oh, let it lie there: I've already seen it. It makes no difference to me. You may have had it reserved for some one."

Then I went out of the shop. It was raining. I looked at my watch and saw that it was 7 o'clock. Hang it! Now I've missed the better part of the performance, especially the part with Margaret and those fine monologues of "Faust."

Here I awakened in a bath of perspiration, and got a fearful tickling in the throat with a subsequent attack of coughing. About an hour later, I fell asleep again.

We recall the first dream he had about the prima donna. In this dream, he repeats the same theme with a slight variation. The chief member of the audience here is the mother (queen). Indeed, her diadem sits somewhat askew on her head, but this is simply the first bit of depreciation in the dream. He must bend himself (bow) somewhat in order to see the prince regent (father and father images). We know, also, that he had witnessed his parents during intercourse. The ovation is to be introduced by a man in a black full dress who also wears a large white apron. He recognizes this man as a "German." This name reminds him of the name of his hated rival, that brother-in-law (Schermann) who apparently represents the king here and appears as the prince regent. He is, in short, doubly represented—once as the man he is and again as the representative of the honoring public.

The two girls with the lion represent both the children of his parents, i.e., himself and his sister. He thus appears in a female rôle, but the lion is a symbolization of his restrained virility, his aggressive tendencies. He desires to be rid of the animal in him, the lion, and flees. We recall that he left Munich because he could no longer stand it there. The baker is his rival, the brother-in-law. The bakeshop is his mother. He can no longer get any love (the corn bread that was so desirable during the war). The bake woman only has a few rolls left. She certainly had his father well rolled up. The rolls are in a glass show case where everyone can see them; only his father could not notice.

And now we come to those mysterious numbers which remind us of his other dream with numerals. In the other dream he presented the figures 208 and 802. 422 is the same, since 4 times 2 is 8 and that makes 82. 71 also discloses the number 8 in 7 plus 1, but the number 93 is still a puzzle. He notices, however, that the baker still has bread. He has seen something ("I have already seen it"). We know that the play in the first dream was also "Faust," but this dream becomes clearer when we learn that his mother's name was Margaret.

He analyzes on the numbers for a few days, and it soon appears that they all have something to do with birthdates of his family members. The most important factor is yet to be told, however. He is not sure whether he has mentioned it to me already or not, but he is sure that he witnessed a coitus scene between his mother and her brother-in-law. One day in the summer—it was in August—he came home somewhat early and heard a suspicious noise. He saw his mother performing fellatio on the brother-in-law and he performing cunnilingus on his mother. He also remembers the date now. It was the 2 August (8), 1893. He was born in 1887 and was thus seven years old at the time. His birthday is the 2 September (11), and that of his mother the 22 March (3), or 223.

This date engraved itself forever on his mind. He hated the uncle who robbed him of his mother's love. It was on that critical day that he made use of his well-known weapon. He coughed in order to make his presence known. His mother quickly stopped the love scene and, at the express command of the brother-in-law, who claimed that he had left the store too early, he was severely punished. The brother-in-law was not a baker, but he had a pastry shop and also sold bread and rolls, which Alfred, of course, had to deliver. And now we understand the basis of his resistances. He had always known of this scene, but he believes that he actually told me about it. His first tales, however, were either phantasies or screen memories.

He dreamed again.

I was on the way home (at night) and was carrying a chair of a writing desk set before me. I was nearly at the door of the house when I saw a man go in before me and soon after come right out again. He had no hat on and it appeared that he had no key with which to go in again, and was therefore waiting for me.

At the moment that I arrived in front of the door, I noticed a woman, dressed in a hat and jacket, appear at my side; and before I could realize or notice who she was, I felt myself seized upon by her and grasped by the throat. I could not free myself immediately and began to yell for my wife, who ran out and helped to liberate me.

Then I wanted to continue on my way, but was attacked a few more times; suddenly I saw myself attacked from both sides, a man being among the attackers.

I cried for help again, but I can't recall whether my wife came to my aid or not. At any rate, I was able to shake off my attackers each time, until the woman was left behind. At least she didn't fall upon me any more, but only the man continued pursuing me. I asked him what he wanted from me, what I had done to him; told him that he should mind his own business and leave me alone. Finally, he went into some store —I think a fruit store—and used that opportunity to sneak off into some hallway. My wife came after me, calling my name. I think there was a café in the first floor of the house. I went into it later to look out for my attacker, but I saw nothing further of him.

In essence, this dream continues the subject of the former dream. To understand both this and the "butcher's apron," we must know that he wanted to kill the brother-in-law. He would have liked to slaughter him like a swine. He really left Munich in order that he might not give way to his murderous passions (the lion). He also wanted to let his father know about it, to write to him, but he didn't have the courage (the stool for the writing desk). The man in the dream is the brother-in-law and the woman is his mother. He cannot free himself from either. He also wanted to strangle the brother-in-law (coughing), and in the dream it is he who is grasped by the throat (principle of the lex talionis. Singular similarity, also, to the Hamlet motif). His wife, i.e., his marriage is to liberate him from the bonds of his mother and homosexuality (father and physician). The brother-in-law also becomes the representative of homosexuality. The patient realizes now that he was originally attached to that brother-in-law and actually respected him. As long as he had been a little boy, the brother-in-law had played with him and had given him little gifts. He had changed his attitude towards the boy as soon as he noticed that the boy's jealousy had made him unpleasant; particularly since the boy was in a position to tell the father about the whole affair.

The pastry man also sold coffee in his shop and that explains the last part of the dream. In the first floor of the shop, he had a little café.

He wants to know why he can never write the letter l in combination with the letter d. When I asked him what first came to his mind on that matter he said: "Low down."

That was what he thought of his mother, but had never said.

He brings me another little essay entitled:

### CONTRIBUTION TO THE PSYCHOLOGY OF MY COUGH

"The basis of my unhappiness is my completely distorted upbringing. It broke my back and also destroyed my self-respect. I have lost my sense of individuality. The worst of it was the manner in which my mother treated me. If I stopped to play with a comrade or if I did not return rapidly enough from one of my never-ending errands—and I could never return too quickly for her—she would put her head out the window and crow: 'Alfred! Where are you?' Her calls could be heard in the whole neighborhood. And if I didn't show up immediately, she began to curse, swear, froth in such a manner that all the neighbors laughed. My schoolmates all laughed at me and called after me: 'Alfred! Where are you?' That was my nickname.

"Often she would get red in the face when she threatened me with: 'Just you wait, you scamp, you. You'll be tickled when you get upstairs. You'll get what's coming to you. Then I knew that I'd get it, and the whole block knew it, too. I whimpered and shrunk, I wanted to fade away or disappear into the earth. I bounded upstairs quickly, so that no one would see my disgrace.

"But I loved this woman despite all this mistreatment.

"I became bashful and reticent, however. I suffer from a feeling of inferiority which I shall never overcome. Where would I not be to-day if I had not been burdened with the onus of this depressing feeling of imperfection!

"In Trieste, I was the head of the department, and yet I trembled before every new addition to the force, indeed, before every one of the errand boys. The matter of being introduced or having anyone introduced to me was very painful. I thought that every new person was far more educated or knew much more than I; that they would recognize this at the first glance and realize that I was an inferior person. I would blush terribly, stammer foolish words, gasp for air. Oh, I tell you it was unbearable.

"Receiving new customers or having to do with any other important personages was also a martyrdom for me. I trembled in my whole body, became weak to the point of being unable to stand. Frequently I was so afraid that I had to run to the toilet every fifteen minutes.

"The whole thing began in Ala when I was seventeen and alone in the world. I was living with a rather well-educated family and soon saw that I knew nothing. I studied day and night in order to fill the breaches; but I didn't have the proper guidance, the result being that I simply gathered a lot of undigested facts together without having any systematic understanding of what they meant.

"The almost insurmountable obstacle was the first step in becoming acquainted with a person. This situation forced me into a side path for aid. I began to cough discreetly. I would cough my way out of any embarrassing situation, so to speak. I didn't have to say anything right away for I had time during the cough to think of what I wanted to say. This method doubtless was discovered or invented by my second ego. It is only now that I am conscious that the other part of me chose this means perhaps in memory of my mother who used to soothe me so during my attack of whooping cough. It was as if I were actually inviting the sympathy of all mankind just as I had gained hers.

"I now recall many remarks I heard about my coughing

which should have made me think a little. But you are the first who opened my eyes. You said yesterday: 'You always greet me with a cough.' And recently you said: 'Whenever you have something important to say, you cough instead.'

"That made me think and review my life a little. I saw that you were right. The cough expresses my embarrassment and my excitement. It helps me over the dead spots.

"I'm like the fire department, always ready and always putting something out. It is my cough that is always ready. The cough of embarrassment is about the best description for it.

"I make use of the cough as a defense of my weak position. It helps me change the subject of a conversation, it awakens sympathy, covers my faults, enables me to spar for time.

"More and more, I am retiring into myself. I don't seem to be capable of feeling my way into the spirits of others or of giving them any joy. I seem to live as in a dream and pass life by.

"I know very well that my reticence has something to do with my criminal tendencies, too; that I have already learned from you. But why am I so shy in the presence of every new acquaintance? What is it that I expect? What do I fear from them?

"You see, therefore, that the beginning of my unhappiness was a flight into the coughing spell. I do not deny the sexual significance of the cough. I understand it completely. But I am speaking here only of the beginning of my condition when I exploited the cough as a disguise for my inferiority."

It is necessary to complete the patient's essay in some respects. The cough also represents a memory of his faithless mother, his good mother, his sins. The tickling in his throat is the desire for fellatio which he wanted to perform originally on the brother-in-law and in place of his mother. He is obsessed by the fixed idea: "Where can I find a friend whom I can love in this way?" That is why he is so embarrassed in the presence of every new acquaintance. He is full of the expectation that his wishes may be realized, but one of the means he employs ambivalently, i.e., in a bipolar manner. He protects himself against failure by pausing in his speech to cough. The cough is a spiritual betrayal, it insinuates a desire on his part for a sexual contact.

During the first few days of the analysis, this asthmatic cough was always the preface to an impassioned eulogy of the new treatment, that was how he always introduced his expressions of transference. The stronger the transference became, the stronger became the cough.

The asthma and the cough are just as complicated in their sources and structure as his apron fetishism. Numerous components have combined to form just this coughing spell.

He now recalls that when he was a child, his mother always kept him close to her; to such an extent that the neighbors all said: "That kid has grown to her apron strings!" He says that he sometimes has the feeling that an apron is not made of cloth, but is some sort of skin, something living.

He is the mother. He would like to be the mother.

The next dream explains the apron and the fellatio phantasy in another light.

I am in a circus which looks like a ball of crystal. Red light. I am sitting in a small loge and look through a small window into the circus which is as yet unlit. Suddenly some man stuck a long bar of sugar right through the window into my mouth. I bit a piece off . . . and awoke with a great erection.

This dream is a typical maternal womb dream. He is within his mother's body, peeps out of a small opening; his father appears and he bites his father's penis off.

His first association to this dream, the interpretation of which I did not disclose to him, is: flea circus. He once saw a flea circus and found it very amusing. Then he tells me that he once wrote a little story about a flea which is supposed to be sitting on the edge of a woman's vulva and relating in a humorous manner all the divers things that it witnessed. He also confessed to a phantasy of being a very minute little human, a Lilliputian, living in the body of a giantess.

Spontaneously he then continues as follows: "I am sometimes very uncomfortable in small rooms. I get the feeling that I'm in a coffin, and fear that I might be buried alive.

And yet, every evening before I fall asleep, I play as if I'm digging my way in. I literally bury myself in the bed, roll up like an armadillo and pull the covers over me. My wife has often told me that that was not good for my cough.

"I like to smell my own wind, too. I haven't the slightest disgust with my own body. As a matter of fact, I've tasted everything my body produces: what's between my toes, the cheesy formation under the foreskin, ear wax, my own urine, everything. I can't understand why a man should be repelled by his own physical products. One's mother doesn't feel that way about it."

From here his thoughts again passed to his mother and his infantile days. He thinks about his birth and says: "I was born with a lucky hood on my head, but I never had any luck in life. I think that the hood is also a representative of the apron and my mother's skin. When I think of apron, I often think of what they call the Hottentot apron [the artificially elongated labia of Hottentot women—Trans.] When performing cunnilingus, I like to look at the labia and would like to elongate them. I really desired a wife with long labia—with a Hottentot apron.

"I now remember several dreams I had in which I was buried alive. In many instances, I was very small in those dreams. It is as if I wanted to crawl back into my mother's womb. Yes, now I'm sure of it, the apron is nothing but my mother's skin. I remember a dream I had before I ever came to see you. It quite excited me without my having been able to understand why.

"I thought myself dressed in a wet apron which felt absolutely smooth, almost like silk. I could not have enough of feeling my belly, punching it, kneading it, stroking it, as if it were the Holiest of Holies, the dearest and most cherished thing I possessed. In the course of the dream, I wanted to have intercourse with my wife, but it did not succeed. Her vagina was too narrow; and that because my wife began to get smaller and smaller, and finally turned into a child. . . ."

In this dream, the apron is really the skin of his mother. His mother actually was the Holiest of Holies for him, the dearest and most cherished thing he possessed. Before her, his wife dwindles and shrinks to nothing and goes through just those changes that he would like to experience, i.e., she becomes a child again.

He effects an identification with his mother in this dream, and when he puts on an apron, he becomes his mother.

He could pray before an apron. He would like to clothe all the holy statues in aprons and then perform his prayers before them.

His apron fetishism is at an end. An apron no longer possesses a sexual appeal to him. He produces several corroborations of his womb phantasies. He is now interested in cannibalism and revelled in the thought that the embryo in the womb really lives on the blood and tissue of the mother. Suckling is a substitute for such blood sucking.

Thoughts of necrophilia and vampiric trends announce themselves.

He has become indisposed and sends me the following associations without being able to come to the office.

"A business friend of mine recently related to me his impressions during the transportation of cadavers, which he had to accompany, from Arco, Riva, Gardone and Salo [frequented resorts for the tuberculous on Lake Garda, Italy—Trans.].

"His descriptions of the things he saw there awakened a horror in me at the suffering those undergo who are afflicted with that disease. The result was that I had several torturous dreams during the days that I listened to his tales.

"Thus, I dreamed once that I was to receive a cadaver in Arco and accompany it home. The relatives of the deceased invited me to dinner which was to be served in the dining salon of the sanatorium where the patient had lived.

"I felt a surge of distaste come over me at the thought of sitting down to eat in that room filled with consumptives. I finally refused to come there and managed to get them to change the dinner to a private room where there were no consumptives. But I don't recall whether I was actually able to eat in the dream or not.

"Another time I dreamed again of being in some resort which was frequented by the tuberculous and everywhere I looked, on all the walls, stairs, walks, and railings, there were nothing but spitting cups and more spitting cups. I watched the strolling guests coughing into portable cups or into their handkerchiefs. I was utterly disgusted and had a terrible fear of being infected.

"Still another time I accompanied a body in a freight car. Despite my certain knowledge that the cadaver was enclosed in the coffins, I was in mortal fear that the dead man would rise up again. The train also seemed to move so slowly; there were always obstacles in the way.

"When it came to delivering the body, the relatives didn't want to pay the bill and said they would pay later. But I was not permitted to do this. My firm had given me strict orders in the matter. The result was a lot of bargaining, and such bartering over the dead body was very mortifying to me.

"It is probable that I had many more such dreams at about that time, but I can't recall any more very clearly. But from that time on, I looked upon consumptives as non-existent for this life. They excite my sympathy and I can already see them in their coffins, being eaten by the worms.

"The memory of this tale must have had some connection with my attitude towards my wife. It may have been the result of the impression these stories of my friend made upon me.

"My wife's parents both died of tuberculosis; the father had often been a visitor in southern sanatoria; the mother contracted it during her puerperal period.

"These facts made me somewhat anxious about my wife; I feared that she might have inherited the deadly germ and would, perhaps, infect me, too. As I can now see it clearly, I was especially anxious during the first years of our married life whenever I would kiss her or have intercourse with her.

"Furthermore, it now seems to me that the apron which I so greatly desired my wife to wear during intercourse, and which I also invariably grasped firmly in one hand, appeared to me to be a sort of protecting spirit; lying between us, it protected me from infection ( ??). [The question marks were added by the patient.]

"But when I was diagnosed last year as suffering from a 'pulmonary catarrh,' the very opposite mechanism set in. I circumscribed my sexual activities with my wife and also

stopped kissing her so frequently—from fear that I might infect her!

"It is barely possible that this was also the basis for the
criminal in me coming to the fore. Perhaps I wanted to act
murderously towards my wife in order to prevent her death
post partum.

"Frequently I was irritated and tortured by thoughts which
made me fear that my wife and I would die as her parents had,
and leave the children behind as orphans. Whenever I wanted
to sleep with my wife, these tormenting notions danced before
my eyes.

"My persistent anxiety about pulmonary tuberculosis is still
indicated by the great interest I have in my sputum, my inces-
sant desire 'to examine it,' look for things (bacilli?) in it,
etc.

"I can put that even more clearly: I often see myself and my
wife as cadavers. I see both of us dead, and often when I want
to cohabit with my wife, these pictures of death and disintegra-
tion arise before me. It kills my desire and my appetite, my
erection changes to collapse, but I continue to clasp the apron
firmly in my hand; I fall asleep a little and dream something,
then awaken with a renewed erection which I lose promptly
when I turn to coitus. All that has been improved, however.
I can now cohabit without the use of the apron, but the death
ideas still torment me occasionally."

Here we have learned of another fact which he had hitherto
withheld from us. It is that his wife had to wear an apron
during coitus, otherwise he was impotent. This apron he would
clasp firmly in his hand. He would crumple it. That means
that he incorporated the memory of his mother in his cohabitation with his wife. His wife became his mother, quite contrary to the situation in that other dream in which she was
transformed into a child. He sees his wife dead, which leads
us to surmise that he must have had necrophilic ideas about his
mother. He is the worm (womb phantasies—being buried
alive) who eats away his mother's body. Indeed, in the very
next hour, he spoke about his fears that his wife might die during pregnancy and take a living child into the grave with her.

His fear of cadavers corresponds to a desire on his part to have something to do with the dead.

It is a frequent habit for people to hold something in their hands during intercourse. I know a woman who must always crumple a piece of paper in her hand if she is to achieve orgasm. She thus expresses strangling phantasies.

"I notice that my ascetic tendency is becoming more marked. I have apparently lost my impotence and have no need of the apron any more. But I'm constantly wondering whether I shouldn't cut down on sexual intercourse; it's the fear that I might die of consumption, I guess. They say I have a touch of it. I can't say. When I was in the army, they said at first it was on the left and then they said I had it on the right side. It's probably all a fake. Nevertheless, I make use of everything that may excuse me from my 'manly duties,' and that despite the fact that I know my wife expects me to fulfill them.

"I have also observed myself a little more closely by day and I must say that you were right when you told me that the cause of my distracted state lies in the wealth of my phantasies. I never realized that I worked with only half my mind. But now I see that I'm always dabbling in my sexual phantasies. Yesterday I caught myself humming some lullaby that I learned from mother. I often think of her and would like best of all to return to Munich and visit her. But I know that that would be foolish; it would only drive me deeper into my illness. I have also caught myself playing with innumerable other phantasies which I would have considered impossible not long ago. It seems that I think of nothing but my childhood and my mother from morn till night. I'm still dreaming of revenge against that brother-in-law although he is now an old and broken man."

And finally he begins to say something about his father:

"I consider that my father's lack of love for me had a great deal to do with my present condition.

"My father was the only son of a rather well-to-do workman. His father died when he was young and his mother married a second and then a third time (the helper in their own shop). My step-grandfather III was a crass egoist, a notorious brawler, gambler and drunkard. My father was nine years old at the time and had to live with strangers because his step-father drove him out of the house. Father became a goldsmith and had to work hard all his life, while my step-grandfather squandered all the money. The shop and the house came under the hammer. Father's life was a bitter one from the very start: deprivation, lack of love, need, constant fear and excitement. That may have influenced his character, too. His only pleasure was singing. He had a strong, clear tenor voice and was proud as a peacock whenever he could shine forth in his choral society.

"He was also very strict with me, but beat me very seldom. He was powerless against my mother and had nothing to say at home. It is possible that he was quite tender with me during my infancy, but I later heard nary a tender word from him. He was always quiet at home, and the only one with whom he spoke was my sister. He nevertheless took her waywardness very much to heart, and subsequently became more serious and shut in than ever. I think that he knew of my mother's habits, perhaps even of her relations with her brother-in-law. But he kept quiet because he didn't want any disturbance; he always tried to get out of the house and meet with his choral society. That was why I was always in my mother's hands, and never had an opportunity to enjoy my father's love. At present the relationship between my parents seems to be somewhat better; I suppose because they are old now and need each other more. I also want to mention the fact that despite my sorry financial position I still send them money. I always send it to mother, who never fails to write me thanks."

He brings me a dream which is a stereotype for him. He has already had it in various forms.

I have rented a room in a brothel, but I don't live or sleep there; I only come occasionally to collect my mail. Arrived in my room on the third floor, I seem always to be awaiting something special. The visit of a pretty girl who never comes. Instead there always appears a woman from the next room, dressed as if ready to go out. She doubtless has designs upon me, for she invariably seeks to draw me into a conversation. But because this woman never interests me and I find her altogether repulsive, the conversation lasts a very short time. A few letters are carelessly strewn across the table which stands in the middle of the room. I catch sight of a marriage notice. In the further course of the dream, I always demand a glass of beer, but I don't get that either; there's always some excuse for the delay or else something turns up meanwhile.

At the last visit to my room, I found the saloon on the ground floor empty; the bartender was not there. I took this opportunity finally to get myself a glass of beer, got a glass, filled it at the beer faucet and wanted to take it up to my room. But I was unsuccessful for I spilt the brew on the way up the stairs, and arrived in my room with an empty glass. The empty glass didn't appear to be just an empty glass, however, but rather more like a large spoon, with beer running down the left side and then the right side.

Such stereotyped dreams usually contain a situation which is expressive of the parapathia. The symbolization runs according to the law of psychic parallelism.

We must first of all note the affective side of the dream. He is in a state of expectancy. But instead of the person he is awaiting, another appears to whom he is either indifferent or who is repulsive. The affect of the expected enjoyment which is never realized is then further portrayed in the second part of the dream by the drink of beer which he would like to have but never gets.

It is the spoon which runs over, which reveals the true infantile situation, however. He expects milk and gets, instead, porridge. It is nothing but the trauma of weaning which is being expressed again in the dream. He was two years old before he was weaned, and at that age it was certainly a very emotional experience for him. The faithlessness of his mother is portrayed by his living in a brothel. Instead of the young mother (the pretty girl), he meets with an aging mother (who will soon die, i.e., soon leave him and pass out). This dream represents all his feelings of disappointment in his mother's lack of love for him. But he is still yearning for the days when she was nursing him. He is an eternal nursling. His affective attitude towards tips also is based upon his phantasies. He would want to drink of the love of every man.

He then openly ventilates his criminal thoughts as follows:

"When my first son grew to be able to stand up in his carriage he would frequently jump about in such a lively fashion that he would fall out of the carriage when not watched. At such moments, two entirely antithetical thoughts would shoot through my brain. The first one was the hope that the fall had not harmed him, that he should not have received some injury to the brain and that I should not be cursed with an idiotic child as a result.

The other thought, however, plainly disclosed the hope that the child's life might be snuffed out; probably in order that I might thus be freed from the bonds of marriage.

"I went to a concert to-day. They played the 'Eroica' first and then the funeral march from the Götterdämmerung. Whereas I had been quite composed until the first intermission, the beginning of the funeral march provoked a strong tickling in my throat which I could not keep from developing into a cough. It all embarrassed me very much. I felt oppressed, the concert hall seemed too hot. The tickling sensation became worse. I felt shivers running through my whole body. Goose flesh.

"I caught myself in the phantasy of following the funeral of my wife and children. . . .

"Up to the time they were about two, both my boys had choking spells several times. The attacks were so severe that they would become livid and their eyes would bulge out. These attacks occurred every time they were required to do something against their will (fits of anger).

"We would hold the children under running water and beat them with wet cloths in order to restore them to consciousness, but I always helped only half-heartedly. I was usually no more than a passive witness to the scene.

"While, on the one hand, I would fear that they were about to die in such an attack, another thought would also occupy my mind, viz., 'that other man' in me seemed to feel that it would be better for them to die then and there rather than return to life.

"Every time I cough, I am afraid that I'm going to choke to death. I know now why I so frequently wished my children

to choke. Why am I such an unhappy man? I want everybody to be happy, want to help everyone; I can't think of myself doing anyone the least harm, and yet I find myself daily
harboring wishes for the death of my family. Am I still en-
slaved by the thought of returning to my mother to make the
last days of her life happier? My intelligence makes me laugh
at this idea of yours, but my unconscious recognizes it as true."

"Sometimes I think the apron is a reflection of my inner soul.
I became infected with a venereal disease during my marriage
and kept it quiet from my wife. It is ever since then that I
notice an increase in my taste for dirty aprons. I always became irritated whenever my wife changed a dirty one for a
clean or laundered one. Why do I droop my eyes whenever her
own seek me out lovingly? Because I feel myself an unclean,
vile man. It is really laughable that I should want to preach
a religion of love to all the world. I, the criminal, who wants
to kill his wife and children, his own flesh and blood; who
wishes them death daily, simply for the sake of his own paltry
egoistic ideas.

"Often I tell myself that I must be free before I can live for
mankind. But now I realize that all that is nothing but a
roundabout expression of my egoistic self, that which you call
rationalizations. I've hitched my wagon to a star, I'm ambitious and would like to excel all men. My day-dreams are iden-
tical with my dreams in sleep. I have phantasied that I could
fly high above all other men without a machine, without wings,
without even so much as the movement of my arms. I possess
a magic cap with which I can fly through all of space; give
orders which must be followed without being seen by anyone."

He dreams:
I found myself back in the old shop in Munich, only the
office had been moved. On the side where the windows were,
the room had an oblique wall, in short, it was like an attic
room. I was just in the process of discussing a possible change
of rooms with my former chief bookkeeper (next to it there
was a large, airy room which caught the sun, but it had the disadvantage of having a small window onto the office of the di.

rector which meant that one would be observed all day) when a sickly and haggard-looking young woman started to hurry through the room. I immediately recognized her as a former office friend, Miss K., and called her back. We greeted each other. She: "Well, Alfred!" and I: "You here again? Is that the bit of baggage I thought I had left on board the *Bo.'.emia?"*

" 'Yes, I'm unhappiness itself and that's why I didn't give you a good-bye kiss as you wanted to have me do.' With that she disappeared. I had a lot of sympathy for that girl, perhaps I even loved her. More than mere friendship might have come out of our relationship had she not led such a free and easy life. She was too good for me. I was after money, too, however, and she had nothing. She, on the other hand, wanted wealth herself, clothes, good times, and all the rest. I lost sight of her soon, but I must mention that we often joked about getting married. I was afraid of her, however, and left Munich. I was after money. I had been in Trieste two years when in she walked into the office and told me about getting married to someone in India and being off on the *Bohemia.* She stopped over in Trieste for three days before she left, and I kept her company. She said that she was coming back in three years. It was during those three days that I noticed how much I liked her. She had a cheerful disposition which provoked me very much. I hardly believe that I had any death wishes with her, for last night I was constantly dreaming about the death of my wife and children; first one and then the next would go off."

The more he talked of Miss K., the more I realize that he had really loved her deeply, but had suppressed his affection for her purely out of ulterior intellectual motives. It is she who was represented by the singer, the prima donna, of the first dream, and Hedwig turns out to have been but a screen figure for this woman whom he wished to suppress in his mind. He confesses to dreams about her, many of them, dreams in which he was married to her. In the above dream, he changes rooms, his old home (marriage) is too oblique and bare for him. With this girl he would have a "larger and airier room which caught the sun." He praises her sunny disposition, her charms, her figure; she was like a gazelle. To be sure, she was a little too clever and sure of herself to suit him. But he would have been able to dispense with the aprons with her. She had suspected that there was something wrong with him and had often told him: "I'd first have to get your childish ideas out of your head." He felt himself transparent under her gaze (in the dream he felt himself observed by the director through the little window). He was often bashful in her presence.

But he is certain that his apron mania would have crumbled in her presence. And yet he fled from her, left Munich for another country (the second time; I am not now speaking of the first trip). He later married without love, but only to improve his financial condition. He chose a simple woman whom he could tyrannize and compel to submit to his apron mania.

And what was the result of this violation of his innermost desires? An unhappy marriage and the progressive development of his parapathia. He suffered the torments of the damned because he felt that he hated his family, wished them dead that he might return to Miss K.

In the dream she, too, seems to be suffering, she looks sickly. She yearns for him. She is unhappy. The *Bohemia*, that great ship, sped her away into the land of suffering. She is unhappy, just as he is. They belong together, to each other. She is the incarnation of unhappiness. And again the scene where she takes leave of him forever appears before his mind's eye.

After three days of utter happiness together, they found themselves aboard the ship. He was to bid her good-bye. They had been very dear to each other, but he had not touched her. She was too proud and said: "The man who kisses me is the man who'll marry me." But she nevertheless promised to give him a good-bye kiss. At the last moment, however, she refused to keep her promise and said: "I think it would be better if we didn't kiss each other. We'd never be able to part." She turned away and cried bitterly. He, too, was deeply affected and left the ship disconsolate. As the ship moved out of the harbor, he felt as if it were bearing his happiness away with it forever.

During those three days a terrific struggle had been going on within him. He wanted to tell her to stay and become his wife.

He wanted to sacrifice his whole fetishism, his mother, his aprons, everything. But some demon within his breast compelled him to change his view of her, to depreciate her, to find little faults in her, to tell himself that they would not suit each other.

But now he realizes that she would have been the only one to cure him through the medium of her love. She would have made him forget all his old fixations. He destroyed his happiness and future when he let her go. Every man has an inner voice—a prima donna—which he must follow. His own conscience had told him: marry this girl (she would never have agreed to an affair). But he began to brood within himself, to introspect (he was the man who wanted to get behind the scenes). And the result was that the singer lost her voice. Love flew out the window. And he returned to the chains of his fetishism. That is the meaning of his first dream. In it he had told of the unhappiness of his love life, and how he himself was to blame for it.

He has committed the greatest crime which a man can commit against himself: he has passed up the opportunity of love for the sake of the base god Mammon.

Still another significance of the dream has reference to his relation to the director of the business. There are several things he has on his conscience and in this room he would feel himself too constantly under the director's eye. His work gives him no pleasure. He would much prefer to stay in bed and excuse himself on account of his asthma. Every morning he feels tired and weighted with lassitude.

I shall omit several dreams which had to do with the development of his criminal phantasies. The very fact that he crumples the apron in one hand while cohabiting is an indication of his phantasy of choking his wife. That is unquestionably a major component of his cough. One of his dreams makes it more or less plain that he was hounded by the impulse to attack a salesgirl in a shop, choke her and then gag her with an apron. He struggles manfully against the impulse, but he is compelled to play at least the first part of the phantasy, he seems to need at least a remnant of reality to satisfy him. That is why he is always looking for shops where there is only one salesgirl. That is why he is so shy and reticent and full of guilt feelings. He has been indulging in criminal phantasies to such an extent that he has begun to see them in reality.

His mother had often said to him: "You're a light-headed kid. You ought to be hanged." He frequently had day-dreams of being thrown in prison, turned over to the executioner, etc.

The idea of becoming an executioner himself had often provoked his fancy. The henchmen of the torturers and inquisitors in the olden days all wore aprons while at work. The apron of the butchers is nothing but a more sociable expression of the executioner's apron (here again we meet with the sado-masochistic component of fetishism which never fails to appear in any case).

His asthma has finally disappeared completely. He knows now that he was simply manifesting the choking on himself. He has, however, also noticed that his wife's libido has cooled considerably. He has been paying attentions to his wife's sister (see the dream about the sister and his becoming a brother-in-law). She appeals to him, he is interested in her child and likes to watch her nurse the baby. As her brother-in-law he would like to start something with her, obviously as an expression of the old, old constellation in his own life.

He saw the baby once sucking on the corner of a pillow and recalled that he had sucked on the lappets of aprons as a baby. "As I have already told you, an apron was never an inanimate thing for me. It was a puzzling, mysterious bit of life. It was God and the Devil, Punishment and Lust, a warning and a temptation all in one. It is even more difficult for me to express the feeling I often got that I myself were the apron. At times I was also subject to a mysterious confusion of all my concepts. The apron was I and I was the apron, an *unio mystica,* which can only be felt but not described.

"I know also that one of the reasons why I held on so firmly to the aprons during coitus was because I didn't want to lose the old one. What you call autistic thought is very characteristic of me. Lately I have been torn by frightful conflicts. The aprons seem to speak to me with living voices: 'Don't leave me! Don't give me up!' And I become weak and feel as if I'll fall back into my old ways and whims. But no! I must not give in. Last night was the first time I was able to have intercourse without the aid of an apron. I'll get my sister-in-law out of my head, too; particularly since I have learned that I'm interested only in reviving the scene between my mother and her brother-in-law."

"Yesterday I went to the bathhouse and became sexually excited. I was able to restrain my emotions, however, except when I was soaping my genitals. At that moment, I saw the light as if blinds had dropped from my eyes. My mother used to soap my genitals in the bath until I would get an erection. She did the same thing with my nephew, too. To take a bath was a real party. And that's why I get so excited in the bath. That's why I like the water so. I want to be a boy again, be splashed with water, and pleasantly soaped by my mother.

"While bathing me, mother would always wear a dirty old apron to protect herself from my splashing.

"Yesterday I thought all day about that girl I let go. You were right. I always was afraid of love because I didn't want to give up my old love. I married my wife, after all, simply because she was not dangerous, because she never threatened to monopolize my heart. But I have been bitterly disappointed. I yearn for my mother, for my childhood. I yearn for the impossible. I'd like to see the dead alive again, the past resurrected. A dead apron revived in the form of my living mother. I really must give up my phantasies, my day-dreams will be the ruin of me. I feel happy when I am not at work because then I can indulge myself in building castles in the air. I'm really struggling against my day-dreaming habits. I'm forcing myself to work.

"I'm also plagued by a feeling of superiority in my work and am doing my best to get rid of it. I know that I'll never amount to very much. I'll be satisfied to be a man like other men. You have shown me my goal: I shall seek my happiness in reality and find it in some quiet corner of the earth. I'll live for my wife and my children. I'll be a forthright man in the office.

My resolutions are of the best. I hope that I shall be able to realize them."

He visited the family physician who had been unable to find anything organically wrong with him and had advised a change of air.

He feels that his apron fetishism has been cured. He senses a certain new pleasure in his wife and can play with the children. He has realized that he was chasing dreams which were incapable of fulfillment. He still has the best of resolutions.

In the last hour he said: "I have just thought of something which doubtless represents the end of my apron fetishism. As a small boy of about seven, I frequently had to go to the cellar and get wood and coal, but I was always supposed to knock the coal in little pieces first and make kindling sticks out of the wood. They told me to wear an apron, but I refused to do so because I felt that the neighbors would see me. But I am sure that I already had a separate apron up in the attic at that time which I used for my onanistic acts. I can't tell, however, whether I had begun the habit at the time I was bringing in wood. But I do know that I frequently used to chop and cut my aprons into thousands of pieces with an axe or hatchet. I can't count the number of aprons which I sacrificed in this way. I was markedly vicious in this respect whenever mother was in the room with the brother-in-law and I was sent for coal and wood. Then I would furiously cut an apron to pieces and throw it on the coal pile or burn it up. I was jealous and wanted to kill mother and the brother-in-law. I even played with the thought of setting fire to the house while they were in the room together. But when father would come home at night and take off his working apron, I would get so depressed that I could have cried.

"My mother was really bad to me. It was only when I was ill that she would show signs of affection. That's why I got sick so often, and that's the reason why I'm still in the habit of getting sympathy by means of suffering. I can wriggle out of any responsible task by simply increasing my cough. Then

I can lie in bed and indulge myself in day-dreams to my heart's content, as you already know.

"I have already told you the last detail: I wanted to kill my mother and her brother-in-law with the axe or smoke them out, i.e., burn them to death, but I was too weak and cowardly. Later I read the story of Orestes and Agamemnon. It scared me. That was just my conflict. I often have a feeling that I must revenge my father. Once when father was ill, I thought that mother had poisoned him. But I dropped that idea. I know that he will die a natural death, and he is probably not blind at all. He was probably glad that his brother-in-law had taken that wild and domineering woman off his hands and left him in peace. . . .

"But that woman ruined my life. Of that I'm sure. . . ."

He went to the mountains for a rest, resolved to begin life anew and shake off his past after the "breathing spell." But he was destined never to realize his intentions.

A friend invited him on an automobile trip to Mariazell, a famous pilgrimage in the Viennese Alps. On one of the serpentine roads in the hills, the automobile skidded, he was thrown out of the car, and died instantly from a fractured skull.

The analysis is at an end. For scientific reasons, I conducted the analysis in such a manner as to direct no leading questions at the patient. I wanted to use this analysis as an example, to show that we analysts do not read anything into the patient's mind, that we do not guide him in certain paths. This patient had never read any of my books. He produced his material in an entirely spontaneous fashion, and his most illuminating communications were his dreams. I interrupted his own words only to give him the most necessary interpretations and assurances.

And now the question of the diagnosis. This is manifestly a case of genuine fetishism. Alfred was, indeed, no ascetic, but he was well on the way towards becoming one. Certain recuperative tendencies always impelled him to cohabitation, but we may recall that he was able to effect intercourse only with the aid of an apron. He also disclosed a tendency to col-

lect his fetishes, for we know that he had quite a stock of them
at home and gave many of them to his wife who had to humor
her husband's whims if only in order to gain sexual gratification herself.  Most marriages are characterized by such com-
promises.  Alfred also reveals the typical compulsions and the
artful system of a fetishistic parapathia.

The most striking factor is the very extraordinary condensation contained in the apron as a symbol.  We begin to realize
how schematic and superficial is the explanation given by Binet
that fetishism is due to a single infantile impression.

Freud [10] correctly writes: "Deep driving psychoanalytical
studies have led us to a justified criticism of Binet's position.
All of the observations I have mentioned have to do with the
patient's first contact with the fetish, and that at a time when
the fetish already possessed sexual interest without it being apparent from the attendant circumstances how the fetish acquired those sexual properties.  Furthermore, these 'early' impressions are said to have occurred after the fifth and sixth
years, whereas psychoanalysis has made us suspicious of the
possibility of such fixations being formed anew at that late age.
The actual situation is rather that behind the memory of the
first appearance of the fetish there lies hidden a repressed and
forgotten phase of sexual development which is represented by
the fetish as by a screen memory.  The fetish thus represents
the remainder, the precipitation of that sexual phase.  The
transformation of this phase of sexual development in the
earliest years of infancy to fetishism, as well as the choice of
the fetish itself, are constitutionally determined."

In a later publication,[11] Freud still clung to this point of view
although he stated it somewhat more precisely.  He writes here
of a primary perversion.

"One of the components of the sexual function is to be conceived as having developed faster than the others, became independent sooner, became fixed and thus diverted from the further
stream of development.  This independent fixation, however,
may be conceived as a sign of a special and anomalous constitution.  We know that such a perversion need not at all be
present for life, it may later suffer repression and be replaced
by a reaction formation or transformed by sublimation.  If

these changes fail to take place, however, the perversion persists throughout the adult life of the individual. Wherever we find such a sexual deviation—perversion, fetishism or inversion —there we may justifiably expect to find such a fixating experience in the early life of the individual through the means of careful anamnestic analysis. Indeed, long before the days of psychoanalysis, careful observers such as Binet were able to trace such sexual deviations of adults back to experiences in the fifth or sixth years of age. True enough, such explanations met with intellectual resistance on the part of some because the fixating experiences were in no wise traumatic in nature, they were, on the contrary, banal occurrences which lacked any effect on others. It was not possible to say just why the sexual life of the individual had become anchored to these experiences. But the significance of such experiences may be sought in the fact that they may have offered the precociously developed sexual component of which we spoke an opportunity for fixation, albeit accidental in nature; and we must be prepared to see the chain of causal connections which we construct end somewhere, at least temporarily. It is precisely the concept of the hereditary constitution which appears to meet all the requirements of such a fixation point."

These theoretical statements contain a sound and solid nucleus. The allegedly first memory is actually a screen memory in most instances. But there are unquestionably cases in which the fixating experience may take place between the sixth and even eighteenth year, as long as the experience is sufficiently emotional. What I consider to be incorrect and unfounded in these elucidations is the concept of a constitutionally conditioned fetishistic leaning. Our case doesn't show a trace of the constitutional disposition which is always used as umbrage whenever the psychological puzzles are not solved.

Sadger's declaration that the fetish is the representative of the mother's (or the father's) genital is just as abstruse. But let us suppose that this statement contains a kernel of truth, especially in view of the fact that our last patient actually strove to return to his mother. What would we gain by the supposition? Is the apron really nothing but a substitute for the mother's vagina? We have seen that the fetishism in this case was a myriad of components, a veritable mosaic of divers strivings. The picture is composed of innumerable stones, and only the composite of them all can form the true picture of the fetishism.

And now let us analyze the various component mechanism contained in the last case.

1. The apron is symbol of his infancy, of his psycho-sexual infantilism. The whole form of his masturbatory practices shows us that he strives to return to the first two years of his life, particularly to the time when he was swaddled in diapers. The apron is thus also a symbol of the diaper and the apron of his mother. The organic feelings of pleasure which he had when he became wet in diapers, smeared himself with feces and urine, are preserved and revived in his present habits (see the numerous examples in "Infantile Psycho-sexuality" in this series; but there the individuals did not reach the fetishistic stage). The apron is thus a memory of his nursing days.

2. His regression in phantasy goes even further. It goes back to his mother's womb. This phantasy cannot be conceived as an engram; it must have appeared later and expresses an anagogic wish to begin life anew (Silberer) and simultaneously the wish to unite with the mother without the guilt of sexual intercourse. The apron thus becomes a symbol of the mother's womb and of the mother as a whole (mother's womb phantasy).

3. The phantasy of intercourse with his mother—provoked by the numerous escapades she had, and enhanced by traumatic observations of her—is emphasized by his crumpling an apron in his hand during intercourse. He clings to his mother. He desires intercourse with her.

4. The apron is for him distinctly bisexual in meaning. Men in aprons; thus his father as the first perhaps, although this was only vaguely expressed in the analysis; but later there were ideal men in aprons. He is just as interested in the phallus as in the vagina. The apron is thus also the symbol of his father's phallus, of the phallus of men altogether, as well as of the vagina (the Hottentot skirt).

5. The apron is the symbol of his humiliation. His first humiliating experience was related to an apron. The apron expresses his disgrace and demands his revenge. It is an

eternal mememto (Adler) and serves to irritate his ambition.

6. The dirty apron reflects to him the viciousness of his soul, full of criminal thoughts. The apron speaks for his conscience, it expresses his criminal tendencies (criminal phantasies), and simultaneously the protection against these trends as given in his moral denouncement of them.

7. The apron is also something holy and elevated, something to which he can pray. It expresses his yearning for the pure mother, the woman who could become the mother of God. It covers the genitals of Christ. It requires him to atone and practise self-denial. Bipolar tendencies just as in the case of a taboo. The apron is taboo, it is God. It is the symbol of his Christ neurosis.

8. The apron is a protective mechanism and also his very own invention. It is the creation of his own phantasies, the one thing which divides him from the general average of man (solipsism and autistic thought). The apron is the triumph of his personality, the symbolization of his individuality, his independence of all the sexual objects of the world. It liberates him from the tyranny of the female. The apron is his very own!

9. The apron is something alive and pulsating and simultaneously the representative of the dead. He identifies himself with his apron. He is the apron and the apron is he (animism).

10. The apron is covered with blood; it is the apron of the butcher, the executioner. It symbolizes the crime and his expiation, his criminal phantasies and his atonement (sadism).

11. The apron must be tightly tied. It symbolizes the compulsion and his impulse. He simply must run after every apron and skirt he sees. He is firmly bound to the impressions of his childhood. His very attitude during coitus (holding and crumpling the apron) is a distinct manifestation of this compulsive obsession, this fixation to his mother. The apron is a symbol of this compulsion.

12. The apron possesses a mystical significance. It has a magic power, a charm; it is a talisman; it makes him potent and impotent. It is not dead, but alive.

Out of a living human he formed a symbol and then infused this symbol with all the qualities of a human, indeed, with divine features. The apron is veritably a fetish, a secret god, his hidden religion. This religion finds its chief expression in the adoration of his mother. The combined figures of his mother and the Virgin Mary are fused to a mystic unity which contains the features of the father, the mother and the child.

The apron is his trinity.

These determinants partly clarify his fetishism. But the condensation goes much deeper than that. He exploits every occurrence in life in terms of his apron. It is the hub of his mental universe, the center of gravity about which his thoughts gravitate.

We can arrive at an explanation of the genesis of this fetishism only by supposing that there was some greatly affective experience which became the crystallization nucleus for a system. So far we agree with Binet. But the crystallization is formed about the nucleus (Stendhal), there is systematization, layer by layer is added until there appears a complicated structure which resembles a true compulsion neurosis. Each new apron impression is added to the structure like a new onion coat about the old onion. Finally, this tumor so pervades the tissues of normal life that the major portion of the normal spiritual life is monopolized by it.

When do such fetishists come to the analyst? Why do they come altogether? Certainly never because of their fetishism, but only because their fetishism has made them incapable of working or enjoying life. Our patient, too, constantly emphasized his distractability, his unhappiness, his lack of concentration. It cost him more and more energy to do the same amount of work. His day-dreams became more and more active, he needed an ever-increasing perseverance in order to keep himself from fleeing into the arms of illness (his cough).

But what is behind the whole thing? The repression of an affect, a pathological impulse, by means of a protective mechanism; displacement and symbolization enter; distortion and theatricality. The whole problem is switched to a side track.

The nucleus of the syndrome is the impulse. This impulse is of a complex nature and derives from several other divers impulses. The most important basic impulse is doubtless his trend towards the past. The desire to revive a dead life. This is expressed in the hidden wish to return to his mother, embrace her, kiss her, recapture her and—perhaps possess her.

His mother is an old woman who would be distasteful to him if he could differentiate between reality and phantasy. What he is really acting upon is the memory of another mother, the woman who was his mother in his infancy, the mother who soothed him when he had whooping cough, and played with his penis. But such realities are ethereal to the parapathic; he is oblivious of them. He demands the impossible. He reveals the prelogical thought which Levy-Brühl described so well as typical of aboriginal and primitive peoples. The impulse is an aboriginal, a primitive reaction with him. An unfulfilled wish strives towards realization, but expresses itself in the form of a symbol. The entire clinical picture, the illness, is an "as if" situation (Vaihinger), in which only the laws of the pleasure principle operate. The incestuous impulses are experienced in a strictly fictitious world of day-dreams. The reality principle appears to have been cast into oblivion.

Still other impulses are of a criminal nature. He would like to kill his mother and murder that hated brother-in-law (as well as the father) with an axe.

His upbringing destroyed his feeling of self-respect. He was humiliated and might just as well have become a criminal as a parapathic. A criminal who would revenge himself upon society for the crimes committed against him in his youth. But, instead, he saves himself in his religious faith and in savior phantasies. He is the good, the noble, the sympathetic and compassionate soul who would give a beggar all he had. This noble man has, however, never learned the one thing which characterizes the true savior: humility. He cannot bend to the desires and needs of others, he cannot thank anyone for anything. He wants to rule. Even in love he was unable to give himself up to the one he wanted to love, i.e., he was unable to bow to her, and fled. He recognizes but one mistress: his apron. He looks up to her, submits, acclaims her. This apron protects him against any and all other failures and humiliations. He can play the paraphilic and also live the life of an ascetic. It was not without foundation that he joined a dramatic club. He learned an art which was not in the least strange to him.

Has he not always been playing a game, acting before himself and all the world? Who would ever suspect that this shy, reticent, trembling, embarrassed and bashful man were a boundless tyrant at heart, possessed of the utmost cruelty? He has reason enough to be shy and retiring. We have seen how close to the surface of his soul his criminal intent against his wife and children came. We have heard that his uprightness was shaken only during the war—unfortunately just as in many other persons who had hitherto practised honesty and faithfulness, and would have continued to practise them unto death, if the war had not shaken all our social feelings to their roots.

Unfortunately, too, death took him all too soon, before the stability of his reorganized spirit could be tested and tried. It was characteristic that his friend and he should have been on the way to a pilgrimage. On the way to his God, he met death. Secretly, he believed in miracles and had often told me that he expected his final cure to be effected by a miracle.

That also disclosed his relation to the primitive mind. All these fetishists await their salvation in miracles, through enlightenment and sudden premonitions. Many of the wanderings of these patients are nothing but pilgrimages into the land of wonders. What Alfred expected was the absolutely miraculous, the impossible: he expected to find his mother young, good and loving, as she had once been; he would begin life anew with her. He, who had wished his wife and family dead, had left her alone and had gone on a pilgrimage into the land where he had desired to send them.

# XIII

## HEELS AND NAILS IN LOVE-LIFE

There is not an organ of the human body, not a single article of clothing or of daily use which may not become an object of fetishism.  In the case studied in the last chapter, we observed an almost inconceivable condensation in the fetishistic symbol of the apron.  The symbol, the fetish, is the focus of all the rays of the individual's consciousness.  And as long as one has not understood this phenomenon of condensation, the cases of this kind will remain an eternal mystery.

In this chapter, I shall present two cases which will demonstrate a special type of shoe fetishism.  The patients were attracted to shoe nails or tacks.  The first case was not analyzed, but the second was thoroughly studied.

Case 56.  Charcot and Magnan reported the case of an eccentric man who was sexually provoked only by the nails of women's shoes.  His peculiarity drove him to most strikingly extravagant acts.

He strives always to get a look at the tacks or nails in women's shoes, carefully examines the traces of the nails in the snow or wet earth, listens for the sound of nailed heels on the sidewalk.  He finds ineffable pleasure also in repeating words or phases to himself which may conjure up in his mind the image of these things.  In short, he comprises the essence of his bliss in one phrase: "to shoe a woman" (*ferrer une femme*).

This patient also indulges in masturbation which, to use the happy expression of Binet, acts as a sort of resonance chamber for his feelings.  Throughout his onanistic practices, he thinks constantly of shoe nails, and that with all the intensity which the sexual excitement of these habits is wont to evoke.  It was thus that he was one day apprehended while masturbating before the display windows of a shoe store.

As early as six or seven years of age, this patient was impelled by an irresistible and instinctive impulse to observe the feet of

women in order to see whether their shoes had nails in the soles
or not. As soon as he caught sight of a nail anywhere on the shoe,
he was inexpressibly happy. Two female relatives of his lived with
his family. He would sneak into their room after their shoes,
tremblingly pick them up, touch and count the nails and become
lost in rapture. At night in bed, he would conjure up the image
of one of the girls and have her play a phantastic rôle in his mind.
Thus, for example, he would see her mother taking her to a shoemaker and hear her telling the cobbler to put soles on the shoes
with nails. Then he would see the shoemaker nailing the soles
on and afterwards give the shoes to the girl. Then again, he would
try to imagine the girl's feelings on putting on the shoes and walking in them. Finally, his phantasies would subject the girl to the
cruelest tortures, he would imagine nailing horseshoes on her feet
or actually cutting off her feet (sadistic hyperbolism of his phantasies). Simultaneously he would masturbate, but not alone in
order to achieve the direct physical gratification which it afforded,
but primarily as a sort of accompaniment to his phantastic dramas.

All these habits were repeated through the years without the
patient having made the least effort to overcome them. Without
a single pang of conscience, he enjoyed these sensual pleasures,
as oblivious of their significance as the child that he was at heart.
After completing his studies, he went to live with a relative in
the country and there had frequent opportunity to meet with two
young women, nieces of his, who lived in the vicinity. Whenever
he was alone, he would sit himself down upon a bench in the
garden and begin to spin a phantastic tale aloud, his two nieces
naturally being the heroines of the stories. At the same time,
he would play with himself in the most lascivious manner, and
even continued the practices for the next few days without actually
masturbating. When he would see the girls again, he would always
try to catch sight of the nails in their shoes. One of the girls,
who had become aware of his desire, used to touch his foot with
hers in order that he might also feel them. He had not asked her
for the favor, but she took pleasure in doing this, especially when
she had new shoes on. Such tactile sensations would provoke a
prompt orgasm, but it must be emphasized that the nailed heels
and not the girl were responsible for the result. Frequently, he
would sneak a shoe away from the girls and then lay the head of
his penis on one of the nails in the heel. Ejaculation was the immediate result, even though he may not have touched the phallus
otherwise.

At eighteen he came to Paris and there experienced the thrill of his life every time he passed a fashionable bootery in the windows of which the women's shoes of that period were displayed. Aside from his sexual excitement, however, the patient also finds himself frequently pursued by his phantasies at other times, too. Despite his attempts to put them out of his mind occasionally, they hound him like furies. At such moments, he feels as if a veil is cast upon his thought, his mind is plunged into the blackest night. His eyelids droop, his eyes become heavy and he begins in a crooning and hardly audible voice to spin one of his phantastic tales to himself. Meanwhile, he will almost automatically begin to masturbate, either directly *per manum* or indirectly by rubbing his phallus between his thighs or by sitting himself down upon it with all his weight. At the time when he may sense his being filled with the acme of creative ability, he gives the impression of exaltation. The hyper-excited condition of his brain is sometimes so marked that he suffers from illusions and almost from hallucinations. This is especially true when he struggles to put down his phantasies. It is then that he feels as if a second person were standing next to him and whispering the words into his ear which he speaks, giving him the advice to beat off this purposeless habit. As in most cases, this deviation of emotion is distinctly based upon a biological degeneration.

Now, it is easy and comfortable to brand such cases unconcernedly as degenerate, and to let a psychological explanation go hang. It seems to me, however—and that quite apart from any other determinants in the case—that this man was suffering from an identification of the female with the horse. Nevertheless, it may be idle to throw up questions about the matter without an exhaustive analysis. One thing, however, is certain, and that is that a monomania for nails must have a plurality of determinants in order to achieve the rank of an autocratic fetish.

In pleasant contrast to this purely descriptive case, we have the "Analysis of an Hysterical Phobia" which was reported in exemplary and exhaustive manner by Ludwig Binswanger.[1]

Case 57. This concerns a twenty-year-old girl who came to Binswanger because of a phobia which has been present for fifteen years. She was afraid to go into any shoe shop, but was nevertheless impelled to look at the shoes of every person she saw. Her prime fear was that the heel might drop from the shoe and thus disclose the nails or tacks. The time the condition first manifested itself is well known and can be related to a definite experience.[2]

"It was one January morning on the ice that our (at that time) five years and nine months old patient—we shall call her Gerda—went with her sister and governess to learn to skate. Suddenly the girl's sisters laughingly called her attention to the fact that her heels had been torn off by the skates and were barely hanging to one side of the shoes. Gerda looked down at them and began to cry bitterly. She was soon taken home by her governess and on the way they met her youngest brother Max, who was being taken for an airing. Gerda began to cry again. She hardly remembers how she got home, but once arrived, she fell upon her mother's neck and cried out: 'I saw the nails!' Hereupon her mother took off her shoes, and Gerda promptly fainted. She awakened on the sofa. Afterwards, her sisters and brothers laughed at her for the way she acted.

"According to the mother, Gerda again fainted while skating when she was seven. This second time, she lost her heel completely. From that time on, they had her soles nailed well and the heels were attached with screws. And yet, when she was nine, the same experience repeated itself."

I must interrupt the report to call attention to the fact that Gerda began to cry again when she met her youngest brother Max as she was on the way home. It is also very significant that she fell in a faint at home, and repeated the scene several times afterwards. When she was eleven years old, she became dizzy on the occasion of losing the bottom layer of leather and a few nails off one heel. She felt "as if she dragged a tremendous load on the foot," and twice when she was fifteen, she fainted at the sight of loose or run-down heels. Even new shoes made her dizzy. She continues herself:

"Once when I was seventeen, I fainted while trying on new shoes in a boot shop, and ever since then I cannot enter one without a certain feeling of anxiety.

"Standing on the rear platform of the street car one day as it was going around a curve, I had the feeling that something had happened to my heel and promptly fell into a protracted faint. Of course, I looked down and assured myself that everything was all right, but it seems that my feelings in the matter were too powerful. When I was eighteen, I lost the heel off one of my shoes at a ball, but I did not faint, because the heel was not nailed but glued on, and so nothing really was torn. Secondly, the heel was of one solid piece, and also, it was not from a shoe, but from a pump.

"In the train about a year ago, I overheard a woman say to her husband: 'Your shoe is torn.' I didn't look to see, but the very words cut me to the kidney, and I had to struggle to keep from fainting. The thought of having to sit for two hours in the same coupé with that man and his loose heel was torturing. I couldn't stand it any longer and fell in a faint. I could hardly remain conscious until the train finally reached X. And for the next three or four days after that experience, I was absolutely incapable of thought; my whole body, and especially my head, was as heavy as lead; I could neither eat nor sleep.—Ever since that attack, whenever I am in the street car or in any room together with strangers, a feeling of anxiety comes over me as if something might happen. The same is true when I take a trip or a hike with several others. And once the anxiety has taken hold of me, it doesn't leave me for the day. I'm terribly upset and restless, and must be left alone to quiet my nerves. It is at such times that I feel totally unhappy and repelled by everything.

"While in the faint, I have the feeling that my legs are gone, that they have been left on the ground. As if my body reached only to my hips, the rest having been removed.[8] No one dared approach me. I was not in the least responsible and did not need to worry about anyone. I was afraid to awaken from my sleep and feared that I might fall to earth."

This restlessness in the company of strange men is undoubtedly derived from sexualized expectancy mixed with anxiety. This also explains the last fainting spell that Gerda had, viz., when a friend of hers told Gerda of a proposal she (the friend) had received.

When she was eleven or twelve years old, Gerda was sexually enlightened. Consciously, she has no sexual distaste. She claims, also, that she is not noticeably interested in sex differences or in the process of birth.

"Whenever Gerda hears the word 'heel' or so much as thinks the word herself, she imagines a half-torn heel hanging by a thread to the shoe and showing the nails or tacks; she is simultaneously provoked by the clean, light color of the inside leather thus disclosed. Or she may imagine to herself that a skate has been torn from her foot, leaving some part still attached. Or she produces the phantasy that some man grasps her foot between his legs, quickly puts a skate on her, and then turns the screw clamps. She feels anxious that he might turn the screw up too quickly and tightly. And this is the worst thought for her. She feels that such a situation in reality could end in nothing else but her fainting. Another time she says: 'The very worst is to feel the clamps slowly biting into the heel when a skate is put on.' She feels as if she herself were being clamped. This displacement of feeling from the foot to the whole person is noteworthy. It is also interesting to learn that when she walks in the street, Gerda feels impelled to look at the heels of everyone who is walking ahead of her. But she feels quite embarrassed if anyone else looks at her feet." [4]

If Dr. Binswanger even placed a finger on the heel, she would become upset and threaten to drop into a faint. It was also a feeling as if someone had pressed a button, as if a stroke of lightning had passed through her body. She has no more control over herself, she feels absolutely without will, as if she were completely at the mercy of someone else. She fears that she and heel could not be compatible. She closes her eyes when she sees one loose and has no more knowledge of what is being done with her.

This, of course, is manifestly the description of a sexual feeling. The heel appears to have taken on the importance of some erogenous zone; indeed, her strongest erogenous zone.

She experiences most singular sensations in her fainting spell; she has no legs, only a trunk, can feel only her hips, thinks the rest of her has removed itself, etc. No one can approach her. (When she thinks of a birth, her own "bottom" becomes weaker and seems to be no part of her.) She feels herself without responsibility.

But she would like to lay her hand on the heel. She has a feeling of being "open" at the sole. She would like to rub and press her heel, she says. Her foot often itches and tickles her, and sometimes it feels numb and dead.

It is plain that she has sexualized her heels. She has taken a sexual attitude towards them. Her conception of them has become animistic.

"As a child, I liked my shoes so. I can't say why. When a heel fell off, it hurt me as if the heel had been a living thing."

Before that trauma on the ice, Gerda had been in the habit of masturbating with the aid of a shoe. Binswanger looks upon this shoe masturbation as an expression of her anal erotism. Since childhood, she has been suffering from obstinate constipation, has a tendency to vomit, but also an insane fear of actually doing so. She never uses any but the toilet at home, and is even afraid of that one. She is afraid of the black hole, and, of course, afraid that she might fall in.

"Even as a child, Gerda had already disclosed a distinct phobia for human and animal excrements. When a friend of her sister's once accidentally stepped in feces in the woods, Gerda refused to go further. When her sister was teased by her brothers because she had happened to smear one knee against some filth, Gerda ran out of the room.[5] In the dark, she was afraid to walk because of a fear that she might step in some filth, and to walk across a meadow was enough to 'scare her to death.' She paid meticulous attention to her shoes and kept them spotlessly clean. Her phobia in the matter of filth went so far that she would refuse to play with other children in the garden if any dogs had been there before them. And dogs themselves were a source of dislike to her because of their 'uncleanliness.' 'Thin stools' are the limit of disgust for her, and whenever she suffers from a diarrhœa, she believes herself on her death bed. In view of this marked anal complex, it would pay us to present a symptomatic act of hers from the period of her life when she had not yet effected this transformation of her instincts and when her interest in anal things was still an undisguised one. Gerda related how she and her brother Albert, two years her junior, had torn out the tail of their rocking horse, and had then dug around in the hole until the sawdust fell out upon the floor. 'We were interested to see,' she said, 'what was in there when the tail was gone.' Then they got on the horse and rocked on it as hard as they could to see how much more would come out. In the evening they put the tail back and took it out the next morning in order 'to examine' the thing again. This all took place before the scene on the ice."

She often complained of itching around the anus and tried to alleviate the condition by "pressing and opening" it. Defecation was pleasurable [6] because it stopped the itch. She had the habit of pressing so hard while defecating that a governess told her she had better stop because otherwise something would "burst." She compares the itching about her anus with the sensation when a foot falls asleep and then the blood rushes back into the limb. She would often induce this prickling sensation by sitting for a while with her legs crossed. "I often sat in the most abstruse positions, and then I would have to stamp to get the blood back in my legs."

"Here we come upon connections between the foot and the alimentary canal (the rectum) for the first time. In both places she would get the prickling or itching sensation, and in both cases Gerda resorted to the same methods of relief. She presses against the organ, i.e., she either stamps on her feet or contracts the rectum.

"Now, the warning of the governess that if she pressed too hard, something would burst, seems not to have passed by Gerda unnoticed, for she later related that she frequently felt during defecation that 'my rectum couldn't do it; it felt as if it would burst, be torn; it simply would not go.' But these are precisely the words she used so frequently in respect of heels and shoes.

"Gerda also had the 'same feelings in the head' when defecating as she had when falling in a faint: her eyes seemed dimmed, lassitude set in and she felt a dull, tired feeling in the body. The difference being that these feelings disappeared more quickly after defecation than following a faint. She also cries easily after both acts when she is spoken to and she is also afraid to speak about either of these experiences. When she sees a shoe pulled open before being put on, she becomes afraid that 'something will crack.' 'Oh! please don't step into it! Please, don't stand on it hard or else I'll feel it in my head!'"

Binswanger then goes on exhaustively [7] to elucidate the relationship between the defecation and the fainting spells. The belly filled with feces becomes a profitable point of departure on a study of her pregnancy complex. Both the feces and the heels show close connection with her anal erotism. Gerda had imagined that the feces become attached to and grow in the intestines as with roots. Some glue makes it stick to the intestinal wall. The tearing away of the heel finds its prototype in the tearing away and protrusion of the feces in the abdomen (infantile excremental theories). Before that event on the ice rink, she had occasionally dirtied her bed. She manifests patent anal erotism, but also a distinct urine sexuality.

"In connection with a remark that she must frequently urinate when she becomes excited, Gerda mentioned that urinating had always made her feel 'good,' particularly if she would press. At seven she often played with those parts, usually when she was sitting on her pot (one of her favorite pastimes). She said that she had been in the habit of compressing that region just as she contracted her rectum. 'I really didn't want to do it, but I did it just the same. I have the feeling that it wasn't right.' She was still doing it as late as eleven or twelve years of age.

"Here we gain a new relationship: that between the 'front part,' as we called the vulva during the analysis, and the anal region (pressing). Both regions are erogenous zones for her, as becomes progressively more clear in the analysis. The third erogenous zone is that of the ankle and heel. The closer connections between all three of these will become still more clear to us later on.

"First she would press in front, then she would put her hands down there, then came the urgency to urinate, and lastly an 'open feeling,' as if something in front were not closed. Gerda would be impelled to enhance this feeling by the use of her hands, she 'simply could not keep from doing it.'

"Involuntarily we recall the 'open feeling' she had upon pulling at the heel, and also her 'irresistible impulse to press against it.'

"In the process of those manipulations on her parts, Gerda was able to increase the intensity of her feelings by working herself into a depressed state, by thinking that her parents would die, that something might happen to Albert, etc. The feelings were also intensified if she would think of yellow shoes."

Whoever knows the relationships between sadism and anal sexuality will easily recognize that Gerda's fears that something would happen to Albert were nothing but the transposed wishes that something should happen to him (her first attack actually was related to her youngest brother). She liked to cower together in such a fashion that no one could approach her. In that way she would press her shoes between her legs. But as soon as she tries this trick, she gets the feeling that her heels slip away, and she must cry (death of her brother?).

As in the case of all fetishists, the compulsion is repeatedly expressed through the medium of a symbol. Gerda's obsessional compulsion is expressed by the skate clamp.

The heel is her ideal, her child, her fetish; she feels she must sit on it to derive pleasure from it. But later she felt she could not sit on it any more for fear that it might break off. She confesses:

"I must have created an ideal out of the shoes. After that accident on the ice, I thought to myself: I liked them so once, and now I must preserve them in my heart because they're so weak. It was simply my duty. That is, duty replaced love.[8]

"I: 'But you must also have hated your shoes, too, because you could no longer use them in your practices.'

"She: 'Whenever I later saw worn-out shoes, I'd throw them away; my hate broke through. I had the feeling I didn't deserve that from them. I felt that I had taken just as much care of them as others of theirs and yet others didn't have such troubles, although they didn't pay as much attention to them as I. I felt unjustly hurt. I looked upon the shoes as something alive. When the heel fell off it was a true disappointment.' "

It becomes rather clear that the shoe represented the mother and the heel the child which was pried loose and torn from the mother's body. That will soon become clearer. There was her hatred of her brothers and sisters, especially of Max. That is why these thoughts are attended by a marked feeling of guilt. Pressing out feces and losing a heel appear psychically equivalent here. Binswanger continues:

"Hitherto we have considered only the genital component of her masturbation somewhat closely, but the anal component is just as important. We must remember that Gerda used the shoe to masturbate both in front and behind simultaneously. Pressing against her anus was also a 'pleasant sensation' for her.

" 'I knew that nothing could come out (feces drop out) for I had my anus covered up with my shoe and the feces were too hard anyhow. That was why I was so scared when it did come out at night and that's why I'm now so afraid of dreams.[9] I must admit that I busied myself with my intestines, feces and the shoes largely when I was alone. These things went hand in hand, they belonged together in my mind. They were my personal form of amusement. When I dirtied the bed that night, I was terribly ashamed, and feared that the others would learn of it. I avoided them. Then two months later, the same thing happened with the shoe. And I thought that it would be able to stand anything (I had taken such good care of the shoes), and yet, just like my rectum, it was not able to be firm and came apart, opened up. Now it was the shoe which disappointed me. One after the other they fell apart and I lost them, and everything that I had conceived so surely was turned upside down (refers ultimately to her infantile sexual theories as we shall see later). When my rectum had failed me, I felt that the heels were my sole resort (i.e., in order to be able to masturbate). But as soon as those, too, collapsed, I felt myself quite forlorn. I had nothing more with which to stop up the bottom; my foot alone was not sufficient.' "

Binswanger conceives the heel trauma on the ice as the rejection of her genital and anal shoe masturbation. "This rejection must, however, signify much more than that. It is probable that the heel represented mother and child to her. Shortly before the above-mentioned trauma, her little brother Max was born."

"The experience which influenced Gerda's life greatest before that occurrence on the ice rink, and the one whose traces we shall be finding more and more clearly in the analysis, was the birth of her youngest brother Max. Gerda was five years and three months old at the time (the trauma on the rink occurred when she was five years and nine months).

"Before we can get a clear notion of the effect of this event upon Gerda's spirit, we must consider her infantile sexual theories which, on the other hand, were also greatly aggravated by the birth.[10] The event after, came at a time in her life at which such studies and researches on the part of the child are at their highest. In Gerda's own words: 'I always considered children as offshoots of the mother. If she wanted to have a child, she had to eat [11] something special, rolled oats or something like that,

in order to get fat.  When her body became big enough it would
burst.  First the belly button [12] would protrude, then the belly
would rip open and tear along that dark line down the middle
(linea alba).  The child would then gradually push its way out [13]—
a fully formed human, only very, very small.[14]  At one point the
child was still connected with the mother, and that part didn't
loosen up by itself but had to be cut off.  The doctor would then
sew everything up.  As soon as the child would see the light of
day, it would begin to grow very rapidly until it would reach the
size of a normal baby.  I imagined the spiritual relationships between mother and child to be a sort of counterpart of the physical
connection as I have described it.' "

The belly button is, of course, the navel (does the word navel
sometimes act as a screen for the word nail?).  We will recall
that the pressure of the heel sometimes made her feel as if a
button were being pressed.  One should pay especial attention
to the sadistic conception of birth in this infantile theory.  The
mother's body is supposed to burst at birth just as she supposed
the rectum to burst.  The child tears itself away from the
mother just as the heel from the shoe and the feces from the
rectum are supposed to do.

"Gerda's conception that children were the offshoots of the
mother derives from her observations of flowers and plants.
" 'I feel myself absolutely a branch or offshoot of my mother,'
she writes.  'I often found that to be the case in flowers; the
young plants grow out of the mother plant.  When they are large
enough, they are then cut off and put in a pot by themselves.  I
distinctly recall an amaryllis from whose bulbs new sprouts grew
out.  I looked after them every day, and hardly had the patience
to wait until I could separate them from the mother plant.  It was
really a small wonder.  The small one was an exact facsimile of
the large plant.  Gradually the little plant tried to gain a foothold
in the earth; its roots already touched the ground, but it still had to
be nurtured by the mother plant.  Then leaves gradually appeared
on top and slowly pushed their heads up towards the light.  By
then I was ready to cut them loose.  Carefully I separated the
sprouts and tried hard not to tear anything.  Having covered them
with good, rich earth, I put them in my little hot-house so that
every ray of sun would strike them.  But I waited in vain for new
shoots.  The plant gradually wilted although I watered and fer-

tilized it assiduously. Just that may have been my mistake. The little plant probably did not have the capacity for assimilating all the rich nutrition which was offered to it from without. It drooped and disintegrated. I had torn it from the old plant too early; while it was still being well nourished. It would have been better for it to have been naturally cared for, but instead I choked it with too much care and attention.' "

More material for the explanation of the symbolism of nails and tacks comes to light. They are small and white; they gleam through the cracks between the heel and sole. She is pained by the thought that they are alive (a child?).

"During a walk in the wood one day, we came upon an old and torn shoe on the ground, and when, the following day, I asked Gerda why she had manifested no signs of feeling, she answered: 'I had the feeling that it was no longer alive; the nails were no longer alive and fresh; they were not bright, but dead and decayed.'

"In contrast to this she recalled that the nails she saw in her own shoe when the heel came off on the ice were 'snow white.' 'It's curious,' she continued, 'but I felt yesterday as if we had come upon a fresh green branch or even an old and dry one that had been cut off. It is the fresh scar which reminds me of everything, the white line. And what a color contrast in that black shoe! And the yellowish part of the heel; everything looked alive there. When one cuts off a branch, the inside is white, there is a marrow there, and that reminds me of the nails in shoes. As children (Albert and she) we used to cut off branches of elder wood and make whips of them. When the long branches have died, they dry up, the marrow and the strength is gone and they're no good any more. They're dead. That's what an old worn-out shoe reminds me of. The nails don't bother me then. But a shoe that's worn, that has shiny nails, they're alive. Like a stick with fresh marrow. The tacks remind me of fresh marrow full of sap. I have often thought that there is more sap, more life in the nails of baby shoes. In men's shoes they're stiffer and more dried out; they're older and stronger. I imagine that when shoes become old, the nails become old and lifeless, too. But that's not so bad. Children's shoes are worse, because they are younger. When I have worn a pair of shoes a long time, I get the feeling that now they can last. I felt that I could judge what they were worth, what they were good for. That was especially clear to me yesterday when I saw all of nature so alive, and that shoe dead.' "

Her sadistic phantasies (killing of newborn babies?) betray still further associations which become understandable when instead of elder juice we read blood. Elder branches are botanical genitals, they look like nails. In this connection, she declares: "I never wanted to hear anything said about heels in terms of reproduction or creation."

"The following (seventy-nine) day, we learned more.

" 'In the Spring, everything still looked alike in nature, but it was only when one cut off branches that one could tell whether life were present or whether the limbs were dead. We were not supposed to cut off the budding branches, and we were told to be careful how we cut roses, for they might easily 'bleed' and lose much sap. Especially when the flowers are torn off, and not all of the stem comes off but some of it remains hanging by a shred. That really kills them, ruins the plant because the sap cannot rise. I couldn't take it with me, however, because the stem clung so tenaciously to the bush. Otherwise I would have put the roses in water. Instead, I had destroyed the plant without having any use or pleasure from it. Whenever I would see such a broken twig the following day, I would get a pang of guilt.[15]

"Eighty-one day. Elder? 'It was a riddle to me how the leaves and blossoms came out of that ordinary wood. And red blossoms, too! One must certainly be able to find some sort of red color and blossoms in there to begin with. They used to tell me that the sap did it, but I could not get it into my head how that were possible. I often used to ask them how they knew what kind of a flower would come out on the branch, e.g., how I would know what was coming when I would sow seeds in the ground. I insisted upon the question just because they had told me that such and such a color or flower would always appear and that was all there was to it. That then made me feel that I could determine the color that was to come. I was terribly irritated when they corrected me. I was always of the opinion that whenever I wanted anything badly enough I would get my wish.[16]

We are thus forced to the assumption that she was distinctly pained by Max's birth and produced all kinds of sadistic phantasies as to how she might be rid of him. But how does that rhyme with her request of her mother that the latter should present the family with twins? On the one hand, we could assume that, in addition to her bipolar attitude, she may have displayed a certain hypocrisy or theatricality such as we often may see in children. One the other hand, she may have imagined that her mother's body would then surely burst. Her animosity must then reasonably have been engendered by the birth of the little brother.

It must also be mentioned that Gerda made use of a shoe as a hen would a hatching egg; she sat on it, hatched it, and hoped that an egg would come out. The bursting of the shoe is thus even more clearly the bursting of the mother's body. We will recall again that she always conceived shoe nails, heels and shoes as something alive.

"We thus come to the realization that at this level of the analysis, the heel phobia means: It is the protection against the appearance of a birth phantasy in consciousness. The heel or, rather, that connection between the heel and the sole, is disclosed as a sort of incubator or, as Gerda put it, a seed, an organ from which new life is created. This organ is usually hidden by the attached heel, but when the heel is loosened and the crack is widened, the new creature begins to grow and become ready for birth. The further analysis will corroborate this conception in divers ways.

"In this connection we may mention a dream of hers which will occupy us later on again. At this point it will serve simply to show us that Gerda also transferred her theory of the development of chickens to the creation of humans. The dream reads:

" 'I was bathing with mama. As we got out, a piece of mucus dropped from mama and remained in the water. But there was something else, something dark; I don't know whether it was feces or not, but it was stuck together with the mucus. Then I looked at it for just a moment and a child was suddenly developed out of it. I saw it becoming more and more distinct. I asked mama what that was, and she said it was a dead child that she had had in her. I thought that was awfully gruesome when mother said that she had had that baby in her. It floated in the water. Then I awoke.'

"Addenda: 'Everything developed from the nucleus and the limbs from the shreds. The baby sat there with limbs drawn up against its body, just as I had seen in the pictures in our doctor book (at twelve). The very moment when mother said that it was her baby, I no longer felt that I was hers. I was astounded that she could have said such a thing, I hated her. I thought it atrocious of her to say that. I was shocked that she showed so little feeling. Moreover, I believed in the dream that the child really had been in her, perhaps for years, and that it was only by accident that it had fallen out.' "

The first part of the dream clearly reveals her various birth phantasies, and also her fear that mother might really give birth to another child. She transfers her own heartlessness to her mother in this dream, becomes her mother's antagonist and rationalizes her hate and revulsion. It was she, however, who awaited each new baby with hatred in her heart, and manifestly was all trembling for fear that it might become just another rival. According to her infantile sexual theory, also, the babies may remain within the mother's body for years.

It is she who is gruesome, she has no feeling for the child and wishes it might be born dead. Her eldest sister's pregnancy was also a time of trial and tribulation for her. She was afraid her sister would fall, stumble or trip; that her foot might slip or her ankle give way while she would be climbing stairs.[17] Gerda herself felt weak in the knees and legs whenever she was together with her sister during the latter's "critical" period. Her heels especially seemed wobbly to her.

When the child was finally born, she felt that something was finally accomplished, that something had died within her. She felt as if she were again burying something. That was manifestly the wish that the new rival (a nephew) might die or be born dead; that she might bury him. Her whole pregnancy complex leads, in the analysis, to the discovery of her sadistic attitudes: operation, appendicitis, slitting the belly open during consciousness, tearing something to pieces, disembowelment— defecation, fainting. If, experimentally, the heel is even so much as touched during the analysis, she gets the prompt feeling that her intestines are being torn asunder, that she is being stabbed through and through, that she is being disembowled. Touching the heel makes her feel as if she were undergoing narcosis, and some other feeling in addition.

It is apparent that the heel primarily represents her sadistic complex. The masochistic element is introduced by her fear of punishment (talion principle).

It is at this level of the analysis that she arrives at the great trauma of her life, in my opinion the original trauma: the birth of Max. The heel is later shown by the course of her analysis to be her brother Max.

" 'I did have the feeling that I was privy to something that no one else knew. I had always listened with such innocence while the others had acted so incautiously. Mama left us for about three weeks, and it was especially at first that I missed her. Then she returned and I was overjoyed, but the relationship was quite a different one. From that time on, I had a little brother who monopolized all of mama's attention. I was only his elder sister. I had the nurse show me exactly how he was cared for, so that I might do the same with my dolls. She also taught me how to care for my little brother and told me that it was my duty as his older sister. She said that being older, I was also responsible for him. And so I gradually came to like my new position and felt much more independent. Realizing that I was responsible for him to some extent, I also became somewhat better behaved. But when they began to attempt to break me of my obstinacy and unwillingness in certain things by exploiting this responsibility, I began to mutiny and found the whole business irksome and onerous.

" 'Following the birth of Max I seem to have been displaced from my former position in the house. I began to demand less of my mother, apparently because a strong motherly feeling also awakened in me. I became less selfish and felt entirely responsible for everything that occurred in the nursery. I wanted to become indispensable, to mean something to my brothers and sisters. For that reason, I didn't dare say anything foolish or ask any silly questions; simply that they might not laugh at me.' "

The trauma on the ice becomes clear. The brother is born and dies. She is insanely jealous and in love with her mother.

"Gerda originally possessed a very strong mother transference. As a small child, the mother or some substitute such as the nursemaid or governess, had to look after her once more after being put to bed, otherwise she would cry for hours on end. Often she had embraced her mother after the latter had fallen asleep. She liked especially to 'climb upon her mother's lap, so that no one else could approach mama.' Whenever she was depressed or tearful, she would make herself as small as possible, so that she might be petted and protected by mama. Then she would like to lay her head on mother's breast, almost under mother's arm. That made her feel very happy. She 'pressed her head against' her mother's side while mother would have to tell her sad tales. Gerda was proud of the fact that her mother had nursed her herself, whereas the younger brothers were not nursed by mama. As an expression and further proof of this strong transference, we find that Gerda manifested a neurotic anxiety of other people, of life itself, and especially a fear of any change in her environment. 'When I would thus be sitting with mama, and would think of the possibility that it could ever be otherwise, I would be seized with a fear of the world, life, all people. That was why I always wanted to be at home.' When her mother talked of death, Gerda became nearly wild with anxiety and pain. She wanted always to be 'small,' and always 'to keep mama.' That was also why she hated to change any bit of clothing, especially any of her shoes. It made her feel the passage of time, that she was ageing."

In other words, she identified herself with her shoes.

Her attitude towards her mother, however, is not solely positive, but bipolar: Love and hate (the hate being due to her jealousy).

"Before Max's birth, Gerda spent most of her time with her mother. She often lay next to her mother on the sofa of an afternoon and would devotedly follow the latter's regular breathing. Then mother might suddenly go down town and Gerda would be left alone. 'No one was able to substitute for my mother,' said she, 'and I liked to be only with her. Aside from that, I was supposed to look more like her than any of my sisters or brothers. We understood each other perfectly, and I was devoted to her with all the fibres of my heart. But with Max's birth, something seemed to come between us.' [18]

"Gerda told me how impressed she was by the following tale which her mother told her. She heard it for the first time when she was about four, i.e., before the episode on the skating rink. When her mother was about six, her grandmother died. In order to get a look at her grandmother lying in the coffin, her mother had to stand on a chair, but some one pulled her down off that and said she shouldn't be so curious, that it wasn't proper, etc. 'That was the story which always impressed me more than any other,' said our patient. Alone in bed at night, she often thought shudderingly of that and felt very sympathetic towards her mother. But then she began to have these thoughts as if she were the sufferer, as if she had lost her mother! She would imagine that *her* mother lay in her coffin, that she herself had opened the cover of the coffin and crawled in beside her mother. She had made herself as small as possible and closed the top.

"Although this makes us only suspect that phantasies of a return to the mother's womb are here presented, we find them manifestly expressed in Gerda's statement that she had imagined as a child that she had died and would again be born by her mother. A sort of night would steal upon them, everything would be at an end and then, in the morning, everything would begin anew. 'I wanted to know how everything was created, everything that was being done during the time that I could not recall anything—when Max and Albert were not yet born.' Then she wanted to recall her—baptism(?)!"

A typical womb phantasy, such as we have been able to find in all of our cases. Yet let us hear how she was affected by Max's birth.

"A strange bit of conduct on Gerda's part at the time her mother was pregnant became known to us through a dream she reported on the one hundred and forty-seventh day of the analysis.

"'A pair of black button shoes which belonged to my mother stood before me. The heels were quite good, but the leather at the ankles showed holes.[19] In a way, that disgusted and repelled me, but I was also so hurt by the sight that I would have liked to cry. I must say that I was so deeply hurt that I awakened and could not fall asleep again until I took my mind off the subject and thought of other things.'"

In this dream, which speaks for itself, the patient thinks of a certain scene from the period when Max was born. She described it as follows:

"'I can still see mama sitting herself down in her comfortable easy chair and pulling on a pair of shoes, but they weren't the usual button shoes; instead they were again those laced shoes. I wasn't used to change and didn't like it. At any rate, I at first

sort of avoided those shoes.  Mama laughed at my resistance to
changes and explained to me that she was given to swollen feet
and therefore had to wear laced shoes which she could lace either
tightly or loosely, as she chose.  But a certain something seemed
to glide between mama and me during the few days following,
something strange.  It seemed that the strangeness was attached to
my mother, too, and that was why I often looked askance at those
shoes of hers.'

"Gerda must therefore have conceived her mother's swollen feet
as a sign of pregnancy, and that was actually the case.  The swollen
feet may simply have attracted her attention at that time a little
more than the swollen body of her mother."

A subsequent appendix to that dream is also important.

"'The thought that I might some day have to have my shoes
made by some other shoemaker, or buy them ready made, or perhaps wear laced shoes rather than the ones I had, was in itself
horrifying to me.  That was why I paid special attention to my
shoes, that they might not be spoiled.'" [20]

This dream reveals a quite transparent symbolism.  The
black shoes are apparent death symbols.  The child (the heels)
is saved, but its mother dies (the holes in the leather), and the
shoe is torn.  Feelings of disgust and revulsion (disgust with
herself!), and deep sadness (sorrow at the loss of her mother).
This all overcomes her and she awakens.  The swollen feet
may have reminded her of disease and death, but also of phallic
erection (although this latter is not yet proven, since practically
no phallic symbolism has, as yet, appeared in the course of
the analysis).  The shoemaker is probably her father, who,
symbolically, produced new shoes in his children.  She will
not leave her parents' home.  Even the thought is horrifying.

"Further associations on Max's birth: 'With Max's arrival,
something new cut into my life.[21]  Mama left all the old things
behind her.[22]  She had nothing further to do with old habits.  All
of a sudden, something new and strange was upon us; something
that really didn't belong; something I didn't want at all.  But that
was all the more reason for my clinging to the old more than ever;
just because mother had given it up.'  Gerda was supposed to go
to Max's baptism clad in new shoes.  They had to fight with

her for some time before she would consent, but when the parents weren't looking she quickly changed them for her old ones. 'It was simply impossible for me to wear new shoes. As if the rest were not enough!'

"In reference to that episode on the ice, she says: 'My shoes tore, too. As soon as I looked at the torn shoe, something seemed to tear within me. The shoe seemed to go to pieces suddenly. Everything had been all right up to then. I liked those shoes so. It was at that moment that a veil seemed to be lifted from my eyes, I don't know just how it was, but I seemed to understand for the first time. I know that I began to remember things when Maxie was born. Up to that time, everything had been nice and quiet in the house.'

The last few explanations have made the coming psychic conflict of the girl more understandable to us, but before we proceed, I must call attention to one more experience which Gerda had just before Max's birth. It concerned her greatly. That was the death of a cousin which occurred a week before Max's birth. She had seen her cousin two days before he died. At his death she "asked heaven itself how that could have happened, and the answer was that he would never awaken again."

" 'I couldn't grasp the meaning of the word: "forever asleep." I asked everybody all kinds of questions in order to get a conception of the death of a human.'

" 'I wanted to know the exact cause of his death. It was just like a hole; something was suddenly missing. I couldn't get away from the "never again" part of the fact; it was awful. Moreover, why are they put into the ground while they're still whole? I tried hard to get a notion of what it meant to have everything over with.' "

It is easy to see from these statements how birth and death monopolized her thought, and also how all these ideas returned in the symbolical form of the shoe-heel pictures and thus again forced themselves upon her mind.

There is something more to be added to the question of her pregnancy complex and its relation to the shoes.

"Whenever Gerda sees an obese woman who is laced in, she must think: 'Just like a skate clamp cutting into a heel. Something is being destroyed, something protrudes above or below. The same with a heel. The leather is stretched. That's why I can't stand curved heels on ladies' shoes. It's just as if they had a belt on. Whenever I see a woman with shoes like that walking or running, I get the feeling that she's simply cutting herself to pieces. I'm especially affected if I see pregnant women wearing such heels.'

" 'When pregnant women wear belts or lace themselves, something must tear, something is destroyed, and the child will be born either prematurely or will die.'

"Another indicative expression of hers is: 'When a woman laces herself, her pelvis begins to wobble like a loose heel.' Gerda has never worn a corset except once for about a half hour. She was afraid she would die. She has always worn her dresses very loosely. 'Nothing tight around the body, otherwise they'll all see right away as soon as your body begins to swell.' She positively hates those corsets that cut into the inguinal region."

The reader who has understood the discussion of the relationship between fetishism and compulsion in the earlier chapters will understand the significance of the above and also the following excerpts.

"In short, neither the body nor the heel may be laced or crowded or cut into. Nothing of either must be injured or destroyed. In this connection, another observation is interesting, although it occurred some time before the episode mentioned above. Gerda had seen a heel torn loose on a little girl in the street. She had the feeling that she must tell that little girl to stand still or else other people would be able to look into the crack; that they shouldn't see what had happened. But she seemed paralyzed and thought:

" 'That child is going through an experience which must overcome it in short time. It can't understand the importance of the whole thing because of its youth and naïveté. If that kid walks any further, trouble will start; her heel will come off; that'll be the catastrophe.[28] The child is certainly exhibiting itself. I should have thrown myself upon it, covered it with my own body, with my own clothing.'

"It is striking, but illustrative, that Gerda never had a thought of the same thing happening to little boys. Naïvely she states: 'Girls are not so protected as are boys and that's why it's easier for something to happen to them.' It need hardly be stressed that such statements clearly reveal a connection between the heel phobia and sexuality."

Indeed, boys can't bear children and thus their bodies cannot burst. On the other hand, we have here indications of her castration complex and an attitude which, further developed, leads to her "struggle of the sexes."

The heel is a phallic symbol; tearing it off is castration, and disclosing it is exhibitionism.

" 'When something happens to a man's heel, it means that the nails show. Then I'm excited, I can't help or protect myself. I simply fall. I'm down. I'm weak and completely in his power. In my faint, I have no idea what happens to me. But I must always look to see what has happened. The attraction is too great. But I fall immediately after having looked. He, too, has something like that in him. As soon as I see it, I'm gone. I was twelve or thirteen when I first saw a loose heel on a man's shoe. I had a sudden feeling that that must be a rude and ordinary fellow. I also couldn't help telling him (the exhibitionist in her eyes) that.' "

But Gerda's symbolism is not restricted to shoes alone. It affects anything which comes in contact with shoes. Thus, the skate becomes a symbol of the child which clings closely to its mother. Binswanger executed the following experiment with her. He put on a skate and then, by a sudden movement of the hand, lifted off a part of his heel. She became deathly pale, her pulse sank to forty-eight, she became nauseous and vomited, and beads of perspiration stood out upon her forehead. But she took both the skate and shoe in her arms and held it as if she were holding a little baby to her breast.

Her nail symbolism is also variously determined. The shoe is a bisexual symbol, but the heel is a phallic representative. She is a male and possesses a penis. "The shoe and heel are one and inseparable; one without the other is useless."

" 'That I realized when Mama took Maxie to her heart and figuratively became united with him. That displaced me. As long as I was so close to her, nothing strange should have come between us. Max was like some foreign body between us. I was pushed aside.'

" 'The shoe nails meant the same to me as a sort of destiny which intrudes upon one's life and disturbs the smooth running of some whole. Max's birth was a fatal intrusion which displaced me.' "

And now we see clearly and unambiguously in her own words that the nails are nothing but a symbolical representation of her little brother Max. The determination of the symbol goes much further, however.

"Referring again to Gerda's conception of the shoe as something whole, indivisible and inseparable, let us make mention of just one more point. 'One must wait until what is inside the heel is mature and full grown; then it'll die off and then it's quite immaterial what happens, whether the shoe is torn or ripped or what. The life of the shoe is then naturally at an end; everything has been all right; but finally the life of both the shoe and its contents is at an end; both clung together and suffered all shocks in common.'

"I: 'In other words, you wished to die with your mother?'

"She: 'The thought that my mother would die first was unbearable to me. There would be nothing left for me.'

"If her mother would die before her, that would free her completely. But that was precisely what bothered her. Something new would happen, life would be fraught with problems, would have to begin all over again.

" 'I always had the feeling that mother stood over me, that I was beneath her; that I clung to her with all my heart. Those were the nails which bound the heel to the shoe. If mother had died or were to die before me, I would have to take her place. I would have to be on top, as it were. Then I would have to get a child. At such a moment my feelings would settle on my shoes, on my bottom. The moment the nails in shoes would show, that was a sign that I had been delivered of something. But how could I do that! I didn't dare! Max had just been born. Mother was still very much alive and wasn't even beginning to die.'

"Gerda graphically described these conditions as follows: Life is like a vertical circle (later she said 'like a perpetual steamshovel') around which the various persons took their positions according to their age. At the top stands mother, at the evening of her life. In the middle is her sister, and at the bottom the patient. After that episode on the ice, however, the positions are changed; so that her mother had passed beyond the vertex of the circle and she herself had practically approached the position her mother had formerly occupied.

" 'In this second position, something seemed to follow me (from below). That should not have been. I had almost reached mother's former position. That pushed mother further along; shall I say further along towards death? That makes me her rival. I've taken an immense stride forwards. That's all so clear to me. I don't understand why I couldn't have said it right away.' " [24]

We begin to see how the patient's attitude towards power begins to appear; the relations between "over" and "under" (Adler). She steps hard on the shoe. She is "over" the heel. The shoe and the heel thus take on the meaning of that which is tyrannized and trod, and that actually corresponds to the practices of many peoples. The Slavs, for example, have the custom of permitting the bride to tread upon the bridegroom's foot during the wedding ceremony. That appears to be a good omen, for afterwards they shall become the "masters" in the house. Treading with one's feet also has the significance of taking possession. She cannot stand her mother being above her. When she faints, something down below grows more rapidly. She falls from above downwards, i.e., she gives up the mastery (of herself?).

Her dream about the dead child takes on a new meaning in the following:

" 'I would rather have been the child that was still in her. Then everything would have been different. But we two were beside each other and that which was in her was dead. That is how she injured me. I was practically pushed aside. In the dream I had to give up the position I had formerly held. Formerly I had been beneath mama, and I was also her pet. But I had to give it all up. As a recompense, I demanded that she be alone, but she went ahead and created an extra, something of which she gave me no knowledge; she never told me what it was and how it lived. If she had only told me that she had a child within her body, or if she had only told me of it when it came out. If she had only told me about it in another way, then everything would have been all right. As it was, she ripped asunder the last shred of feeling I had for her, and I began to feel that something had cooled within me.' "

She submits to her mother, she loves to be beneath her, but she wants to be paid with love and can't stand her love being disturbed by another rival (Max). She can't divide or share her affections. In the dream, she stands beside her mother, she is her mother's equal. Her attacks have particular reference to this relationship with her mother. That is why she cannot speak with her mother about her seizures. She cannot be approached.

And yet she clings to her mother with every fibre of her soul. She cannot be separated from her.

" 'In the course of years, something came between us and separated us. Nothing seemed to bind us together as formerly. It may be that mama didn't influence me sufficiently, that she let me go in the course of time, pushed me aside; and that is just what I can't stand. That is why I became more and more withdrawn. I went my own way. And yet I am not entirely independent for deep within me—perhaps repressed and pushed aside—there is still a feeling that I am very close to my mother. It is a feeling which gives me no peace but always seems to be dragging me along after it. I can't seem to shake it off, perhaps because I feel too strongly about it.' "

The reader should observe the tone of this passage carefully, note the choice of words. She is like a heel which has been torn from the shoe, but still clings by a shred and can't come off. She cannot separate herself from her mother. It is the separation of the heel from the shoe which is shocking to her. "The nails tear wounds in the shoe leather—in mother's heart."

The shoe is thus also the mother's heart; she is the heel, the appendage, that hangs and clings to it. The nails are, however, also fingers (phalli?). She says of hand-shaking: "The fingers of one hand mix with the fingers of the other. The closer friends the two people are, the more intimate are the things they talk about and the more closely do their fingers entwine when shaking hands."

She realizes that she was somewhat precocious, and that the problems of birth and death agitated her too early.

" 'Destiny entered my life too early and overcame me with its power. I had little understanding as yet, nor was I strong-minded enough or sufficiently resistive to have the right conception of what was taking place. I only felt the power of fate and was afraid of life. It became my fable about the shoe and the heel. That contained the most horrible and at once the most beautiful part of life for me: life and death.

Indeed, the shoe was for her the loveliest of things: love. And the most horrible: death.

It must not be forgotten that in this exemplary analysis, her relation to her father also appeared. The death and burial of her father were horrible experiences for her. She noted that her feelings at her father's funeral and during that last heel experiment were very similar. The heel is thus also her father. Her mother had often laughingly said that her father was in love with her. She felt that she had to care for him and minister to his wants, but then she had also the feeling that she was mama's equal and had the same rights as the latter. The shoe and heel thus become the symbol of marriage: the shoe is mother, the heel is father, and both together a lingam.

Binswanger goes exhaustively into the sexual significance of the shoe.

"In the course of her masturbatory practices, the shoe had become her friend, her darling, her worry, her loveliest plaything, her ideal. She showered attentions upon the shoe, cared for it, indeed, one could say that she spoiled it. She sheltered it from the profane glances of others and practised a veritable purity cult with it. Her shoes were her very own, they were inseparably bound to her, almost attached to her person. Whoever injured her shoes, injured her, too. Her deep attachment to the shoes was so beautiful in her eyes, that she could lose herself in blissful dreams about them, lose all contact with the world in her indulgence.

"With legs crossed like a dervish, her shoes pressed close to her perineum, so that they touched her vulva and her anus, there she sat. The cutting and pressure of the hard sole or the heel gave her pleasant sensations (as a gratification of the masochistic component of her sexuality). This we find in both the autoerotic and the alloerotic phases. Her feet would naturally fall asleep in that position and that would provoke a pleasant prickling and tingling. Urinary urgency would set in and urinating would then become very enjoyable. Whenever Gerda sat thus and pressed against 'her bottom,' she had the soothing feeling that everything 'down below' in the vulva and anus was well closed. That no one could attack or approach her. Especially since her legs and trunk were well covered with clothing. But the shoe was not only a sort of cork which might relieve her feeling that 'everything was open'; it was also to serve as a sort of stopper, which expression recalls something that is used to stop up an opening. It also brings back to mind the symptomatic acts which she manifested when examining her rocking horse.

"But this shoe erotism was not at all the most primary form of anal erotism with Gerda. This must have been preceded by those voluntary acts which consist in opening and closing the anal sphincter and thus holding back the fecal masses in the rectum. Gerda also described these habits very carefully and stated that they were provoked by an itching around the anus. But this is a frequent etiology for that type of onanism. She told us that whenever she defecated, the itching ceased of itself, a circumstance that was very pleasant to her. And by holding back her feces she could postpone this pleasure as long as she wanted.[25] Only after she had learned this trick can the shoe and heel have been added as aids. Aside from the direct irritation of the anal region in this manner, the shoe could not but have promoted the habit already established in view of the fact that it closed off the rectum and prevented the possibility of involuntary defecation."

This brings us to a new determinant in the matter of the heel. Like a column of feces, it closes off the anus. But we must add the experiences of her upbringing which enlarge upon the determination of her symbolic life and increase it.

"This autoerotic practice soon found all manner of obstacles, however. Once the governess had scared the poor child by telling her that if she pressed too hard something would burst (and what the governess said was as good as the word of the Bible). Then there came that involuntary defecation in bed which so frightened Gerda. That experience showed her that she could not depend upon her control of the muscles alone while masturbating. And yet she had to feel that no feces would come out. Firstly, because she did not want to become the laughingstock of the other children; secondly because she did not want to be punished by her parents; and thirdly, and primarily, because she had by this time become fearfully disgusted by feces."

I must refer the reader to Binswanger's original paper for the rest of the exhaustive details on the sexual history of this patient. We can present only the most important points in our summary. He recognizes that the entire instinctual and social life of the child is changingly represented in the symbolism of the shoe. He sees the origin of the phobia clearly.

"Now that we have worked through the symbolism of the heel in this case, have shown the byways of her associations, it is time that we demonstrate the occurrence which we must conceive as the origin of this whole phobia; the experience without which her heel phobia would not have been possible, i.e., the birth of Max. I need not go into too great detail since all the more important points in this connection have already been presented exhaustively in the analysis itself.[26] We find here Gerda's 'family romance,' the kernel of her neurosis, everything that Freud so long ago set down in his interpretation of dreams and his infantile sexuality: the relations of the child to its parents and to all the children born after it; everything which is to be found in the child analyses of Freud and Jung.[27] In short, that the four- or five-year-old girl noticed her mother's pregnancy, that it became set against the new rival in the family and actually wanted to kill it; that these impulses were soon veiled in a motherly sort of care and interest in the child; that she could not forgive her mother the secrecy about the pregnancy; that she felt herself pushed aside, lied to, disappointed; that she blamed her mother severely for having taken on something 'extra,' a new being with whom Gerda had to share her mother's love. And the results: that she wants to revenge herself for her mother's faithlessness and betrayal, first by creating children herself in her phantasy (dolls, friends, the new-born child itself, and, in our case, the heel), and secondly, by disposing of the mother (the child, the father) and putting herself in her mother's place; degrading her, making an evil stepmother of her or an animal, as in the fables or, as in our case, symbolizing her in the degraded form of the shoe.

"That is how the first great psychic conflict arose in this child, an expression of her love and hate for one of her parents. Her attitude towards the repaired shoe after it had come back from the shoemaker's following that episode on the ice is very illuminating. She would rather have had the old heel back on the shoe, despite the bent condition of the nails, because it belonged to the shoe in the first place. 'Rather than this strange heel, anyhow, which doesn't belong to such an old shoe.' She would have been glad to be more than careful of the old heel, until she would have been sure that it was all right. Gerda thus expressed a desire to take up her old position again with respect to her mother. She was willing to make up, forgive her mother, and try to regain her old confidence. But the heels persisted in coming loose, all attempts to make up and restore the *status quo* were in vain. We can also hear her saying to her mother: 'What do you need another child for at your age!' "

The birth of Max was her original trauma. Max was the intruder, the stranger, the foreign body which came between her and her mother. She wanted to be everything to her mother, even a man. It appears that she even wanted to displace her father. She feels that she is just a castrated boy: "Mama is at fault for my being a girl."

Binswanger emphasizes the wealthy over-determination of the heel symbolism, and adds valuable pointers on foot and shoe symbolism.

The success of the analysis was complete. Two weeks after the end of the analysis, Gerda was able to walk into a shoe store and buy herself a pair of shoes. She was engaged to be married within six weeks. She married and was able to overcome many other hysterical symptoms.

Binswanger does not look upon the case as one of shoe fetishism. He says: "This is a case of simple sexual symbolism. The shoe, and particularly the heel, is simply a representative of the phallus." Gerda reacts to the symbol as if she were reacting to a phallus. That, he feels, is something different from the value taken on by a shoe or any other piece of clothing belonging to a beloved person. In such a case the object is sexually over-rated, becomes a fetish, and achieves an independent sexual standing. He considers this case as one of negative fetishism and adds it to the cases of anti-fetishism which Hirschfeld described.

I am of a different opinion, however. This is a somewhat atypical case of fetishism which was cured and straightened out by a thorough analysis. What would have been Gerda's fate if she had not been treated? Would she have been capable of liberating herself from her psycho-sexual infantilism and her fixation on her family? Would she have returned to her shoe as to a sexual object? Or, in other words, would she not have remained in the situation she was in? The shoes constituted her sole interest. Her sexual life was bound up in them, tied up in the negative components which they represented to her (disgust, anxiety, shame and horror).

Gerda definitely revealed a deviation from normal sexuality, just as we have been able to see in all our other cases. But I refrain from repeating myself endlessly. The reader will find in this case all the signs of condensation to be seen in the previous case of apron fetishism. The shoe is her ideal and her sorrow, her god and her devil. Her outlook on life is determined by the shoe and the heel.

I am therefore not afraid to consider this case as a cardinal example of genuine fetishism. Binswanger's success indicates the path we must take in all similar cases. It is true that most patients come to us when it is almost too late. It is also much more difficult to readjust a man sexually for the reason that his natural rôle is one of activity in contradistinction to the natural passivity of the female. It would be important to know whether Gerda was frigid in her marital relations. One might almost fear that she were.[28]

## XIV

## THE MASKS OF SADISM (PARS PRO TOTO)

In all the cases of genuine fetishism we have been able to note a marked admixture of sadism. At first sight, they all look like distinctly masochistic persons. They torture themselves, subject themselves to compulsions, deny themselves the joys of life. But the analysis reveals this masochism as the superstructure founded upon a highly original form of sadism. Guilt feelings and the pangs of conscience are added to make of the fetishist a lamentable picture of humanity.

The fetish lover's suffering derives from an almost invincible spirit of expiation and atonement. But, we ask, what does he have to expiate? What is his great sin? The previous analyses have given us the answer: fetishism is a self-inflicted punishment for the individual's cruel attitudes and phantasies. We were also able, in every case, to demonstrate the presence of this sadistic component in the fetishistic ideal itself. The compulsion must be marked by unpleasantness, pain or coercion if it is to fulfill its fetishistic purpose.

This disguised sadism is the key to many otherwise insoluble psychological puzzles in the field of fetishism. I am in the favorable position of being able to present to my readers the complete analysis of such a case, but before we undertake the study of this patient, it behooves us to go into the literature of this form of fetishism to some extent. In this chapter I intend to consider such forms of fetishism which cannot be included in the categories we have discussed hitherto.

In general, the fetishist is a passive character. He may steal handkerchiefs, corsets, collect all kinds of objects, in short, he may follow his object religiously, but he rarely acts, he almost never injures the object in question. He is satisfied with the possession of a harmless symbol and in most cases he is even gratified by the sight of that which inflames his easily ignited phantasy. Like most parapathics, the fetishist is a criminal without the courage of his impulses. His actual criminal acts are merely symbolizations, substitutes, pale and lifeless schemes as compared with his bloodthirsty phantasies.

Sometimes, however, he seizes upon some easily gained part of the body. Hair and pig-tails are preferred objects in the world of fetishists. Cutting off hair or pig-tails is already a great step forward in the serious damage of the object which may thus lose one of its chief adornments. It is just as unpleasant for a woman to have her clothing damaged or soiled.

The last-mentioned form of fetishism is manifested in divers forms. Recently there was a man in Paris who created quite a furore in the city by going about and ruining women's furs by means of some acid. The police were unable to get hold of him. Still other fetishists of this type sprinkle vitriol on finery, while others may be found who enjoy cutting holes in clothing by means of small scissors.

All such acts are effected under the stress of considerable affect in a hyponoic state. The individuals themselves are rarely conscious of the sexual nature of the act. The occurrence usually takes place, like theft or pick-pocketing, in crowds, preferably in public places such as theatres, street cars, busses, trains, etc. Pressing against the object is often attended by manifest pleasurable excitement, while other individuals, such as the case described by Jastrowitz, deny any thrill whatever. This case hardly belongs in this category, but it so excellently illustrates the excitement I mean and is so distinctly marked by an absence of the conscious sexual motive that I must mention it here.

Case 58. "A thirty-one-year-old father of five healthy children, who lives in compatible relations with his wife since their marriage nine years ago, has been impelled of late to acquire the belongings of women, although he denies that this stealing gives him any pleasure. It was thus that he found himself picking the pocket of a rather pretty woman behind whom he was standing one day. As he touched the woman, his nerves twitched and vibrated, he felt oppressed in the breast and sensed a choking in the throat. He began to shiver as if he were ducked in cold water; wanted to find another place for himself in order to shake off this feeling, but in the crowded car, he could hardly move. Witnesses corroborated his excitement during the act. He was a piano tuner and had been working rather hard of late; this, it was said, had caused a nervous breakdown. He was acquitted of the charge of theft." (Jastrowitz, *Deutsche med. Wochenschrift.*)

The shivering and the anxiety reveal this act as a symbolical one. In his phantasies, this man undoubtedly goes much further than in reality. He approximates the type of patient whose deeds I have called "pars pro toto." It is a characteristic of that type that they aspire to the possession of objects violently separated, cut or torn from the person of their object. It is here that we must class the finger nail collectors who amass a pile of women's finger nails; the collectors of genuine and false teeth; but primarily the pig-tail fetishist who shall constitute a paradigm of this type of fetishist.

Petersen reported the case of such a switch cutter in the *Münchener med. Wochenschrift,* Vol. 69, No. 14, 1921.

Case 59. "A thirty-year-old business man, single, was caught on Easter Sunday, 1920, just as he was in the act of cutting off the pig-tail of a blonde girl. This man is greatly stigmatized in his hereditary line. Two aunts are in an asylum, an uncle is feeble-minded, and another uncle is a drunkard. Of ten brothers and sisters, five died in infancy as a result of convulsions, and of the five alive, one is feeble-minded and four others have eye diseases. The patient is physically negative, but somewhat retarded mentally. Ten years ago he fell into a fifteen-foot hole, landed on his head, and broke his arm. The fracture healed so poorly that he was operated on a second time. The result was that for months he suffered from a state of excitement and insomnia. During the war, he was in the field for four full years, took part in twenty-seven battles, but was not seriously wounded once.

"Referring to his paraphilia, he gave the following information: When he was eight years old, he had to fetch food from a saloon-restaurant for several months. There he was a witness to the regular care which an eight-year-old blonde girl gave her hair. In the course of time, his desire for the girl's hair increased to such a degree that he was often physically and psychically unbalanced for days at a time. Every time he would see a blonde, he would become excited, sleepless, anxious, would get headaches, perspired freely, breathed heavily, etc. He could not work, and his emotional disturbance led him into difficulties with his employer who was otherwise satisfied with him.

"No one had the faintest notion of his paraphilia—nor of the conflicts in his bosom—until that Easter Sunday, 1920. On that afternoon, he had drunk a half bottle of wine in a restaurant and saw, as he stepped out of the place, a pretty blonde girl. In a flash he was so overcome by the surging impulse to gain possession of the blond hair, that he blindly and obliviously pulled out an ordinary pair of scissors, seized the girl by the hair, and started cutting off about two inches of her coil. He was, of course, promptly arrested. He was able to give no information about the motives behind this act, either at the moment or later at the police station. He was certainly not drunk, although the alcohol may have washed away some of the inhibition otherwise present. He persisted in his story that the desire for the possession of that blonde hair came over him with such irresistible suddenness that he involuntarily acted as if under coercion. He said he felt at that moment as if he had to do it.

"The magistrate's court sentenced him to a month in jail on the ground that the attack constituted physical assault with a dangerous weapon, and battery; it was added that the attack must have included a painful injury. The appellate division was not able to find that a 'painful injury' was present, but also decided—that is the usual judicial conception of such a matter—that assault with a dangerous weapon was present and fined the patient on the ground that his mental retardation was a mitigating factor.

"A striking feature of the patient's history is the hereditary stigmatization. The later circumstances of the man, the accident he had suffered as well as the many battles he had been in, were also of indubitable influence upon his nervous system. Altogether, these factors must seriously have shaken his integrity and reduced his psychic resistances. Special attention must also be paid the fact that his impulse first appeared in childhood and then gradually developed. It is seldom that one is in a position to find the first appearance of a perversion without the aid of psychoanalysis, as in this case. It is interesting, furthermore, to note the clear description the patient gives us of how he was simply overcome by his impulse at the time of the act, that he was so suddenly and so completely overwhelmed by his emotions that, at least at the moment of 'the act,' there was no question that his consciousness was clouded and his free volition considerably circumscribed if not totally abated. It was like a transient psychic disturbance;

all the ingrained inhibitions of his upbringing, education, religion and social status were simply cast overboard, and his natural impulse, like a mountain torrent, swept everything before it with a primitive force.

"It is of further interest to mention that when he caught sight of the eight-year-old girl, he had a violent erection, and later, whenever he saw blondes, he would afterwards masturbate.

"It is noteworthy that he denied himself intercourse out of religious motives, but permitted himself masturbation; a phenomenon which may frequently be observed in fetishists.

"Following his sentence, he submitted to a completely successful course of hypnotic treatment.

"Three months later, he married and is now said to be a normal, steady father, without any interests in the hair or switches of blonde girls."

Thus the report. It is, of course, questionable whether the eight-year-old girl with the blonde hair was really the first definitive impression of his life. We must say that the hair cutting is much deeper determined than that and probably derives from his castration complex. I have unfortunately never been able to analyze such a case. The overwhelming nature of the impulse is, however, beautifully described here. He allegedly went out without any special intention to cut off anyone's hair, but we must state that that does not rhyme very well with other information. Many of these patients always carry a little scissors with them. It is, indeed, frequently the case that the impulse may occur at home, the scissors may then be taken from a drawer when the individual leaves to run in search of a satisfactory object.

I take the following case from the collection of Krafft-Ebing.

Case 60. "A pig-tail cutter, P., forty years old, locksmith, single, is the son of a man who was transiently insane and a woman who was very nervous. He developed well, was intelligent, but early manifested tics and obsessional ideas. He claims never to have masturbated, loved only in a Platonic fashion, intended many times to marry, had intercourse very seldom and then only with a prostitute, but found coitus rather unsatisfactory and rather repulsive. Three years ago, he was the victim of serious financial losses and also suffered a severe febrile disease which provoked delirium. These experiences distinctly damaged the nervous system of one who was already stigmatized from birth. On the evening of the 18th of August, 1889, P. was arrested *in flagranti* in front of the Trocadero in Paris just after he had cut off the coil of a young woman in a crowd. He had the coil in his hand and a scissors in his pocket. He excused himself on the ground of transient confusion, unhappy and irresistible passions, and confessed to having cut off ten coils or pig-tails at different times which he collected and enjoyed at home in blissful happiness.

"When his quarters were searched, sixty-five switches, pig-tails, coils of all sorts, were found carefully packed away in separate paper sacks. P. had already been arrested once for a similar act on the 15th of December, 1886, but lack of evidence had acquitted him.

"P. stated that for the past three years he would always feel unwell, restless, anxious and nervously dizzy when at home alone of an evening, and that he would then be overcome by the desire to touch and feel female hair. Once he had actually held a girl's hair in his hands, libidine valde excitatus est neque amplius puella tacta, erectio et ejaculatio evenit. Arrived at home, he felt ashamed of what had happened, but the desire to hold a coil or switch in his hands, quite lustfully colored in his mind, became ever more powerful. He wondered to himself that he had never previously been animated in this way during intercourse with women. One evening, finally, he could not resist the impulse to cut off a girl's coil. Arrived at home with the spoils, his previous lascivious experience repeated itself. He felt impelled to stroke his body with the hair, to wrap his genitals in it. Being finally exhausted with these practices, he felt very much ashamed of himself and didn't dare to leave the room for several days. After an interval of a few months, he was again impelled to acquire some female hair, regardless of whom it belonged to. Once next to his prey, he felt himself the cat's-paw of some supernatural power, incapable of letting go of his possession. If, however, he was unable to achieve his end, he became deeply dejected and disconsolate, worked his passions into a violent orgasm and satisfied himself by masturbating. He was, by the way, not at all interested in the switches displayed in barber's or hair goods stores. The hair he desired was the living coil of a woman's head.

"At the height of his attack upon a woman's hair, he claims to be in such a state of excitement that his powers of volition and knowledge are only incompletely active. As soon as he would touch the hair with his scissors, he would get an erection, and the moment he had cut the hair off, he would have an ejaculation.

"Ever since his losses and his illness of three years ago, he claims to suffer from a weakness of memory, rapid exhaustion, insomnia and nightmares. P. claims to regret his acts deeply.

"A search of his collection disclosed not only coils of hair, but also hair pins, ribbons and other female articles of hair dressing. These he had received as gifts, he said. As long as he can remember, he has had a mania for collecting such things, as well as newspapers, pieces of wood, and a lot of other articles which were of no earthly use to him. He also expressed a totally inexplicable resistance against passing a certain street in the city. Whenever he tried to go there, he became quite ill.

"The forensic opinion stressed his hereditary make-up, the compulsive, impulsive, definitely involuntary character of the act. The attack had the character of an obsession, provoked by an obsessional idea which was further irritated by abnormal sexual emotions. He was acquitted but committed to an asylum." (Voisin, Soquet, Hotet. *Annales d'hygiene,* April, 1890.)

In this case, we see again the disgust the patient has for women. He has intercourse only infrequently and even then he is not satisfied. He is rather repelled. He reveals the characteristic cult of a fetishistic harem, but this does not include coils or hair alone. The deed is effected in a hyponoic state. The next case is partly by Leppman, a leading specialist of this type of material, and partly by Wulffen. The first part is taken from A. Leppman's report in the *Aerztliche Sachverständigenzeitung.*

Case 61. "The twenty-three-year-old university student A., distinctly stigmatized from heredity, was charged with having cut off the coils of divers females, especially little girls and children, during the past three months. Sixteen cases are represented in the charge; thirty-one switches and coils of hair were found in his rooms. The explanations he offered the police as an excuse for his eccentric acts corresponded in detail with the information he gave me in regard to his sexual history.

"He was always a dreamy, withdrawn and shut-in person. Although he was a good and unselfish son, despite the fact that he was well liked by everyone, he never confided his feelings in anyone. None of his friends had ever become intimate with him on this subject. He never gave the impression of self-complacency, but was rather always modest. The attorney in the case received letters to the effect that friends of his in the best classes of society found his actions a complete riddle.

"Recently, following a sea trip, he appeared more than usually quiet and reticent. His conversation revealed that he was one-sidedly interested in mathematical and technical subjects. He had little interest in literature and public events. His social contacts seemed markedly lifeless and devoid of interest of late. He even manifested a distinct loss of his former capacity to play chess well.

"He had never shown the faintest trace of sensuality. Nothing in the way of sexual talk or conversations about girls seemed to attract his attention. At the request of a friend of his, he joined a fraternity which made it obligatory to remain chaste. He declared that such a promise was the easiest thing for him. He nevertheless manifested no trace of fanatical fervor when discussing the matter. One occurrence, however, has turned up in the minds of his friends as singular now that he has been discovered. Once when he had become drunk at a students' affair, contrary to his usual habits, he was brought home by his colleague and when his landlady opened the door for him, he sprang at her and began to ruffle her hair.

"The interview with his mother which had particular reference to any possible nervousness he may have shown, revealed the following: He had always slept lightly, and sometimes not at all. Even as a child, he often complained of headaches, but he had never suffered from spontaneous dizziness or fainting spells, except when he saw blood. He was not able to carry on any exercise which necessitated his bending over or hanging head downwards.

"He himself gave the following information with respect to his emotional life, mentioning the basis of his quiet manner and reticence particularly.

"As far as he can remember, he always had a feeling of oppression and sadness. He was under the impression that he was not noticed by young people, either male or female; as if, as he put it, he could not get into them, although inwardly he felt that he was capable of almost anything. Indeed, he felt that he was cut out for something great. This feeling of depression increased after the sea trip and his studying for his examinations. He felt somewhat freer only when in the company of elder persons.

"He never sensed any sexual attraction to a person of the opposite sex. This first became quite clear to him when, one time, a discussion on the difficulties of resisting temptation was started in his society. At that time, he had honestly declared that he could guarantee his chastity, and that he had not conceived how difficult it was for others to resist temptations. Nor had he ever had any sexual attraction to males. He had really never thought of the possibility that his feelings were perhaps abnormal as regards the sexual side of man. It had never occurred to him that he was probably so different from others in this respect.

"He gave the following description of these feelings:

"As early as his eighth year, he had been pleased to look at the hair of a friend of his sister, and, as he now recognizes, this pleasure provoked unconscious sensual stirrings within him. He then got the same sensations from the hair of his sister and it must be added that his lust was primarily aroused by cutting off some of his sister's locks. It was thus that at about twelve or thirteen he first came to masturbate. He would indulge in phantasies about hair and rub his phallus on the bed. He never used his hands for that was unpleasant and disgusting to him. Nor did he later ever touch his genitals with the hair he collected. As he put it, those coils were much too holy in his eyes for such practices. He would wind them about his head, lay them on his heart or lay himself upon them. In earlier years, he was seldom aroused to such habits, but his feelings became more marked after a trip at sea and after his studies for the examination, i.e., after considerable physical and mental exertion. He then got the idea of cutting off locks of hair or coils in order to acquire material as a basis for his sexual phantasies. He had never given a thought to the fact that such an act would damage the person from whom he had cut off the hair or disfigure her. He claimed never to have been sexually animated by the thought that he might harm or pain a person. As a matter of fact, the persons from whom he wanted to get the hair were quite negligible quantities in his mind. Whether they were old or young was immaterial to him. He had chosen children and young girls for the simple reason that these individuals more frequently wore loose locks or coils of hair which he could easily grasp. He would feel a lustful thrill run through his body at the moment of cutting off the hair, but the most important part of his practice came when he would later coddle and play with his booty.

"The habit of masturbating in his manner so increased in strength during the past year that he began to masturbate about twice a day. Each time, he would lose himself in a world of phantasy. He would imagine that he were a powerful potentate with a palatial castle on an island; that he had the power to make himself unseen and was thus able to fetch himself lovely girls from all the lands of the earth, especially, of course, girls with blonde, silky hair.

"These girls would serve him at table and afterwards he would cut off their hair and let them go. The hair he would then use to excite his sensuous feeling, a most provocative thought being that he might collect enough of it to cover the walls of his rooms. It is to be stressed that he did not conceive the service of the girls as something humiliating or unworthy.

"His striving for the possession of girl's hair finally became so importunate that he would have given way constantly to his desire for stealing it had he not occasionally been caught and arrested. Just now he feels as if he had awakened from a drunken spell. Now is the first time in his life that he has reflected upon his conduct; he thinks, however, that he will be able to control himself. He says he cannot blame himself for having acted as he did; he feels that he was but a child, devoid of any understanding of the emotions to which he submitted. He now speaks of them as 'crazy.'

"A. was indicted, but, on the report of the forensic psychiatrists who looked upon him as mentally unbalanced, he was acquitted. During the proceedings, the court asked A. whether he could guarantee that he would in future desist from cutting off girl's coils. A. answered that he could not guarantee anything of the kind, since his instincts were more powerful than his will. This proved also to be the case. After A. was released from the asylum (as recovered), he moved to Hamburg and there again began indulging in his old habits. He had made the following statements to the psychiatrist about his sexual life; they complete the information we have heard thus far, and afford us a rather deep insight into the psychic make-up of the habitual hair thief.

"The real motive for his being susceptible to these hair cutting episodes had not been clear to him before. He was sure, however, that it was the hair alone, and not the person, which attracted him. That is one of his explanations for the fact that he cut some of his sister's hair off. Like most of the other boys, he had also paid attentions to the girls in school, but denies that he had any sexual feelings or thoughts in doing so; indeed, not even when he once kissed one of the girls. He was still very young when he began to dream and day-dream of hair and coils and switches.

"The following vivid dream is an example which he gave:

"He found himself in a very lonely, mountainous region surrounded by much underbrush. There were many hidden caves in these cliffs; before the caves stood blonde girls with long pigtails; and in the girls' locks and pig-tails hung the keys to the caves.

"Plaits and tresses had begun to play a leading rôle in his emotional life while he was still a little boy. Just when this first took hold of his mind is something he cannot tell, nor was it at all conscious when he first took to cutting hair off. He felt as if it were rather some physical urge to which he had to submit. His first real enlightenment on sexual matters came to him during the first trial against him. He claims never to have had the slightest intimate contact with a woman and even felt estranged and repelled by male friends of whom he knew that they cultivated intimacies with women. He was particularly revolted by obscene or vulgar conversation about such things. That was the real reason why he had joined that chaste society called Ethos. Following his acquittal in B., he had firmly resolved never to succumb to his habits again, but he was adamant only for a year, and in 1917 he had a relapse. He now fears that he can never withstand the pressure of his abnormal feelings and would embrace help from wherever it came. He feels considerably relieved here in the hospital, but he cannot say that he is completely at rest in his heart. He always asks himself when peace will come to his soul. During the spring semester of 1917 in Br., he was quite alone, and that was when things became more acute with him. There was to be a party, and for weeks in advance he had suspected that the situation would afford him a real opportunity to cut off several tresses; this knowledge tortured and tormented him. Ever since that time in Berlin, he never carried any scissors with him, not even a nail clipper. About a fortnight before the party, he walked up and down in front of a cutlery shop, struggling with himself whether he should buy a pair of scissors or not. Finally, however, he was able to master his impulse. Nevertheless, a few days later he did buy himself a pair of scissors and that, he feels, was the end. From then on it was all up with him. He then often felt like throwing the scissors away, but decided that despite the presence of the instrument in his pocket, he would convince himself that he could withstand his impulses just the same. Also, it would be easy to fool himself into believing that it wasn't a real pair of scissors, but just a nail clipper, which he had to have anyway. On the day of the party, he wandered about the streets looking at all the tresses and coils of the ladies, avoiding any friends whom he may have met casually. But, despite his great emotional tension on that day, he had been able to control himself. The next day, however, he succumbed. There was a great ovation in front of the palace in the evening, and in the crowd he took the opportunity to cut off several coils. The first attempt didn't succeed completely, because the switch was a little too thick to be cut through. The second was easy. The third was a girl with strikingly long and beautifully combed hair which reached almost to the knees. This inflamed him to the highest pitch of excitement. He begins to feel the luxuriousness of the crop; the girl switches it all over her shoulder forwards. That was a slap in the face, but he did not budge from the spot, hoping that she would soon throw her plaits back over her shoulders. When he saw that this would not be the case, he finally tore himself away from her and looked about for other prey; but all the girls had thrown their hair over their shoulders towards the front. As a last resort, he pulled some hair back over the shoulder of one girl and quickly cut it off. Towards the end of the ovation, he was in a terrible state of excitement which was doubtless partly anger at not having been able to get what lovely hair he had seen.

"Arrived at home, he took out the hair and looked it over lovingly, coddled it, pressed it to his face, kissed it and finally cut it to a powder with his scissors and threw the pieces away. Why he did that is beyond him. He went out again and ran into a few friends who invited him to come and have a glass of beer with them—and he actually went.

"It was apparent that A. was quite excited and nervous as he was telling all this to the specialists, and even the following day, he stated that once having reactivated all those memories he was now constantly plagued by the memory of that beautiful long coil. He would see the thick cue in bed, hanging over him, keeping him from falling asleep. He got painful erections. 'Is it possible that there are such long and thick pig-tails?' He would measure on his body about how long such a cue could be. He would imagine the proud possessor of such a tress sleeping, he approaches her bed, takes the magnificent cue in his hands and feels its gorgeous thickness, presses it to his lips and nose, inhales the perfume of the hair; and finally takes the scissors and cuts it off. Then he would groan and moan, struggle not to succumb to that awful impulse. He can't sleep. He rolls over on his back, on his side. Nothing helps. Out of the blackness of night come the pictures and memories of all the hundreds of pig-tails and cues, the real ones as well as those he has dreamed about. His excitement grows upon him, he becomes terribly restless. All in vain. The phantasies, the old pictures, arise again in his mind: His castle; the girls with tresses are brought in, whole cities are plundered for girls with cues; Berlin, Hamburg, London, Stockholm; only the loveliest of pig-tails; from the schools, the streets from all over, the prettiest girls are brought in. They are cared for by the girls he already has. Their hair is combed and plaited, pretty ribbons are tied above and below, and little labels are attached telling of the age and birthplace of the girl, the color of her parents' hair, her name, and the information as to whether her hair has already been cut or not. Then fifty at a time are brought into a special hall. Formerly he had passed them all in review and had cut off the locks of each, but now he has invented a special machine in his phantasy with which all fifty heads are cleared like lightning of their hair.

"The cues and tresses are then placed in a special glass case where they are hung up in rows. Beside these girls, he would have favorites whose hair he would cut off himself, with great ceremony and then place the locks with his own hands pompously in a special wooden chest lined with colored silks. Then there would be his wife, who would have two of the loveliest blonde pig-tails in creation, much longer than her own height. At night he would sleep next to her, play with her tresses as she slept, and in the morning he would comb and plait her hair himself on a special stool which could be raised and lowered like a barber's chair, so that her hair might hang free. Then he would have her die young and at the bier he would cut off her cues and close the coffin. He would have similar orgies on a private yacht, but of that he would rather not speak. Sometimes he has the feeling that his whole pillow is made of switches and that several perfumed locks have floated onto him. Into the pillow he would bury his face and breast; his arms and face played with the locks and whirled them about. After he had had an ejaculation and had masturbated, he would feel weak, and when his excitement had died down, he would be able to fall asleep, but this was usually only after several hours. Not infrequently he would have an ejaculation several times in a night. He never touches his penis with his hands, but lies on his right side and rubs it on the bed.

That may take some time before he will achieve satisfaction, but if he would bury his face in hair, he would get a prompt ejaculation. A. was declared to be irresponsible. (Communication of the Police department of Hamburg.)

"The further destiny of Robert St. is to be found in Vol. X, No. 1, 1921, of *Geschlecht und Charakter* (Sex and Character). St. went from Hamburg to Buenos Aires as an engineer and there again was brought to court. He begged his judges to sentence him to life imprisonment in order that he might be protected from his pathological impulses. But he was again acquitted. The thirty-seven-year-old man was later again arrested in Berlin as he was jostling young girls in a crowd. They found one hundred and fifty (!) pig-tails in his rooms which he claimed to have collected in Valparaiso. But there were also eight women's pocket-books. He appears to have become a pickpocket since last seen; perhaps altogether a kleptomaniac."

This is a typical case of fetishism. A. avoids heterosexual intercourse, he has collected a harem of fetishes, he indulges and revels in characteristic phantasies, such as we have described in our chapter on the "Bible of the Fetishist." It is probable that every fetishist has a stock of such singular and eccentric phantasies.

His avoidance of sexuality is also demonstrated by his alleged indifference to obscene talk. He can't stand vulgar jokes. It must be stated that this trait is characteristic of most of these patients, and they are just as prudish and modest in their exterior lives as their phantasies are extravagant and lascivious. That is just why their friends are so astonished to find Joseph or John suddenly disclosed as a fetishist or exhibitionist. We see, however, that a little alcohol dissolves the outer man and reveals the true fetishist in A. He begins to ruffle his landlady's hair. On the occasion of his last act, also, he even manifested violence (he cut some stolen hair to pieces). He manifests just that type of over-compensated sadism which we analysts, who study the reverse sides of psychic experiences, know only too well. Even as a child, he fainted whenever he saw blood. His first memory seems to be the sister's hair. It was her friend's hair which attracted the eight-year-old boy, but he confesses that his sister's hair was his chief source of delight, and that he actually cut off some of her locks.   But there seems to be a fixation on his mother, too, for he says that he was indifferent to whether the hair came from old or young.

He manifests a rather marked feeling of inferiority which is probably what sent him along his fetishistic path.   He does not believe that he could please any woman or man ('sic!).   But his sense of power exhausts itself in his phantasies.   He is a potentate, has castles, the women are in his power.   That is a sufficient testimony to the fact that he is afraid of them in reality, and that his fear of the female is a contributing factor to his paraphilia.

The dream, too, is interesting.   His real goal is hidden.   The pig-tail is but a symbol.   The keys to the caves hang in the tresses of the girls.   The hidden caves are doubtless the caverns of his soul into which no one may peep.

The cues which contain the keys to his paraphilia also lock the door to normal sexuality for him (the caves with the girls).

The theatrical character of the paraphilic is also beautifully expressed here.   He buys himself a pair of scissors just to show himself that he can control his passions despite the instrument in his pocket.   And yet this assures him that he has it ready in case of need.   He stages a real comedy, and even rationalizes the situation by saying that it is a nail clipper and not a pair of scissors.   But why, we must ask, doesn't he leave this "clipper" at home?   Simply because he really wants to have it with him in case of need.

That the cues are distinctly phallic symbols is revealed by his divers descriptions of them.   The plait must be long and thick; he even measures to see how long they might be.   He gets the feeling of their "wonderful" thickness, and presses them to his lips and nose (fellatio?).

His abstinence shows that he is suffering from a psychic castration.   Is it possible that that is the *poena talionis* for a castration which he desired to carry out on a rival?   It is probable that womb phantasies are present in these cases, as we have already observed so frequently.   I would suspect that he had the phantasy of castrating his father while he himself was lodged in his mother's womb.   That, however, is only a supposition which may be buttressed by the strength of much experience. Nevertheless, only an exhaustive analysis could give us complete insight into the singular motives behind such a case. The signs of sadism are rather clear in this man, however. We remember that his phantasy constructed a special hair-cutting machine which could shear fifty heads at a time. The pig-tail appears to be a substitute for the head in this case, and the phantasy would thus ultimately mean decapitation. We must not forget that this patient hates women because he feels that he cannot cope with them. He is excluded from normal love, ostracized from the community of pleasure. It may be assumed that his cue fetishism is a complicated condensation such as we have found to be the case in all our other patients.

Nor is it improbable that this may be a case of self-castration. In many of our previous cases, we observed that the patients masturbated with the fetish in front of a mirror. That is a sign that they are seeking themselves, they cut off something from their own bodies, they are the girls, they rob themselves of their own virility. They identify themselves with their object, just as with their reflection in the mirror. And the *lex talionis* has its effect here, too. Whoever wanted to attack another, here attacks himself. This is the explanation for such cases as the following one.

Case 62. Pt. is overcome by a marked depression which is associated with indifference and inactivity described by him as a "crisis of lifelessness." In order to tear himself out of this state, as he says, he tried for six months to keep himself drunk and well amused. But that was unsuccessful. Then he decided to commit suicide, but from the moment that he had decided to kill himself, he felt much relieved, and happier. The excitement engendered by the decision to die, put more life into him than all his other attempts to awaken his interest. He felt much better while writing all his friends the most touching letters of farewell. He even amused himself by firing at his reflection in the mirror. When he finally fired a bullet at his own breast (which, incidentally, caused him only a scratch), he felt better than he had for several months. The usual suicidal impulse is certainly not of this character, but it is possible that such abstruse attitudes may be present on occasion (Janet).

The underlying relationships between plait cutting and sadism are illuminated with the clarity of lightning by the following case of H. Gross (Gross' Archiv, Vol. XII. "Ein Fall von psychopathischem Aberglauben"). (A case of psychopathic superstition.)

Case 63. The product of an orphan asylum, under constant and severe disciplinary measures while in the army, marked by a psychopathic inferiority, attacked a ten-year-old girl at the age of twenty-nine for purposes of rape. He threw her to the ground, pressed one knee against her throat, pulled a knife out of his pocket, and—upon a sudden impulse—cut off her tresses. He did not attempt coitus, but simply put his finger in her vagina. He claimed that he cut off her hair because he needed it for a brush. At fifty-four, after having served a sentence, he comes out and sees a sixteen-year-old girl whom he desires to attack. He desisted, however, "because the lightning hadn't struck" him as yet (acute symbolization of the impulse). Shortly thereafter, however, he attacked an elderly woman and demanded intercourse with her, which she refused. Thereupon, he choked her to death and cut off her breasts and genitals. These he took home and cooked into a sour stew which he ate in the course of the following three days (cannibalism). His excuse was an inordinate inner desire and greed. He also manifests a pathological reaction to whistling. Whenever he hears someone whistle, he flies into a fit of rage.

Gross correctly calls attention to the invalid and weak rationalization of the cue-cutting episode and feels that this was due to superstition which demanded certain parts of the human body for certain mystical rituals. What a classical case of transposition! The cue cutting as a substitute for cutting out the genitals.

Various cases of picacism (Eulenburg's expression for sexual "gourmandise") are to be explained on a sadistic basis; they derive from a sudden feeling of superiority whenever the object is an inferior or weak person (see the chapters on "Special love

conditions" in Vol. III and "Conditions of male potency" in
*Impotence in the Male* in this series). Hirschfeld (l.c.) has
many cases of picacism in his broad experience.

One of my cases of hermaphrodite fetishism is mentioned in
Bloch's *Sexual Life.* This man, a riding master, was completely filled with the striving to find any and every hermaphrodite
he could. These he would approach with a view to starting up
sexual relations. I also know of men who felt especially attracted
to women with speech defects (such as lisping), and there is a
woman in my collection of cases who preferred stutterers to all
others. Indeed, even serious diseases such as anemia, jaundice,
consumption, may be the bases for pronounced fetishistic tendencies, and, what is more astounding, even venereal diseases have
been known to be the condition of a sexual attachment. An elegant lady who consulted me once was attracted sexually by the
presence of warts, calluses and corns. Fetishists for wooden
legs and women with beards have also been observed. Not long
ago I saw a most interesting case: a man who had an irresistible
passion for pregnant women. He always looked for them on the
streets and would follow them for hours. And the more pronounced the pregnancy was, the greater was his passion.

This collection of Hirschfeld's tends to create some confusion
in the understanding of the deeper motives behind the several
cases. Men with marked homosexual components will seek a
bisexual ideal, such as hermaphrodites and bearded women
(see "Onanism and Homosexuality" in this series on "Masks
of Homosexuality"). Other cases may be based upon a fear
of the sexual partner (Adler), the infantile impressions being
of paramount importance here. The attraction to pregnant
women often has a sadistic basis as I have found in two cases
of my own observation. There was present the phantasy that
the child in the mother's womb might be spiked on the penis.
It may also be that the early impressions of one's own pregnant mother have been fixed. Nevertheless, such cases should
not be conceived as fetishistic; they belong rather to the cases
which we defined as being marked by specific love conditions.
It is only when the patient has become fixed to the symbol
itself that we may be permitted, as I have often repeated, to
speak of fetishism.

Now, there are curious cases which have already achieved a certain notoriety in the literature. For example, a mania for crutches or amputated persons. I shall present such cases here because I am able to illustrate the material with a well-analyzed case of my own. But, before we go into the details of this case (in the following chapter), I would like to pave the way by mentioning some similar cases from the literature.

These are, particularly, men who feel attracted by crutches and prostheses or false limbs. During the war a wealthy Englishman published advertisements in all the papers of the Continent. He had prostheses made for all girls who had lost a limb and is said finally to have married such a girl. The susceptibility to crutches may appear as true fetishism. The crutch then monopolizes the man's interests or it offers a mode of approaching certain women. But in both cases we have to deal with a masked form of sadism. Such patients are subject to the unconscious phantasy of injuring someone else, amputating a leg (displaced castration complex); but, by circumventing their direct sadism, they arrive at what we have already called the principle of the finished product.

Hirschfeld (l.c.) has given us a description of a case of crutch mania:

Case 64. Dr. S., an author of Dutch extraction, thirty years of age, was sent by his wife for a consultation. He insists that she use crutches in walking and demands that she take them to bed with her during intercourse. The patient states that his first sexual animation appeared when he was about five years old; at that time he was watching another little boy walk on crutches. Ever since then, the sight of crutches has a fascinating effect upon him and provokes him sexually. For many years he never considered woman as a sexual creature. Since puberty he has been revelling in phantasies of crutches and even bought himself a few pairs at various times, only to throw them away afterwards because of disgust and shame. But it wasn't long before he had bought himself another pair. To go out of an evening on these crutches was a great pleasure for him. He emphasizes, however, that it was not the sympathy awakened in others which gave him such enjoyment, but rather feeling of the crutches and the soft crutch caps under his arms. Until his marriage, he had lived in abstinence, and he states that his wife is his first love. She is sixteen years his senior and, aside from her character, attracted him because she always wore so much fur, this being also a thing of powerful influence on him. In the beginning, he says, his wife seemed to understand him completely, and he was especially happy whenever she would seize him under the arms (he is somewhat weak) or whenever he would be able to help her up a flight of stairs in this manner. Now, however, his wife feels that the crutches are his primary love objects and she is but a secondary thing in his life. This is, of course, one of the most frequent complaints of the wives of fetish lovers.

Let us hear the words of this crutch fetishist now. He writes:

"I was born the 15th of May, 1890. My father was about forty-six at the time and my mother thirty-three; both, as far as I know, quite normal. When I was about five and a half, father moved with us to R. There I was able to watch a little boy from our windows who walked about in front of the house almost every day on crutches. His right leg was crippled. I could not take my eyes from him and sensed a curious thrill which, of course, I could not understand at that age. I can also recall several walks which I took with my mother in that city. We would often see a well-dressed man who also wore crutches. As I now recall it, he probably used them in the same way that I have come to use them. In short, they were false.

"After the death of my father, my mother moved to Berlin, and it was there that my first attempts to walk on crutches were made when I was eleven. I'm not very sure of the time. It may have been later, when I was about fifteen. The latter date is more probable. At any rate, it is only from that time on that I have any clear recollection of the progress of events. At fourteen and a half I passed through a severe attack of epidemic meningitis. From that time on—of course, at great intervals—I began to manufacture my own crutches out of broom sticks and the like, and would hobble about the room on them. Later on, as a student in Kiel and also on three other occasions, I bought the usual type of crutches and would use them to walk about on at night. That is, with one exception which occurred just before I met my wife. I had overcome my bashfulness during the winter of 1917 to such an extent that, while I was a legal clerk in L., I hobbled about on crutches for over a fortnight and went everywhere with them except the few steps I had to the court house.

"Until I was twenty-six, I never had the slightest intimacies with a woman. Nor did I have the faintest suggestion of homo-sexual attractions. I was very much afraid of normal intercourse and this was due to several different factors. First of all, I was afraid of infection; I was shy; and I felt that I lacked the neces-sary wherewithal to seek a 'friend' on the street. So I mas-turbated. Usually only once, but sometimes it was twice in a night. I would imagine lovely women, dressed in furs, and hob-bling on crutches."

Kronfeld also reported on this case as follows:

"Extracts from the autobiography of a curious case of fetishism. The author is a not unknown writer, highly talented, but sexually abnormal. He is a marked neuropath, of Christian extraction, stigmatized by a disorganized instinctual and emotional life, shows a tendency to phantastic and hysterical aberrations, a susceptibil-ity to hyperbolic affectivity and obsessive thoughts. He is tall, but of asthenic habitus; has a curvature of the spine and several signs of degeneration. His psycho-sexual make-up is an unusual combination of infantile traits together with the residuum of over-emphasized pubertal impressions and marked, but unfortunate, sexual repression. He reported the following about his life.

" '1. Childhood (from five and one-half to fourteen): As far as I know I was born of quite normal parents [1] in 1889, and moved with them in 1895 to B. In front of our ground floor apartment there played a twelve-year-old boy who was crippled on the right side and wore crutches. My parents never noticed that, instead of playing like any other boy, I would stand at the window and watch this cripple. My mother was also oblivious of the fact that, during our walks, I would stare as if hypnotized after a man whom we often met walking on two crutches. Both these figures, the boy and the man, were forever engraved in my brain.

" 'Autumn of 1896, we moved to F., February, 1900, my father died, and in October, 1900, my mother and her sister opened a boarding house which continued until October, 1918. Until the Spring of 1911, my 'mothers' and my uncle—who was the director of the home for the crippled—cultivated a regular Sunday visit, and there in the home for the crippled I also had further oppor-tunity to observe officers and others walking on crutches.

" 'Summer of 1903 I became dangerously ill with epidemic meningitis. During the course of the disease, I was totally para-lyzed on the right side and could neither speak nor hear. Following my miraculous recovery, I limped on the right side for some time. In addition, I was unable to keep up with the regular course of work in high school for another year, and had to leave for a convalescent stay in the country.

" 'It is since that period of illness that my first active abnormalities have developed.

" '2. Youth (fourteen to twenty-one): October, 1904, we moved to C., but even during the six months preceding this time, my "second nature" was getting the better of me. I had been manufacturing primitive crutches out of broom sticks which I would split lengthwise, connect by cross-pieces of kindling wood and cover with remnants of cloth. Simultaneously, I developed a fur fetishism which I indulged secretly, while the guests of the boarding house were at table, by sneaking into their rooms and feeling the divers fur clothes which they had hanging or lying about, snuggling into them or putting them on. My "mothers," being economical women, had practically no furs at all, and all that I had was a little beaver collar. A fortunate accident moved the widow of a physician to leave her deceased husband's fur coat for sale in our place. During the weeks that the coat hung in our house, it was a source of pleasure and torture for me. Hidden in it, and hobbling about on my primitive crutches, I would revel in my already awakened erotic phantasies and indulge in sexual gratification once or twice every evening, and sometimes even during the day.

" 'Thus time passed until I graduated from high school (Autumn of 1910). When, a year later, I left home for the first time, my second period of activity began.

" '3. Period before beginning work (twenty-one to twenty-eight): In the winter of 1911-12, I was in K. There I bought my first pair of real crutches, but, with one exception, I never used them except in my own room. When, in the Spring of 1912, I returned to B., I first burned the crutches. From the Spring of 1913 to the Spring of 1914, while I was in G., I also bought myself crutches and used to hobble in the park on them at night, but before I left that city, I burned them. I did the same at home after I came back from G., but then I would walk even in the busiest streets at night. The outbreak of the war did not influence me any less than others. Although I was not able to go to the front, my patriotic feelings so overwhelmed my personal desires that I thought of furs and crutches only occasionally at night, simply as a means of gratification. December, 1915, I entered the army and remained there until the Autumn of 1917. January 1, 1916, was the first time I had ever had intercourse with a woman, and my masturbatory habits became considerably deflated after that. But they returned in full force after I reported at the front again as a voluntary soldier in March 1916. My "girl" turned up again when I went home in May 1916 to take my examinations. Then my onanistic habits became stronger and remained powerful until I had completed my twenty-eighth year.

" 'September 1917 I was called back by the courts and assigned to the National division. Back again, I soon bought myself crutches, and during the first fortnight I used them even by day, with the exception of the time I had to go to court (used some nervous disease as an excuse). When I left my position, I consigned the crutches to the reserve hospital of the place.

" 'My fur fetishism also became stronger during the years between 1909 and 1918, i.e., as far as that was possible. This eccentricity was furthered by the fact that ever since 1909 I had had a beaver collar, and in the Autumn of 1916, my mother sent me a regulation fur coat to the trenches. In the Autumn of 1917, back from the front, I had a tailor transform this infantryman's coat (without a collar) to a regular civilian fur coat with a collar (he added my beaver collar). That relieved me of the necessity of "floating loans" among the guests of the house, but my abnormal tendencies expressed themselves only passively, i.e., only when I would look at the fur.

" 'December 1917, my mother died, and in January 1918 I made the acquaintance of my wife (she died in May 1920). Ever since then, my eccentricities have taken somewhat different forms.

" 'Adult (up to the death of my wife): February 1918, I left the service of the state and took up writing. Simultaneously I began to cultivate rather frequent intercourse with my future bride. One relapse occurred in November 1919 when things were nearly broken off between my bride and me. I then bought a pair of crutches. I later took them into marriage with me, as it were, and had them made over to fit my wife. I bought a new pair after our marriage, and still have them.

" 'My wife had received a gift from the front: an airman's fur lining of musk-rat. Since my own fur coat was well worn, she made me a present of this gift from the front and, out of consideration for my tastes, bought herself a heavy seal coat, while I had the tailor make me a heavy winter coat of the musk-rat. Now that my wife is dead, I have had her seal coat turned into a seal-lined coat for me, which gives me two rather heavy winter coats. My crutches—which were well padded to begin with—I had covered with an extra layer of well-padded plush. Succinctly, I have everything that I need, now that my wife is gone, and perhaps the only thing that is lacking is a long and severe winter.

" 'Sex life during the past few years (since about 1916): I sha'n't speak again of those periods in which I indulged myself in onanistic practices. I should like to mention in passing that, aside from my peculiarities of feeling, there were two factors which kept me from normal intercourse. The first is my natural abhorrence of bought love which I have never yet been able to overcome. And the second is my inability to start up anything—even a Platonic little flirtation—with any but my social equals. The very sight of the thick coarse hands of maids, etc., instills an inconquerable disgust in me.

" 'But aside from that: I had my "wooden ladies," what use did I have of the ones of flesh and blood? Thus it was that my defloration, as it were, was more the result of the woman's activity (the wife of an industrialist) than my own. Along with these heterosexual activities, however, I did not leave off my onanistic habits. Nevertheless, those were happy days. That woman, with all the astuteness of a female, soon got wind of my eccentric tastes and began to visit me in her sealskin coat. Afterwards, however, I was again without a woman until I met the one who became my wife in March 1919. She had already transformed me to some degree when she unfortunately died and left me alone again. Or—may it have been for my good that she died?

" 'From February 1918 to December of the same year (when I moved to my wife's), my masturbatory activities diminished considerably and all my other abnormal habits also were nearly wiped out entirely.

" '25 December, 1918, we were officially engaged and on the 11 March, 1919, we were married. During those three months—but only by means of the worst nervous eruptions and hysterical crises—I was so far able to blot out my masturbatory habits that it is only now (in June 1920) that I am beginning again; and even so only about once every week.

" 'In many respects, my marriage helped me considerably. I became intimately acquainted with that intercourse which springs from the natural love of both the man and the woman. I was able to overcome a compulsive habit which had tormented me for so many years and my success was of such thoroughness that I have relapsed only occasionally when I needed physical relief.

" 'My crutches have lost their attribute of provoking onanism. They now serve only the purpose of supporting me after exhaustive and protracted work of a nerve-racking nature. I need them to let myself go in my moments of physical weakness. Their soft padding gives me an unspeakable feeling of well-being and rest, but I must admit that this feeling also thrills my genitals and gives me a prompt erection, although I am not otherwise provoked. Aside from that, I am no longer afflicted by my formerly anomalous habit of looking after everybody who hobbles along on crutches, except, perhaps, when the cripple may be a young and well-dressed woman. That is probably due to the fact that my wife also had to use crutches for a few months. I learned that fact quite accidentally from her during a conversation. And no matter what might have separated us, I firmly believe that the crutches would have reunited us. Occasionally, when my wife would suffer a nervous breakdown, she would make use of the crutches I had made for her. I may add that her seal coat also poured oil on the flames of our sexual attraction.

" 'But, in contrast to the crutches, my fur fetishism has remained unchanged. As always, I look at every girl who wears a fox, and get quite a thrill in winter out of the long fur coats with the great collars. In my room at home, I have collected all kinds of skins and furs. I sleep under a panther skin and in the summer, I lay a light woolen coverlet over it (in the winter I use a feather bed). My summer and winter slippers are lined with fur, and my smoking jacket has a broad seal collar.

" 'My former bashfulness in the matter of using crutches publicly has disappeared to the extent that I often go out on crutches towards evening and even use them at home despite occasional visitors. I must add that these practices are made easier for me by the presence of the daughter of my wife's first marriage, a twenty-six-year-old widow to whom I am sexually indifferent. She understands my habits and keeps house for me.

" 'That is thus my present condition: fur fetishism of the crassest sort. Crutches are now for me only a means of supporting me in times of nervous weakness and not, as formerly, purely erotic objects. Crutches in others: only when worn by young, well-dressed women (preferably also dressed in furs). Masturbation: Formerly every night and now about twice every three weeks or about once in ten days. During my work, I occasionally think of my "wives," but this does not spur me to any form of activity and leaves me without any great animation.

" 'But, aside from that, I cannot forget the memory of the happy two years with my wife which have just passed. I yearn for her; the woman of my heart. Her coarse brunette features, her slender figure, the deathly sad and mystical eyes, her small hands and feet. But my woman would have to have an understanding for my other "wives," even if it were but the understanding that comes of all powerful love. This woman who could inflame my weakened passions by clothing her naked figure in furs and wearing softly padded crutches, such a woman would be my true savior. She would be my heaven on earth, the happiness which my furs and crutches can, after all, only partially afford me. For, to tell the truth, both these objects lack soft arms to embrace me, red, hot lips to kiss me and invite my love.

" 'Crutches and furs! And yet my wife was certainly wrong when she said to me: "You don't need a woman."

" 'But where am I to find the right one, and who is there to help me find her?

> " 'I am perverse; and yet it seems to me,
> With all that makes me "satisfied,"
> With all the means, the glee,
> My deepest spirit is never gratified.
> Furs and crutches are my salvation,
> But only when the heart, my breath, do hold.
> An unearthly love, the heart's pure gold,
> Will be my final liberation.' "

(Taken from "Sexualreform," supplement to "Geschlecht und Gesellschaft." Edited by Ferdinand Freiherr v. Reitzenstein, Vol. X, No. 2, Oct. 1920. Verlag Richard A. Giesecke, Dresden. l.c., pp. 20-23.)

This is a case of rudimentary fetishism. It is quite indicative of his character that he never had intercourse until his twenty-fifth year and that his wife feels herself playing second fiddle to the crutches. Like all such patients, he indulged in much onanism, but weaned himself of the habit with an iron will during his marriage. His relations to his mother are pretty clearly defined. Normally built persons who walk on crutches provoke a prompt erection.

It is this point, which will appear later in the long analysis to follow, that I want to emphasize.

It is the healthy individual hobbling on crutches which catches and provokes the fancy of these patients. That reveals the fact to us that the patients are ultimately attracted by a reflection of themselves; they occasionally play the cripple by hobbling about, too.

He also suspected that the man whom he had seen while on walks with his mother also played the cripple. Beggars and those with amputated legs did not interest him (we shall see an analogy to this later). He claims to use the crutches, not because of their sexual interest, but because of their use as support when he is tired. ". . . It was not the sexual attractiveness of the crutches which caused me to yearn for them again. It is the tired feeling I get when I have had to stand for some time, the weariness I suffer from so much walking in my position as an editor. . . ." This is the most ludicrous type of rationalization. For we know that hobbling on crutches is a most tiring form of locomotion. But the patient needed the sexual stimulation which this afforded him, although he was not conscious of that fact.

Of his potency he tells us that it was not so great as that of a normal male. It took him quite a while before he achieved the first ejaculation, and sometimes even this was impossible until his wife would begin to tell him of the time when she was suffering from rheumatism and wore crutches. That means that only his specific phantasy was able to provoke orgasm. He happily awaits the day when his wife's age will enable him to live in abstinence, and already he sees her hobbling on crutches. He denies that he deflected any of his affections from his wife into such phantasies ("that's untrue"), and yet it is a palpable and saddening fact.

Another form of unique aberration reported in the literature is the type of man who can love only amputated women. Lydston's case (a lecture on sexual perversion, Chicago, 1890) is well known. His patient had a love affair with a woman one of whose legs was amputated and when he lost her, he greedily looked for a substitute. Transitions to such cases are those in which a limping girl is the love object; cases in which the limping is the *conditio sine qua non* of the love affair. Two characteristic cases may be taken from Krafft-Ebing.

Case 65. X., twenty-eight years old, claims that since his seventeenth year, his sexual passions are aroused only by the sight of female cripples, particularly by women who limp and have crippled feet. Ever since puberty he has been the subject of this fetishism which is of the deepest mortification to him. A normal exerts not the slightest influence upon him; his love is inflamed only by a female with a limp and crippled and crooked feet. Any woman, quite regardless of whether she be pretty or ugly, may ignite his passions if only she fulfill the fetishistic requirement. In his wet dreams, he sees pictures of only such crippled women, and occasionally he cannot resist the temptation to ape such a female himself. While doing such tricks, he will get a violent orgasm followed by a prompt ejaculation, attended by the deepest gratification. The patient complained that he was very passionate and suffered from a lack of satisfaction of his instincts. He first had coitus at twenty-two and has since cohabited but five times. Despite good potency, he claims that the intercourse gave him no satisfaction whatever, and he feels that if he ever had the good fortune to sleep with a lame woman, everything would be different. He is sure that he will marry none but a lame girl.

Case 66. A similar case. V., thirty years of age, government official, comes of very neuropathic parents. For several years after he was seven, his sole playmate was a lame girl of his own age.

At the age of twelve, without having been introduced to the habit by anyone else, the hypersexed and nervous boy began to masturbate. At about the same time, he began to show signs of pubertal development and it is beyond a doubt true that his first sexual animation was connected with the sight of lame or limping girls. From that time on, only limping or crippled women provoked his fancy. His fetish was a pretty woman who (like his childhood playmate) limped on the left side. V., who was exclusively heterosexual, and also very passionate, tried his best to satisfy his needs, but found that he was totally impotent when with normal women. His potency and gratification were greatest when the prostitute happened to be lame on the left side, but he was also potent with such as limped on the right side. Since, however, he was able to satisfy his fetishistic demands only occasionally, he resorted to masturbation, despite the fact this appeared to him to be a disgusting and unhappy surrogate. His sexual difficulties so depressed and dejected him that he often considered suicide, but only his devotion to his parents held him back. His moral suffering culminated in the fact that although he had cherished the hope some day to marry a sympathetic and limping woman he felt that he would never appreciate the woman so much as her lameness, and this attitude seemed to him to be a profanity against the holiness of marriage, an unbearable and impossible form of existence. This situation had frequently made him think of having himself castrated.

Case 67. Z., a man of a rather stigmatized family, claims that he manifested a special sympathy for lame and limping people even as a child. He would hobble about the kitchen on two broom sticks as crutches, but had, as yet, no open sexual excitation as a consequence. He would also play the cripple in an empty side street. Gradually the idea developed that he, as a handsome, crippled child, would approach a pretty young girl and thus gain its sympathy. The sympathy of men would have been repellent to him. Z., who was reared privately in the best of homes, claims to have known nothing of sex or intercourse until he was twenty-one. The feelings he had were as yet innocent in his eyes; they consisted of phantasies of being pitied by a healthy girl while hobbling on crutches or himself expressing sympathy with a lame girl. Gradually, these phantasies were more and more sexualized and, at twenty, he succumbed to masturbation under the force of such day-dreams. His increasingly onanistic and phantastic life developed into a sexual neurasthenia and he was finally so hyper-irritable in this respect that the very sight of a lame girl on the street would excite an ejaculation. Of course, all his onanistic activities and his wet dreams were also accompanied by such phantasies. Z. himself came to realize that the person who was lame was quite a negligible factor in his eyes, and that his interest was directed solely at the lame foot. Z. has never yet tried to have intercourse with any of the women who manifest his fetishistic conditions. He does not feel in the mood to attempt such a thing nor does he trust his potency. His phantasies are strictly confined to masturbating with the feet of lame women. Occasionally he collects himself sufficiently to think of gaining the love of a limping girl, and believes that overjoyed at the fact that he loves her very greatest handicap, the girl would free him from his fetishism by lifting his love "from the soul of her foot to the foot of her soul." That would be his salvation, he thinks. In his present condition, he feels himself the unhappiest of men.

In all of these cases we see a characteristic retreat from the female, from active sexual duty. Z. never attempted coitus and H. fled from the possibility of marriage under the hypocritical rationalization that he would probably not love the woman but the lameness.

V. bases his paraphilia on a protracted experience which began when he was seven, but both the others have no good ground for the incidence of their present condition. X. identifies himself with the limping woman; he even apes her. He fails to achieve orgasm in intercourse.

In all these cases sympathy, the cruelty of the weak, plays an important rôle.

The following letter from a colleague gives us a good idea of the picture of an amputation fetishist.

Case 68. "Dear Colleague: I shall leave it to your good judgment as to whether you may be able to use the information contained in this letter for your scientific writings. In order first to give you an idea as to who I am and, as it were, introducing myself, let me preface my statements with a sort of *curriculum vitae*.

"I was born in 1894 in N., the son of an official. My childhood disclosed nothing of special importance. I went through public and high school with success, I might even say with ease. My upbringing was the best possible. I honor and respect my parents greatly, my father particularly. From an early age, both my brother, who is four years younger than I, and myself were reared to become capable men, if I may say so, by a life judiciously divided between work, all kinds of athletic exercise and noble diversion. Through a number of trips and hikes, undertaken with my father, I came to know and understand both man and nature at an early age. After graduating from high school, I served my year of military time and then entered the University of Innsbruck to study medicine. My studies were suddenly interrupted in August 1914. I was called immediately to the colors and served for four full years at the front as an artillery officer. It seems that my luck carried me through considerable danger without injury to the end of the war. It was with a veritable voracity that I returned to my studies and graduated in medicine in 1920. As a student I had been either a voluntary or second assistant in various theoretical departments. At the present time I am an assistant in a surgical clinic. I may add that my professional activities satisfy and fulfill all the hopes of my life.

"As regards any further medical information, I could not say very much more. My parents are alive and well, as is also my brother. No one of my relatives has ever been seriously ill. I myself was also never seriously ill, aside from the usual children's diseases. At present I find myself in the best of physical health.

"After this rather long-winded introduction, permit me to speak of my pathological *vita sexualis*. To begin with, I must say that I suffer from a most eccentric form of fetishism, although I know, my dear colleague, that you no longer call this form by the name of fetishism. Any woman who has had a leg amputated exerts a most marked sexual influence upon me. Like all other fetishists, I have also become specialized: I am most deeply affected by a pretty young girl who has been amputated at the thigh and wears a wooden leg. Amputated men do not interest me at all. If I may put it in such terms, I have 'practised' this specialty only very seldom. Occasionally, like the foolish pup that I was, I followed a girl who may have worn a wooden leg or a prosthesis. Once, I can still recall the day clearly, I sat on a bench in the courtyard of the hospital and greedily watched a young girl with a wooden leg walking about the yard. I was always too bashful to start up a flirtation with an amputated girl. The case of that medical student cited by Merzbach always used to excite my envy because he had a girl. I have never practised masturbation, but I have often achieved erections and ejaculations by prolonged and oblivious indulgence in phantasies of my idol; in other words, a purely psychic form of masturbation. Otherwise, my sex life has been the usual thing, i.e., I have frequently and satisfactorily effected intercourse. I never went to prostitutes, but took the opportunity whenever it presented itself with so-called 'nice girls.' If no opportunity for intercourse presented itself, I would be subject to pollutions about every two weeks, and these wet dreams would frequently, but not always, be attended by dreams of amputated girls. Finally, I would like to say that my eccentric sexual habits have begun to wane, particularly since I have become acquainted with a girl whom I love dearly and whom I intend to marry soon. As soon as our relationship had become somewhat more intimate than usual, I confessed my whole condition to my girl, and I was overjoyed to find a love of my person and an understanding of my weaknesses which gave me courage. I now know that this marriage will completely cure me of my perversion.

"Now, my dear colleague, you will doubtless have several questions to ask me, being a specialist in these matters and a psychologist. Nevertheless, I shall try to answer some of these questions in advance if possible. I am, to be sure, not at all specialized in the field of sexology, but I have looked through the literature for similar cases, and I could cite several cases of the same type. And yet, with all my reading, I am still in the dark as to the nature and origin of my sexual or psycho-sexual condition. First of all, as regards the initial appearance of this disease. Try as I may, I cannot possibly find an 'infantile root' to this thing. I can only remember that, as a fourteen-year-old boy, I saw a girl lift her skirts and fix something on her wooden leg. I got a prompt erection without, however, realizing what the connection was. Later, when the sight of a person with an amputated leg invariably provoked an erection, I began to be puzzled, searched for an explanation in all kinds of writings and books. To-day I am finally in a position to judge the condition a little better."

Since this colleague was not able to come to Vienna for an analysis, I sent him a questionnaire to fill out, among the more important questions being such as would evoke answers about his earliest memories; these usually containing the nucleus of a paraphilia.

After some time had passed, I received the following answer:

"Dear Doctor:

"You have put a number of questions to me which I shall now try—as well as I can—to answer.

"First of all, I cannot quite share your opinion that my condition consists of a disguised form of sadism. I can answer all your questions in that regard (pulling out insects' wings, breaking toys, etc.) with a definite 'No.' Your next question as to whether a naked leg ever caught my fancy in youth must be answered in the affirmative, if I am to consider puberty as equivalent to youth. I must add, however, that an elegantly stockinged leg acts with greater effect upon my sensibilities than a naked one.  I must also mention the fact that my 'love condition' further insists upon having the single leg of the girl well stockinged and shod; this holds for my dreams as well as for my phantasies.  And yet I am positive that this is not a case of fetishism which has to do with the idolatry of these articles of clothing.  Still another factor appears to be of significance: the sight, image or even intercourse with a woman amputated on both sides would leave me absolutely cold.  As regards your request for dreams containing images of amputated women, I must say that it is impossible for me to offer you dreams of the past for analysis, but I assure you that I shall promptly inform you of the very next dream of this kind that I may have, all the apparently unimportant details included.  Your last question about my earliest memories is not quite clear to me for I think I mentioned what appears to me to be my earliest memory in my first letter to you.  It is possible that that experience simply reactivated memories of a much deeper stratum, but I cannot at present recall any special occurrence of an earlier age which might be of significance in this respect.

"Thanking you for your interest in my case, I remain

"Yours truly,

"N. N."

After sending a second letter which specifically explained the meaning and intent of my questionnaire, explained the castration phantasies and searched for his daily dreams, I received no answer.

Aside from these cases from the literature, I have nothing further to say on this theme.  One thing is manifest: there is a colossal difference between the descriptive period of psychopathology and the analytical.  Once we have undertaken a thorough analysis of such a case we are able to arrive at roots of the condition, the sources of the condensations, and the motives of the parapathia.

All the cases we have studied in this chapter reveal to us an intimate welding of fetishism and sadism.  As I have mentioned at the outset, the fetishist may look like a lamb, a masochist, at first sight.  He administers pain to himself, inflicts all kinds of punishment upon himself, binds and chains his body and limbs, he suffers for his paraphilia.  But behind this masochism is hidden a boundless cruelty and sadism. The aggressiveness which was originally directed towards objects in the outer world has been turned upon the individual himself. It is precisely this gruesomeness which drives the fetishist into the arms of religion. God must protect him against himself and his wild impulses. We now begin to understand why the fetishist avoids a partner and remains satisfied with a symbol. He is like a homosexual who, because of an aggressiveness towards the opposite sex, flees to his own. That is also the reason why fetishists reveal a combination of both paraphilias. They become homosexual fetishists. The next case will demonstrate to us such a combined paraphilia.

## XV

## A CASE OF ORTHOPEDIC FETISHISM

The patient whose analysis follows is a twenty-seven-year-old physician who comes from Riga. His mother is Russian, his father German. His grandmother was a Jewess. Ten years before the outbreak of the war, his father moved from Riga to Germany, where he founded a factory and amassed a fortune sufficient for him to live well and educate his children in the best manner. Our patient—we shall call him Otto—was always a very healthy child. He was very sensitive about his ancestry because he wanted to be a "real German."

Because of a very complicated form of fetishism which shall be exhaustively described later on, he turned to Professor X. for advice. Professor X. referred him to me. Otto had already become acquainted with several volumes of my works and himself understood that nothing but an analysis could help him. He decided to undertake treatment, but wanted to do so without the knowledge of his father which would then make it financially difficult for him to carry out.

Before we go into Otto's analysis, let us hear what he has to say about himself. He wrote me a long letter, in which he treated of the psychogenesis of his difficulty at great length. This letter is very valuable because it was written by a physician who understood the significance of various psychological factors. In this letter he stresses certain details which will appear as important high lights in his analysis.

Case 69.
"DEAR DOCTOR:

"Having read through several volumes of your works on *Disturbances of the Instincts and the Emotions,* I have gained an entirely different attitude towards my own sexual difficulties.

"In consequence, I visited Professor X. to-day and asked him for his advice. He told me that, according to the information I gave him, you would be the person who could advise me best; that he himself was not in a sufficiently experienced position to treat me with specialized knowledge.

"In the following, I shall try to give you as accurate a description of my present sexual situation and its development as I can.

"I am twenty-seven years old, physician, and intend to start upon an academic medical career. At the present time I am in the midst of preparing a rather large work on orthopedic subjects.

"My parents are alive and well. I love my mother very much, but have always been troubled with considerable inhibition in the presence of my father who is a rather nervous man.

"I lay this to his complete inability to understand my sexual states (masturbation, homosexuality) and to the rather strained relations which existed between us during my school days. That was due to the fact that, despite my talents, I had great difficulty in advancing without outside aid.

"I also have three sisters: twenty-eight, twenty-two, and seventeen. The middle one is happily married, the other two are still unmarried.

"I can remember that as a child I liked to play with my sisters' dolls and also found enjoyment in doing girl's work (such as knitting and the like). I believe that that was before I went to school. I was closer to my eldest sister than to any of the others.

"When I was about nine or ten, we always used to wrestle and fight about in bed every morning, and also amused ourselves at night (our rooms were next to each other) by playing through the door; I was the king of ghosts and she was the queen of the elves.

"In the course of the subsequent years, I suffered from nocturnal fears which persisted until I was about fourteen years of age. As far as I can recall, these conditions were connected with two houses which my parents lived in, one after the other. I would get certain visions which introduced the nightmares. Far out on a plain I would see a little bundle of something which would gradually enlarge like a hurricane, approach me and take my breath away, so that I finally awoke in frightful anxiety. Before this would occur and before I fell asleep (at about thirteen or fourteen), I would have the feeling that my fingers had become very thick, everything seemed to sound unusually loud, my body felt pathologically large, and the room seemed to have turned into a great plain with all the furniture very far off. The latter feeling later appeared by day, too.

"I can distinctly recall my first emission. I was about ten and a half years old. I dreamed that I jumped up on the step of a coach which was in motion and pressed my body against the coach door.

"I cannot recall having had sexual experiences before that time.

"When I was about eleven, I got up nights and would walk about in a state of somnambulism. They usually found me crying in the dining room. I must have banged myself against the edge of the table, awakened, and begun to cry because I was afraid and didn't know at first where I was. One night my parents came into my room to find me standing on the edge of the window sill.

"When I was eleven, a schoolmate who was several years my senior took me along with him to some place and had me masturbate with him. I can't very well remember just what he did with me or what the first moves were.

"He also satisfied his leanings on several of the other boys of my own age, but with me he only masturbated. I was somewhat shy in complying with his demand that we practise mutual masturbation. I think the feel of his phallus must have disgusted me as much as his whole person did. What attracted me about him was the thrill of the thing and the fact that he did me many little favors. He would give me postage stamps for my collection, a penny now and then, bits of cake or cookies, etc.

"When we masturbated, he would bind me fast. I can't recall anything else that was in my mind. He would tie me to the sofa with ropes and straps. That only heightened my pleasures (I must have been about twelve). Once I had ejaculated, I would demand that he untie me again. Once we bound a third boy in this way, but performed no sexual act on him.

"One psychic filip still remains in my memory: A boy came to our school who, because of a crippled condition, had to wear nickel shanks on his legs. They used to tease him a lot. The vision of this boy provoked my fancy every time I would masturbate.

"I also recall the day I finally refused to continue those practices with my friend. That was probably due to certain rising ethical and moral or esthetic feelings. But I continued to masturbate alone as usual. It is probable that I exploited both methods together for a while, but gradually neither his promises nor his pleading could get me to continue serving him. By that time, however, he must have been using me for his onanistic practices for years. Always per manum. Neither he nor I ever demanded pederasty. It is also possible that he took my phallus into his mouth, but that must have been seldom.

"The autoerotic period which followed my fourteenth year was marked by my binding myself, tying myself in bed, bandaging, beating, hanging myself between two ironing boards, etc. One hand, of course, had to remain free for the masturbation. I also dressed dolls, and found especial interest in the bust of a youth which stood in my room. After carrying out my manipulations on myself, I would use this statue as a substitute and take it to bed with me. It was life size. Then I resorted to my imagination which I naturally augmented by divers printed matter that I had collected. I was markedly provoked by any kind of description of binding, tying or anything which put a human in a very uncomfortable position, regardless of whether the victim were man or woman. The chief thing was that they had to be young and handsome persons. I would also complete the pictures in the books to my taste by sketching chains, bandages, and the like.

"Very dimly I recall having seen a boy come out of the house of an orthopedist in my home city, and it seems to me now that he must have worn an orthopedic corset. I was struck by the lack of movement which it permitted in the neck especially. I must have searched for a picture of that for some time. I can't recall how old I was. But often, when I would ramble in the streets in order somehow to get away from myself and my impulses, this memory would shadow me. That boy was accompanied by a woman who held him with her left hand.

"For the sake of clarity, I sha'n't go into the struggles and mental conflicts which have burdened me ever since my fourteenth year. They are the conflicts which arise from the upbringing and the esthetic and ethical attitude that one grows up with; they are also typical of the state of most onanists.

"I wish only to mention that I constantly collected provocative material, and although I was always burning my collections on the occasion of a reactive depression, the collection of books, papers and cuts grew steadily larger and the burnings just as steadily less frequent.

"And as my desire for new material grew, I would become increasingly irritated by the loss of the old. For my autoerotic practices were by now completely occupying the time I had to myself and my whole life during those school days was taken up with the striving for new material.

"In my worst days, I probably masturbated three times daily.

Later, I began to have more to do with my schoolmates than formerly, when I was rather withdrawn. I began to avoid being alone and tried hard to rid myself of my habits. Now my memory fades.

"I can hardly recall any sexual practices, either of a heterosexual or homosexual nature. But between 1912 and 1914, I lived in a period of marked erotic experience. First of all, I joined the Boy Scouts, where I came in close contact with several other boys. As far as I am concerned, these contacts were distinctly physical in nature. I even tried to touch the genitals of a comrade of mine one night in camp, but he prevented this.

"Somewhat later, I again had opportunities to touch the genitals of another comrade, but that was a wish of mine only in so far as I was altogether desirous of a physical contact. I was beginning to strive towards some physical feeling, that *contact des epidermes.*

"That is to-day the only desire I possess aside from my auto-erotic activity. But now that wish presents itself only in the presence of my friends. And if it should present itself in the presence of a woman, I promptly and forcibly repress it.

"But first as to my heterosexual experiences. A twenty-three-year-old married woman who had started up a friendship with me, finally achieved her ends on Good Friday 1913, after having tried in vain during my visits in Berlin (i.e., vainly for her, for I had amused myself considerably). We were sitting together on the sofa. The moon was full. She suddenly fell upon me with all her blonde weight (four children!), pressed me to her bosom and covered me with kisses which I ardently returned. I fell into a violent but paralyzing excitement, my whole body trembled, and it was all very easy for me because of this state to resist sleeping with her. I gave divers moralities as an excuse. Following this, we cultivated an intimate, ardent and sexually provocative correspondence for over a year. My burning sexuality drove me to verses.

"This affair broke up at Easter 1914 as I was falling into my third affair.

"After her, there was a short-lived affair with a small blonde with whom I had acted in a little play. On the stage we had kissed each other and continued to do so afterwards. But she did not satisfy my discriminating esthetic tastes and since her mother irritated me, too, I gave her up after a week.

"The third one took place just before I graduated from high

school.  She was a friend of a friend of mine who was plentifully
supplied with girls.  I laid siege to the castle and scaled the
heights in one grand sortie.  She pouted and I gave her an ultima-
tum.  After that I had all the bodily feeling and contact I wanted,
as well as kisses and hugs.[1]

"Nor was this affair lacking in the spiritual superstructure which
I so desired.  We liked each other and my sexuality (the physical
contact) was completely gratified.

"I then went off to the university and she to a girls' school.  The
separation was so hard on me that, when my father called me
down for my actions, I ran out of the room bawling (nineteen).

"In addition to these, there were a few other girls who attracted
me, physically as well as otherwise, but they were so surrounded
with boys, and so coquettish, that I had to leave off.  Whenever
I was with a girl, I wanted her wholly, i.e., totally in my way,
and if that were not possible if I had to flirt with her, then I
was dissatisfied.  Aside from all these, I was friendly with a lot
of other girls, without having any physical contact with them.
They were usually friends of my sister.

"My heterosexual period was criss-crossed by divers attractions
to men, too (e.g., the twelve-year-old brother of my third girl).
During this period, my autoerotic habits raised their head again,
but were easily put down.  The whole phase was finally ended
by a farewell letter which my girl wrote me at the instigation of
her mother.  She gave me up and I felt very down-hearted and
depressed.  Thereupon my autoerotic practices came to the fore
again.

"The books I read were mainly from the sadistic press in Leipsic.
But I also found some expression for my spirit in the friendship
of young fellows and boys with whom I was living as a Boy
Scout.  That was a happy time for me, as I recall.  I felt very
much attached to several boys of my own age, some of them
younger and one of them also older.  But I had a deep sense of
responsibility and rejected every homosexual offer that came from
one of the other boys.  The ideals which I had been forming ever
since the last days of my school period were being more clearly
fixed in my mind.

"Keep clean!  That means: don't masturbate, as well as anything else.  Ascetic!  Even in school, I had been the only one
among all the boys who was abstinent, didn't smoke, didn't frequent the cafés and didn't swap dirty stories.

"Keep clean for the great love of your life! A very pretty ideal, I should say.

"Well, instead of the great love there came the great war, together with a whole horde of divers homosexual and sadistic attacks upon a man's person.

"I went in as a volunteer. The close-fitting uniform was a provocative agent for me, and the downright sharp treatment we got in the army was nothing short of pabulum for my autoerotic strivings. Among the traumata for my sexual make-up, I might mention the special exercises for punishment, the harsh commands and cursing, being hauled up before the commanding officer, and, later, the divers punishments and sentences which led to one's being bound, chained or handcuffed. Not the least of my delights was the sight of wounded soldiers who, of course, were well represented and fully satisfied my autoerotism or, rather, sadism.

"After this period began, I ceased to have any contact with women altogether. From December 1914 to January 1919, I was constantly at the front, and from May 1916 on, I was a lieutenant in the artillery.

"My heterosexual affairs were thus made more difficult during the war. I also threw my principles of abstinence overboard, and the longer the war lasted, especially after I had become an officer, the more I drank and smoked in my attempt to keep up with my comrades in arms. Later on, also, I had to do something to fight off the growing necessity to revert to onanism.

"I masturbated particularly during the winter of 1917 at a time when we were in the midst of terrific close encounters. But I would also surge through a period of onanism whenever I suffered any sexual trauma, such as those which affected my sadistic complex particularly.

"I never found it necessary to torment anyone unusually, and although I was firm and resolved in my military manner, I never acted like the sabre-rattlers and rowdies that some of the men were. On the contrary, I sublimated my lust to sympathy and astonishment that such things could pass as handcuffing when simple arrest would have been enough. As a matter of fact, I would have loved nothing better than to see handcuffing all round, just in order that I might express my sympathy and sorrow all the more. This sympathetic and helpful attitude is what really determined me in my choice of a profession.

"I am very clear on that point. The deciding factor was: you must become a doctor, so that you may sublimate your sadistic tendencies to sympathy and help. There is, of course, the question as to whether, because of this attitude, I might be forced to do something that would be strictly unethical and dangerous.

"But I believe that the spark of self-preservation would prevent me from any aberration in that direction. After all, I have no real need of a sadistic activity, and the normal professional work (agreed that it might also be replete with sexual provocations for me) would doubtless satisfy me even if it turned out that my present condition were incurable.

"Now, please pardon me if I seem to digress somewhat. But I must tell you, in reference to my medical activities, that my present situation is such that my autoerotism gratifies me completely, but the autoerotism is solely directed towards irritations and provocations of an orthopedic nature—the orthopedic corset. Not fetishism, but simply an animation which is connected with the conscious relationship between the corset and a person. Formerly, the female played an equal rôle in my phantasies with the male; as a matter of fact, in my binding and tying phantasies, she was preferred. But now she has been almost completely displaced. She's now only a surrogate, a sort of walking on crutches. The splint on an arm. By the way, splints, etc., are most delectable provocations for me. Bandaging a patient can form one of the most consciously pleasurable experiences, i.e., if the patient satisfies my homosexual attitudes. He must be between fifteen and twenty-five, although the age limit is constantly changing as my own age changes. Formerly, e.g., I was attached to much younger men. I must add that a mustache is disturbing, but a few hairs are not so bad.

"When I consider my abhorrence of women now in the light of the information I have gained from a perusal of your works, I must admit that my sister was right when she said: 'You're afraid to be together with a woman.' Women are not simply indifferent material as far as I am concerned. On the contrary, the more sexualized and attractive they may appear, the more they repel me. I myself often feel that I'm anxious because something might happen. I might really do something. Summer of 1919, I was together with a highly sexed girl, a friend of my sister's, who sort of 'thawed' me out. It went so far that I finally got some pleasure out of tormenting her, a thought which almost made me feel that I might, under this influence, be able to effect intercourse with a prostitute.

"I acted in the same way in the winter of 1920, when a female student of rather libidinous make-up made advances to me, and also got me excited during a dance.

"Just because of her markedly sexualized and erotic attitude, I am moved to a strong dislike. And when we were to do some tableaux, I expressed my feelings in the matter by packing her into a box which was supposed to be my appurtenance as a Hindu fakir. I then proceeded to play as if I had the swords these fakirs are supposed to have, and stabbed through the box several times. But I wasn't thrilled or delighted at being able to express my feelings in this manner; it was rather a feeling of disgust that followed my having given way to my distaste to such an extent that I was able to humiliate her in this fashion.

"I frequently get the thought: What use is a woman to you when you can't live with her as a woman would live with her.

"But I'm always becoming infatuated with young men, i.e., with more or less intensity. Regular homosexuals, i.e., men who call themselves that, are repulsive to me and do not animate me in the least. My whole attitude is summed up when I say that I have dedicated myself entirely to my own sex, but my potency and erotism stop with the achievement of spiritual and bodily contact. All my attempts at homosexual intercourse, such as frequently took place during the war, were just as much a failure as any attempt would be to have intercourse with a prostitute. I tried the latter method twice without success. Nor could any form of perverse provocation bring about sufficient libido as to promote even an erection.

"Succinctly, I emphasize the old Greek relationship in its ideal form, without, however, desiring it to arrive at the final erotic goal of actual intercourse. The libido which is signified in the erect phallus, the desire which drives me to masturbate, is no wise related to my attachment to men, despite the fact that in those relationships I may also get an erection. It is, rather, related strictly to myself, I produce it only through my own phantasies and thoughts and satisfy myself on myself by means of onanism.

"I have noticed that these autoerotic and sadistic phantasies may be diluted and diminished in force through the agency of love, such as was the case in the affairs I mentioned before (heterosexual as well as homosexual) ; but the homosexual forms of attachment were less effective in this respect for the simple reason that they were directed at heterosexual men with whom it was either difficult or impossible to gain any contact.

"Furthermore, all these autoerotic complexes, i.e., my obsession on sadistic phantasies, died away whenever the opportunity presented itself to sublimate my sadism into sympathy, e.g., during my activity in the surgical clinic. I must say, however, that those persons who acted as the objects of my sublimated feelings, thereafter played a leading rôle in my autoerotic phantasies and images. I could give you good examples but I need not do so at this time.

"All the men whom I like to any extent, also drop out when it comes to my sadistic notions. I protect them, as it were, from myself, and if I do try to include them, my libido fades.

"The objects of sadistic phantasies are the people I may have seen on the street; patients who have been seen by me in the hospital; and pictures which I have collected from medical text-books and magazines.

"In the period of my having succumbed to one of my obsessive attacks, I feel impelled to collect whatever books and magazines, pictures or sketches I can lay my hands on. I buy up books only after considerable struggle with myself and perhaps after days of restlessness; and often I even steal what I want.

"One of the greatest bits of print in this respect is, e.g., Wullstein's monograph on the treatment of scoliosis. I acquired this big book along with many others when I was in Berlin for a post graduate course in January 1918.

"A book which contains a prototype of my essential phantasies is Neumann's *John Bull as Educator;* another is Rüdiger's *A Bitter Childhood.* The chief virtues of the latter, as far as I am concerned, lay in the descriptions of the upbringing of the young boys by severe governesses who use corsets, straight-laced gloves, stiff collars, female dresses, etc. R. H. Dohrn's stories about the witches' tower also excited me, although I had to transpose the masochistic language into sadistic terms.

"The attitude of the masochist is thus plainly foreign to me, but the attachment of masochist ideas to the objects of my sadistic pleasure is distinctly advantageous to my feeling.

"Since about the end of the war, I have been living in a world of the following composition:

"'I extended my ante bellum ideas and said to myself: there was no war. Every sign of sexual aberration that you show is due to hyper-irritability of the nervous system.   So, see to it that you cure yourself and get busy.

"That I would become a physician if I ever got out of that war alive was a determined fact with me.

"When I did come out, I went into divers social reform and 'Jugend' movements with all my soul and was thus able to sublimate my sadistic strivings to some extent.   Being with those young men and boys helped me considerably.   But, unfortunately, a few months of success was usually followed by a depressing relapse.   But I held out.   You're not homosexual, I said.   The foundations of your conduct are noble and pure, and not dictated by a perverted sexuality.   Reform activities, uplift, abstinence, vegetarianism, etc., were all a wide field for my sublimations.   And I had good reasons, too.   Blüher attracted me, and I was able to support him well, just as I had always been able to support anyone who preached a sound and sensible attitude towards onanism and homosexuality.   But I could not support his ideals of manhood.

"And with all my searching, loving and hating, I missed the one person from whom I separated myself more and more (my mother).   Perhaps because I feared that I might exert my sadism upon her, too.   I believe that a woman, femaleness, could save me and bring me peace.   She could be my salvation, whereas my autoerotism and my love for men cannot afford me that peace which I seek.   The unselfish love of a woman is simply something which is not an attribute of a man.

"I believe that I am one of those infantilistic individuals whom you say you can help.   Consciously, I am in love with neither my perversion nor my homosexuality.   How much I am unconsciously attached to these tendencies is something I cannot tell.   I suffer from my thoughts while at work, although I realize full well that I frequently revert to them in order to provoke some tension in myself.

"Whether I am sufficiently socialized to produce inhibitions and repressions, or whether I may yet develop in this direction, is something I cannot foresee.

"The human in me is suffering, and it is my greatest wish to do something for humanity, a desire which I cannot believe to be related in any way to my phallus.

"I now remember that I have completely forgotten to mention anything about my dreams.   I have already mentioned my first wet dream.   For years afterwards, I never had such a dream, but in the past few years, that is, when onanistic activities did not intervene, I have had emissions with considerable regularity. As far as I can recall, these emissions were attended by anxiety and the feeling: don't you dare to masturbate, or: now you've masturbated again; but later these reproaches were dropped from the dreams. I accepted the wet dreams as something which relieved me from tension. The provocative origins of such dreams were usually taken from autoerotic tendencies.

"In future, I shall try to note down my dreams in order to be able to put them at your disposal. I might add that I dream very much. Hardly a night passes that I do not dream something, many of them being of a sexual nature, but some of them often having an asexual tinge. Frequently, I awaken in the morning with a full recollection of what I have dreamed.

"Many times I have dreamed of the war, that I had to return to my company, was looking for it under great excitement and couldn't find it. Then I see myself as an infantryman again, although I am an officer. Very often I dream that I'm on horse (one of my dearest wishes, even consciously, is to ride again). Again, I am seriously wounded; horrible wounds which, strangely, don't hurt me.

"Or, I may have one or two wooden legs, but my walking seems unimpaired. Everybody is happy to see me back again. We are attacked. The artillery begins a furious barrage, etc., etc.

"The periodic dreams attended by anxiety and awakening, which occurred after my pavor nocturnus had ceased, were marked by a regular and schematic make-up. I would be in a certain house, and would feel that now those men would be coming, usually Indians, but frequently also other men. I try to hide and always run into the same room where, although I know that I shall be found, I crawl under the bed. The room does not exist in reality. I hear the men coming closer and closer and finally, with the greatest of anxiety, I am discovered and awaken.

"I believe that this dream has not occurred since 1914. Recently, however, I have had more frequent dreams which are marked by my unprincipled habits of smoking and drinking. At first, I tried to resist these habits in the dream and would awaken in despair. But gradually I accustomed myself to smoking and drinking in the dream, the reproaches became less frequent, as if I realized that it were all a dream. Lately, these dreams have also disappeared.

"It seems that dreams of a heterosexual nature were seldom, but they also occurred. Following upon a rather wild dream full of guilt feelings, I would see myself pursued because of some delinquency, would get away under difficulty; I married a certain Nelly K. whom I had met in the Wandervögel (a German youth movement—Trans.) and whom I found very sympathetic. We were coming from the justice of the peace, I had given her my arm, and my sister was also present (who also studied in Riga and with whom I had just previously had a conversation on sexual questions). I was quite happy and felt that everything would now be all right.

"On another day, I took a look at the girl and I must confess that, of all the girls I know, she is the most appealing to me. Why? Nevertheless, these conscious feelings do not corroborate my dream. I promptly produced a manifest resistance against all this by saying to myself that she could never become my wife even if I did have a physical striving towards her, etc., etc. I must also have had a dream not long ago in which a woman excited me sexually, but I haven't the faintest recollection of what it was all about.

"But I can assure you that when necessary I could manage to remember all my heterosexual dreams. Recently, after I had busied myself with the library of a masochist (for 'scientific reasons') in which I found many references to flagellantistic scenes, I had a military dream in which I was a witness to a whipping scene. Otherwise I am not given to the ideas and strivings of flagellants, although my onanistic passions are heightened by the mental picture of having the loved object whipped as a sort of stimulant.

"Otherwise, I may dream that some young man is lying next to me in bed, presses against me, seizes my genitals; and I softly repel him (just as I would do in reality) although I find the advance very pleasant. I must add that scratching around my genitals is never unpleasant to me. It must have been even more delightful in those days when I was more uninhibited in my homosexual trends than I am now. Nevertheless, I must have possessed a budding inhibition against further advances even then.

"That was all during the war—winter of 1916 and spring of 1917.

"Before I became infatuated with my third girl in 1914, I had a little affair with a schoolmate of mine who was three years my junior. I had him sleep with me twice. Although I was powerfully impelled to fondle his genitals, my inhibitions were so strong that nothing more happened than that we simply lay there next to each other. I later prided myself on having been so full of control.

"There is something more I would say about my perverse tendencies. I may be walking on the street and feeling in the best of moods; optimistic. I may suddenly see some youngster who may be wearing an apparatus on the right leg which is intended to prevent a contracture of the muscles following an inflammation of the knee joint. I am suddenly overcome with a strange feeling. If I were able in that moment to speak with the boy, treat him medically, I would have an opportunity to react my feelings. But I am moved to follow him, to note his walk. In the marked cases of this kind, in which the object also corresponds to my usual homosexual fixations, I feel as if drunk.

"Although I was very regular in my clinical attendance, such an occurrence would drive my industry and conscientiousness out of my mind. Regardless of whether school kept or not, I had to follow the boy, I had to try to dispose of my emotion, and if I didn't, then it would follow me and ruin my days. I would have to go out in search of the same boy again or try to relieve myself in autoerotic manipulations or find some other reaction. But if I am in a position to start up a conversation with the boy and express my interest, then the effect is marvelous. My excitement ceases immediately and the obsession is removed. I feel at ease and restful. That's just an example. I could tell you of many others. Whenever my autoerotic complex begins to rise within me, as it does after I have been abstinent in that regard for some time, then I get the feeling: if I could only see somebody now who would really provoke my deepest sympathy. But if that is not possible because I am at home or because for some other reason I am not in a position to catch sight of just that type of surgical or orthopedic case which is necessary to me; and if, on the other hand, I don't wish to succumb to masturbation for relief, then I am impelled to ramble in the streets, to wander about town until I find just the sort of person I want. And then the whole thing starts all over again. That is, I either act as I have described to you above, or I am actually forced to masturbate, although this step is always depressing and repelling to me.

"Of course, I have a whole stock of methods whereby I can help myself. I take long walks, ride a bicycle, exercise, or seek the company of nice men the sight of whom may take my mind off the other things.

"But inevitably my delight in painful conditions and the desires of the sadist will break through.

"I am in the best of physical health, stand almost six feet, and am considered to be a fairly handsome fellow, even among men.

"One of the chief points I have to make is a pathological anxiety which I manifest. I have for years been suffering from a fear of dentists. I disguise the anxiety in every possible manner, but always excuse myself from visiting a dentist, with the result that all my teeth, especially the rear molars, are in a poor condition. But the very thought of the drill nearly prostrates me, and I am sure that I could never get further than the dentist's door.

"My mother ceased trying to take me to the dentist after I was thirteen. I must have created the wildest scenes in those days whenever she tried.

"I must also tell you that whenever I would masturbate I would invariably interrupt the manipulation in order thus to prolong the pleasure antecedent to the ejaculation. This was especially the case ever since I have been trying to rid myself of the habit. It would sometimes last for hours, and in this manner I would often be able to stop it altogether. Infrequently I would extend the period of manipulation and interruption for days and then end in ejaculation and orgasm.

"As soon as I might feel the first prickling sensation of the orgasm coming on, I would seize the penis at the deepest portion of the pars cavernosa, in order thus to stop the flow mechanically and also interrupt the nervous thrill, run about the room to deflate the orgasm and then begin all over again. I was disgusted by the specific odor of semen. In this manner I have been able to prevent a free spurting of semen ever since I was fourteen.

"My phallus is unusually well developed, also the testes. I had a slight phimosis, but this was so stretched by my onanistic manipulations, that now I can pull the foreskin back over the frenulum even when the penis is erect. When it is not erect, the foreskin will not stay behind the corona, but is in infantile position.

"I usually awaken in the morning with an erection. Depending upon how I feel about my sexual complexes, I either disregard it or give myself a taste of introductory pleasures. To the thorough execution of a complete masturbatory act, it is necessary for me to draw up the complete artillery of my collection: all my pictures, sketches and accounts of sadistic scenes (now about fifteen).

"Such habits are definitely fixed with me ever since I have been about eleven or twelve, and certainly since my thirteenth year. One of my schoolmates suddenly became important and interesting in my eyes when he broke an arm and had to carry it in a sling. Even at that time, the image or the sight of this boy carrying his arm in a splint was very pleasing to me. Then, too, the sources of my provocation were boys of my own or a slightly younger age. An older student in the school attracted me but once and that was when we all went out to the beach one day. There I noticed that one of the boys was wearing an orthopedic corset (brass rack with some sort of cervical support). I could see only the neck part of it, but it animated me immediately. At that time, I was not yet so intimately cognizant of all the meanings of my emotional life, and it was easy for me to turn my eyes from the sight under the influence of other things; but even so I would have liked to look longer. Later on, I missed this picture very much.

"On the basis of a long series of such experiences, the phantasies which made up the basis of my onanistic practices were founded. They gradually took permanent shape and tended to displace the female entirely. I was always striving to transform the image of the female to that of a male. The only type of woman who found any consideration at all was the full-breasted, buxom type that is so often used as an illustration in the cheap novels which I, like all the other boys, read so assiduously. But even that type is important only because of its relationship to the male.

"I am also very susceptible to the influence of catheters, and the thought of a permanent catheter attached to the object of my phantasy greatly enhances the effect of my feelings. If the virility of the male is emphasized in a picture, it should be through the clarity and size of the genitals.

"The female element in my own sketches (of which I have only a few at present) is invariably a governess, a severe teacher or nurse. Occasionally bound and tortured women were also an essential addition to my pictures of tormented men; to heighten the effect, as it were. But never alone; only together with drawings of the men.

"I may add here that during my student days, I was always pained by the necessary visits to the gynecological clinic. I had but one feeling during a gynecological examination: disgust; and that was especially true whenever I would get a whiff of the vaginal odor. Gynecological operations, blood, the pains of the patients, the examination, all these are possible to me only when I paralyze my feelings by a scientific seriousness.   Here, too, any unnecessary brutality on the part of the physician irritates me, and I am not at all excited or sympathetic in such situations as I would be if the same thing were happening to some man who appealed to me.

"I never have the feeling that such a thing is necessary and simply suffer that part of the curriculum because I know that I would never graduate if I didn't learn it along with the rest.   I might add, however, that my ideas about helping humanity include women as well as anybody else, and I took the trouble to learn everything well, so that I might be of service to mothers and women as well as men.

"Nevertheless, I can't help but feel a distaste for the female and the skin specialties.   My strivings are directed primarily at surgery and also indirectly at psychiatry.   Ever since I have collected some knowledge of my condition, however, and have privately burrowed into books and works on this subject, my taste for psychiatry has been dulled somewhat.   I am afraid that a psychiatric practice would have a bad effect upon me; and since I cannot be very objective because of my greatly neurotic tendencies, I am afraid that my psychotherapeutic and suggestion treatments would be a failure.

"As regards surgery, the technical part of major surgery bores me to death, and even years ago, my tendencies were well expressed by my desire to become a nurse or a stretcher bearer in the war.   But other influences and my fight against such ideas made that impossible.

"In short, I find a great pleasure in my surgical practice because of my psycho-sexual sadism.   The study of medicine was infused with interest through my attachment to this branch of medicine alone; at times, this even instills a greater capacity for work into me.   But my desire for care and treatment of the crippled and wounded does not extend to women.

"At the time when I was about to become a clerk or interne in the surgical department, I thought that I would expire if they ever sent me to the obstetrical or gynecological clinic.   I decided that if that happened, I would excuse myself by saying that I didn't know enough about the technical methods, or something of the sort.

"Although I prefer my men to have a trace of the girlish (though not of the womanly), I am not at all repelled by men of a more robust nature as regards the indulgence of my sadistic complex. The type I favor, i.e., the somewhat feminine type, is a rather common thing among the students of my part of the country.

"During our military advance in the Ukraine, I was sexually attracted to several of my subordinates, without, however, ever having given way to my desires, excepting in one instance when I would wrestle with one subordinate officer and thus react some of my emotions. I might say that I found this an excellent method of relieving myself whenever my tension became too great, and I made frequent use of it with prompt and satisfactory results. The effect lasted for days, I would regain my composure and my strivings would abate.

"In the Ukraine, I had an affair with a girl who attracted me, and practised the same habits that I have described above with the other girls. The reason for this attachment was that the girl had a brother who was quite a handsome male. I loved the brother through the medium of his sister, and that enabled me to overcome my inhibitions. I soon separated from her, however.

"I was forever impressed by what my parents had once told me: 'Whenever you have anything to do with a girl, think of what you would say if some other man were to do that with your own sister.'

"I had more than my share of morality. My father always preached to me about chastity to the day of my marriage. He doubtless hoped that I would achieve the aim which he, as he once intimated to me, had not been able to achieve. Always told me I should fall in love and marry. Even wanted to help me (during the war) to find a wife. But, unfortunately, every avenue was closed to me and there were a thousand reasons besides the one chief factor which made it impossible for me to love. All my attempts to fall in love with one or the other of the women who appealed to me, were wrecked by the resistance offered by that other part of my soul.

"I enclose a photograph of myself. It was taken in November of last year. There is another man in the picture, a friend of my own age who also once tendered me intimate feelings. I wanted to have full possession of him, but he was engaged. He married soon after this was taken and is quite infatuated with his wife. I visited them once and noticed that I developed a hatred of this woman. Or, perhaps, I was only envious of her. At any rate, I had lost him to her. I removed myself from the scene.

"I am sending you the entire picture. I feel that I may do this, but I beg you to destroy that part of the photo which shows my friend. I am the blond at the left, and my friend is the one at the right without the mustache. I have a small beard, a closely cropped mustache and parted hair. I am afraid to shave off my beard and mustache because I think that I will look feminine.

"I have never consulted a physician, and my visit yesterday to Professor X. was the first of its kind.

"Yours very truly,<br>"Otto N.

"P.S. I have just remembered that when I was about fourteen, in the summer of 1910, I tried to realize my binding phantasies in playing Indian and robber with other boys. I sensed a certain excitement in this, but I think I was able to control myself by some conscious volition. I tried these experiments in other plays and games, too, but the most I felt was a slight erection, but never orgasm or ejaculation. In one of my earliest memories, I see the lovely park at home where we boys used to play: A girl is tied to a tree and the boys throw burning pieces of absorbent cotton at her. It seems that the girl wore a vaccination bandage about her arm (as is usual in public schools), and I think that they were all larger and older children than I was. This memory quite thrilled me.

"The very earliest memory that I have is the following one: As a very small child, I was sitting on a blanket in the woods. My nurse had on a light colored washable dress, probably linen. She had been picking huckleberries, and had accidentally sat down on some of the berries with the result that there was a big stain on her light dress. She was bent over and I could see the dark purple stain on her dress. I have always remembered that scene."

This closes the patient's first confession. I invited him to come to Vienna and undergo gratis treatment—but with the condition that I might be permitted to make use of his case in my works. He accepted.

I would like to add a few remarks to his letter. We see here a distinct tendency to collect his fetishes and form a sort of fetishistic Bible with them. Then he destroys the Bible, regrets his act and forms another. We also note an accompanying parapathia which, in my opinion, is never missing in any case.

At an early age, anxiety states appear as a sign of the inner conflicts of the boy. His dentist phobia is a kernel of his condition. It reveals to us the fact that his mouth was one of his erogenous zones and that there must be a connection between his genitalized buccal zone and his fetishism.

He also reports noteworthy somnambulistic states (such as we have discussed in *Peculiarities of Behavior*) and these states indicate the presence of an impulse which must be constrained by the fetishistic impulses. There is also the onanism with its characteristic sado-masochistic make-up; the avoidance of the female and the development of a homosexuality. His experiences with women were very few and the ones he did have stopped short of intercourse. Coitus is a sin, to which is added the strict preachment of his father who appears as a condition between his sister's purity and his own (the patient's) experiences.

His father had commanded him to remain pure and chaste and he had complied with the aid of his paraphilia. The compulsions and obsessions he executed upon himself are beautifully symbolized and effected in the choice of orthopedic instruments. He is like a horse with a curb-bit.

His stereotype dreams are quite characteristic. He must return to his company, i.e., he wants to get back to his past, his childhood. As in all of our cases, he manifests a retropulsive tendency. His artificial legs in another dream symbolize his parapathia. In his dreams of Indians, he is attacked by males; the well-known traits of pubertal dreams. Naturally, he also breaks all his good resolutions in the dreams and drinks and smokes to his heart's content; indeed, he even marries, but the presence of his sister seems to indicate that the girl is but a substitute for the sister.

A noteworthy piece of virtuosity is described in his *masturbatio prolongata,* in which he is able to protract or even to circumvent the ejaculation. That cannot be due to the fear of seminal loss alone. In the course of the analysis we shall learn that this was a sort of preparatory game, a playful act, such as the preparatory character which Gross has been able to demonstrate in the games of humans and animals. Even in the onanistic act itself, we meet with the use of pressure which is so well known to us by now. He clamps his phallus so hard that he prevents not only the ejaculation, but also the orgasm, from coming on.

His first memory—a spot on the dress of his nurse—will be revealed in the analysis as having the greatest significance.

The specific form of his fetishism shows a development which could be produced in hardly anyone else but a physician. It is doubtless true that his paraphilia determined his choice of a profession.

The analysis will probably meet with the greatest obstacles and resistances, since the patient already has a good idea of analysis. The preliminaries themselves give a taste of the struggles that are to come.

Under considerable resistance, the patient arrived for treatment. The first thing he did was to start derogatory measures. He gladly accepted my invitation to come to Vienna and receive treatment gratis as a physician. But he finds my letter ludicrous and its appearance indicative of self-advertisement.[2] He wrote a special delivery letter which didn't arrive (the address was probably incorrect, so that it was sure not to be delivered. Symptomatic act). He becomes furious. I let him wait. Finally, he writes a second letter which was received. He promised to note down all his dreams with assiduity and without my having asked him to do so. But from that moment on, he can't recall a one. In the morning they've all faded.

He can recall nothing but his guitar dreams. He lives entirely in the guitar now, and acquired the instrument in order to have some sort of diversion which might keep him from sinking beneath the waves of his fetishism. He strives towards the ideal. Just because he is half Slav, he wants to become an exemplary German to the Germans. He wants to excel the Germans themselves and for that reason he would like to rid himself of all his pathologically sensual feelings.

Let us begin with three dreams which constitute all that he could save from the period between his first letter and the time he arrived in Vienna (three weeks!). These were dreamed before the treatment, of course.

1. I had given my mother my guitar to have it repaired. She came back and returned the guitar to me, and I saw that false pegs had been inserted. I said: those are not the right pegs. I

must go down there and see that I get my right pegs back. On the corner, I passed a music store in front of which there were piles of old and dirty snow and filth. Two men from the street-cleaning department were standing there. All kinds and sizes of pegs were lying in the piles of dirt. Most of them, however, were of the size of bass pegs. I asked if I might look for my pegs and they said yes. I began to search for them, but couldn't find the right ones.

2. There were lots of people in a crowd. It was like a congress of the Boy Scouts or the Wandervögel. We were about to break up, but I couldn't find my guitar. I searched and searched but all I saw was innumerable guitars of the most unusual sizes and shapes lying about. Among them, too—as far as I can remember—there were also parts of cadavers. Suddenly I had my guitar back, but some youngster, whom I didn't know at all, took it away from me again, and refused to return it despite my protest.

3. I am standing in front of a company. I'm the subaltern. The grand duke with his wife and some others were standing at my right and before the front. I was supposed to hold a sermon, but I knew that they would all laugh at it. But I went ahead. I don't know whether it was my purpose to be comical, but they all laughed continuously at what I said. Then they all left and I was alone. I followed them, but I couldn't find the way although I knew it well. Once I thought that I was in the offices of the North German Lloyd or some ship company. Then I found myself on the path, but it led to some privy, some dark and hideous structure. . . . Interruption. . . . I am walking on a (right) path with three friends. We are on a hike. For some reason, I suddenly had to run back down the path. They waited for me, and as I came back, I noticed, to the right and left, that the remains of Ernst Haeckel were erected there. It was all a pile of bones and bronze figures—like a museum. I wanted to take something with me, but the pieces were all too heavy. I was already heavily laden. Finally, I picked up two small figures and a centimeter rule and went back to my friends who were waiting for me.

These dreams are largely resistance dreams, and become clearer when we know that the guitar represents his soul and his sexuality. In the first dream, he notices that his soul hasn't the right pegs; they are all hidden in the dirt among other pegs. His soul is tainted. He can't find the right pegs. That expresses his maladjustment in life. He hasn't yet found the right path. His volition and his capacity are shown to be markedly maladjusted. The pegs he does find are all too large for his guitar.

Also, relations between his condition and his mother. His mother has given him life, but he cannot seem to make use of it properly. The interpretation of the materials in the dream is still unclear.

In the second dream, life is represented as a walking tour. He cannot find his soul. Life produces the most inconceivable men, the most divers forms (he is interested in psychology). His guitar possesses young offspring (his infantilism, his youth). He has lost his soul and his sexuality in youth (fixation on infantile impressions).

The third dream begins with an indication of his piety which, as we have seen, is present in every case of fetishism. But he is afraid that he will become a laughingstock. He is afraid I might be amused by his eccentricities. His family (the grand duke) doesn't understand him. His father hasn't the faintest idea of his condition. The patient didn't tell him why he was coming to Vienna. He would have laughed or been in despair. That is why he feels alone and cannot find his way. He must undertake the trip (North German Lloyd) of his life into the new world (Stekel) alone. His conscious thought tells him that he may be preached to by the analyst. In the dream, however, he fears that I shall lead him to a privy, lead him to a woman and conduce to his immorality. He must return for a while (the analysis, the road to childhood). But only for a short while. Then he returns to his old habits (the three friends are a symbol of his parapathia). Ernst Haeckel should be read as Wilhelm Stekel. He likes Haeckel for the bold political stand he took. But Haeckel is dead. Before he begins the analysis, he is already consigning me to the dead. He doesn't want to be burdened with all my knowledge and science. He will be satisfied with a couple small figures and a small measure (the rule; an infantile measure). Then he will return to his former practices.

Poor analytical prospects, indeed.

Like most fetishists he has, of course, a Bible, a collection of pictures and sketches and excerpts from books, which he uses during his onanistic practices. He had already burned six such collections, but only after considerable inner struggle and resistance. A short time ago, he put aside such a collection and now turns it over to me. It consisted of cuts from orthopedic books and magazines.  His desire makes him nearly mad, and he will do almost anything to get hold of a fine example of his taste.  He is not afraid to steal if necessary.  He suffers the tortures of the damned and finds no peace until he has acquired the book or picture he desires.  Lately, he has been making sketches of his own, such as are illustrated in the text.  And if the pictures he gets don't suit him, he makes changes himself.  Women are changed to men and girls to boys.  He says that he avoids all pictures of women because they don't provoke him sexually.[3]  Women don't attract him. His collection contains a great number of transformed pictures. He cuts off the heads and legs of the figures and puts others in their place.  Cutting things out seems to give him pleasure (disguised sadism).  Hair is shorn off the illustrated head, and thus a girl is transformed into a boy.[4]

In his own pictures and sketches, the cardinal rôle is played by a domineering woman.  It is in such pictures that he submits to the female, although he seems to scorn—and fear—her in reality.

Our patient introduces his analysis by what we may call a "dream diarrhœa."  He reproaches himself for having dreamed so little all the while, resolves to watch out for his dreams, sleeps restlessly, even criticizes the dream while dreaming and begins to analyze it as soon as he recalls it.  These dreams are not very valuable, and that is just the difficulty one meets when one analyzes physicians who have a knowledge of psychoanalysis.  The naïveté is not there.  Instead, there is an antagonist awaiting the analyst. Nevertheless, these dreams present us with some material.

These are the dreams brought to his first hour:

1.  I have a lot of porcelain figures which I made myself.  They are varicolored, and many of them look like small religious idols or large tin soldiers.  They are very brittle and fragile.

One of the series has a book of sketches and drawings.  A trumpeter is blowing his trumpet and behind him stand God and the devil.  The effect of the blowing is to be seen in three of the groups fashioned.  Three drawings, one of which shows a trumpeter who has had to blow his horn just as he was about to defecate. That made me say at the end of the dream: if Freud were to see that he would certainly say: hole.  Otherwise, I noticed nothing erotic or sexual in the groups of figures.

2.  I feel my chin and find that I'm already rather rough in the face again, although I had shaved just yesterday.

3.  I am on the way towards a little company that is sitting out under the trees in a café.  We arrive at a broad river where

there is a breakwater of great planks. As we climb up on it, some of the planks rise up vertically and I become afraid. The other fellow gave me courage. Then we crossed a swamp, and I purposely acted funny in order to hide my anxiety. I fell several times. From the other side I see the Wagner family coming towards us, and at their head is the deceased Mr. Wagner himself. Mrs. Wagner said: My husband is not dead. I get the feeling that I must not speak to him. Then we were across and that dream about the porcelain figures followed.

4. "Jugend" meeting. I am wearing a sailor blouse, knee pants and short socks and feel very well in that get-up. Gradually, however, I noticed that the blouse didn't fit me. It seems to change its size. I then have my gray shirt on. I wanted to buckle a belt on, but it was too short. I awaken.

5. We are lying out on the grass. A girl is supposed to make up her mind as to which one of us she'll take. I wanted her to choose me. Dim memory of Miss Sänger. When she finally decided, I noticed that it was Rosa, a girl I knew in the "Jugend" bunch. She never meant the least bit to me. And then I said to someone else who had passed a remark to me: Why, I've known her since I was two years old.

The first dream is quite characteristic. His neurotic playthings (his infantilism) are symbolized by porcelain figures which are half playthings and half religious relics (religious idols). He's very much afraid of what may happen to his idols. They are fragile, these fictions of his. The drawings refer to the collection of drawings he gave me yesterday, doubtless only after a great inner conflict. A normal person could never understand the importance of such a step in the life of one of these patients. The bipolarity of the soul is expressed in the figures of God and the devil. The trumpeter is an anagogic expression, the voice of God which calls to him to destroy his parapathia. (The trumpeter of Jericho.) The three groups represent defecating individuals, and it is probable that the symbolic form here has it that the trumpeter calls to them to give up their dirty habits. The connections with his anal complex are quite clear. The patient declares that Freud's triad of miserliness, obstinacy and fussiness as the sign of the anal erotic quite fit his character. As a child, he liked to control and play with the passage of his wind; he even collected the hydrogen sulfide of his wind in a bottle and had a lot of fun lighting it with a match. He also liked to make bubbles rise in the bath tub by letting wind, got a great deal of pleasure from defecating, and even withheld it for long periods in order to increase the pleasure of the act. His remark about Freud in the dream is really directed at me and is intended to depreciate the anal indications of the dream.

The second dream expresses the fact that the analytical shave he has had but yesterday has not cleansed him as yet.

In the third dream, his sexuality is represented as a broad river. He has protected himself against the currents of his soul by erecting a great breakwater (his parapathia), but the planks are not very solid and he is afraid to give up his parapathia and run the risk of falling into the swamp. Up until now, he has desisted from any form of sexual activity, and he is afraid the analysis may conduce to his immorality. The meaning of the fetishism is clear: a protection against woman and active sexuality. He finds that this anxiety has made him ludicrous and that all his attempts to disguise it are laughable. The Wagner family is his family. He had often wished his father, who lorded over the house and domineered his mother, sudden death. Even as a child, he had often dreamed that his father were dead, and he would have great feelings of guilt as if he had been the cause of his father's death. He would then be relieved upon awakening to find that it had all been a dream.

His relation to his father, which had already appeared in the first dream (addendum: behind God and the devil stands the king) was a rather curious one. He feels a physical abhorrence of his father; he manifests an inexplicable shyness in his father's presence and cannot remain in the same room with him. Whenever his father embraces him, something in him congeals. He cannot be tender with his father at any time. From afar, he was willing to recognize his father's virtues and merits, but when he saw him naked once he felt a chill shiver run down his back. He also reproaches his father, claiming the latter made certain mistakes in rearing him; he blames him (unjustly, as he realizes) for having conduced to the development of his present condition. At home, father was a papal lord, and his word was law. Mother always loved Otto very dearly and invariably took Otto's part against father. His older sister is parapathic (washing mania), has nothing to do with men; the middle one is the only really feminine person in the family; that is doubtless why she married early. The youngest is also "peculiar" (washing mania, infantilism and naïveté mixed with cynicism). In this part of the dream, he reaches dream 1 only after he has passed the barrier.

The fourth dream is manifestly infantile. He is dressed in boy's clothes. The shirt doesn't fit the collar and the belt is too short. This is a symbolical representation of the antithesis between his parapathia (infantilism) and the demands of life. The belt is, furthermore, a symbolization of a compulsion. He is growing out of his infantile attitude and wants to coerce himself somewhere else. Gray shirt and belt are equivalent to penance garb and monk's cord.

Now to dream 5. Miss Sänger is the one girl whom he has known in the last few years who made even a slight sexual impression upon him. But we know that he always tried to depreciate the value of women who impressed him, acted in a derogatory way with them, desexualized them. The same occurs in this dream. She becomes Rosa, who never meant anything to him. Later dream analyses will show us what relation Rosa had to his sister complex.

He realizes the extent of his resistances. He feels as if he had had a key to his soul before, but that now the key were lost. He is succumbing more and more to his phantasies and is retreating accordingly from reality—even in homosexual respects. He has so arranged his masturbatory practice that he never achieves orgasm (we know that he interrupts the onset of the orgasm and the ejaculation by means of squeezing the phallus very hard at the root; this expresses his compulsive obsession). His last adventure was with a patient. A man who wanted to be liberated from his homosexual and masturbatory habits consulted him in regard to hypnotic treatments. The hypnosis was easy, but during the treatment our patient experienced the full force of his own homosexual phantasies. He undressed himself and masturbated, but he withheld the orgasm. The patient then tried to grasp the physician's penis—and the later at first permitted him to do so, but when the former became bolder, he gave him the command to stop.

Otto manifests several distinct signs of infantilism. He cannot stand the odor of certain persons, e.g., his father and his sister. The odor of some of his comrades nearly drives him mad. The specific vaginal odor of women is abhorrent to him. Yet he likes to smell of his own smegma and the odor of his feet. His paraphilia is closely connected with his olfactory instincts.

Naturally, the patient is aggressive towards me in his attitude. He dislikes anything that reminds him of Philistinism. He classes me among the Philistines and bourgeois, of course. I smoke a

pipe during the analysis. That's the mark of a Philistine. Everything that indicates adjustment or satisfaction is humdrum. If a
fellow is ambitious he's a Philistine. Whatever happens, he doesn't
want to be like the rest. He wants to be different and go his own
way.

The resistance to the treatment is expressed in the following
dream.

In front of the mail boxes, I meet with Lieutenant Colonel Vormann. He extends me his left hand and grips my own left hand
hard. I feel how weak my own hand is in his palm. He thinks
that's lamentable and grabs my right hand with his left. I try as
hard as I can to resist him, but he crushes my right hand, too.

Then he takes hold of both my hands with both his. I feel as
if he's going to tear my hands from my wrists and want to protest.
I awaken with the feeling that my lower jaw has been dislocated
forwards.

He dreamed this dream in the afternoon, after he had written
two letters. One of the letters was sent to his father and demanded that papa send a larger monthly allowance. The second
was sent to his sister and discussed the question as to whether—
as I had advised him—he should let his father know of his condition or not. He also told his sister that I had prophesied to him
that he would leave the analysis within a fortnight.[5]

But let us turn to the dream analysis. Vormann is an officer,
handsome, slender, blond, energetic, the very picture of a German.
He's a spirited fellow. In the dream, he was at least two heads
taller than our patient, who is dissatisfied with his stature. He
would like to be much larger. Whenever he looks in the mirror,
as is often the case, he will admire his naked body, but frequently
he will find fault with himself. Vormann is his ideal. He would
like to achieve the almost impossible, i.e., the control of his passions. His instincts, especially the left side of them (homosexuality) are held in check by his ideal demands which make him
follow, although he submits unwillingly. Now, however, both his
hands are tied, the normal (right) satisfaction, as well as the paraphilic (left) one. His ascetic tendencies impel him to complete
self-denial. He doesn't smoke and would like to be a vegetarian.
But he knows that he has totally deformed himself through his
ideals and resolutions. He is certainly no Philistine, but what was
the price! His wrists are twisted, his jaw dislocated; he can
neither act nor speak.

The second determination of the dream is that Vormann is his father and the analyst his father's representative. His father bound both his hands. Otto associates that Vormann uses his left hand because he wants to do something which is not right. We can thus assume that this physical contact was something forbidden, something which he expects of the physician, too, just as all patients with a father transference. He really admired his father and was unhappy at the strictness which ruled at home. This compulsion is pictorially represented in the dream. It also indicates the compulsions he feels at my hands, I who have given him certain orders, against whom he is powerless. With a dislocated jaw, of course, he cannot talk, and that ends the analysis. In addition, he'll become even crazier than he already is if he stays with it. That is the true sense of the dream; the point of it is directed at me. He wants to protest, but his weak voice is not heard. He must sacrifice his parapathia. I must call the reader's attention to the beautiful illustration in this dream of the pressure and coercion character of fetishism.

A number of associations follow. He first tells me about some stereotype dreams he had. He often dreams, he says, of swimming through water with the speed of a torpedo; swimming dreams are altogether frequent with him (spermatozoon dreams?). His typical railway dream is that he has climbed into the wrong train, that he has forgotten his baggage or has failed to pack up the most important thing. As he is about to get in the train, he finds all his suitcases and bags opened by strangers. These are quite characteristic fetishist's dreams. The train is the ride of his life. He cannot find the right road, cannot reach his destination; he hasn't even prepared sufficiently for the trip. His fear of being betrayed and recognized for what he is shows up in his anxiety that all his bags have been opened.

Like all ambitious people, he produces flying and gliding dreams. He also dreams frequently about falling into a deep hole or falling off something. He still remembers such a dream which he had before the analysis began. It made quite an impression on him. It is a stereotype riding dream with him.

First I ride past a company and salute its officers. The road then becomes progressively narrower, and I find myself sitting atop a former schoolmate of mine as a horse. We find ourselves then on a bridge which is dizzily high above the bottom. It is built upon the highest of conceivable tree trunks as piers, and the bridge itself is only the thickness of a tree trunk. I hold fast, but he springs off into the bed of the river. It took us four seconds, and despite the rock cliffs, he landed unhurt. I didn't know whether I should jump or not. I was terribly afraid and couldn't go back.

In this dream, he expresses the violation of his second ego by a schoolmate whom he uses as a horse (a homosexual picture). The whole scene is completed by his great drop, the gradual fall of the other boy and his great anxiety. Similar dreams showing a gradual drop from dizzy heights occur frequently.

He possesses wild instincts against which he must protect himself. What are these impulses? We may get an idea as to what they are through the fact that before he falls asleep he must bite into the coverlet or the blanket; he bites his nails or a handkerchief. He is also afflicted with the evil habit of crunching his teeth in his sleep. He presses the blanket close to his abdomen before he falls asleep (memory of being swaddled in diapers?).

As a boy he used to steal a good deal, and would then buy himself candy with the money. He cannot bear to throw anything away (fear of losing his parapathia). He was practically reared to his anal sexuality by being the subject of constant purgatives and enemas as a child. At the slightest sign of some malaise or indisposition, they would take his temperature per rectum.

Up until very recently he manifested all kinds of infantile habits. He would put nasal crusts into his mouth and interested himself in all his excrements. He would stick everything he possibly could into the external cavities of his body; beans would be hidden in his nose or rectum or ears. Once an ear specialist found a bean in one of his ears which must have lain there for years.

We have just mentioned his cannibalistic tendencies (biting into the blanket). In conformity with this, it may be stated that he liked to lick his own blood, called the various meat dishes at table "animal cadavers or corpses," and always used to say to his colleagues at lunch: "Now I'll have the corpse of a steer," etc.

Even when he was fourteen or fifteen, he still had the habit of talking to himself before he fell asleep. He would address himself and then a dialogue would ensue, he being both parties. Sometimes he would begin to bawl, and his mother would either come running into the room or call him to her.

He would like to be a hero. At the front, he would take a walk while bombs were falling, just to show how brave he was, but he wasn't sure whether he were really brave or was just showing off.

This reveals to us a primitive type of sadism which has been present in every case of fetishism that we have considered.

The tendency to splitting of his personality is disclosed in his monologues in which he plays the part of both parties. This is a phenomenon which is observable in many compulsion neurotics. It expresses their peculiar type of thought. It deals with the two poles of their make-up: primitive or civilized man. The meaning of his dropping off dizzy heights is that he has dropped from the heights of civilization to the depths of bestiality.

He dreamed:
I met my patient on the street and he wanted to be hypnotized again. He became importunate, but I coolly refused him.

The physician who is a patient of mine sees himself as the master in the dream. He also discloses the ability to resist the homosexual advances of his patient. He is again at home. His own analysis is over and he is analyzing others.

He then touches upon his pathological anxiety of dentists. It began to plague him when he was yet young, and now he has a mouth full of carious teeth. In his phantasies, he always sees himself going to the dentist. About three months ago, he got as far as the door of a dentist whom he knows, but didn't have the courage to ring the bell. Among his phantasies, a sarcoma of the jaw takes on an important part. An important question with him is whether, in such a case, he would permit himself to be operated on by an oral surgeon. He is ashamed to go to a dentist. What would the dentist say when he saw this row of rotten teeth? Furthermore, the bad teeth are also a protection against his kissing anyone. What would she or he think upon smelling such a foul odor before a kiss? Wouldn't his partner be disgusted?

During the war, when he was showing off his bravery, he always had the notion that if he would permit any of his teeth to be pulled, he would fall the next day. This reveals an association between tooth and death, quite in accordance with a general superstitious belief (see my *Language of Dreams,* the chapter on tooth dreams).

He is very religious and superstitious. Although he is a protestant, he loves to go into Catholic churches because they excite his "mysticism." With the aid of his religion and his superstitious beliefs, he has formed all kinds of conditions which keep him from going to the dentist. It appears that the dentist is altogether one of his basic problems. He frequently has tooth dreams; someone

hits him on the mouth and knocks out a tooth. Or: he is supposed
to go to the dentist, but there are all kinds of obstacles; he gets
as far as the door and then fails to go in.

Even toothaches afford him pleasure. He likes to suck on the
aching tooth. He is tickled by it and also gets a thrill at the tip
of his penis.

He has thought of extracting his bad teeth himself. The longer
he procrastinates, the more ashamed he is of himself. His carious
teeth are symbols of his foul spirit. He could not stand the
thought of being under the power of the dentist, being betrayed to
him. He is more afraid of the drill than of the forceps and even
the sharpening of a knife or scalpel is unbearable, not to speak of
the boring noise of a trephining drill. He cannot stand the noise
of skull operations.

In early youth he already manifested a "skull complex." He
would knock off the heads of thistles as he walked along and would
imagine that they were the heads of his enemies.

He is marked by a distinct destructive tendency. He would
frequently break bottles, pots and other fragile objects and get a
tickling sensation in the urethra. On visiting the torture chamber (in Kastan's puppet cabinet in Berlin), his feelings were those
of lust mixed with disgust and horror. As a boy, he had a Hermes
head which he loved very much; he painted it and dressed it up
to make it look more like real. Dissecting the anatomical speci-
mens at first interested him greatly, but later on—as with all his
interests—his appetite became jaded.

He is always restless and can't sit still anywhere; he seems to
be driven. When he first entered the dissection room in the
anatomy laboratory, he was calmed by a great peace, but this, unfortunately, soon fled.

He again became unstable and fought a constant battle between
his duties and his paraphilia. Then he suddenly stopped studying
and began to dedicate himself to his drawings and cuts. During
the war, he masturbated before a book on oral surgery, opening
the book to the plates which showed jaw wounds and dressings.

His particular mouth gag shows his interest in buccal and
pharyngeal things. He is distinctly of an oral erotic make-up.
For a long time he sucked his fingers or a baby sucker; he loves
candy and sweets, smoked heavily during the war. Then, with
some friends, he resolved to keep away from sweets. His ascetic
tendencies invariably conquer his desires. But he frequently has

dreams of candy. He sees himself walking into candy stores and taking bags and boxes full of it with him. He has the same kind of dreams about stamp-collecting stores. He used to be a passionate stamp collector and even stole some examples that he wanted.

One of the first books he ever had in his hands was the Bible illustrated by Doré. He made out the letters with difficulty at that age, and was always awed by the words God or Jehovah which were printed in large letters. He would then spell it out G—O—D. Doré's pictures excited him terribly. They showed him all kinds of fiendish deeds and he believes that this may have been one of the infantile sources of his condition.

He dimly recalls (at four) having crawled under the skirts of one of the maids in the house. He often wrestled and fought with his elder sister with whom he shared the room for some time. For many years she was the stronger of the two, until he grew up. After that she didn't find any fun in the matches and their playing stopped. Lately they wanted him to share the room with her again, but he was against it. He can't stand her odor. The air in her room is revolting to him. She is apparently the prototype of the governess in his sketches. For a short time she wore a lorgnon and now wears a *pince-nez*. She complains of all kinds of ailments.

She once wanted him to hypnotize her and, according to the method of Forel, cure her of her dysmenorrhœa. But the hypnosis was a failure. Manifestly, the patient of the hypnosis dream which he related to us was not the man, but his sister.

He had a vivid phantasy as a child and was always asked to tell the other children fairy tales. That used to take place in a garden where there was an open privy for which he disclosed considerable interest. He would run in and look to see the differences in the color and size of the feces.

One of the earliest of his memories (two to three) is of a babies' home. His sister had been ill with the measles; they took him to this babies' hospital and there he saw a little boy who had no arms (they had been amputated); this made a lasting impression upon him.

He fights against a ridiculous thought. He came to Vienna after all, in order to cure himself of his paraphilia. But he's always thinking: What have I got out of life? How shall I find satisfaction? I can't stand women, or at least they don't attract me. On the other hand, I would be disgusted by a homosexual act. So what shall I do?

He was an habitué of the movies at an early age. As a twelve-year-old, he would sit and be filled with pleasurable excitement whenever the film would show some woman being tormented by a villain. But now he is interested only in males.

At seventeen, he experienced his great disappointment in love. He had been insanely infatuated with a girl and was even a laughingstock at home. He had been able to repress his satistic habits for a time, and they were well in the background of his sexual interest. He recalls the circumstances of his collapse very clearly. It was at the railway station. His ideal was about to go away and he was on the verge of tears. She suddenly handed him a letter and then climbed aboard the train which left almost immediately. The letter contained an unambiguous rejection of his attentions. That was a severe blow for him. At eighteen there was a rather pale affair with an English girl—and then he was through with the ladies forever.

He wouldn't permit himself to be humiliated any more.

Two ways were open to him. One of them led to woman, but that road was impassable now. The other led to the male. But he had a terror of homosexual intercourse. Thus, he chose the middle path of chastity. He would keep himself clean, pure and chaste for his ideal.

He began to live a life of abstinence which was extended to smoking and drinking, too. Formerly he had liked to drink. Drinking *per se* made him feel well, and somewhat elevated afterwards. But he was able to stick to his resolutions.

In Vienna, he was once offered a glass of brandy and drank it down with a feeling of satisfaction. Then he began to think of giving up his abstinence altogether. I smell a rat in this and feel that he intends to carry out his ideas only in order that he may squander his money in drink, women and all the rest, and then go home because he has run out of funds. I call his attention to this and tell him that during the analysis he is not to make any changes in his usual habits. I have no wish to be made the instrument of his seductive anagogic tendencies.

He is horribly afraid of loneliness, nor can a woman banish this feeling from his heart. There is nothing he could discuss with a woman. Small talk at the best and that's soon over. But with comrades, he can talk for hours. He really stages this attitude towards women whom he hates ever since his rejection at seventeen and a half, only because he wants to keep them at a distance. That is betrayed by the fact that he can very well converse with older women. But, he says, they don't count. Only sexual possibilities count. As a result of his attitude, he avoids company and hates to go visiting. As long as he gets into a conversation, he likes to spin out his sociological problems and opinions. He talks about the nonsense in modern conversation. Everybody thinks about something else and talks about something else. He likes to talk about this point. He is also interested in the viciousness of our sexual morals. He stands for sexual freedom and openness. But, like every true prophet, he demands this freedom for the others but not for himself (e.g., Nietzsche). The discrepancy between what is preached and what is practised is unbearable to him.

Otto also likes to talk about the sexual hunger of youth and about the failure of teachers to understand their pupils. He found the first trace of uprightness in these matters in my books.

When sleeping, he always lies on his right side, rolls himself up like a snail, takes up a fœtal position and then pulls the covers over his ears.

One of his early memories is also a kind of orthopedic apparatus; his first suspenders (four). He went to the toilet, but couldn't undo his suspenders; he began to cry and the nursemaid came and helped him. When he was about six or eight, he was mortally afraid of water and hair cutting. He was always very sensitive and afraid of pain. Once when his sister had an upset stomach and vomited, he ran about the house bawling and crying that his sister was going to die. He was told that when he was born they were afraid he was going to die. He was lying on a bundle of old clothes and cried fearfully. When they unwrapped him, they found that his whole body had been bitten by bed-bugs. But these bed-bugs had really saved his life, for when the nurse unwrapped him, she saw that his navel dressing had come off and he was bleeding to death. They had to dress him again in a hurry and later told him when he grew up that he had nearly died from the loss of blood. This accident seems to have been engraved in his memory and appears also to have determined his interest in bandages to some degree.

He was precocious, very phantastic, susceptible to every form of passion, jealous and given to fits of temper. He often produced phantasies that his father had died and he would become the head of the family and support his mother. He greeted the advent of his younger sisters with mixed feelings, for they robbed him of some of the attentions of his parents. He recalls how angry he was one day when he came into the nursery just in time to see his father kissing his newborn sister on the buttocks (he cites Wilhelm Busch—the German humorous poet: *"Auf die Backe mit Genuss, drückt er seinen Vaterkuss"*).

The death of his younger sister, who succumbed to the measles, appears to have constituted a severe shock for him. He sees the picture clearly. The little one in bed, his grandmother, who touchingly nursed each of the children during diseases, sitting at a table, a lamp burning. He also recalls how, after his sister was born, he went up to his mother's bed and she told him that the stork had bitten her great toe. Then she showed him her great toe which was dressed with some bandage. It was really some old rag. He was somewhat dubious about the truth of the story, but wasn't able to learn the truth, despite the fact that he had always pored over the encyclopedias in his father's library and had dragged out all kinds of old books.

That seems to have been his first period of curiosity, but it was soon repressed. While he was in the army, he had been made the butt of many jokes and jibes because he couldn't differentiate between a stud, a stallion and a gelding. He would have to lift up the tails before he could tell the difference. He claims that he couldn't tell what the difference between a man and a woman was when he was ten or twelve years old. That, however, does not rhyme well with the fact that he used to watch them bathe his little sister and manifested a curiosity mixed with envy and jealousy. He was taken at an early age to the picture gallery and found one painting in particular of great interest: Konrad's farewell before his execution. The paintings of battles and executions all attracted his attention. He also recalls a painting of a caravan full of slaves who were being taken to the slave market. What interested him most about the execution of Konrad was the lopping off of his head.

Many of his memories indicate a markedly developed castration complex. First of all a dim memory in which he thinks his mother said to him: "If you don't stop that or that, I'll cut something off you!" It may have meant the penis or perhaps the thumb. The story of Struwelpeter (who had his thumbs cut off), the verses of which he can repeat to this day, made a powerful impression upon him. In that story, there is a little boy, Wupps-schwupps, who had his thumbs cut off by the tailor because he sucked on them. He felt that all this little boy's bad points were reflected in himself. Nor has he given up any of these bad habits yet. Whenever he catches flies, he tears their heads off. He has always been an impassioned fly catcher and in the field, he became a past master at the art, sometimes using his hands and sometimes the fly swatter. When he catches them with his hands, he tears off their heads out of "sympathy because they die more quickly that way."

Another root of his orthopedic mania: in childhood they threatened him with all kinds of apparatus if he didn't behave. If he didn't sit straight while writing, they would draw a fearful machine on the board which was called a straightener; if he tipped his letters too much to one side, they would threaten him with splints and the like. In short, his attention was called to orthopedic apparatuses at a very early age. He made a joke of all these threats, i.e., he took the sting out of them by depreciating their effect; he would also imagine them being attached to other boys and would derive pleasure from these phantasies. He finally began to wish himself placed in one himself. Like the old Dutch beggars, he turned a threat into a promise, a curse into an honor.

I want to stress particularly this very principle of transforming all feeling into its opposite. It is a mechanism which plays a leading rôle in every case of fetishism and constitutes one of the chief psychological methods of self-protection.

He is afraid of illness and of the female nurses that might care for him. He appears to hate the thought of being ill at home and having mother and grandmother pamper him. Out in the field, being ill meant being among men with male nurses, and that pleased him. He hates nurses (or the Catholic "sisters") with their sympathy on their sleeves. He takes care to show no sign of his feelings at home. He masks and hides his true emotions; if he feels sentimentally about something, he will talk in a cynical or ironic manner. He manhandles his sentiments just as if he were reducing a joint and laying on the shackles of an orthopedic instrument.

One his early memories (between three and four) is about his lying in the grass with his nursemaid. His parents came up on bicycles, got off, exchanged a few words with the girl, got on their bicycles again and rode off. He envied their free and rapid movements.

As a child he had yearned to become big and grown-up. He was burning with a desire to possess the rights of an adult, to be able to do something. Then the phantasies appeared which we have just mentioned. He would have his father die and he would become the head of the family. Of course, in all these phantasies he played the part of a child wonder. His mother had a much better time of it in his air castles than in the home his father had built.

His resistances are on the job. He can't remember a single dream. Like all physicians who are treated by me, he begins to take an interest in my differences with Freud. He expects me to give him a lecture on the subject. He is deeply absorbed in the conflict. I explain the matter to him in a few moments. I tell him that this is only another form of resistance, and he is able to corroborate that by another example. He had been in the university library where, to help me out, he was to look up a certain criminological article for me. He liked that. But it wasn't long before he had them bring him the *Zeitschrift f. Chirurgie und Orthopädie* which pleased him much more than helping me out. He enjoyed himself hugely over the pictures, but had sufficient control over himself as not to cut out any of the magazine.

He is tired the whole day long and would like to sleep. To-day he went to a park and wanted to read, but fell asleep instead. He is under the influence of his innermost complexes. The pictures from the orthopedic and surgical magazines dangle before his eyes. He also knows definitely that he has had rather pleasant orthopedic dreams lately. He remembers one such dream, and would like to dream it over again. He had this dream before he wrote to me.

I am at home. I have to climb several stairs and then enter a hall which is filled with all the figures of my phantasies. There are young men shackled in divers orthopedic instruments. I get the feeling that there's nothing for me in this place. I don't belong here. I'm an intruder. For this reason, I didn't dare open my mouth. Suddenly my mother appeared and brought me something (blankets?). She then retires to have her lunch. Meanwhile I write. Then she returns. I don't know what happened after that. I think I had an emission.

His feeling was: "What's my mother doing here?" The interpretation is not at all difficult. The hall is his brain which is filled with all his phantasies. But there's something about it all which doesn't sound genuine. He transforms the fact that these phantasies are not his, that they are intruders, that they hide something (blanket) from the passive into the active. He is the in-, truder, he doesn't belong to these phantasied figures, which is, of course, somewhat of a truth. He doesn't dare open his mouth. That also corresponds to the facts, for he has never had the courage to talk with his father about his paraphilia and now feels somewhat relieved that he can talk it over with me (his conscience refuses to acknowledge this euphoria. He feels that he's having it too good in Vienna). He did say something to his mother about masturbation and homosexuality, but he doesn't dare say too much because he knows that she'll tell his father everything.

The dream shows us that he has touched upon threads which lead to his mother. The emission at the end of it could be an indication of incestuous strivings of which he has no conscious knowledge. As a little boy he had been taken into his parents' bed, and whenever he was ill, they put his bed in their bedroom; but he never was the object of too much petting or pampering. On the contrary, his mother was rather cool and reserved. She even became strict, energetic and aggressive at times. Whenever his parents did beat him, they hit him on the head, to such an extent, as a matter of fact, that he once told his father that the latter had knocked all the intelligence out of his head.

They would suddenly hit him in an outburst of temper over some little thing. Once he had misbehaved and they spanked him. His father caught him just as he was standing before the wash basin in his night shirt and brushing his teeth. Papa lifted up his shirt and spanked him so hard that the toothbrush knocked against his teeth and he thought he had knocked a tooth out. It is possible that his habit of sketching a gag into the mouths of his figures is a fixation of this scene. The gag would thus be a memento of resentment against his father. Otherwise he can speak only well of his mother. She possesses control, is cool and haughty, submits to her husband and is therefore the object of her son's sympathy. She is said to have been a beauty.

He also recalls an Easter custom of theirs which gave him quite a lot of fun. As early as his fourth year, he and the other children would come into their parents' room carrying cat-tails which they would then use to beat on their father and mother; the parents would then crawl under their covers and play as if they were suffering terrible pain. Then the parents would lay an Easter egg for each child; sometimes they were quite large. They gave him a book-case for Easter once and claimed they had laid it.

We have learned here that his dentist phobia is at least partly a fixation of the time when he was beaten by his father and nearly lost a tooth. It is as if this were his childish way of showing resentment against his father and punishing the latter for what he did. "It's all your fault that I'm losing my teeth." It is at least plain that the dentist is for him a father image and that his anxiety of the dentist is really the fear and bashfulness he manifests before his father. The dentist extracts one's teeth—the father either did or nearly did knock out one of his teeth; he can't remember just what happened. But that scene is forever engraved in his memory. Unfortunately, he cannot give us the exact cause for that little tempest, but he thinks that he had perhaps spoiled or broken something that belonged to his sister.

He is too peaceful now to do any work. He has to have steam up to do anything and without considerable emotional pressure, he can't live in comfort. He always used to make his sketches in a sort of ecstatic state. The series of drawing used as illustrations in this text were drawn from four in the afternoon to two in the morning. Then he went to bed, got up, and worked until two in the afternoon again. After that he was exhausted and felt depleted emotionally. He couldn't do any more.

It is only in such moments that he can express any artistic talent. If he should try to execute some fetishistic sketch at a time like the present when he is at peace with the world, the result would turn out to be a lamentable failure.

He dreamed:

1. I am standing in the street and watch some men working in a garden; one of them looks very familiar to me. He is a certain L. who was one of the subalterns in my group. While I am considering whether I should address him or not, the others turn out to be acquaintances, too. We recognize and salute each other and then a lot of other soldiers suddenly appear on the scene also. They are all familiar to me, all from the front. They're all glad to see me, and I feel the same. Suddenly they all get into formation because the colonel wants to review them. There's a lot of running about. I consider the matter of getting into line myself. I'm an officer, indeed, but at the present I'm a civilian physician or something of the sort. Just as I was going through both halls in which they were lining up, the lieutenant, an impossible fellow in a hussar's uniform, lunged past me. Everything awaits the colonel. But he doesn't appear. The lieutenant's aide is said to have spread the rumor.

2. I am standing on the corner with Mr. W. He talks with several other people and I get angry that he keeps me waiting and doesn't say anything to me. Then I go with him to a family known to both of us and spend some time with my sister and her four children. Later on, grandfather, who is a little senile by now, comes along and asks me about my physique and whether my penis is well developed or not. I boast and tell him: "I couldn't wish for a better one." He asks my eldest sister the same thing, and she answered him something or other. My second sister then said to him: "You know that we always get hysterical fits at such questions." The old man laughed. Suddenly he became a little weak and I had to support him. He acted as if he were going to collapse, but I held him up and he was soon better.

His association on the first dream is that the men were working on a high wall surrounding the garden. Then they sprang over the wall and it appeared to be only a fence. It looked like an orchard. That subaltern L. was a middle-aged, weak sort of man who was quite intelligent and an excellent conversationalist. He had the habit, however, of talking in his sleep, and it was thus that the patient once heard him say: "Oh, God! What have I committed now!" He thinks of a few addenda to the dream. When the soldiers got into the hall they first went through some very curious exercises. He was not sure whether he should join them or not. On the one hand, he felt that he should line up with the rest, and yet, on the other, he felt that the colonel had no jurisdiction over him whatever.

The lieutenant was blond and looked like a very unpleasant German nationalist. The aide was even larger than the lieutenant, but was dark. The beginning of the dream was marked by a happy affect at being together with so many friends again. But in that hall, most of them seemed strange to him (feeling of loneliness). Then he thought: "The colonel will be here soon. What are you doing around here?"

The interpretation of this dream follows the general lines of the other soldier dream we analyzed in an earlier chapter apropos of the case of the breeches fetishist. The expression made by L. in his sleep is in itself an indication of the patient's evil conscience. The soldiers represent the pious who submit to the word of God and pray assiduously (exercises). The lieutenant is the spirited man who bends to the will of God and creates an example for the others; he is himself a demi-god in the eyes of the others. The aide represents the Slav (or Semite) as a contrast to the Christian. He is fearful of the last judgment, the truths he will learn before God. Anxiety in the analysis. Guilt consciousness and doubts as to whether he should tell the truth or not speak out from the dream (the will to power against the will to submit). We shall learn of another determinant later on.

The W. of the second part of the dream was a tutor who gave him lessons outside of school. He was the patient's favorite teacher. Otto liked him because he knew how to attract the boy's interest in the work. W. was a parapathic who suffered from anxiety of examinations which was the reason he never became a professor. Like the grandfather, W. is a representative of myself. He has a transference to me and is jealous of my other patients ("he speaks with the others and lets me wait"). Yet as a physician he has received much more than the usual consideration from me. He makes me appear as a parapathic. In addition to which, I'm the impotent old grandfather, suffering from senile dementia, needing his aid and support. Whereas, in the analysis, I seem to pay no attention to the question of his genitals, he has me ask about them in the dream (primitive reaction). I'm also interested in the sex-life of his sisters, a circumstance that seems to displease him. He has his second sister in the dream repel my curiosity. Feebly a little glimmer shines through the network of the dream and throws light on the fact that the hysterical attacks must have had some connection with the sex-life of his sisters. The colonel, W., and his grandfather also represent his own father. He always wanted to catch sight of his father's phallus, but it was not a pleasant sight. It was "a worn-out" member; the foreskin entirely covered the retracted phallus. He doesn't like to look at a penis. It disgusts him (and yet the penis is always emphasized in his sketches). Old members are disgusting. He prefers to look at fresh young bloods. As an officer, he always was thrilled by the so-called "prick parade," and was thwarted at the thought that the men were not permitted to wait in line with their penis hanging out, but were required to show their phallus only when their turn arrived. It sometimes looked as if the company doctor permitted himself all kinds of jokes (projection of his own wishes?). Recalls a comrade in arms who always got an erection when bathing. He crawled into this fellow's bed one night, but he was ticklish and squeaked every time Otto touched him.

His own grandfather has been dead many years. In the dream, this grandfather represents his father and me. There appear to be relations between the father and his sisters. The dream presents a striking collection of deceased persons. The father of the four children fell at the front. W. is dead, perhaps also L., and, like his grandfather, he has me represented by a dead person. He has me die, but also has me collapse. That would keep me from being a danger to him and his paraphilia. He'll have me dead before the analysis is over. His appreciation of death is determined by his infantile impressions. His father is very pious and suffers from a fear of death.

After the question about the size of his own penis, there follows a question addressed to his eldest sister. Is it possible that something was up between the two? Such a question is visibly unpleasant to him. That's why he had me die. That would insure the secrecy of what ever passed between them, and he would be able to return home uncured.

We begin to see clearly that his parapathia is closely related to his sister complex.

He is well aware of his great resistances. Before he came for treatment he was a productive and vivid dreamer, but now he finds it very difficult to preserve even a part of a dream. Last night he dreamed that he was training recruits, i.e., that he was a commander. He feels ill at ease and coerced in the analysis. He knows that it is his plan to remain here and resist any changes; so that he may then say: "Well, you did the best you could to get well. You even went to Dr. Stekel, and it's not your fault that you're still ill."

He knows very well that he cannot count on my company or intimate friendship during the analysis, but he is nevertheless affronted that I do not permit him the liberty of my society outside the treatment. He feels alone, needs a friend who attracts him homosexually, and with whom he would not need to have intercourse. He denies the possibility of a transference to me. He refuses to see it, just as he refused to see his love for his father. He nevertheless admits that up to three years ago, older people attracted him (see the grandfather dream). He had a manifest transference to his tutor W., to certain officers, and to several university professors. But he knows how to repress any feeling or emotion which may cause him unrest. Unfortunately, he had read all of my works before beginning treatment and came to Vienna with the ready-made resolution not to transfer to me.

He understands fully that what he seeks in these orthopedic figures is himself. When he had finished the series of sketches which we have used as illustration here, he noticed with astonishment and fright that two of the pictures betrayed his own features distinctly. He erased them quickly and changed their features until they were unrecognizable.

He had formerly masturbated before a mirror, but later gave up such "foolish tricks." He once fell in love with a fellow who resembled him remarkably; he says they might have passed for twins.

He is told that his paraphilia is the expression of a compulsive obsession which he has effected upon himself. His spiritual orthopedics have the purpose of preserving his asceticism. What does he do with men? The worst that he will permit himself is a little fondling and lying next to his object (fully dressed) on the sofa. He has already found himself a friend here in Vienna; some one with whom he can take hikes, a person for whom he can yearn. He is looking for some experience which may put an end to the analysis.

He dreamed:

I was somewhere in the kitchen. We were doing target practice. Someone else was with us and was holding up various targets for us. I aimed, fired and set again. Then the shot would ring out, and each time the bullet would fly in another direction. Once through the mirror which was hanging from the ceiling like a candelabra. Then I shot again. Then there was a forest outside and I felt as if I had done something wrong. I think I must have shot at a deer. We were in a blockhouse. A man came running through the wood with his trunk and head all aflame. That was my fault. He tried to force his way into the house, but I protected myself.

I came upon a married couple that was sitting out in the garden having lunch. I was invited to sit down with them because my parents recommended me. The man was at first rather abrupt, hardly noticed me. In a little while, he became friendlier. Then I found myself riding in an auto through wonderful parks and fine, old castles, everything very medieval. One of the castles belonged to the married couple. They must have been very elegant people. The auto rides through very narrow paths, and I wondered that we were able to pass. Then I looked to the right and saw a very curious landscape: jagged cliffs with deep ravines, castles and eccentric buildings. We rode on. I think we arrived at my uncle S.'s place, but he sent me on. I arrived and saw my grandmother and my dead uncle Rudolph and his wife. They were very happy to see me. Curiously enough, instead of the auto which I thought brought me there, I see a baby carriage standing in the road. Two old porters were there too. I don't know whether I should give them something or not. I recall that when I left, my grandmother had said that she would give them something. I ask: "Shall I give them something? I have only Austrian crowns with me." The first of the servants waited for me to give him something, but finally he left, irritated that I hadn't given him anything. I said to the other one: "My grandmother will take care of you."—Then I had to get over a fence that was woven of willow branches. A couple of chickens flew over it. I sat up on the fence and it began to bend (it may have been of straw) towards where my aunt and uncle were standing. Then I slid off onto the path.

He says he knows that a very important dream preceded this one, but the moment he wanted to write it down, it had faded from his mind. Adding to the first portion of the dream, he says that some old man was also in the kitchen, commanded his shots and laughed every time the bullet went astray.—Of course it always went astray. The bullet always came out in a different direction from that in which he had sighted. Every time he set his rifle down on his shoulder, the weapon went off by itself. He recalls loading in the dream. The bullets were small, little things, flat in front, like no bullet he had ever used. And at every shot, the old man would say: "Now, look where that one went." To the last shot, each one was a failure. But by that time, he was no longer in the kitchen, but in a blockhouse. The man he saw— it was a deer at first—was half dead (half rotten) and half aflame. The flames seemed to come from within. Like a dryad, half tree, half man; like a figure from Ovid's Metamorphoses.

He had always been interested in shooting. At twelve, he had acquired a bow and arrow and shot arrows at everything he saw in the house or yard. His first target practice in the army was a little unpleasant because he was frightened by the noise. At the front, he had to get used to the rattle before he was able to say that he was a soldier. Then he recalls the fable of the little brother and sister. The brother was a deer, under a spell, and was finally released. He can't remember the details.

The connections between the dream and the analysis are not hard to find. I am naturally the older man who commands him and forces him to shoot at his own brother (the paraphilia). **He** doesn't really want to kill his inner ego, but, against his own will, he hits valuable objects (the mirror). He also hits his little brother, that antagonist of his, who is half dead, half aflame. On the other hand, we see him struggling against his paraphilic impulses which threaten to overcome and inflame him.

A second meaning of the dream appears to refer to the death of his sister. He must have had death wishes against her. Still other references to his elder sister will become clear later on.

The second part of the dream is understandable when it becomes known that he came here with the phantasy that he would live in my house, eat at my table, and enjoy my company. But these beautiful phantasies have faded. Not far away from here, however, there lives a wealthy uncle of his. He wanted very much to look him up. He calculated that his own money would soon have run out, and that that would put an end to the analysis. He would then still be able to visit his rich uncle S. whom he had visited once already. Besides, his mother had sent him several recommendations and introductions to fashionable and wealthy people in Vienna. In this dream he already sees himself as the guest of a married couple. This couple represents, of course, myself and my wife. He takes a trip back into babyland (the baby carriage). Uncle S. has been dead for some years; he was very dear to Otto. But the identification shows that he has had me die, too. He is also rather stingy with his tips. He likes to tip only young and handsome fellows who excite his erotic sensibilities. He also makes a servant out of me and gives me a tip for the trip. The payment is an expression of his guilt feelings. The fenced-off garden lies between him and his uncle (who is in the cemetery). But this last part is still somewhat vague and must be analyzed further.

Like all physicians undergoing analysis, he talks about it to all his friends and colleagues. He is tickled whenever he hears a derogatory opinion. Yesterday he made the acquaintance of a physician who stated that analysis was nothing but a big swindle. And, of course, there are plenty of criticisms of Freud and Stekel. He snaps up every such declaration in the interests of his resistance and then exploits them against me.

His dreams betray his resistances.

1. Dr. Stekel sits in front of me, looks at me, and at his left

on the wall hangs my guitar. I see the sound-hole particularly. Then he says to me: "You can drink beer just as well as your guitar."

2. I am supposed to go to a funeral. A boy is supposed to be buried, younger than myself, perhaps a schoolmate. But I don't go. Then that old H. is sitting there and asks me why I don't go along. Everybody else was going. I told him I didn't feel like going.

3. I'm lying lengthwise on a man's back. He's a husky fellow and sometimes it seems as if he is much larger than I. I try to swaddle him in a sort of cloth or diaper, and get quite a thrill. He struggles to prevent me, and just as I thought that I had bound his arms tightly, I see that he gets away from me.

Whenever he becomes excited or nervous, he likes to play the guitar. In reference to the first dream he says that the last sentence may very well have meant: "You can drink beer just as well as you can play the guitar." He evidently wants to play his guitar for me, and is a little hurt that I haven't invited him to do so. The guitar betrays its anal significance by the "sound-hole." He confesses that he has had the desire and phantasy of having pederastic relations with a man, but he adds that he could never agree to any passive pederasty. Beer is a symbol of virility, but it is also urine here. As a child, he often put his finger in his urine and tasted it. This dream is a distinct sign of transference.

The second dream, too, is an expression of his unwillingness to have his paraphilia buried. The schoolmate is his *alter ego*. That old H. is their former family physician, a confirmed celibate. His name is also indicative of the patient's religious complex.

In the third dream, he embraces his antagonist and will not let him go. (His father was accustomed to permitting the children to roll him tightly in the covers before he fell asleep; manifestly a reminiscence of the infantile days when, as a baby, he was well wrapped in the diapers.) Otto naturally doesn't want to give up his infantilism, either. He embraces it and fears that his second nature may yet shake itself off. As a matter of fact, the only part of his sexuality of which he does make use is what Moll calls the contrectation instinct, i.e., he is satisfied with simply coming in tactile contact with the partner, and, as with his masturbatory habits, never letting himself arrive at detumescence.

There must be some experience in his childhood which causes him to hold so fast to his paraphilia, some occurrence which he cannot forget. As he was thinking of the second dream, he recalled an old dream which had so excited him at the time that he could not forget it.

I see one of my sisters, probably my youngest. She has wounds all over her body, like pricks. She is bleeding. She is about four years old. I'm supposed to have killed her; I'm in a state of terrible anxiety as the family comes together for a conference. Our family doctor is also there and I begin to feel much better when I hear that she is still alive. My father suggests that they take up a collection with which I may go away for a rest. Dr. H. said he would give fifty marks, but then he only gave me two, red and white one-mark bills.

Again we see the family physician and the burial. That was his youngest sister who died of measles. In the dream he also saw his father laying a large sum of money on the table. But the dream really annuls the death of the sister, and we will remember that when he was in the hospital with measles he showed the first signs of his paraphilia. It was there that he saw the boy without arms. His little sister has spots on her skin in this dream, spots which look like bed-bug bites (this is also an indication of the bites that once saved his own life). She has the measles, the lesions are bloody and hemorrhagic, such as the exanthema frequently is in lethal cases of morbilli. His sister died when he was four; this number is further indicated by the amount of the mark bills, whose color also emphasizes the color of the measles. The fifty might be a reference to his father, who is in his late fifties. It seems that the money in this dream is an indication of his guilt consciousness. A small guilt for the sister's death (perhaps he's also blaming Dr. H. to some extent for her death) and a large obligation towards his father. The guilt feelings are derived from the fact that he had wished his little sister dead, and was therefore guilty of her decease. His conscience is bothering him.

I believe that this occurrence was the nucleus of his subsequent paraphilia. The death of his little sister is the guilt which he must expiate in his illness.

He claims to have no recollection of the burial, but suddenly he sees an old picture: his mother in a black dress and a black funeral hat. In this moment he goes off into a peculiar mental state, a sort of trance. He says that he used to have such states when he was a little boy, but even when he was fifteen or older he would also get dreamy periods.

He begins to feel as if space were limitless and that he is in an infinitely wide and broad room. His legs become longer and longer, his arms are stretched immensely (in the earlier attacks, his fingers would become very thick, but this doesn't seem to be the case in this period). Everything seems to be far off and away. My voice seems to come to him from great distances, and his own voice sounds unusually loud to him. All the noises which come from without seem to be a roar. He feels a little dizzy; as if all his limbs had been elevated and his trunk, which lies upon the sofa, had remained grown together with the furniture. It seems to him that his limbs float in the air. Something seems to be turning in his head; like a tornado. I and everything in the room appear to him as if he were looking through the wrong end of an opera glass: very small and far away.

In earlier years, these states would invariably preface an attack of great anxiety. First his fingers would begin to feel as if asleep, then his anxiety would begin to develop and he would say to himself: "Say! You're dreaming, old boy. Wake up!" But it was of no avail. The anxiety continued to develop like a rising tornado, he felt a terrific oppression in the breast and would sink gradually until he was able to free himself from the spell with one yell.

He had frequently complained of micropsia and macropsia as a boy (twelve). They took him to the eye specialist who said that he was tired out and needed glasses.

He states that he gets a similar attack sometimes which transforms his usually friendly face into a militaristic glare. He goes about with a dark visage and can't seem to shake it off. It is like a compulsive state which will not liberate him.

The explanation of the first described attack is quite difficult. In part, it is probably a symbolical death with infinite dissolution. On the other hand, we see that he becomes the great one and the great (in real comparison with him) become small. He feels as if he could fly and yet is attached to the earth. The violent feelings of anxiety show us with greater clarity that this attack is a phantastic representation of death. The anxiety is thus a fear of death. Is it that he is dying together with his little sister? I hope that the analysis will help us solve this problem.

Yesterday's attack is disclosed as a sort of retreat into the past. Everything of the present, e.g., my voice, seems so far away to him. Every distant thing, on the other hand, appears to be very near. He seems to be looking through the large end of an opera glass. He's looking at his childhood.

Yesterday he had a decided relapse. We were taking a walk together when a very crippled man hobbled past us. He seemed to be suffering from a coxitis. The patient said: "You see. Formerly this man would have been an ideal of mine. But he is not handsome enough." Nevertheless, he later reproached himself for not having gone after that man and taken a good, long look at him. He even produced phantasies about him. He was quieted only after he had come upon the sympathetic face of a young criminal in a criminological magazine. The photo showed the fellow's hands bound to an iron bar in the middle of the picture.

I had noticed that his attack of the other day and his subsequent excitement were introduced by a letter which he had received shortly before from his eldest sister. It must be recalled, too, that the dreams about his sisters both referred to a living sister. He evidently desired to overcome his sister, to bury her in his mind, as it were, but this he was not able to do.

The patient then confessed that he had lately become a little suspicious himself of his affective attitude towards this sister. First of all, the very marked physical disgust and secondly, the embarrassment which he manifests in her presence. When he was a little over ten, his sister had a serious case of rheumatic arthritis. She often had many bandages about her limbs. He also remembers that Dr. H. once laid on a cardboard splint in order to immobilize one of her legs. This same sister also suffered from a disease of one ear later and had to be operated on, with the result that for a long time she wore a head-bandage. He doesn't recall the bandage itself, probably because he was himself in the hospital at the time with the measles. His sister had her head closely cropped, and he remembers this because he himself had long locks. He was a very handsome boy and was very much pampered and even taken for a girl occasionally. He also remembers that both he and sister used to be bathed together and that in later years they always bathed after each other. At night they would tell each other stories in which she would be the queen of the elves and he would be the king of the ghosts.

When his youngest sister was born, they tried to take the

sting out of the arrival of another rival by presenting him with a large bag of candy. They said that sister had brought it with her for him. During the first few months, he would always be on hand when she was bathed and powdered. They called the powdering "miller tickling" (yesterday he felt a tickling sensation in the genital region all day long; that was manifestly his desire to be a nursling again and be well powdered and swaddled). His phantasies often take him back to the days when he was a baby and was bathed and powdered. He envied his little sister the pleasures of "miller tickling."

It is striking that corsets play such a leading rôle in his orthopedic phantasies. His mother had always worn a strong and large-sized corset, but his sisters wore only well-fitting elastics. When he was having that affair with the married woman, he found her corset very disturbing and unpleasant. She was quite an obese and luxurious woman and naturally kept herself tightly laced up. The feel of the corset and the scraping sounds it made were quite a pleasure to him in the case of that bound-up girl in the park, but touching the corset of the married woman gave him precisely the opposite feeling. The married woman was a mother image, but the girl had a mother herself who was probably well laced together. In the one case, the corset was an attraction and in the other it was an inhibition. He states that he has never put on a corset himself, but supposes, since he bandaged himself, that he also had corset phantasies and wishes.

His dreams of last night are characteristic.

We are in a room and there is a war raging. Whenever we open the door, the others shoot in. The first shot hits my baggage. Then I'm supposed to pursue some one together with a third person. I'm supposed to disguise myself with a false beard. But because it looked so unnatural, I trimmed it down with a nail clipper and turned it up a little. The revolvers don't function properly. Besides, there is no ammunition and I can't find any. Then we were in a large house and I had to get down from some roof. I was afraid, and I don't know how I got down altogether. Finally, I dreamed that I was looking at some orthopedic magazines and masturbating.

He is always struggling with himself. Now it is I who is his enemy. He is afraid my shots might hit him whenever he opens the door of his soul. He wants to keep it tightly closed. The pursuit is against his other ego, of course, and his companion and aid is none other than myself. He pastes a sign of virility on his face which he doesn't possess in reality (it is false). Yesterday he suddenly got the idea that he ought to have his beard shaved off. He would like to be a woman and a child. He is no man, for his revolver (phallus) doesn't function properly and he has no ammunition.

But, aside from this impotence feature, there seems to be another complex which is worrying him. We know that all these fetishists are really seeking to preserve an infantile impression. Originally, it seems, his desires were directed against his sister with whom he wrestled and fought so much. That alone might explain his need of simple tactile relationships. His so-called bodily feeling is nothing but the fixation of those pleasurable scenes with her. It is she that he is pursuing, she whom he desires to catch. He sees her with all her bandages, just as she lay in bed that time. Did he have anything to do with her at that time? Otto believes that behind his dreamy attacks, there lurks some experience which he probably dare not reveal or bring to consciousness. This experience and the repetition compulsion appear to be his symbolization of the original sin. He has had dreams in which he falls or drops or has a great fear of falling. In the present dream, he is supposed to come down off the roof; he is afraid, but finally he lands at the bottom. Just how he got down is hidden in memory. But he also dreamed of masturbating with the aid of orthopedic magazines. The original sin and masturbation are thus identified, i.e., he masturbates with the aid of a specific phantasy. It is important to record that he did not have an emission nor could he find any trace of one on the bed clothing. The dream shows only the relationship between his onanism and the orthopedic picture behind which his sister seems to be hidden. The trimming of the beard recalls his castration complex which is further indicated by his desire to have himself clean shaven. He doesn't want to be a man. He is afraid of his virility, but he didn't shave off his beard because he is consciously resisting his ever-growing feminine tendencies. He wants to display himself as real he-man. The failure of the pistol shows that he probably has had failures with his virility. The impotence, on the other hand, is a self-protective mechanism against the forbidden sexual desires.

I want to stress the relations between his paraphilia and his sister. That man in the splints represents to him his sister who also had to wear splints for a while. The false beard in this dream also shows us that he wants to disguise himself from his analyst.

Before the hour yesterday, he was sitting in a café and looking expectantly out the window, when along hobbled his ideal. He followed him for the simple reason that his tension had become unbearable and he felt the need of a little reality. Then the struggle within him was sharpened. But a voice said to him: "That's pure nonsense. You're running after your own reflection. Remember what Dr. Stekel told you." But another voice answered: "If you don't follow this man, you'll be impelled to steal and cut pictures out of books; so go ahead." He followed after the man and, sure enough, it wasn't a coxitis at all; the man went into Prof. Lorenz's orthopedic dispensary. Our fetishist went into the waiting room and looked over the patients who were sitting there, but saw none who met with his approval. Then he waited outside for over an hour until his ideal came out. Then he continued to follow him, happy at the fact that the cripple had picked up the company of another. They both went into the city hall. He thought he would wait again, but it was lunch hour and he had to give up his shadowing. Meanwhile, he had indulged constantly in phantasies which were heightened by regular observations of the men. He said to himself that if he had not succumbed to his impulse, the memory of the cripple would have plagued him for weeks. He would have to begin a new collection. Or he would have to masturbate, but onanism with his specific phantasy would only drive him deeper into the underbrush of his fetishism. When he masturbates before the pictures of his collection, he has at least a semblance of reality before him, but, unfortunately for him, he has given me the entire collection. He now has been fighting off the tendency to start a new one.

Ever since the sight of that cripple on the street, he has not been provoked by the picture of that criminal with the handcuffs. He did not address the cripple, however, nor would he do such a thing now. Moreover, the man was not handsome enough for him. His friend had one leg amputated and wore a prosthesis. He is not attracted by such types. He is provoked only by handsome young men with whole limbs which are pressed into splints or trusses of some kind.  Crutches also animate his fancy.  But if a man has only one leg then his pleasure is but a tithe of that which he derives from a whole man.

In the afternoon he wandered about the Prater for a while and then went to some performance which the Wandervögel were putting on in the evening.  It didn't please him.  But he can't work. He is waiting for me to force him, admonish him, press him to go to the dentist, but that is just what I have been avoiding.  Last night he had a toothache again and wondered why I didn't send him to the "tooth plumber."  He envies the crocodiles because when they get old their teeth fall out and new ones grow in again. This crocodile complex must be of some importance to him for he said: "If some much more vicious evil lurks behind my fetishism, such as a desire to eat little children or suck blood like a vampyre, wouldn't it be better for me to stick by my fetishism?"

He is then told that even were the analysis to disclose such roots at the basis of his paraphilia, he would never actually succumb to those desires; in addition to which, he is expressing his paraphilia in some symbolic way at all times.  He had to understand and then openly give up his idea.

I then told him that his paraphilia somehow had to show connections with his sister's suffering (the mastoid operation).  It seems also that his dentist phobia is covered in the maze of these memories.  The beginning of the paraphilia must have taken place on some part of the head.  He then corroborated this suspicion by telling me that he had begun by making himself several head bandages.  And then he divulges this important bit of information:

His first bandages had been made of some flannel pieces which belonged to his mother; she had once used them for something or other.

The most important question we would have to ask would be: did his mother use these flannel cloths to bind her legs during her pregnancy?  Or: whether these bandages were not used by his sister during her rheumatism?  He said he couldn't answer those questions, but he would write and ask.

It is of great significance that his first bandages were pieces of flannel which had lain upon his mother's body (see the guitar dream which disclosed relations to his mother).

He was about twelve or thirteen when he began to make bandages industriously.  He would also gag himself and walk about on home-made crutches of broom sticks.  He fabricated all kinds of fantastic dressings out of handkerchiefs, towels and other linens. His mother seems to have suspected him of something for she would often burst suddenly into his room; but this only gave him greater practice in divesting himself quickly of his bandages. Once, however, they found a bundle of knotted towels behind the stove, and he had to stand up under a rather uncomfortable cross-examination. At eleven he was introduced to masturbation by a schoolmate and afterwards his mother used to find the well-known stains in the linens. She would also observe him at night, but she never spoke openly with him.

One of his greatest sources of excitement during masturbation was the so-called stretcher-bed. When he was about nine, he received a calendar as a gift from the society for the prevention of cruelty to animals. One of the pictures on the calendar showed a man with a curb-bit in his mouth. This was a metaphoric manner of showing the inhumanness of the curb-bit as compared with the regular snaffle-bit. The curb-bit in the man's mouth made a deep impression upon him (curb-bits pull the jaw upwards). His first drawings were of men with curb-bits in their mouths (a contribution to his dentist phobia, also).

At eleven his kleptomaniacal tendencies were at their height. He stole a great deal from his grandmother because she always left her pocketbook lying about. Always he would take a single gold piece (twenty marks). Only once did he take a one-mark piece and then they caught him. And whenever he would go visiting with his parents he would steal, too. He would steal stamps in the collector's shops to such an extent that his stamp collection consisted almost entirely of stolen goods.

He dreamed:

A small boy had a stamp collection which I wanted very much. He was willing to sell it and finally demanded two one-mark pieces. I was willing to give him five marks, but in reality it seems that I gave him a ten-mark bill. I thought that was quite swell, giving him more than he had asked; but in my heart I knew that he deserved more.

I find myself at a big congress, a Socialist congress, I think. All kinds of important personages and leaders are there. Tchicherin and others. It seems that the others there looked up to me; I was somebody; clear and composed. I even spoke sometimes.

I follow the captain through the rooms and everything seems to be dropping from my arms, all kinds of trivial things from the service. The captain is a very nervous man who has lost most of

the respect he commanded by his yelling and cursing. I resolve
with clarity and firmness to see that the situation is remedied.

The first dream shows that he is battling against his paraphilia.
His fetishism is represented as a little boy (infantilism). He
doesn't know whether the price that he is paying for his cure (the
loss of his collection) is not too high for the loss of his pleasures.
The numbers are quite characteristic. They have already appeared
to some extent in the other dream about numerals. The two ones
are to be explained by the fact that he was born on the eleventh.
The number fifty also appears again. We have already seen that
it was connected with the family physician. Is it possible that his
sister died the fifth of August (ten)? The most he can say is that
it was in the Autumn. He had a secret calendar at home, however, and he will write and ask. It is possible that the date was
preserved.

The second dream fulfills his wishes for a great historical mission. He is a famous leader and talks very little, in contrast to
the analysis where he is a follower and must talk a great deal.
In the dream he is a respected and honored man.

He thinks the captain in the third dream is his father. The
latter was a very nervous man and so tyrannized the house that
everybody had to be as still as a mouse when he was home. Manifestly, Otto has resolved to be different from his father and not
have so much to say. His attitude towards me is clear; he doesn't
respect me and doubts whether the analysis is going to be a success.

Yesterday he again followed an "ideal" type, and afterwards
felt very industrious. He thought he would work and study a
great deal, but he was quite distracted.

He had the following dream:

I had the scabies. All over my body little mites crawled about.
They were like little wood-ticks, but they sat there on my skin and
I seized them between my fingers and cracked them.

I am at home. My mother must have had quite a lot of cake.
I was in a room at home, lying in bed. A girl of about the size
of a twelve-year-old, with red hair, came in, approached my bed,
then crawled into bed with me and put her hand on my phallus.
She had a pimply sort of rash with large red bumps. It seemed
to be on her trunk. Over that she had a loosely knitted jacket
of heavy wool. Then she seemed to be large, but still of an infantile appearance. I told her to get out of the bed, but I was quite
pleased at her being there. Then the door was opened and a still
smaller girl, about three or four years old, came in and also

wanted to get into bed with me.  I let her come in.  She also had
a rash on her body.  She knows that her sister had been there
before her.  She, too, put her hand on my genitals, but just before
the ejaculation, I collected myself and pushed her out of the bed.
My second sister came in and said that mother had been angry
that I had had the first girl in bed with me because diphtheria was
going around.  I got up and went into the dining room to talk
with my mother.  She was packing away the silverware.  I took
a piece of coffee cake and then, because she didn't speak to me, I
left the room.

After thought: The little girl said to me just as she was leaving:
"You have to come down now because we have got everything
ready for you, hot water and everything."

Upon awakening, he told himself that this dream must certainly
be of considerable importance; that it probably contained the key
to his paraphilia.  But he promptly began to undermine its value
and would have forgotten it entirely if he had not put it on paper
immediately.

He can hardly understand how it was possible that "the fine
tickling feeling" was provoked by a girl in the dream.  He believes
that he is a thorough "homo," and that only handsome youths and
young men could animate his senses.  He often gets that "fine
feeling" in the genitals when he is following his ideal type on the
street and imagining that they were touching his genitals.  He
finally comes to the realization that he has come to this attitude
by a displacement, a transposition from the female members of
his family to men.

It is remarkable how frequently infections and rashes occur in
this dream.  He himself has the scabies, the itch.  Ticks are well
dug into the skin and whenever they are torn or picked out,
wounds and inflammations are left.  It is thus that evil and vicious
thoughts hide in his brain, and he shall suffer much pain before
they are picked out.

Associating on "cake," he says that he was always a passionate
cake-eater and never seemed to get enough of it.  He valued the
divers birthday visits he used to make on the basis of the amount
of cake he used to receive.  He used the money he stole as a boy
either for stamps or cake and cookies.  In the dream, his mother
is the mistress of the cakes and sweets, a circumstance which
further indicates her relation to his parapathia.  The red-haired
girl first reminded him of a red-haired nursemaid they had had,
Rike, by name.  That was the girl under whose dresses he had

crawled or wanted to crawl when he was four. She seems to have appeared twice in the dream, for he had the impression that both girls who played with him in bed were one and the same person, only at different ages. Her rash looked almost like a furunculosis. One could see the boils through the netting of her loosely woven woollen jacket. But her face was quite clean and healthy. He had a curious certainty that the people lived under them. The very first time he was touched he was somewhat astonished at the oncoming orgasm, and this astonishment grew with the second girl. Even in the dream he had thought: "You imagine yourself to be nothing but a homosexual, but here you see very well that you get a thrill out of women too."

For the past several years his wet dreams have had to do only with youths and he cannot recall having seen girls in any of them before the analysis began.

He believes that both the girls in the dream were his sisters. Indeed we know that they were conceived as two sisters in the dream. We also recall that Otto and his sisters used to visit each other in bed as little children and even continued these customs when they grew up to have separate rooms. Later still, the visits in night shirts ended at the edge of the bed where one or the other of the children would sit down and talk with the one in bed. Even as late as a few years ago, his second sister, who often offered her services as a hot-water bottle, would come to his bed for a little chat with him.

In reference to the family silver, he states that his mother liked to put it away herself, especially the fine silver which would appear only on special occasions. His mother reproaches him for something in the dream. He did something he should not have done. He thinks of the little sister who died of the measles and how he may have crawled into her bed and done something. As if his mother had said to him: "You shouldn't do such things. Your little sister could die that way and then you would become sick, too." But such a memory is very hazy in his mind. Perhaps not even a memory but only a construction, a fabrication. He is struck by the frequency of rashes in his dreams; a red exanthema which reminds him of the measles. He can't recall any more just how the children lay next to him in bed; he says also that they didn't exactly play with his phallus, but only somewhere in the perineal region—only soft touches of the hand. He had the feeling in the dream that he could not be responsible for such acts; that they were forbidden.

His mother had also had a miscarriage, but he hadn't even mentioned that until to-day. It was a little brother who was named Archibald by the family. He has no recollection of when the abortion took place. He now states that those flannel bandages of his mother's attracted him because of their odor. He is always animated by the odor of linens or clothing belonging to persons who appeal to him. The jackets that some of his favorite "Wandervögel" wore excited him greatly; he would virtually drink in the odor of the sweat. His friend's suit also had a strong odor, and this was a direct sexual stimulant for him. One of the most provoking parts of the masochistic books would be a scene in which the masochist would have to put on a woman's petticoat. He would frequently think of a worn petticoat and what a pleasant odor it must have (especially a certain scene from the memoirs of Viscount Robinson).

We begin to see the contours of those infantile experiences which have engendered his parapathia somewhat more clearly.

What is it that passed between him and his sisters?

What was the rôle of the nursemaids who appear in his memories? It also seems that he must have had some sweet experience with his mother (the cake and sweets).

We will patiently await developments in the further course of the analysis.

He had a terrible reaction yesterday. Memories struggled to the surface but he fought them back. He reconnoitred about the streets again for a vision of his ideals and was quite disconsolate that none appeared upon the scene. He didn't know what to do next. In the evening he went to a concert and soon caught sight of a handsome young fellow—blond, of course, and slender. But the man showed him no receptivity. He envied others who seemed to have discovered each other there. Finally, he approached a nice youngster and looked over his shoulder at the score. But he got a little dizzy and felt faint. He lost track of the music and struggled hard to put down his heterosexual strivings in favor of the homosexual ones.

Let us return to the last part of the last dream he had ("Come down now, the water is hot"). He thinks it might also have meant: "Hurry, the water will get cold." That reminds him of his third sister who always sneaked things when the soup was on the table. She was a reddish blonde and was four years old when he was twelve. That then explains the numbers in his dream. Vague and hazy memory of her having often come into his bed of a morning. Even to-day she is "terribly delicate." She was dubbed the "hot pack" or the "hot-water bottle" in the family. She could kiss and pet the whole day long. That was the sister who said: "I have to have a man or I'll get a stick to hug." She suffered from nocturnal frights as a child. His second sister was also in love with him. She was terribly cut up whenever he did anything which spoiled his good looks. She thought him the dandiest of men and was especially infatuated with his photograph in uniform. Once he stuffed a pillow under his vest and danced about the room as the caricature of a Jewish banker. His sister cried because he looked so ugly.

This stuffing of a pillow under his vest leads us to the subject of pregnancy. Formerly pregnant women were abhorrent to him, but he seems to have overcome that attitude of disgust. He also states that there was a time when he was attracted by breasts. He had seen the photograph of a negress who was so tightly laced about the abdomen that her breasts stood forth plastically. This quite excited him.

Suddenly in the middle of the analysis he begins to sing an aria from Troubadour: Oh, dearest mother, thou shalt not die!

If we are to believe the indications of this last dream, it seems that the turning point in the development of his parapathia was his twelfth year. He had doubtless masturbated even earlier than that and had had masochistic phantasies, but the systematization began to take place at about this time. Did something take place between him and his sisters which burdened his conscience? In the dream, his sister appears aggressive, she is warm; it's high time (the water is hot).

At home, he is always inhibited, moody and very susceptible to great sexual excitement. He masturbates frequently and practices his special habit of protracted onanism. He has sometimes been able to masturbate at short intervals for three weeks at a time without actually permitting the orgasm to come on. He thus forces himself to go about in a state of permanent expectancy and irritation. He stages a yearning the realization of which is postponed. It is probable that what he is waiting for is the miracle which will bring his sister back into his bed as in the dream. But he wouldn't do anything even then. That is why he is always upset, unhappy and excitable at home.

But if he gets an opportunity to take a long walk or outing with a comrade, then he is able to react every vestige of his feelings. The most superficial intimacies are enough to make his days happy.

Yesterday was Sunday. Since it had rained on Saturday, I had arranged that he might come for an hour on Sunday, and that was to hold good for any week-end when it was bad weather. He enjoyed the coming Sunday hour in advance, indulged in all kinds of phantasies about getting better acquainted with me, that I would invite him to afternoon tea, etc., but it appears that his phantasies overstepped their bounds. He seems to have put an unconscious stop to them himself, for he suddenly got the idea that he would go to the opera to hear Tristan with a friend who had mentioned that he was going. He went very early to get tickets. The weather became doubtful, the sky overcast. What to do? He decided to stay. Then it began to rain and he thought he had better come back to the appointment with me. He struggled back and forth in his mind and finally decided to stay at the opera. But he was manifestly torn between the two tendencies and did not enjoy the opera at all.

He treats me just as he did his father with whom he would have liked to become somewhat better acquainted. But he depreciates his father at every opportunity. From the front, he used to write the warmest of letters, but at home it seemed as if an insurmountable wall stood between them. This wall is his sexual attitude, and I took the pains to explain to him that it was just the same type of inhibition which was disclosed in his transference to me.

He related the following fragmentary dreams about war and imprisonment:

The colonel wanted to return with us to our quarters. The road becomes narrower. On the left stands a house and at the right there is a wire fence. The colonel told us we would have to get through. In the house we found an old and withered woman who cursed us. I wanted to get past, but I seemed to be caught fast in that barbed-wire fence. My suit was caught. I would wriggle myself loose and then get caught again.

And still more war. I was taken prisoner once by the English. I was deathly afraid of the shooting. But I felt safer after I was taken prisoner.

This is the third time that we meet with the motif of the

fenced-in field. He has manifestly fenced off a certain part of his soul, and this is the part which represents his parapathia. I (the colonel) command him to climb over the fence. But he can't succeed. The old woman reminds him of some working woman, a neighbor, but she has the features of his mother as well as the figure. We recall that his last dream included some reproaches on the part of his mother. It seems as if his mother stands in the way of his getting into that fenced-off piece of land.

The second dream-portion represents the struggle (the war) in his soul. He has been taken prisoner by his pious tendencies (the English) and is happy that he has been taken out of danger.

He is afraid of the struggle for existence. He is afraid of sin and the pitfalls of life. His parapathia protects him from temptation.

The fetishism becomes more distinctly a protective mechanism whereby he may ward off his evil strivings. He feels that he would be entirely at a loss without this protective mantle. Following upon the exciting emotions of the past few days, he is now in a state of apathy. In the theatre the other evening he got the phantasy: how would it be if everything just crashed now? He then got behind a pillar in the foyer to make himself feel that he were protected. Then he imagined the ceiling gradually sinking lower and lower (womb phantasies?).

He can't imagine himself ever becoming cured of his condition and demands a number of theoretical explanations about analysis. Why do I conceive the parapathic as an example of regression? What is the significance of the constitution, etc., etc.? I tell him that all these questions are manifestations of resistance, but he won't have such an answer. He wants to be clear on these matters.

Then he begins to speak about his phantasies. The past two days he had been on the lookout for his love objects, but hadn't been able to find any. He is beginning to get a clear idea as to just what these objects mean in his mind. He uses them as a basis for spinning his phantasies. The objects themselves are only illustrations, as it were. They are the bit of reality in the stories.

He dreamed:
Somewhere and somehow I got to a dentist. There was a middle-aged man there with a Vandyke who was to have a couple teeth pulled. He conducted himself lamentably. Then I looked through a glass door into the dentist's office and saw my sister in there. I recognized her distinctly as my third sister being treated.

Suddenly she became frightened and tried to run out, but I caught her at the door and brought her back. Then I had a fragment of a tooth in my hand and, for a moment, believed that I had already been in the chair myself. I ran my tongue over my teeth to feel for the hole, but I soon realized that the fragment was not mine.

I'm in the army again, have an officer's uniform on with short jacket, silver epaulets; a regulation uniform. With several others I'm standing about a pile of regulation equipment: haversacks, bags, belts, etc. I looked for a knapsack for myself, but found nothing suitable. There were many old shoes and inlay soles, but everything was worn out. Inspecting the articles a little more closely, I find that the knapsacks and bags are also narrow, like small cases. Certainly not suitable for the purposes of a knapsack. Suddenly a lieutenant said to me: "Are you some officer's representative?" I asked him how he got that idea and he ramarked that I had no mirror on my collar.

Then I was with Captain Vormann. He discussed my future with me. He seems to have talked with my father previously. He looked disgruntled, wore a second-hand loden suit (a special woollen weave used for mountaineering in Germany—Trans.) His colored shirt and collar were very dirty. He seemed to be of the opinion that I ought to return to the army, but I wasn't able to explain my reasons against the idea very well. Finally, he got irritable and said, as far as I can remember: "You'd do best to become a cook!"

Then I was somewhere in the company of corps students—not a very clear recollection. It seems I was a robber, too. . . . Then we were in my grandmother's bedroom, but it all looked entirely different. There was a young fellow with me, dark-haired and shorter than myself. My father came in, we played robber and my friend playfully went after my father with a knife. Just trying to keep him from coming into the room. I also had a knife in my hand, but the knife my friend had was very familiar to me. It was a Swedish steel blade with a horn handle and is like the knife my father has in his dressing table. Father was very amiable during the game.

Then the question: did you cry, too?

And the numbers: two times one . . . six . . . ten . . .

This dream brings us a good step forward in our understanding of his fetishism. The first part of it deals with his fear of the dentist. The old man he saw there is myself. I act lamentably, i.e., I seem to be afflicted with the same anxiety he has. Then he forces his sister under the dentist's care. He finds a fragment of a tooth in his hands which is apparently not his own.

At first the dream seemed unclear and he had no associations. In the second part of it, he expresses his feelings of uncertainty and inferiority. Nothing seems to suit him in life. In real life, Captain Vormann, who appears in the third part, is quite elegant, but in the dream he is shabby. He reminds the patient of his father. He himself had similar conversations with his father. The fourth part is quite vague in his mind. He felt as if his little blade was quite inefficient as compared with his father's big knife. That knife had always appealed to him and provoked his phantasies. Thereafter there seemed to be a gap, and he recalls only the apparently irrelevant question as to whether he had cried or not.

We recognize in this dream his attitude towards his father. That is the basic theme throughout the whole (the large and the small knife). The anxiety in the dentist's office is a symbolization of his castration and impotence fears (displacement upwards). The extraction of a tooth is psychically equivalent to the destruction of his penis, castration. His fear of the dentist is his fear of castration. He must have suffered some serious castration threat in early childhood. He recalls his grandmother once walking behind his third sister who seemed to be getting forward too slowly for the old lady. Grandmother thereupon pushed her and said: "Get on with you! If you don't move a little faster I'll poke a hole in your behind with this umbrella!" His sister answered her: "I don't care. I've got one there already!"

In the first part of the dream, he makes me impotent (I've lost all my teeth). His sister is a castrated male and the tooth fragment is a part of her or his penis. But he can't find any hole. This relieves him. The fragment is the lopped-off penis of his sister. This now illuminates the second part for us. The knapsack is a symbol of his scrotum. He feels that his scrotum is too small, and we learn that as a boy he had suffered from the thought that his genitals were too small, an expression of his sense of inferiority. Even to-day he sometimes will suddenly touch his genitals to make sure and relieve his mind that they are quite large enough. The father, however, is the real hero with the mighty phallus (the officer). He himself is only an officer's representative, a second fiddle. That means, of course, that he would like to represent or substitute for his father in respect of his mother. Yet, something is missing on his collar (always a phallic symbol). His father advises him to take up a feminine position in life: to become a cook. His father had frequently complained of the patient's lack of virility, his flaccid posture and character. But he will now revenge himself for this his father's attitude. He will attack him with a knife. It seems that he plainly phantasied himself castrating his father.

The cook is also an indication of a poison complex (did he have the phantasy of poisoning his father?). As a child he had had the ardent wish to become a cook.

And now we get an even clearer bit of insight into his dentist phobia. The dentist is his father who threatens to castrate him. Father will see his rotten teeth (his vicious thoughts).

Manifestly, a deep sense of guilt lurks behind his paraphilia. He wanted to emasculate his father. We remember that he always over-emphasized the size of the genitals in his sketches (it was necessary to tone this down somewhat in the reproductions in the text). The genitals are contrasted with the size of the delicate figures. Is it possible that the bandages were calculated originally as a protection to the phallus and were only later displaced to other limbs and organs?

They talked a great deal about death and burials at home. He was seven and was suffering from a pleurisy when his tutor died. They took occasion at the time to puncture his chest. Hardly had he recovered from the pleurisy but he had to visit the tutor's grave with his father. As a matter of fact, his father's preferred walk always led to the cemetery. And that was how the subject of death and burial was brought up in his mind at an early age.

One would think—if one were inexperienced in analysis—that a physician being analyzed would think about the gain in insight which he had experienced in the course of the treatment and either produce associations to corroborate our constructions or manifest signs which would undermine them. But words flow off this patient's back like water. Indeed, he digs himself deeper into his attitudes and develops new resistances which are calculated to disrupt the analysis. Thus, of course, he ran yesterday to the old stand where he thought his ideal must pass again; looked out of the café window in order not to miss him. Then he walked about the streets and was happy to find some other cripple. It was only a girl, to be sure, but since the beginning of the analysis he has become somewhat friendlier towards females in his thoughts. At a concert in the evening he had even found some pleasure in looking at a couple of flappers.

Apropos of the dentist phobia, he divulged some information which showed that his buccal region is an erogenous zone of the first water, as we had supposed in the first place. First he disclosed relations between his toothaches and his onanistic habits. Whenever he suffered from toothaches, he would masturbate and thus gain relief from the pains. It cannot be determined whether he provoked toothaches in order to have an excuse for masturbation. Defecation also was related to his bad teeth. For instance, whenever he would retain his feces for a long time and then defecate, he would experience a sort of "pleasurable pain" in his teeth. That means: a pain which is distinctly pleasant to him.

He often sucks at his carious teeth and that causes him a sudden, sharp and shooting pain which also feels pleasant to him. He even likes to suck at the foul and abscessed roots. The sweetish taste is enjoyable, he says. He often spits into his handkerchief afterwards in order to be able to smell the odor for a longer time.

He confesses to the most violent death wishes against his father. He also had phantasies such as: "If I were to die now, how they would sympathize with me." He feels himself in a state of permanently delightful expectancy which is expressed in his dreams.

For instance:

I live in a hotel and have a room for myself, but others seem to have got in there and that is unpleasant to me.

I come into the dining room and see a richly spread table. Cakes, cookies, sweets of all kinds. Acquaintances of mine sit at the table, among them a certain G. S. I would like to eat with them, but none of them invites me to sit down and avail myself. And when I wanted to partake, I found that everything was eaten. . . .

I am standing in the bed of a rivulet which seems to be partly dried up. The ground is stony. I notice that the dorsum of my right foot is swollen considerably and there is a small opening in the middle of the swelling, like a fistula. I think that I had best go to the surgical clinic, when suddenly a thick stream spurts out which reminds me of the fluid evacuated from a punctured abdominal dropsy. There seems to be more than could possibly come from such a swelling on the foot. There seems to be a thick and disgusting clump or shred hanging to the foot, like a clump of maggots; I want to wash the foot off in the running water, but that clump clings tightly and I have to brush it off with my hand. It turned out to be a very long, rolled-up tapeworm which has already begun to disintegrate.

On the road there, I came upon a broad ditch, filled with water. It was fenced off with barbed wire, and I couldn't get across. There were several buildings on the other side and a man with a "sister" was over there calling to me. It seems that I heard something about the shocking treatment of the Alsatians. The sister corroborated the information. Then I was holding two beams, one of them about fifteen feet long and the other about half that length. I threw both of them across the river. One fell through the gate into the courtyard. Then I was over there myself and went through the houses at the left looking for the way out. I found myself in a babies' hospital or home which was managed by a certain doctor in R. whom I know. I was looking for the exit; it seemed that I was in the wash room or laundry. Then I met the doctor. He said: "That's not permitted, you know, running around here like that." I ran into the next house, got into the toilet and climbed through a little window and thus got out into the open. The doctor said: "It seems to me that you're a little old to be running and wandering about like that." (Wandervögel passage.) I said that I would get rid of the habit soon enough. My habits of clothing myself like that and wandering about were quite old. Then I found myself together with some friends drinking coffee in the garden of a café. They served me with some of the cake they had, but it wasn't specially good. It seemed to be a certain Mrs. P. and her family.

These dreams are resistance dreams. The pleasurable feeling of tense expectancy refers to me and he transfers the feeling to his paraphilia. He expects me to recognize his sexual urgency and to fulfill his secret wishes. But what are his wishes? The second part of the dream betrays that. I should conduct myself like his comrade G. S., who taught him how to masturbate, i.e., I should practise mutual masturbation with him. I should play with him. That is what he evidently expected of his father, and because this hope was not fulfilled, he became obstinate and resistive.

In the first part of the dream, he has himself living in an elegant room in a hotel, whereas in reality here in Vienna he has to live in a sort of crowded tenement. In the hotel, he could receive visitors; he also could analyze, a thing he cannot do now. At the same time, this expresses his displeasure with the fact that I am becoming privy to the secrets of his soul.

In the second part of the dream, he stands before the richly decked table of life. The sweets are the joys of love; that is what G. S. pointed to. But he seems to be prevented from partaking of these sweets. He is an ascetic. In the third part, then, the analytical cleansing which he is experiencing is symbolized by the burst abscess. The quantity factor indicates that he is full of more complexes and experiences than he had imagined. And, also, there is always a drop of pus or dirt left clinging to him. The analysis is compared with a tapeworm. His paraphilia is a disgustingly long and rolled-up tapeworm (I might add that he had actually had a tapeworm in his youth). In the fourth part we again meet with a fenced-in plot of ground, a ditch. A sister appears on the scene and he is mistreated by me. (Mistreatment of the Alsatians.) I don't take a walk with him nor do I invite him to take tea or coffee. I let him run about alone. But he also declares symbolically that he has no intention of letting his paraphilia go (his Wandervögel habits). Finally, his passion for coffee and cake is gratified in the company of a family which is, unfortunately, not mine. He is not very well satisfied. Mrs. P. is a former landlady of his whose son is a physician and mistreats her. Her daughter had died suddenly. There are also indications of birth and pregnancy phantasies.

The mistreatment of the Alsatians is disclosed in his associations as a mistreatment of Elsa (Elsa of Brabant from Lohengrin —a sister imago).

The plenitude of dreams which he produces (dream diarrhœa) makes it impossible to go into them very deeply and this is his method of making it desirable to lengthen our analytic sessions. It was up to me either to analyze a single dream thoroughly or to finish all of them every day as they came along. I chose the second method because it would be easy to overlook the resistances if one abided by one dream alone. The success of the analysis finally justified my technique.

All patients who suffer from a fear of the dentist reveal some sign of a nursing complex. The associations tend towards either the mother's breast or the father's phallus. Our patient was asked about fellatio phantasies and confessed to a few experiences of this nature. The friend who first taught him to masturbate used to collect his semen in a saucer, it appears, and even tasted it or swallowed it (he was eleven or twelve at the time). He then hesitatingly tells of another friend whom he had at sixteen. That boy also took Otto's penis into his mouth. That this experience actually corresponded to a wish on the part of our patient is revealed by the fact that when he later hypnotized a male patient (of which we learned above), he gave him the suggestion to take his (Otto's) phallus into his mouth.   In the first case, it was an easy matter because the boy actually wished to perform fellatio on him and was very susceptible to the thought of large phalluses. In the second case, the patient at first resisted the suggestion but finally capitulated to our patient's wish.   (This shows us very clearly what the foundations of hypnosis are and how, under certain circumstances, the situation may be exploited.   Many parapathics hope for just such experiences.   The patient mentioned here felt very indebted to our patient who, he claims, improved him considerably, and even writes him long letters.)

We obtain further information from the dreams he had last night.  Again he produces them at great length.

1.  My guitar has been seriously damaged by somebody to such an extent that it comes apart at the joints (I think it was my father's partner, N.).   At first, I produced a few crocodile tears, but then I gradually began to cry as if something very serious had happened to me.

2.  I was back with my company after having been absent from trench duty for some time.  I'm a substitute officer.  I'm supposed to conduct setting-up exercises in some room, but my commands and orders are very faultily executed as if I weren't quite sure of my authority.   Several men who didn't have to join the exercises came into the room and stood near the windows and the beds.

Then A. came in carrying his penis in his hand.   It was very large, about a half yard long and over two inches thick.   It looked like a large worm or snake.   He showed us his phallus and I said: "You've got a phimosis and I also see a red pimple on your penis, like a rash."   The phallus was not straight, but irregularly curved and winding.   I was quite disgusted, and astounded at the whole proceeding.   Then I became afraid of the coming rifle exercises because I hadn't been on duty for so long.   I feared that I would probably make a fool of myself at the targets or something of the sort.

3.  Twice I had to pass down a road which ended in a steep incline (between the two times I seem to have had another dream which I forgot).   From my experience with other dreams of the same kind, I knew that a girl would soon come roaring down that incline in an automobile.   It was some kind of motion picture being filmed.   In the previous dreams, someone always came

riding right behind her in another car. The second time, she would always come down the hill more slowly than the first. And as she would pass by the second time, I would step into the inn. I'm a guest there and go up to my room. There is a double bed in there (the bed of my parents). On the right side of the bed, there lies a young fellow of about sixteen; it is J. H. I am happy at the prospect of lying down with him. Then his father comes into the room and, much to my astonishment, seems agreed with this act. Later, it seemed to me that his father was the professor of political economy, M. Both H. and M. were very big and strong.

Dream 1 is one of his very typical guitar dreams. He adds that his father's partner, N., sat down on the guitar and crushed it with his buttocks. The partner represents his own father. Father is the cause of his condition. Father is an enemy of that guitar, he feels that his son exaggerates his condition. But Otto desires to captivate everyone with that guitar. He wants to sing to me, and is hurt by the fact that I have not yet invited him to do so. In real life, he also identifies himself with his guitar. It is a living instrument for him (animism). He communes with it, talks to it, coddles it and wraps it up when he puts it away, as if he were putting it to sleep. When the guitar screeches or gives off a false note, it is as if his soul were out of tune. When he had decided to come to Vienna, he "tore open the belly of his guitar." He likes to sing to someone and is jealous of the fact that father prefers to have some woman sing to him. He firmly believes in the magic of his voice and feels (half consciously) that I would promptly fall in love with him if I would only listen to him sing. At present he prefers to sing melancholic songs and melodies. For instance, his favorite just now is the "Three Gypsies" by Lenau—people who play or sleep or dream their lives away. And yet some active tendencies seem to break through here. For instance, he was impelled to call out a certain doggerel thirty times in a row:

> " 'Twas great that that did happen;
> When God of me did think.
> A bird of silk and satin;
> But oh! how he did drink!"

He loves his guitar like he loves himself. He can even bring himself to sing and serenade girls. That is, he could do it very well once upon a time, but now he's somewhat inhibited: "Man! What good does it do you! You can't even kiss!"

In regard to dream 2, he remarks that the cardinal feeling there was that of distinct inferiority. He wasn't the true officer, but only the substitute; not the man who possessed the real authority. The men whom he was supposed to command were all younger than he; friends and comrades of his. Those who were not included in the exercises were all older than he. It appears that there is a distinct difference in his mind between the young and the old. But how do these elders conduct themselves? Indeed, that tutor A. comes along with a mightily erect penis. It is the same teacher to whom he had once complained of the masturbation and his sexual hunger. The teacher who had manifested such an understanding of his plight. He seems to have been a homo, but there never was anything between them. In the dream, A.'s phallus is considerably depreciated. It is infected (pimple-lues) and, despite its size, disgusting. It is bent and twisted, wriggly like a snake. Otto is astounded at its size, but disgusted nevertheless.

This teacher is, of course, a representative of his father and myself. He would like to see me exhibit myself (primitive reaction of undressing). He expects some homosexual gesture from me. He would like to perform fellatio on me and at the same time bite off my penis.

The last-mentioned phantasy derives from his castration ideas and appeals to him as a most natural thing. He confesses to it. He recalls that he has repeatedly imagined such sadistic scenes. And yet he cannot see that he would like to execute one of these scenes in his transference situation, and, furthermore, that in the dream he divests himself of the phantasy by depreciating it. After all, I am infected and my phallus is a disgusting, snaky thing. He would much rather execute that so-called M. G. (machine gun) exercise with the girl; but M. G. stands for machine gun exercise, and that is thus the same thing. There he feels himself impotent.

In the analysis of the third dream he associates on "hill": "mother's hill," i.e., mother's abdomen, and then gets around to womb phantasies which are as yet rather dimly outlined.

The extent and power of this parapathia may be guessed from the polar tension between his conscious and his unconscious personality. Consciously he would reject any advances on the part of either myself or his father. But unconsciously (in his phantasies), he indulges his infantile wishes. In his phantasies, he is a child with the wishes and strivings of a child, but in reality he is a man and wants to be a man. The tension between the conscious man and his antagonist in phantasy in tremendous. The bridge between them is the fetishism.

He adds to dream 3 the fact that he felt as if he knew what were coming. It was like a motion picture set; something was being filmed. The girl is about to come shooting down the hill with the man in another car right behind her. The girl's car was red and the man's black. The road was steep and winding. He was quite tense, waiting for something to happen.

Last night he dreamed:

I was in company somewhere with Professor R. and the crown prince. It seems as if R. didn't want to introduce me to the crown prince. But later I talked with the heir to the throne.

The German crown prince was always a favorite figure in his mind [the ex-crown prince of Germany was a universal favorite among the population of Germany, and especially among the youth of the country—Trans.]. But Professor R. was not very appealing in the dream. Otto thought that he was impotent and that his wife had an affair on the side. Otto begins to think all kinds of things about my family and would like to be introduced in my house. He realizes that all these ideas are being exploited by him for resistance.

One of his chief characteristics is a jealous nature which he will not admit to himself. Nevertheless, he was amenable to a little insight in respect of a few points. He had noticed that his elder sister had been pampered and preferred to him by his father, his grandmother and an aunt. It is she who speeds into the vale of life ahead of him. He envies her the fact that she was born first. He thinks his father mistreats him and doesn't take enough interest in him. That is why he cannot suffer his father's company. When he was three years old, he stole the cake that was baked for his sister's first birthday. He had thought to himself: "What'll she know about it, anyhow?"

Then come memories of the painter who painted a life size portrait of him. That man was also adept at "magic." When he was sitting for his picture, the painter would pull gorgeous candies out of his mouth and ears. Otto was also in his studio and received apples, too.

Once when he was a little boy, he slept with his father in one room. He had always wanted to have either father or mother for himself alone. He can't share anything. There were large twin beds in the room and also a child's bed. He refused to sleep in the child's bed and insisted on getting into the bed next to his father.

When he was fifteen, they were together in the Saxon hills south of Dresden. They took a room together. He wanted to keep the light burning all night, but his father wanted to have it dark. He was terribly afraid and excited in the night. Finally he caught sight of a glimmer of light through a crack in the door and felt easier that there was light somewhere.

Two years later he was in Switzerland with his parents. That was an unhappy period for him. He felt so bored, he could hardly decide what to do next. He was always alone and seemed to find no one to play with. He seems to have hoped that father would dedicate some of his free time to him. Distracted, he began to play with a toy bank which they had and stole the money. Then they forbade him to do that. So, what should he do? He wanted desperately to be home again, and hated his whole family. Those well-known family outings on Sundays were hateful to him. He wanted to have one member of the family for himself.

His love for his father was mixed with a dash of wonder. Father had been a sporty and spirited student in his day and had had many friends and admirers. Otto would secretly read his father's letters as they lay on the writing desk or in the drawers. He wanted to possess his father's affections all alone, and if that was not possible, he would act stubbornly. He paid no attention in school and brought home poor report cards. The result, of course, was renewed scenes at home and the situation became impossible. His father would preach lengthy and moral sermons to him, pointing to his own past record. But father was after all, an unapproachable ideal. Father seemed to be so "terribly moral." Out of pure opposition, because father was a Social Democrat, he became a Communist; the result being that his father was deeply hurt by his action.

He can't stand riding in aerial railways (such as they have in the mountains), nor can he suffer rocking motions. It gives him an unpleasant drawing sensation in the pit of his stomach.

His mother replied to his questions by informing him that the death of his sister occurred at a time of the year which actually corresponds with the numbers in his dream.

When he was thirteen, he underwent an operation for adenoid

growths; that wasn't so bad. But his anxiety of dentists seems to derive from that illness which necessitated his transfer to the babies' hospital (at three). He suffered from diphtheria as we know. It is not impossible that he was often plagued with examinations and the frequent discomfort of tongue depressors and laryngoscopes.

He cannot suffer the noise of knife sharpening, chalk on boards or the drilling of teeth or the trephine. He begins to suffer associated toothaches at the noise of such operations and manipulations (he himself crunches his teeth at night). Further questioning on the matter of cannibalistic strivings divulged some openings. He cannot stand crunching or creaking of bones, nor could he eat nuts when he was a child. They had a large nut-cracker at home (king nut-cracker they called it). In his eyes, that instrument was a man-eater. He himself played the part of the man-eater last year in an amateur performance of "The Brave Little Tailor," by the Wandervögel group. At eighteen, he began to oppose meat eating and became a vegetarian. And yet, in a dispute with a vegetarian, who claimed that he was a vegetarian because he did not wish to make man a murderer, he himself had argued that such an attitude only revealed that the man was executing a reaction formation to his own murderous impulses.

In Otto's phantasies, amputations played an extensive rôle as a means of punishment. He claims that such phantasies had nothing to do with castration impulses, since he always felt the need of imagining the sight of the penis at the same time. This seems, however, to be a form of defense. For we know that formerly he frequently indulged in fellatio sketches and drawings which were unpleasant to him as long as the phallus was invisible. He would then erase and sketch anew until at least a part of the phallus had become visible again.

Only recently did any suggestion or indication of feces or urine phantasy appear in his pictures (this indicates a distinct movement and advance in his regression).

He then recalls that as a child, he always tried to be tender with his father, but father would be busy and would send him off.

To-day he has been bothered by the guilt feelings he had when his third sister became ill with a diarrhœa and vomiting. He threw himself on the floor, clasped his hands and prayed: "Oh, dear God! Don't let her die!" He had the feeling as if he would be guilty of her death. Had he given her something suspicious to eat? He can't remember very clearly what had gone before.

A dim recollection of father sitting at his writing desk. He himself is a very small boy and approaches father to embrace his legs. Father appears upset over the annoyance.

In the analysis, this desire for fatherly tenderness becomes a serious impediment and resistance. He is not satisfied with my medical interest in him alone. He is very desirous that my interest in him take on a more personal tone, that I send him to the dentist; he is finally appeased when I give him the name of a dentist acquaintance. He tries to give the impression of having collected himself; he's determined to have his teeth fixed. He believes that they have determined the course of his life. If they had not been so bad, he might have become a singer or an actor. And yet he knows that when he was in high school he had thought: you must become a doctor; then you can indulge your tastes, otherwise you'll do something foolish.

His attitude towards the female is illustrated by what he did yesterday. He had a friend here in Vienna who entrusted him with the company of his girl while he went off on a trip. Yesterday Otto went on an outing with the little Jewess. He felt discomfited by the fact that she was small and a Jewess. Jewesses are not his type (but she was very intelligent, educated and sweet, and that had attracted him). They lay down on the grass. Suddenly she seemed to irk him. He felt physically uncomfortable. Disgusted. He almost wanted to say: "I wish you'd leave me. I'd like to be alone."—This disgust also overcomes him even when he is with a real German blonde; with any woman. Also when he is with his sister whose odor he cannot suffer. Her room is insufferable to him in the winter time when it is rarely aired. It was also the "little Jewess's" odor which primarily annoyed him —her whole femaleness. He got a sudden toothache. The toothaches seem to act as a sort of moral watchman for him; they occur whenever he wants to be distracted. He is afraid of woman. He is afraid of his potency more than of his impotence. He denies his virility because he needs his inferiority and wants to stress and emphasize it at every opportunity.

Yesterday a very husky fellow moved into the tenement where he lives. He felt thoroughly cowed. Hitherto he had been the strongest man in the place, but now he was only second fiddle, and that annoyed him. He envied the virility of the newcomer.

He dreamed:

Last of all, there was a dancing lesson. We were running about the room in a circle. I was in civilian clothes, but, in addition to

myself, there was a substitute officer there from the artillery, a
man who had been present in previous dreams. I wanted to sit
down at a piano which was somewhat in the way. I ran over
the keys and everybody seemed amused. They asked me if that
was dance music, too.

Before that there was a riding lesson. It seems that I rode a
good deal in the dream. We galloped about in a circle, but we
were out in the open. I thought that it would be nice if we would
gallop about on the ring. Finally, we were all running about in a
circle without our horses.

His feeling in the dream was that he was being scoffed at. He
tried it with a small piano (the small Jewess) and made a fool
of himself. The riding and dancing movements resembled coitus
movements. He is incapable of effecting intercourse, but the substitute officer understands his business very well. He feels
humiliated by the potency of the other man just as he felt oppressed by the virility of the newcomer in his house.

Asked to associate on the dream, he first mentioned his sister
and then his jealousy. He dislikes to dance with his sisters although it was from them that he first learned how to dance. His
eldest sister dances too heavily for him. She makes such curious
motions and has such a queer look in her face while doing it.

He recalls watching his mother with absorption when he was a
small boy as she was swaddling his sister in diapers. There was
an aunt with a lorgnon there, too, but he can't understand why
she was so unpleasant to him. He hated her. It seems that she
was the prototype of his harsh governesses in his drawings. It
also appears that he envied his sister especially because of her baby
carriage. He couldn't resign himself to the fact that he was suddenly pushed out of the center of things and that his little sister
became the chief source of excitement in the house. The baby
carriage seems to have remained a vivid memory with him.
Whenever he has a belly ache, he presses himself to a chair and
makes some rhythmic movements; and whenever he gets a toothache he either knocks on the tooth or executes rhythmic move·
ments of the body. He drowns his pains by an infantile form of
pleasure. Up to the time of his parapathic troubles, rocking and
riding were always very delightful to him. His first wet dream
(when he sprang up on a moving carriage) thus becomes clear
as a memory of the baby carriage. The pillow which covered the
bottom of the baby carriage also attracted him. He often played

with it and pressed it to his face. The diaper commode had also
been engraved in his heart.

He sees not only the reflection of himself in his objects, but also
his swaddled sister. He identifies himself with his mother and
the object is a child which he has bundled in diapers.

As we have already mentioned he seemed to have no real understanding of sex differences, although he had been an interested
witness of the bathing of his little sister. And to this very day
this willful ignorance has remained with him. He is a physician,
but he has no very clear idea of the topography of the vulva. It
is as if he had forgotten the time when he was proud of his phallus.
He cannot recall whether or not he envied his sisters because they
were already castrated whereas he, with his appendage, was exposed to the threat of the knife. Since his first anatomical studies
were carried out on his sisters, it is plain that the memory is unpleasant to him and was therefore repressed. The thought of the
vulva is associated with distinct disgust.

The inconceivable became a fact. Our patient visited the
dentist to whom I had recommended him and permitted a lower
molar to be extracted without the least resistance. He is supposed
to return again to-day and I advise him to get the whole business
over with at once.

During the night he had a strange dream which he promptly
put to paper.

The motto of the dream appeared to me in the morning in green
print; like a cinema title.

Ah, Martha, but we could—

Or are you so—

Ah, be so— After Easter (the third line questionable).

Content of the dream: My eldest sister and I are on a pleasure
trip; we come into a place which seems to get progressively more
elegant, and finally takes on the character of a cabaret. My sister
wants to wait for the second show and talks me into saying. There
would also be a discussion about . . . student . . . (???). I decide to remain. But when the ticket girl comes around, sister takes
two tickets and I see the price: 23,000 crowns apiece. I say to sister
in horror: "But we don't need a loge; they must have cheaper ones,
too." The girl showed us tickets at 8,000 crowns, gray ones, and
still others of a rose red color (price?). But I wanted to get
up and leave. The ticket girl seemed to understand that I had

good reason for leaving. I wanted only to drink a large glass of champagne that was standing on the table. But my sister wanted to remain even if she would have no money left for the rest of the trip. I had to walk around the table and stand while drinking the champagne, but I could hardly stand on my feet. But I drank, although I could hardly keep from swaying. Everybody in the place could see that I was drunk.

My father reproaches me because I'm always finding fault with him, whereas I . . . ???

I wanted to bring down some gifts from my parents off a high cupboard (chocolate, boxes with something in them, etc.). It was very hard for me to crawl or reach up so high; something sticky and sweet fell down and broke.

Some one (?) wants to become my servant.

As I came into the barracks, I found all the cots and beds taken. I went over to the left side of the long barrack room and there found a few empty children's cribs. They were of no use to me because they were too short; (nevertheless) I took possession of a press because the first five (or seven) from the left were still free. Another one just in front of mine was promptly taken by another fellow. Then I wanted to stow away my luggage, but because I was deficiently provided with goods, I returned home to fetch my knapsack which was already packed. Now I was dressed in a comfortable officer's uniform, with a soft cap pulled down over my neck. I bounded up the stairs and on the second flight I saw the party from the floor below, blond, about forty, with a red, vexed face, and dressed in a white doctor's gown, looking through a white lacquered door. He did not greet me, but withdrew immediately behind the door, for I was on the way to war (despite my previous notion to the contrary). Arrived at the top, a girl opened the door for me and I promptly began to pack up (a pair of socks, an extra pair of shoes, etc.). I meet a young soldier and ask him where he is posted. He said: with the Thirty-third Regiment, where his brother was. That made me feel a little downhearted because I would have liked to have him in my regiment.

When he awakened, the first three lines of the dream floated before his eyes in large letters. Martha is his eldest sister, but how are the lines to be completed? Are they infantile memories or are they wishes? Are we to read: "Ah, Martha, but we could do something! Or are you so sad as I? Ah, be so good and let's get together after Easter." With the aid of the patient's associations, that is about how the lines were able to be completed.

The thing that strikes him most about the dream, and that which imbued him with the greatest affect, was his swaying there at the table with an immense glass in his hand. He first thought of his mother. He seems to stand there like a little child that cannot yet walk steadily, but wants to walk towards its mother and falls. The dream makes it appear as if he had experienced something with his sister in his childhood (the first show). Then there comes a second show, but the price is too high for him. In reference to 23,000 crowns, he says that he wrote his mother that he had been struggling unconsciously for twenty-three years and consciously for the last ten years (the time of his paraphilia). He explains the 8,000 by saying that from the time of his trauma (at three), eight years passed and then he began to masturbate (eight plus three equals eleven). The girl reminded him of his mother. The liquid in the glass was golden yellow and effervescent (urine?).

The discussion which was announced was to have been on the subject of "The Student as a Devil." The manager of the cabaret, who was also to have conducted the discussion, was quite a dandy. He looked like Mr. F., a former partner of his father's who was a dipsomaniac, married and soon thereafter put a bullet through his head and died. This man appears to him as an "eternal warning." While at the front, our patient drank a great deal, but now he has been living in total abstinence. The meaning of the dream is that he paid a high price for his first pleasures with his sister. The sister is willing to remain in the pleasure palace. She has no love (money) for another. He is drunk, but that only expresses his intoxication over the fun. He is intoxicated by a phantasy, a wish or the memory of an actual experience.

In the next part of the dream, his father reproaches him. He feels that he has unjustly reproached me and that he has been doing nothing to advance the analysis. He is ready to give up his infantile habits. He is willing to serve again, become his own servant; he is willing to struggle; to return to the war.

He realizes that he doesn't fit into the child's crib any more. His infantile traits are antithetical to the demands of real life. The compulsions of his neurosis must cease. He is dressed in a comfortable officer's uniform and has a soft cap. "The party down below" reminds him of phallus. The white lacquered door is a pair of white trousers. He sees a penis which immediately withdraws. The soft cap and the phallus which withdraws from battle indicate his resistance against the female and intercourse. The maid reminds him of a nursemaid of his sister.

The young soldier from the Thirty-third Regiment looked like his sister. He would have liked to have his sister with him in the Thirty-third Regiment. Thirty-three reminds him of a doggerel:

> Thirty-three years—for thirty-three years
> we've gone into action.
> Down with the dogs, the dogs of reaction!
> The blood must rain, rain and rain thick,
> To water the soil of our German Republic.

Here the analysis closed for the day. To-morrow we continue with this interesting theme.

We continue with analysis. He looks upon the child's crib in the barracks as a retreat from the female to his childhood and homosexuality. In the army, among the soldiers, he felt very well. Nothing but men about him.

His associations on "Easter" were: green—mother menagerie—zoo. Then he pictures his eldest sister with closely cropped hair; she looked like a boy. That was after her mastoid illness. He himself wore long curly locks, so that he looked like a girl and his sister like a boy. He prefers young men or boys who wear their hair like the Free Germans, i.e., when they look like his sister did when her hair was closely cropped. That fascinates him. Yesterday he saw a woman with bobbed hair like that and couldn't take his eyes from her. She was sitting on a park bench and he waited until she got up to make sure whether she were a man in female clothing or simply a male type of woman.

Easter reminds him of Faust, and so does the cup. Easter time is the time of examinations and advancements in school. A time of transition. He thinks that means the transition through the analysis. He had again visited the dentist and sacrificed two bad teeth.

His eldest sister tried hard to marry him off to one of her friends. That's what he thought of when he was asked to associate on cabaret. Then he talked about the color of the tickets. One type was of a dirty white (gray) color which reminds him of soiled linens; the next was of a dirty purple color and the last was rose red. Violet is his favorite color. His fixation on this color is doubtless a relic of his childhood days. His sister had a violet dressing gown. Rose reminds him of the delicate blushing of girls, and of red grits. Lilac reminds him of a lovely melody about lovely Lila. She was drowned in the sea and called out at the setting of the glowing sun: not red but lilac. But ever since his sister sang him that song, he dislikes the color. He manifests a distinct capacity for what the French call *audition coloré*. He can see the color violet, for example, whenever the bass or wooden wind instruments play deep notes. Lilac or violet often pass into black in his mind and disclose connections with his death complex.

It seems as if he is filled with a desire to revive some infantile scene with his sister (the first show), and thus put on a second performance. But the price is too high for him. We cannot find any other guiding motifs. There is then also his fear of his father's reproaches and his military service which again discloses a religious significance. The dream again betrays his deep attachment to his sister.

He displays tremendous resistances towards the dentist and is also dejected. He has become restless again and is afraid to lose his paraphilia. He finally hit upon a compromise: "You can have your teeth fixed and still remain ill."

He dreamed:

It seems that we were in the field, and it was towards evening. We were at the edge of a sparsely wooded forest (alder or birch trees). On the right is the castle which houses our staff and on the left is the enemy. But the military character of the scene is not immediately noticeable. Lightning flashed. The bolts strike closer and closer. One of them struck behind the house. One of us said: "He thinks he made a bull's eye." The next shot really struck one of the out-houses of the castle. Attack! The enemy comes! I dash into the hiding where we have our machine guns. I was the first there. The whole scene is enacted in our school yard. The machine gun nest was behind one of the basement windows of one of the school outhouses. I drag up the machine gun and we set it up at the left of the little toilet house. In reality, a little group of birches used to stand there. I get out my guitar and lay it up on a little ledge to the right which was also near that privy. I think I fetched the guitar out of my room where two vice color-sergeants and aspiring officers were sitting at a table. They seemed to be dejected. Then it began to rain and I feared the guitar would get wet.

This dream expresses resistances to the analysis. I am the enemy and my shots are beginning to become uncomfortable for him, especially after he had started by scoffing at my attempts. He arms himself for the repulse. He doesn't want to go to the dentist any more. He gets out his guitar and is afraid that it may be ruined. The guitar, as we know, is a symbol of his paraphilia which is now causing him great worry.

Nevertheless, the dream does help us along a little. The mention of the privy is an introduction to his anal sexuality. His father, too, was a distinct anal erotic. He would sit for long periods of time in the toilet, read newspapers and books, and would thus blockade this most important of rooms. There were frequent quarrels over this valuable place in the family, especially between him and an uncle who had the same habits as he; they finally had to build another toilet in the house. His sister protested constantly that father would drag her books off to the toilet.

As a child, he had often retained his feces and got a great deal of pleasure out of it. Even to-day, he gets a great degree of satisfaction from defecating or urinating after protracted retention. It may be that this is the basic factor in his compulsive make-up (according to Jones, possibly the basis of every obsessional neurosis). It is at any rate the first compulsion which a child exerts upon itself with pleasure as the result.

His anus is an erogenous zone for him. He is filled with desires for active and passive pederasty. But, as we have already mentioned above, when he attempted (at eight) to indulge in active pederasty, he became impotent.

Further analysis shows that his mouth is a substitute for his anus. The foul odor of his breath further enables him to complete the identification. He also confesses hesitatingly to wishes for active and passive anilingus. Behind his orthopedic phantasies, there was hidden an important wish which he had not hitherto disclosed: he desired to be bound hand and foot and then forced to acquiesce in homosexual acts.

He speaks of a book released by the German League which reports the horrors perpetrated by the enemy. The Duc de Vendôme is said to have sexually mistreated a defenceless German prisoner (a vice color-sergeant). That gives a clue to the meaning of the vice color-sergeants and the aspiring officers of the dream. The castle in the dream is the toilet. He had a soft spot in his heart for the toilet and up to the present he has spent hours sitting on the toilet and reading.

The picture is completed by a fear he has of rats. A rat might bite him while he were defecating. He claims that while he was defecating once at the front, he was touched by a rat. The long tail of the beasts is particularly disgusting to him. That clears up his fear of the dentist somewhat more. The dentist is the man who gets into one's mouth (read anus) and messes around.

As a boy he had heard a tale about a caged lion. He often feared that a lion might spring out of a wall at him. Such an anxiety is easy to understand in its symbolism. He has walled off a burning passion and is afraid that it might burst the walls of its cell.

I shall pass over a few dreams in which he continues to express his resistance to the analysis. He is constantly bothered by the matter of the dentist and fears that he shall not be able to go to him any more. But he effected the following symptomatic act. He came to the hour and then excused himself under the pressure of an urgent necessity. Or he stops the session with the declaration that he has to go to the toilet. I tell him that he evidently desires to use the same toilet as his master (*tertium defecationis*). The dream material of the following two days, which I naturally could not know as yet, corroborated my suspicion. He never liked to go to the toilet after his father had made the seat warm by sitting on it for a long time. But he agrees that before that period of dislike there had been a period of positive attraction. He also liked to use his sister's toilet. He believes that every time he went to that toilet, he became sexually excited and that the sexual provocation gave him the urge; an explanation which certainly cannot be refuted.

The following dream brought us still further forward in the analysis.

I dreamed: . . . Then I am at home and see my collection of stamps. I said to myself: "Great, now you can take them back to Vienna with you and sell them." And yet, without manifesting it specially, I seem to be surprised to be at home (in Riga).

I was walking with some other people and, coming from the left, got into the following situation. At the left was the city wall and out of the gate there came a train of monks in gray garb. At the right (on the other side of a stream?), there stood a group of clerics who held the Holy Image before them. There seemed to be an angry sort of tension between both groups, although nothing was said. Along the outer side of the wall, from the left, there came another train of monks which also picked us up. We now belong to the group from the left. Something was demanded of us, but we refused to comply. Someone called to let the younger people fight it out with weapons. Two or three knives flashed among the excited crowd. Then someone from the other side killed our young men and strode among the crowd cutting deep wounds in the arms and legs of the men with a large razor. Panic. Fear. He was a well-nourished, twenty-five-year-old, with a red face and blond locks.

My fear turned to wrath and I killed not only him but about three others in all. The last victim is very clear in my mind. After slitting his throat, he sank back with a gaping windpipe and groaned terribly. I became frightened and gave him another that sank to the spine. A grayish-pink fluid gurgled forth. Remarkably little blood. He was slender, of a grayish pale complexion and about eighteen years old.

The ones I killed were slit from right to left across the throat. I was surprised that the carotids didn't spurt blood.

Immediately upon awakening from this dream, he noted down a few slogans for it, some sort of outline. Then he wrote out the dream without looking at his notes, but afterwards he took a look at the lines he had written first, and noticed with astonishment that he had put down a cannibalistic scene which he had completely repressed by the time he wrote down the whole dream. The following are his first notes:

The winner, a somewhat obese young man, had cut the throat of our man and then began to attack defenceless ones.

Anger seized me; I picked up the dagger and proceeded to slit the throats of three or four young men.

I felt a gruesome oppression. I had to stab them several times before I cut the arteries. Something swelled forth from the wounds. Then we ate of the meat (liver). But I had enough. Two other men began to argue about it, but one of them was in agreement with me.

And now to the analysis of this dream. The stamp collection represents his fetishistic collection. He is ready to give up his paraphilia. Thereupon there starts a mighty struggle between his ascetic tendency and his normal trends. He battles on the left in the ranks of the ascetics. The leader of the Rights has blond locks. Otto thought: he looks like Amor. During the battle, he thought of the Bride of Messina (the fraternal enemies), and of the two choirs that march upon the scene. The razor frightens him somewhat; he never likes to have himself shaven. Yesterday he suddenly went into a barber shop and had his fine locks cut in order to make a more male appearance. His sister had often ruffled his hair and whenever he would have a fight, he would first seize his antagonist's hair. He manifests an affective attitude towards hair. The pubic hair of both men and women disgusts him, especially in women. But the pubis of young girls excites him. Yesterday he wanted to make himself look bad because he was afraid he would attract me and the dentist too easily. He wants to be a man (perhaps as a substitute for his castration; bipolar tendency).

In regard to the battle scene in the dream, he says that he voluntarily helped in the slaughtering of the animals at the front. Once they tried to kill a cow by slitting her throat, but they found they had to put a couple bullets into her besides that; and yet they were forced to kill her finally with an axe. He was covered with blood like a butcher boy.

The cannibalistic scene points to that early cannibalistic period which later appears in the form of an oral parapathia (Abraham).

He is surprised that his dreams do not now lead to emissions. There is always the same excitement and emotion as before an emission but the relief of ejaculation does not turn up. It seems to be some hidden parapathia which has not yet come to the surface. The ejaculation appears to be conditioned by a certain sexual constellation.

Yesterday he had seen three of his love objects, men who had formerly quite excited his passions. Two of them provoked no emotion whatever in him, and the third excited him only very slightly. The whole thing appeared strangely distant to him and had evidently lost all its emotional value for him. He looked at the man and even turned around but did not follow him; nor did he retain the man further in his phantasy.

The dreams of the following night were very characteristic:
Nebulous dream: much riding and stabbing.
Clear: 1. Two figures wrestle with each other in the half-light of an areaway within a block of gray houses of several stories' height. I thought in the dream: my father and I.

2. I am a lieutenant and back in the war again. I was with the Austrians. Dr. H. comes past the hut before which I stand. He does not recognize me at all. Then he seemed worried by my war-like intentions, but accepted them.

3. I met my father, who also wanted to go to congratulate the

man on his birthday. I thought to myself that I had better go
with him. But, after a short while, he left me for a toilet that
was near by, and I went on alone.

4. Dressed in a military coat and a sport cap, with my collar
thrown up, I walked through the poorly lighted streets of the
city at dusk. Some people stop to look at me, especially a certain
fellow. Then I recognize that the reason why I wanted to remain
unnoticed was because I was biting on my handkerchief which
I had knotted together.

5. At the congratulation ceremony (Margy Kolbert). Who are
we waiting for? Later I notice that I am blindfolded, but I can
nevertheless see everything. Gerty Ziegenrucker comes to the
party, too, but her face is all stuck up with a white plaster,
especially the nose. She brought her children along. She nods
towards me, but it seems as if we don't care to notice or know
each other.

6. Old park in Riga. But an electric street car seems to be
running through there now. The neighborhood is very lovely
(meadow), although much digging is going on. We rode under
some ramps and stands covered with dirt and dumpings. I
thought: I hope that doesn't come through. Then we ride through
the low hills. Everything is light and I see the large rocks stuck
in the sand, hanging from the ceiling. Here, too, I had a fear
that they might fall down. By that time, we got off.

I am alone on a wide plain. To the right is a forest and bushes
which do not attract me. To the left the road leads up a hill.
A narrow path leads up the side of the hill (vineyard). At the
top there is a gate in a barbed-wire fence.

Down below there is a sign which reads: "Beware! Dog!"
Somewhere else I read: "The gate is closed." I turned on my
heel and went away.

7. And came to several tremendous blocks of stone. Red sand-
stone. They were chipped and worked. One of the stones was
like a little house, and in its shade the museum commission was
having its meeting. The blocks of stone lay in front of the
museum. Well, there are all my friends and acquaintances, too.
Professor N. was especially clear to me, but there were others.

In the previous battle dream, I had already had a suspicion
that he was having symbolic dreams of the mother's womb. In
that cavern, he kills all his sisters and eats them up. In this
dream, he fights with his father. At the bottom of his soul (at
the bottom of the areaway) there is the struggle with his father.

Perhaps also a womb phantasy, this areaway. He now says that the monstrous action of the dream before may have signified the holy love of the son for the family and his parents, or love in all its meanings. The Amor would help buttress this interpretation.

Dream 2 refers to his present struggle against the paraphilia. I am Dr. H.

Dream 3 offers a toilet scene. He uses the same toilet as his father. *Inter feces et urinas nascimur.* The toilet is also a symbol of the mother's womb.

Dream 4 betrays the fact we have already heard, viz., that he bites a handkerchief every night before falling asleep. He puts the handkerchief between his teeth in order not to crunch during the night and also in order to protect his teeth. He first bites hard into the cloth and then he can fall asleep. He himself associates fellatio phantasies and cannibalism to this fact.

Dream 5 shows a sticky face. Perhaps the memory of his sister's gummy umbilicus when she was born.

Dream 6 a clear-cut womb phantasy with indications of relations to his sister. The illustration of the situation explains the dream. His sister is a virgin, for which reason her introitus is barred by barbed-wire (hymen—thorny rose). The sign: "Beware! Dog!" refers to him. He is a wild dog and must beware of himself.

The resistances become stronger and stronger. They concentrate upon the dentist. The analysis shows that the dentist, the analyst and the father are a single trinity. He was expecting me to show him some sort of special attention and praise because he had gone to the dentist (a thing which he conceived as the greatest heroism). He doesn't understand why it is necessary for him to have his teeth fixed in order to be healthy. Every day I have to admonish him: *tua res agitur!* He does it for my sake. He had also hoped that I would go there with him and help him overcome his resistance. He wants affection and praise. He is again hurt by the fact that I haven't invited him into my house. Consciously, he realizes that such practices are not possible during an analysis, but unconsciously he cannot but insist upon his phantasy. The "pathos of distance" which is so necessary during an analysis dissatisfies him.

It is his eternal complaint: my father doesn't understand me. He doubtless feels that I understand him, but he also realizes that behind his complaint about not being understood there is the feel-ing that he is not being loved.

Despite my explanations and interpretations, he comes to me in the greatest excitement and claims he must use my toilet be-cause his excitement has "gone to his bowels." He says it is all because of the dentist. He doesn't care for the dentist at all because he doesn't talk with him or praise him for his heroic attitude. Although he permitted a tooth to be filled and didn't have any pains, he is nevertheless mortally afraid of the drill. In vain I interpret to him the sexual symbolism of drilling and the affective displacement which makes that operation so fearful for him. He simply will not understand. But the results are never-theless better. He continues to visit the dentist and his treat-ment is progressing.

Yesterday he had another tooth extracted. He even brought it with him and said: "Look at my little pocket penis." He looked at it himself long and lovingly and then put it in his pocketbook.[6] Then he ran about restlessly the whole day; went to Schönbrunn, the famous summer home of the kaiser, and threw the tooth into a trash can.

I pointed out to him the motives behind his use of my toilet. Depriving him of this privilege provoked stubbornness in him. To-day he is quite excitable and gives me all kinds of reasons why he had to use my toilet and no other. The others were dirty, the public ones are expensive, in the cafés one can get an infection, etc. I explain his rationalization to him and he begins to see that he did the same sort of thing with his father. His attitude to-wards his father has improved considerably. He wrote a sensible letter home and told his father how he had come to realize that he had conducted himself ridiculously because of his misunder-standing of the situation, and hoping that they would yet arrive at a reasonable understanding of each other.

In the dreams of last night he was the officer, i.e., the normal self-possessed man. All the dreams began in an interesting man-ner, but they stopped short of action. He remembers only a single short dream.

I take a walk with the little one. But he looked so small, wrinkled and vexed.

He promptly associates penis to the little one. That was very plain. He had once declared that the phallus of old men did not interest him because it was wilted and wrinkled. He likes only full and youthful members. But in this dream, the original attitude comes to the surface.   He claims always to have disliked a hanging scrotum and feels pained by the fact that his own hangs down pendulously.   In the army, they had matched each other to see who could stretch his scrotum out the furthest and he had won. It seems that they were altogether given to disguised expressions of homosexuality in the army.   Recruits had to "shake down the nuts" of the older soldiers.   He had even dreamed of this game one time.

He had watched children playing in the street yesterday and thought to himself: "You'd like to do something to them."   This something would be to tread on them, crush them like worms, kill them.

Whenever he actively pictures the situation at the dentist's, i.e., when he thinks of what he tells the dentist to do, his restlessness grows.   He feels better when he is perfectly passive and lets the dentist do what he pleases.   He manifestly produces phantasies at the dentist's of being shackled to the chair and at the mercy of the man.   He unconsciously expects fellatio, pederasty or castration.

His original phantasy comes to light: Hidden in his mother's womb, he shall bite off his father's penis.   But he cannot say anything further about his castration anxiety.   He is only a little more struck by his former indifference to the difference between the sexes, and how little he apparently was interested in the genitals of man and woman.   He believes that this indifference may have been the result of an early repression.

His paraphilia manifests several variants.   Two divergent attitudes may be noted.   He seeks the glowing young man; that is his purely homosexual attitude.   In that rôle he plays the father dallying with his young son.   In that there is no hate.   Then there is his orthopedic mania.   The young man is a symbol of his sister.   First he wounds her and then he lays on bandages.   His growing tendency to differentiate himself from his sister is indicated by his recent act of having his hair cut.

The patient is in a state of great excitement.   He runs about purposelessly the whole day long and tries to invent some reason for coming to see me more frequently.   His objects have lost all their attractiveness for him.   He feels very tender towards me and his father, and his thoughts are also full of his dentist.   The dentist gave him a day of rest, but that doesn't give him any satisfaction.   He is afraid that he may lose his courage.   It becomes more and more clear to him that he is strongly fixated to his father.   He has not been able to establish himself, to become independent and do the work he had intended, because the umbilicus of money which kept him attached to his father was never separated by him. He wants to remain dependent upon his father. He is very modest in his demands, walks about with an old military coat on, has his shoes hob-nailed to save the leather, looks dilapidated; but he need not live like that because his father would send him all the money he wanted, and even praises his extreme modesty. But behind this reticence there lurks the fear that his father may some day say: "Let's have an end of all this."

The day he was free from the dentist he nevertheless returned to him and had the dentist drill around in one tooth and extract another, so that he might the sooner be through with the job. He felt that he had done something great in going there. It was a heroic deed and the beginning of his independence.

He then went into a church and sat himself down in a corner. The verses Christ had spoken in the temple kept going through his head: "Shall I not be in the house that is my father's?" He got a sudden rush of delusional grandeur. He seemed to himself to have swollen to such imposing proportions as to fill the entire cathedral.

The following night he dreamed:

G. S. writes me that he has become a specialist for kidney and gall stones. But that fellow is not even a doctor! If he doesn't get on, some man . . . (?) will help him (?).

I'm an English officer, a Hussar. Killing uniform and courageous horse. There is a young English soldier with me, whom I am taking to his company. I alighted and we started towards the firing line. It was towards evening. The streets looked like those of a city in the French sector. Everywhere great numbers of soldiers look out of their quarters. I ask where the English troops are and they tell us, but we have difficulty finding them.

G. S. is the boy who was mentioned at the outset of the analysis as having taught him how to masturbate. Here he symbolizes his own paraphilia. The disease is represented as a granular deposit which must be crushed. The crushing process is the analysis. He wants to become an analyst in order to free people from their stones (complaints). I'm to help him. He is not yet a doctor, i.e., he doesn't yet know enough about analysis.

In the second part of the dream, he is an English officer in a splendid uniform. The English symbolize his pious and religious tendencies whereas the French represent the sinfulness of men. His *alter ego* is here portrayed as a young man.

We begin to discuss his piety and it appears that up until a short time ago, he was still in the habit of saying his prayers at night and of going to church. Exploring more deeply, it turns out that yesterday in church he identified his father with God the father, and himself with Christ.

In one of my books, the following sentence made a great impression upon him: "The neurotic has nailed himself to the cross of his neurosis."

He understands now that what he wanted was martyrdom; he wanted to be a second Christ. His toothaches served him in this purpose. Every tooth was a nail which painfully nailed him to the cross. His fear of the dentist was his fear of losing these desirable instruments; his fear of dropping off the cross and falling into the depths, i.e., into the world of human weaknesses.

The handkerchief which he stuck into his mouth every night also indicates his Christ neurosis. It is the sweat cloth. He has lately had a desire for sharp and acetic foods (mushrooms with vinegar—from the New Testament).

He considers that the root of this attitude is to be found in a Bible by Schnorr von Carolsfeld. Therein he had seen the picture of Lazarus. Poor Lazarus lay there before the door of the rich man, covered with ulcers and nibbling a few crumbs. Then he was sitting in the lap of Abraham while the rich man was being tortured in hell.

At that time, child that he was, he thought of becoming a poor Lazarus and sitting in the lap of Abraham in Heaven. We will recall that he walks about in the poorest of clothing even to-day, and in the hottest or the coldest weather he will never wear a hat.

Every patient or beggar with crutches or splints is a living Lazarus for him. His toothaches and his parapathia also make a Lazarus of him. But the most important thing is: he avoids woman and sin; he even struggles against his onanism. Here in Vienna he has been completely abstinent.

Yesterday it seemed to him that he was larger than the newcomer in the house whom he had envied because of his size. He had gained his own soul and all his pains were the tortures which he, as a martyr, had to suffer. But for that the kingdom of heaven was assured him.

His dreams disclose a most obstinate resistance to the discovery of the sexual foundations of his desires. He cannot achieve an emission in his dreams because he observes them too closely. He may begin to develop a wet dream but it breaks off too soon.

The following is such a dream:

My eldest sister approaches me. She was together with some other woman, I think it was my mother. Sister is large and grown up. Her face is somewhat male; her hair pale brown and copious. She seems to have a rash. At first it seemed to affect her whole body, but then I noticed that it was present only on the lower right side of her face and neck; it looked like a trichophytiasis or an actinomycosis profunda. Her dress looked curiously ornamented like antique friezes.

His first association is: Lionel the Lion-hearted. The idol of women and children. Then he recalls the furunculosis from which his sister long suffered (see the dream above in reference to this). She has a poor complexion and also suffers from acne. For a long time he himself suffered from a syphilophobia. He repeatedly reverts to poor Lazarus; how he fashioned bandages out of rags. The dream was marked by pleasure and seemed to be leading up to an emission.

We shall skip a few dreams which continued to display the difficulties of the present situation. He has had all his bad teeth extracted and is now having the rest filled. He is also preparing an exhaustive scientific paper.

I call his attention to the fact that one detail of yesterday's dream has not yet been cleared up: the sister's dress. He says: "At first I thought the rash was all over her body; then I saw that she had on a striped dress. Her breast was marked as with meanders, like the breast of the sphinx."

This sphinx reminds him of Œdipus, who suffered a severe period of stress. Œdipus had been left to the elements after his tendons had been severed. The curious fact appears that his love object represents Œdipus.

He confesses to full-blown murderous impulses against his father (at fourteen), and as late as a year ago he had dreamed that he had killed his father. He attacked him with a knife or a saber in the dream. Many other such dreams followed. As a boy, he had thought: "The dog treats me as if I were not his son. Perhaps I'm an unwanted child, or maybe he hates me because I'm not his." (Family drama.) Of course, he had also phantasied that perhaps he was descended from the kaiser. Or he would day-dream how he might save the kaiser's life and receive a medal for his act.[7]

Otto also produced the rather ridiculous and complicated phantasy that his father were thankful to him because he had been so good as not to kill him. An important factor in these phantasies was an old army revolver which lay in his father's dresser. This all leads us to a new and exceedingly illuminating conclusion: the cripples of his phantasy and striving are father murderers who have overcome their impulses and subjected them to the shackles of the surgical instrument.

A short dream returns us to the subject of his onanism.

I went to S.'s house without being seen by anyone. There was a stamp collection in the room, containing one hundred and seventy-four stamps. They didn't belong to S., however, but to someone else. I then met his mother in the house. . . .

S. is the seducer who led him into all sorts of affectionate little games. S. had tied and bound him, too. S. is the representative of his onanism and his paraphilia.

The number one hundred and seventy-four is explained in the following manner: one hundred and seventy-four is the number of the criminal statute which just precedes the statute pertaining to homosexuality. Section one hundred and seventy-four refers to prostitution and lewdness. There was an officer in the one hundred and seventy-fourth regiment (called Gibraltar) who was a fatherly friend to him; it was he who had sung that ditty about the free German Republic. He says that one hundred and seventy-four is half of three hundred and sixty-five (not quite). He had masturbated about every other day; so that this number represents his yearly output, as it were.

Otto is now quite at ease whenever he goes to the dentist. On one of the first days he had gone there to have a tooth extracted, he had produced an *arc de cercle* (opisthotonos), and felt a sort of pleasurable thrill because it seemed to pain him.

The roots came out easily and he thought to himself: "Well, that went remarkably easy."

The dentist phobia is over, and he feels like a conquering hero. But he arms himself for new struggles. The devil isn't dead yet. Yesterday he saw a girl with a four-in-hand tie and, looking after her, felt that he was getting an erection. He considers it a bit of progress that he is manifesting heterosexual interests.

It is a strange fact that he himself cannot suffer the wearing of a bandage or dressing. At fourteen he gave up his self-binding and tying habits forever and has ever since then been unable to wear a bandage even if he has a severe cut or wound on his body.

At that time (fourteen or fifteen), his ideals were still women.

He read many robber stories in serial form because they invariably carried pictures showing bound or shackled women. He borrowed the books from a circulating library but had no compunctions against cutting out pages and pictures at will and using them as a basis for his first fetishistic album. He was particularly attracted when the female's breasts would stand forth noticeably (as when women were bound to the mast). In one of the stories he read, there was a torture scene in which the breasts of the woman were torn out with a large pincers. This was the favorite picture of his fetishistic harem (his own words) for some time. (Indication of his castration complex.)

But how can he approach women when his father demands abstinence and chastity of him? His father had repeatedly told him to remain pure and clean to the day of his marriage.—When his father heard of his onanism (his mother had naturally told the father of the son's confession), he cried like a baby and said that he would be completely ruined. Whenever papa spoke of women he would invariably repeat: "Treat every girl as if she were your sister and every woman as if she were your mother."

We next begin to speak about his homosexual period. He had also confessed to his mother of some intercourse or relations with another boy. He was twenty-one at the time and a lieutenant. His father was beside himself with rage and said: "You'll land in prison yet, young man. You'll bring down the greatest shame upon your family. Your sisters will never be able to marry and you'll ruin my own career, too." He could have choked the old man, but he also felt love and sympathy for him and the family.

The type of sexual enlightenment which he received from his mother was also strange, to say the least. First, she told him the story of the stork and then she said that a child grew beneath the mother's heart, especially when two people loved each other dearly. He himself had a fear of childbirth, however, for he must have heard somewhere that they take children out with a forceps. He corroborates this suspicion. This brings us to another determinant of the dentist phobia: The dentist is the obstetrician and the tooth is the child.

His attitude towards his father is betrayed by the following rather highly emotional dream:

I am on a gradually sloping hill, a green meadow. Far in the background, the horizon is cut off by the sharp outline of forest and brush. It seems that I was alone at first, and even later I was alone; or was I, after all, the leader of a band of men? Some-one pursues me; no one aids me; I must reach a hole in the barbed-wire fence which runs across the hill halfway up its side, otherwise I am lost. But it is very difficult. Just before I arrive there, "he" catches up with me. The leader of the enemy! The king! It was one of Alexander's battles, and I was right in the middle of it. He stood upon his chariot, with a blond, square-cut beard, and threw his lance at me. He looked like Mr. N. It seems that I threw lances, too; we alternated in the throwing and spearing. The spears were very narrow and had long iron tips. Would I never strike? It seems not. Or did I throw at all? He lanced me every time. Arrows were shot out of the milling crowd, too. I was terribly afraid of the shots, but it seems that I felt no pain. Hagen has betrayed me.

The barbed-wire fence looked like the balustrade in the opera house—antique frieze figures. The leader of the enemy was like Christ. He looked serious and pale, and threw his spears as if to say: "I must do this against my will. I must kill you." "He," however, was invulnerable. He was a God; God the father, and even more—his better self which was killing his paraphilia.

His most important association is that of his father. He is afraid of a quarrel with his father. He would like to find a girl and begin to cultivate normal intercourse. But his father is dead against any extra-marital intercourse. Will I be his ally in this battle, or will I betray him like Hagen betrayed Siegfried? When he was twenty-one, his father wanted to marry him off and sup-port him in his attempt to cure the boy. But that would be much more difficult to-day. He would want to support his own wife. How shall he solve the sexual problem?

He also recalls the famous Pompeian relief of the battle of Alexandria. The battle between Alexander and Darius. That is a symbol of the struggle between him and his father. And then the interpretation suddenly dawned upon him. The rising hill, the barbed-wire fence (also the parapathia in which he feels himself secure), the brush and the wood: He stands before Ther-mopylis and defends his mother's genitals against the attacks of his father. He had formed the notion that each time his father had anything to do with his mother, there was rape, cruelty afoot. But here he stands in the narrow pass, a second Œdipus, and defends his mother. The motif of the battle is jealousy. He doesn't want any sisters. He wants to have his mother for him-self. Mother must not be exposed to the danger of pregnancy.

Aside from this, the dream is also a sperma dream (feathered arrows fly about his head like the swarms of spermatozoa). He is in his mother's womb and kills all his sisters.

His mood vacillates between delusional grandeur and depression. He clearly feels how the second soul within him struggles against cure. He has been working scientifically with an industry which is suspicious even in his own eyes. He has begun to observe his own day-dreams. Some of them find nourishment in his ideas of grandeur. He has his own feelings of fulfilling an historical mission. He will become one of the greatest of psychiatrists. He will open new pathways in psychoanalysis and will be the salvation of innumerable people. Another part of him is strictly sadistic. He knows now that he has been dreaming that his family would die out, that he would inherit all the money and would then be able to live as he pleased without any consideration of their desires, especially of the intentions of his father. He had often seen his father being shaved by the barber and had thought: "If only he would cut his throat." Almost every day he would have his sisters run over by the street car in his day-dreams.

He had a restless night with many dreams of which the following are but a few.

Breakfast table. We're sitting there and I'm across the table from father. The atmosphere of the place is somewhat depressed. Father in his dressing gown and skull cap as usual. And, as usual, I'm in irritable spirits. Finally I say to him: (Franz Moor) "Do you feel better, father dear?" And he answers: "Better than you, at any rate." I feel guilty. Then he says: "But I like you a great deal, and we'll let bygones be bygones. I expect you to take the same attitude."

I'm in a corner to the right and am just pulling on my rather soiled shirt in the process of dressing. Suddenly someone says to me: "Say, the king is sore at you again." But that makes no difference to me. Then the king comes in, short, obese man with a short, dark beard, and says: "You shall immediately leave and overtake Brunhilde. I give you twenty-four hours' time. Ten golden eggs are thine if thou art successful. As a counsellor, I give thee . . ." I think to myself: "What! This false hound!" and feel little assurance of success.

I'm in a buggy riding on the street. There was someone with me whom I did not recognize at first, but then it turned out to be my youngest sister. We turn to the right into a blind street which is closed off by a church or mosque or Greek Catholic prayer house. They turn us away. I turn about and ride back to the main street. On the other side of the river we see the city rising before us. Mighty buildings which tower one above the other (Lucerne?). I point out one building which I call the palace of Cardinal Richelieu. It rises in several stories, a yellowish brown pile, at the foot of the cliff. Over three gates or windows, there was to be seen some shiny red stucco. Those were the cardinal's emblems.

I'm alone on the street; there is a house to the left and one to the right of me. The landlord and his wife are just leaving the house on the right. I say to my aunt (?), "Shall we go into the house they've just left, or shall we go into the other one?"

The first dream anticipates the coming reckoning with father. He manifests the curious superstition that the opposite of his dreams is bound to come true. He frequently used to dream of good marks in school and then naturally got bad ones. He looks upon this dream as an evil omen.

The Brunhilde of the second part of the dream is the representative of femininity. He, of course, is Siegfried. The ten golden eggs are ten one-thousand-mark bills which he had demanded of his father for fixing his teeth.

In the third dream he stages the difficulties put up by religion and symbolizes his parapathia as an artfully constructed building. He is Cardinal Richelieu and thus again expresses his great historical mission. Louis XIV is his father.

In the fourth part, he is about to leave his old house (the parapathia) and move into a new one. The landlord resembled me.

He is no longer the football of his fetishistic emotions, for he can look at his former objects and not feel the least animation, at least not the importunate sensations of before. He recognizes his attitude towards his father as the nucleus of his parapathia and then relates to me various happenings which betray his father's latent homosexuality.

He conceives those infantile wrestling matches with his sister as a serious trauma in his life. They even lay naked next to each other. During the wrestling he would feel her breasts and the "bodily feeling" of her breasts next to his long afterwards excited his memory. He feels afraid of the woman with luxurious breasts (the sphinx).

Still another bit of insight has dawned upon him: The guitar

is also his father. It has the same baritone note that father has.
He can play with it, sing with it, walk with it. He can string
it whenever he wants (a new symptomatic act of the last few
days).

Hope: Will father sing a different tune with me?

He dreamed:

In the half-light of the room, I find myself digging about in
a middle-sized wooden chest. My eldest sister is also there. She
is watching me. Among the rubbish that I have stirred up, I find
the ten thousand crowns which I have been missing, and a pile of
other money, too. I never knew I had it.

I clearly recall a five-thousand-crown bill of a pink color, a
one-hundred-mark bill of blue, and some of the new, grayish-
green one-hundred-mark bills. I was quite tickled at the find.

While I was digging around in the money in the chest,
B. came in from the right. He looked pale and dejected and
said that he would have to sell the watches. Then he
showed me three (?) ladies' watches, one lovelier than the
other. The last one was the finest. It had a black moiré
band attached. He said the watches had cost two hundred and sixty marks (apiece?). I said that if that were the case,
he had better not sell them for now no one would give him that
price for them. Then I thought of my own gold watch and that
I wouldn't sell it.

Then I was (in the barracks?) together with my friends
again. Suddenly somebody hit me over the head with a
square stick about a yard long, or perhaps he hit me with
both sticks in the form of an X. I felt the whack on my
cropped skull. Shall I demand a duel of the fellow? I
must do something, I can't let a thing like that pass. But I
shouldn't like to demand a duel of him, and yet I must do something about it.

Unexpectedly, he finds treasures in the old chest. He has discovered the beauties and wealth of the past and will not let them
go. In reference to the colors, he repeated several experiences
he had had of *audition coloré*. Rose or pink reminds him of the
weave of children's clothing and the style of baby carriages. The
three watches are his three sisters. The two hundred and sixty
stands for his twenty-six years.

The second part of the dream symbolizes the vehement struggle
he is having with his paraphilia (the Christ neurosis). He is
possessed by two divergent tendencies. He is restless because

he had not received a letter from home, but to-day he received one after he had written a full confession home. His father said that he was quite shaken by everything that his son had written, but that he desired very much to see him and could assure him that all misunderstandings would be cleared away. The money for the dentist naturally came, too.

This letter plunged him into a state of considerable excitement. He tries to picture the return scene to himself and feels that he could not stand it. Father might talk with him about his paraphilia—and that would be insufferable. Whereas he had formerly hated his father and loved me, he now turns the spear about. Unfortunately, he saw me walking with a lady and his jealousy is at a high pitch. I also insulted him by clipping my nails once during the session. I wouldn't have done that if there were money in it. He has recognized my deviltry at last. I intend never to have him get well. I intend to keep him a paraphilic as otherwise he might excel me in the business. I must surely be suffering from some severe parapathia myself, only I know well how to disguise the fact. I am afraid of my pupils. But he will revenge himself yet. He will show the world what a real analyst is like. He will excel me and then the world will forget me and get down to business.

His dentist phobia has completely evaporated. Filling teeth is a pleasure now. Whenever the drill begins, he gets a tickling sensation in the penis. As a matter of fact, he seems to have a permanent thrill in that organ. He cannot work because he is filled to bursting with emotion. He has recognized a multitude of his infantile habits for what they are and wants to overcome them. But he would nevertheless like to retain a part of his suffering, and has begun to act so obstreperously that he is courting the danger of being thrown out. His intelligence conquers, however. He realizes that he is going through a period of stress and strife.

Last night he had a very curious dream:

N. . . . (chief porter of the surgical clinic in Riga) or A. . . . (my last aide in the war), comes and says that I had better tell my sister what that means to appropriate my waste-paper basket (?). I go off into the room (association: of the nurse-maid) and there stands the bed, across the middle of the room, and on the other side of the bed, is my parents' clothes hamper full of soiled clothing and linens. The bed, too, is not yet made. There was no one in the room which, by the way, was rather bare. On the bed, I saw a box which, among other things, contained a self-winding tape-measure, like the one I lost. It had a yellow brass case. This one was much larger than mine, however. Then I saw several more such tape measures, and on the second one there was engraved: Schr. Neuburger. I wanted to take it with me, but it wasn't mine, after all. Finally, I found mine, but it was a little dented and I feared that it would not work. My name was engraved on it. I pulled the tape out and then let it fly back in again. But, although the ring on the end had been torn off, the tape didn't fly all the way back, but about an inch remained hanging out; so that it could be pulled out again. The metal case seemed to become larger and there was a lot of engraving on it. Then the circle seemed to become smaller and smaller, changed to an ellipse and finally became a bolt or stick.

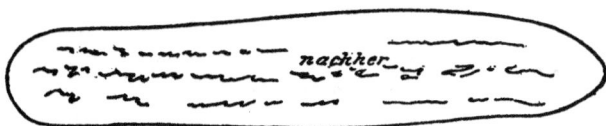

He recalls that old or soiled linen and clothing always fascinated his senses. He used to sniffle in the clothes hamper and smelled each piece he found.

Neuburger is a soldier who is dead; he had nine children. He is thus a representative of family life and the patient's ideal of the future. Otto wants to be a man again. He wants to find his true measure again. He has been measuring life with the wrong tape and needs the old one which he lost. He now has found it. The circle (vagina) is transformed into an ellipse (the phallus). Something in his sexuality has changed. The ring which bound him to his family seems to have been lost.

He went on an outing with his little girl again, played with her, got repeated erections, but shrank back from the final step. He would prefer to have her actively approach him; so that he would not be responsible. He wants pleasure without guilt. Occasionally he would be plunged back into his old phantasies and then the whole thing bored him.

He is still plagued by that constant tickling sensation in the penis.

A marked narcissism begins to appear in his analysis. His family had always indulged in considerable praise of their only son. His grandmother always remarked upon his handsomeness and his sisters had their walls covered with his photos. That must have struck other people because the pastor had warned him against "the desires of man" when he was confirmed.

Gradually memories come to the surface. There was a waggoner who delivered vegetables. He would sit on the box and observe the horses defecating. Also: grandmother had a scratch. Scratching was a direct source of pleasure for him.

He envies bears and lions. He evidently used to bite his sisters.

He then describes a dream he had and adds his own analysis. The following is the analysis in his own words:

Night of twenty-fifth to the twenty-sixth. Interpretation and associations.

I am with others at lunch. The girl who serves us comes along with a platter of all kinds of good things: lemons, oranges, peppermints, desserts. I wanted the others to partake first; then she came around to me, and by that time, it didn't look as appetizing as before. I took half a lemon and a handful of the dessert which was soft, sticky and warm. But none of it stuck to my hand. The girl then said that I should take the orange, too; that it was for me. But I said that I didn't feel like eating an orange, and refused her offer despite her exhortations. I can't remember whether I took it or not.

When I awoke, it seemed that only the rind of the lemon was left and the same of the orange. I promptly associated feces to the dessert and then: my father's feces. Then I recalled the following dream of the same night:

I am in a grocery where I had just previously bought something. But I had left it there because I wanted to look for a new quarters. A half pound of lard was included. I then went back to fetch it. There were several packages on the counter, but I thought that mine wasn't there. I was particularly struck by a certain piece of bake goods among the wares in the store. It was a white, shortened crust. There was marmalade in the middle of a cake about the size of my hand. I had the feeling that that must taste good and sweet.

The cake reminded me of that red spot on the linen dress of my first nursemaid. Then I thought that that experience must screen the memory of my father defecating.

Further associations: My desires as a child always to sit on the box. Whenever I had to ride inside the carriage I was unhappy and pouted.

With distinct pleasure I can recall looking at the swelling buttocks of a horse in gallop. The tail is lifted, the rosette of the rectum is pressed out and there follows the expulsion of the dung. I was tickled at the stiffness of the animal which was forced to defecate while galloping. Also the sharp and tangy odor of horses and everything connected with them. Thus it was that my first homosexual trends were directed towards men who had something to do with horses. Tough stable boys, cavalrymen, coachmen, etc. When I was a soldier I also liked the odor of horses and the stable. I would always tear out the tail of my rocking horses as a boy, put the tail between my legs and play horse with that. But my chief source of delight was the black horse's tail on a rug-beater or duster we had at home. I would clamp that between my legs with the handle in front (erect penis) and the tail behind. I even coddled that beater, pressed my face in the horse hairs and tickled myself with it. That was a magnificent horse for me.

I love horses to this day and I would like to be riding again. The only conscious zoophilic tendencies I can recall were my affections for my horse. He was my comrade, I liked to stroke his neck and press my head against it. Both from the saddle and when I would stand next to him. I always liked to be in a stable, but in the city I rarely had occasion to be near horses. Only during the summer in Misdroy when I would be together with the gardener who delivered the vegetables. I liked to steal fruit from him, too.

It would be a great day for me whenever we would take a ride to Lake Jordan and I would sit on the box with the driver of the omnibus or coach. I am left cold by the thin lips of the women I kiss because my ideal would be the lusciously thick lips symbolized by the great, red anal rosette which the horses used to bulge out when defecating. I like the meatier zones. I prefer to kiss women's breasts, but the best would be the anus, if that would be permitted. When I was fourteen, I got into a furore of emotional excitement one day when I had to fetch my mother some fertilizer from the creamery with which she wanted to leaven up some earth on the balcony. I reacted with such disgust, however, to my original attraction that I later lost all desire to continue with the business. I always liked to feel the bellies of the horses when we would curry them. The hair of men and women is a powerful stimulus to my senses. I like to bury my face in the hair and to kiss women's necks. This reveals other parallels. But I am always dissatisfied, however, despite my comparative enjoyment.

The horse is yoked; the iron curb is put in his mouth. Is it that I feel the iron on my own teeth, the clatter of forks or the dentist's drilling in my mouth? I always found a lot of fun in annoying others.

Again I see in my mind the picture of a man yoked and in the traces like a horse, his head thrown back into his neck by the pulling, his face a lamentable sight. Such an image can still animate me.

This is a picture I saw (when about eight or ten) on a calendar given out by the society for the prevention of cruelty to animals. The horse is terribly laced and whipped. As a boy I often played the coachman on chairs (rocking chairs especially) and on ironing boards. They would wobble and shake but never fell over. I got even more fun out of being the horse myself (little Claus and big Claus: Hee-up! my seven horses!).

After I had overcome my fear of horses as an adult, I liked to have them eat out of my hand. The feel of the thick, soft, wet lips gave me a thrill.

That's why even to-day the most exciting phantasy for me is an orthopedic picture of a corset which hinders the head and neck from any movement because it reaches that high up (get strong erection). I get the thought that I must promptly run out and look up such a picture in a text-book of orthopedic surgery. But I fled from school at the appearance of that thought, although it was not yet midday or time for lunch.

The platter is full of symbols of various sorts.

The half lemon: 1—Symbol of the pointed female breast. 2—After the first sharp taste, the acid of the lemon is pleasant: a lemon is sour but the sharpness can also be a pleasure.

The lemon as a symbol of masochism: it is pressed dry; tendency to depreciate or an indication of the influence of the youngest sister.

The dessert which progressively takes on a more and more fecal appearance symbolizes the infantile oral and anal erotism. Nothing sticks to the hand: self-protection and censoring. No one eats feces. Whoever touches it dirties himself.

Orange: symbol of fruitfulness, of mother, of female. Particularly: coitus, the fruit that must be broken open.

The girl even offers the fruit to me herself, she exhorts me to take it, but I can't do it. The same as with my little friend, the difference being that she is small and dark and the girl in the dream is tall and blonde.

From some more dreams:

". . . I am with a girl to whom I am engaged in a bare and white room. At the right near the window, there stands the mother and the imposing gentleman. It isn't my mother, however, for she is blonde and has a nose like a vulture's beak. She mistreats the girl and is aided and abetted by the 'faithful servant.' The man is kindlier, however.

"The shameless dog finally leaves the room and is about to go downstairs with me after him. He has on a sky-blue stiff cap. Then I see that it has a broad red silk band. I grab him on the stairs and crush him so in my embrace that he squawks and loses the last vestige of breath within him. That satisfied my thirst for revenge."

Associations: Following this dream, I awakened with an erection and, as is usual, pressed it to my body with both hands.

Dr. Stekel "called attention to the identification of the person with the penis and vice versa. The man in the corset is an erect penis, a rigid symbol." I agree and cite the erect position of an impotent man. The goal is, therefore, to have a permanently erect penis.

Dr. Stekel: "The desire to meet every emergency. The ejaculation is avoided and only the anticipatory pleasure of the masturbatory act is enjoyed. The ejaculation is never permitted."

I recall the attempt once to bandage my penis in both the erect and then the flaccid state; the latter in order to be able to enjoy the pain when it became erect again.

The attempt was spoiled, however, when the dressing came off as soon as the phallus began to become soft.

I cannot be provoked by the thought of that sliding mechanism they have for impotent men.

But a catheter! A permanent catheter! What delights!

Another dream:

A bedroom in which I am sleeping with several other young fellows. One of them who was sleeping at some distance from me so irritated me that I got up, went over to him, and crushed him so in my embrace that his limbs and trunk were squeezed together. He was quite powerless. I carried him about the room and then bumped his head or his buttocks several times on the floor. I continued to press him until I thought he had enough.

He is half dead, but I am satisfied, although I had a little touch of a guilty conscience.

Associations: I promptly thought to myself: that's how people carry little children when they shield them while they drop their excrements. The memory of having been held in that manner must have been pleasurable. The legs are spread (as at a gynecological examination), the abdomen is compressed and the back and head lie against the holder's clothing. A very uncomfortable position, at any rate. Had pleasant sensations whenever I crouched on military toilets and defecated in a squatting position. Even to-day I get some thrill out of seeing women hold their children that way while the latter defecate or urinate. The wiping that comes afterwards was very important and pleasurable to me.

I always used to get a terrific effect (and still get a pleasant feeling) out of the imagination of two fellows being chained together, transported under the supervision of another in a train to a reformatory, and seeing them have to go to the toilet together. They would also be dressed in some sort of corset or strait jacket. I get this especially when riding in the train. I used to repeat this phantasy regularly, both in word and picture. The matter of unbuttoning the trousers, especially the flap, the necessary touching of the penis, and the necessity of looking on while the other did it; perhaps the necessity, the coercion to perform anilingus; all under pressure. All this excited me.

Then fellatio, or one of them urinates into the other's mouth. The other always younger. Had many pictures of this type, but they are all burned.

The fellow with red bandage is the erect penis. He squeaks. Desire of emission? He squeaks like the little Teddy bears. The rubber balloons that look like sausage. The little toy pig into which you plug a rod to ignite; the result is a long ash-sausage which looks like feces. And then the favorite game of pouring alcohol over some cellulose wafers and then igniting them to watch the long, snaky ashes.

I used to like the trick scissors which would stretch out when they were closed. Was one of my special delights as a child. In other words, all symbols of erection.

I am represented three times in the dream.

1. The dream-ego: the neurotic who yearns for a woman and engages himself to a blonde ideal.

2. The serious gentleman: the male, analyzing part of me that desires my cure.

3. The coarse fellow: my physical sexuality which strives for coitus.

The woman with the vulture-like beak who pitilessly banged away at my blonde ideal is Dr. Stekel, who has made it clear to me that I shall never be satisfied with this woman because I seek something entirely different. You will never find gratification in this Platonic ideal because you need physical satisfaction. The coarse fellow, that third ego, bellows his approbation.

The serious-minded gentleman has nothing against Dr. Stekel's attitude and is much more kindly disposed towards my wishes and myself. Just as the third fellow, the phallus, begins to go down stairs, i.e., into the vagina, and the glans is red instead of bluish-gray as before, the neurotic chases after him and squeezes him until the erection, the desire for physical gratification, subsides.

The whole situation is taken from a detective story which I had read just previously. In the story, the mother of a son tries to deter him from marrying the girl by saying unpleasant things about the girl's past in front of him.

The second part:

The young man. A neurotic I know. Irritates me. Provokes homosexual feelings in me. But I am energetic and strive to put them down. The young man is thus the symbol of the conquered homosexuality. It is half dead by now, and that makes me feel a little sad; perhaps anxious that I sha'n't be able to have any homosexual pleasures any more.

The compressed young man is also my own penis which I used to compress until the erection subsided; just as he did.

I have already mentioned the associations. Here are some more:

Went to a wrestling match once with a friend of mine, a short, rotund, husky laborer, who was so susceptible to the emotions engendered by the match that he frequently became over-excited and seized me about the waist and butted me with his head and shoulders until I would fall to the floor.

The *arc de cercle,* the bodily stiffness during the tooth extraction. The resulting pleasure.

Did I bang my sisters to the floor like that or did I, perhaps, have notions of killing them? Where I live, they knock the fish against a sharp edge, so that their necks will be broken and they will die faster. I often watched them do it at the beach.

Dreams from the twenty-eighth to the twenty-ninth.

The day before the dreams, I had developed an increasing anxiety that my family would not understand me. A letter which arrived the twenty-seventh incited the emotional tension in the form of a disaffection from woman, marked recharging of my old homosexual and fetishistic feelings. The amnesia I produced of the dreams in the night of the twenty-seventh to the twenty-eighth speaks sufficiently of my resistance. Then the following dream:

I am at lunch and two corps students from Riga whom I know sit opposite me. One of them is red-faced and I don't like him. He asks me: "Are you a Catholic or a Christian?" I: "I'm a Christian." He: "Is it possible that you are not a Christian?" I: "Yes, I'm a Jew." He: "And you dare to sit in here?" The other one who was a little more sympathetic also said that I would have to leave. I: "I've paid for my ticket and I intend to stay," but I thought to myself that to-morrow I wouldn't come back.

In the night between the twenty-eighth and the twenty-ninth, there were only a few fragments to 4:15 in the morning. "Continuous and marked depression and lack of courage." "Examination anxiety." "The part of a tooth that was remaining, which the dentist wanted to use as a sort of anchor for a bridge, has fallen out; I've got it in my hand and think how angry the dentist will be."

I noted these few fragments down after I could not bring myself to write down anything during the first time I had awakened. Then I fell asleep again and had the following dreams in the order in which they are arranged.

1. I am with my father and experience the scene which gives me the greatest anxiety. He doesn't understand my condition. Dr. Stekel is a charlatan. He understands as much about analysis as Stekel. I'm lazy and good for nothing. With some misgiving but plenty of energy, I defended Dr. Stekel. My father walks up and down and the tension seems to be getting worse.

Addition: This dream contains the same emotions which I tried to express in my letter answering my parents; it is somewhat more theatrical here, and the tension is not alleviated.

2. I am in a room and seem to be in a peculiar position. I seem to be in it from above. The room was filled with youngsters; it is a Jugend society and there is but one other adult there; the Turnverein leader. It seems that I was on a sort of balcony under the ceiling.

I seized a young boy and held him hanging in the air by one leg. At first I was afraid I might let him drop, but then his kicking and twisting amused me. He tried to catch hold of something, but I let him do it only after considerable wriggling; then I let him go and he was very much afraid. I repeated this several times and each time I saw a penis at the end of the play; a child's penis: small and phimotic, so that when it is erect only a small part of the glans shows through the foreskin. One or two light-colored, urine-like drops hung on the end. I thought that the penis must be mine.

3. I see an officer whose trousers are too short; he has a dagger in a nickel scabbard on the left side and a broad silver border around his cap. . . . Then there was a flower store there. The officer is in some bushes at one side. I found a silver tie clasp and gave it to the girl in the florist's shop; by that time it had become a silver opera glass.—Then I am supposed to have insulted the officer. He approaches me with his retinue, several men and some girls. But they are not sure whether they should demand a duel of me or not. I recognize in the officer one of the brothers Rehtaler, the younger one is also along. I beg his pardon, we make up and then proceed conversing with each other.

Then I am together with the younger brother. Homosexual tendencies awaken in me; we lie close by each other and he puts his hand on my forehead. I feel his body and look through the cracks between his fingers which lie across my face. As he takes away his hands, I turn over on my back and a girl lies down upon me, his sister. She pulls up her dress in front and lies down upon me. I am surprised suddenly to feel the soft parts of her vagina about my penis; she writhes with pleasure but I don't seem to have the slightest feelings. My thoughts were of two kinds: 1. I hope she's not diseased and infects me. 2. I'll show her how potent I am. Just a little technique, and I'll give her a real orgasm.

The girl seemed to be satisfied; at any rate we had got up from the sofa, and I wanted to wipe off my phallus which was still half erect. The head was all smeared with semen or something of the sort, and even the shaft was covered with some cheese-like bits.  But the faucets of the wash basin were not to be reached because the basin was too high.  It seemed as if I was to have slept with her friend, too.

While the girl was lying on top of me and I was trying anxiously to push in rhythm with her, my friend seemed to be getting much larger.  He was still sitting at my side, but he appeared to be a much larger person than I.

It was about 6 o'clock when I suddenly awakened.  I thought that I was actually wet, but upon looking, I found everything dry.

I felt certain that the girl of the dream was my eldest sister, especially because she so resembled the childhood pictures of my sister.  The happy laughter during the cohabitation was particularly that of my eldest sister.  My first association about the big person next to me was that it was the nursemaid.  I also noticed during the washing in the dream that my penis was phimotic, the glans could hardly penetrate the foreskin.  But the member was not as infantile as it had been in the second dream.

That was what made me feel that the basis of both the third and the second dreams must have been infantile experiences.

The reaction displayed in the course of my few associations was a very marked one, but, buttressed by other unanalyzed resistances, my own analysis produced no further associations.

I must mention further in this connection something you already know, i.e., that I had formerly been afflicted by a moderate phimosis which was stretched only by considerable onanistic activity.  Before I was 12, I was not able to pull the foreskin back over the head of my erect penis, and even to-day it is not an absolutely painless business.  But after the little band of skin had been stretched or torn at about 13, it became easier for me, and I enjoyed pulling the foreskin back over the swollen glans, despite the pains.

Dr. Stekel calls my attention to the possibility of interpreting my corset fetishism as a symbolism of the phimosis which constricts the penis just as the orthopedic corset the patient; especially the head and neck.  I agree with this and wish to emphasize particularly the constriction of the lips and cheeks in the Glisson straps or in Wallstein's apparatus or in the corsets which have head and neck supports.  Dr. Stekel thinks the phimosis may have been the basis for the development of the compulsive fetishism.

He also points out that the masturbation is a preparation for later life. Whatever one wishes in adult life is first tried out during onanism. My habit of prolonging and avoiding an ejaculation during masturbation would thus be a sign of my desire and ability to cohabit with women and satisfy them without impregnating them. That would also be an explanation for the fact that I have not had an emission for over two months now and am yet constantly under sexual pressure and constantly plagued by a stiff phallus.

My desire not to capitulate to any further psychic experiences at the dentist's has transformed itself into a hypersensitivity towards drilling phantasies and the noises which I can hear through the door from his office.

My wish not to discover anything further also expressed itself in the fact that, despite my intention to ask Dr. Stekel for some paper, I desisted from doing so. But one day when he was not in, I happened to come into his room and took five sheets. The five is the symbol of the hand and everything that one might do with it (masturbate, grasp the phallus). I must say that I am hounded by the desire to have some "bodily feeling" with him, even if only externally, as in going to the theatre together; but my disappointment in this matter is naturally quite marked. When Dr. Stekel offered me a theatre ticket which he had bought (i.e., for myself alone) I was quite overjoyed, but I thanked him and refused to accept his favor. I was still waiting for an invitation to tea.

Dream three also aided me in the understanding of the most impressive part of my physical contact with women. I always think: now she's going to start something. In the dream, I lie on my back, close my eyes (they were closed for me in the dream), and wait for her to climb upon my penis.

It seems, also, that "lifting up her dress and lying down upon me with her clothes on," as in the dream, is an indication of my sexual desires. It is not impossible that the dream was but a coitus-like act and not actually cohabitation, although it seemed so to me afterwards. Nevertheless, the feelings in the dream were so pleasant that I am inclined to lay them to the fact that I was actually in the vagina.

Rehtaler, the officer who wants to duel with me and whom I am supposed to have insulted, is a mask of Dr. Stekel. Afterwards we got along rather well and at the place where he led me I became rather intimate with his brother and sister. The complicated splitting of the figure of the officer is doubtless due to many factors of which he is a symbol. For example, my own neurotic ego, Dr. Stekel and my father.

Let us follow up one of the interpretations. My father hides in the bushes at the left and keeps watch over the flower store, the virgins, my sisters. Under the impression of the opinion I have gained of father (the silver clasp) and grandmother (who was always associated with that silver clasp whenever I thought of it), I decided to go into the florist's shop. That insulted my father, who watched me from the bushes but didn't dare come in.

In other words: I dare not communicate my new knowledge to my sisters because that would insult my father. Material: going into the flower shop, i.e., the defloration of the sisters. After the dream, I felt that I had been in there; at least I went in to give up something I had found. That is, it seems that I made use of some infantile experience as far as my infantile understanding had conceived it.

My father hides in the bushes, i.e., he has mother, the bushes being the pubic hair. But he's always on the lookout for what happens to the daughters, for he is jealous of them.

Conceiving the officer as my neurosis: the short trousers, the shining dagger which was not a battle dagger at all (the penis); the cap is gray (the head of the penis), silver-gray. He stands there like a cock on a dung pile. That, in reference to my father and Dr. Stekel, would divulge important material on my present attitude towards them and on my present emotional situation altogether.

As regards the second dream, one could imagine the basic infantile experience about as follows: I may have seized upon my littlest sister and played with her while she writhed and kicked. Or is that only a wish? And yet, the repeated phantasy and dreaming of the infantile penis with the couple of drops of urine clinging to the end, makes me feel that such a situation must actually have taken place and afforded me considerable pleasure.

Exercises on the cross-bar, or any kind of gymnastics, always filled me with anxiety, and I would invariably lose my balance and fall over. I liked to toy with frogs and caterpillars and see them writhe. The frogs I would dangle by one leg and the caterpillars I would let drop from the particular thing to which they would want to cling.

To Dream 3: I was a voluntary soldier with the Rehtaler

brothers. I liked the younger a lot, but he was cross-eyed. We never had any intercourse because he, and also his brother, ran after the girls.

At this point I should like to interrupt the patient's material in order to make a few clarifying remarks. It is of interest that he has forgotten a few things. First of all, he did not express the fact with any clearness that Pauline, the nurse-maid, held her hands over his face after she had staged the coitus scene between him and his sister. His very first memory (the stain in her dress) would rhyme well with this. He seems to recall this rather vaguely.

He also forgot to describe satisfactorily what masturbation as a preparation for his sexual duties means. He was afraid that he might impregnate his sister, and that was why he practised masturbation without ejaculating. He was able, as we know, to prolong his onanistic act without ejaculating for hours or days. That means that he can learn to cohabit with his sister or any other woman without running the danger of impregnating her. His masturbation is thus a preparation for his sexual practices with his private harem, i.e., with his sister and her friends. The whole period of the analysis in which he has erotic dreams without achieving ejaculation also indicates that he suffers from some fixed notion. That is to say: I have learned how to provoke an orgasm in the women without achieving more than the anticipatory pleasure myself. That protects me from danger. The danger is his father. If his sister should ever become pregnant, his father would learn all.

Last Sunday he went out into the woods with his girl. He played with her but did not succumb to the temptation of coitus. He was expecting the same situation as in the dream, i.e., he wanted her to take the active rôle and climb upon him while he remained passive. That is why he always stretched out upon the grass and awaited the activity and aggressiveness of his partner. She, however, remained passive. She wanted to be taken and overcome. She told him that she could not meet him this Sunday, manifestly because she could not stand the sexual tension without relief.

The patient reports:

The night produced a mass of dreams of which, against the flood of marked resistances, I shall report three.

1. I am in a kind of surgical lecture hall in which an operation has just been completed. The patient, a Lithuanian from my barracks (castrated stallion) looks at me and goes out. I saw a large wound on the side of his right thigh just above the knee. Then I was supposed to be next, but I thought: I certainly won't permit myself to be operated on; I'll wait a bit first.

The right hand was to be sutured to the thigh or the knee and then be lopped off. "But I don't want my right hand hacked off. Can't I have it yet. I need it." "No, but you can have it done in two stages." Then I awoke.

2. . . . N. N. comes to me and says that a court martial awaits me. The kaiser (Napoleon) is ill. I think to myself: "just irritated." I'm sure that his indisposition is due to irritation.

I'm supposed to have disclosed treasonable information to the Russians through the medium of one of my men by the name of Atophan (?). I said: "I can't even understand the fellow, how is it possible that I can be responsible for what he said."

3. My father and I together in a room. Something seems to be hanging from the ceiling or standing on the table in the old room. Then I thought that it was a large bell (a child's bell) which hung in a frame. It couldn't ring because it would always bump against the frame. I wanted to look into the matter, but my father took a hammer and chisel and went after the pretty bell until it was all bent and twisted. I cried: "You're breaking everything to pieces!" He was angry that I had butted in. Finally, the bell was all dented and ruined, but it seems that it could still ring.

Dr. Stekel considers one and three very important because they indicate my castration complex, but I find only a few well-known connections in this respect. Dr. Stekel is dissatisfied with me because I can't help him. My desire to stop the analysis has been growing. I sing: "Blow, blow, blowing wind," and "The wind blows me home" and other similar songs.

Then there was a feeble attempt to have myself thrown out by remarking skeptically about his telepathic dreams. Nevertheless, the last time sharpened my wits. Dr. Stekel grimaced again. His old Medusa face.

In short, I recognize my resistances to the analysis, but that helps me very little and the inhibitions are still there. My experience with my sister also remains fruitless as regards the analysis. Dr. Stekel believes that I want to hide the importance of the nursemaid. I wonder that he doesn't pay any attention to my grandmother. As far as I can see, this also covers unpleasant notions about the analysis. Am sorry for the old lady.

But as regards the analysis itself. That Lithuanian really looked castrated. The right hand was always related to the penis in my mind, the left much less because I never liked to use it in masturbating. Possible that the hand is a symbol of the penis itself. It was supposed to be sutured. Like the auto-transplantations in two stages. That operation invariably forced the patients into a stressed and uncomfortable position which frequently provoked me to masturbate.

Dream 3. First of all: father: Dr. Stekel. The child's bell of my infantile days must be made to fit the frame of reality in order that I may be able to do something. For that purpose he makes use of the hammer and chisel of the dentist. The dentist always uses that to pound upon the crowns and make them sit fast. A hellish pleasure.

In short, more resistance to the analysis. Or anxiety that father might—or rage against him because he wants to force me to adjust to reality by education and strictness (banging against the head). Whereas I am trying to find out where the inhibitions lie, he wants to cripple me in the attempt to have me live according to his wishes.

Dream 2. Father has heard that I have given his enemies information about his affairs through the medium of Atophan, i.e. (taken etymologically), through the medium of a healthy person, i.e., without tophi. He is sick with fear and will revenge himself yet. His enemies are all those who have derived new information about my father and my family. On the other hand, I myself am Napoleon, the great man who so impresses me; the man who also treated women so badly. I have betrayed myself and am putting myself on trial. In that case, the enemy would be Dr. Stekel.

The courts-martial can also make one lose one's head (penis). According to the way one looks at it, this might also be an indication of the castration complex.

That which I don't want to divulge is again about to be born. These written notes are becoming stagnant. I am strongly moved to get out. No special fixation; only marked restlessness.

In the evening: A restless day behind me. I had to go to the library, but was unable to work with any directness or purpose there.

After lunch, my path took me past the number thirty-eight street car line. I obeyed an impulse and got on the car, but promptly wanted to get off again. But I rode out to Grinzing (a suburb of Vienna—Trans.). The last chapter of your *Infantile Psycho-Sexuality* increased my depression. But number one was brought back to me again. I returned to the city.

The following is a résumé of all that may have reference to the castration complex:

1. The tailor with the shears. I liked to suck my thumbs and was afraid that they would be cut off. They often threatened with just that.

2. My father is circumcised. At an early age I found out that the foreskin on my penis is something valueless. I would pull it back, but it always slipped forward again.

3. At various times I wanted to bind away my penis, the first time, as far as I can recall, being when I was in my bandaging period. I also had the desire to tie it up when it was erect because the constant erections made me feel uncomfortable in the trousers. On the other hand, I often felt sorry that I was not a woman; so that I might have some place to put the penis of my partner. *Paedicatio in anum* was not at all desirable to me, but I would have considered the matter from in front. I always used to be afraid of all cutting and cracking instruments. The noisy ones especially. Fire-crackers were a nuisance to me, and I was afraid of them. I was altogether a coward and overcame my cowardice only very late. I can't say that I am at all courageous even to-day.

I might say that I had others cut and manicure my nails for the longest time. My oldest sister was not able to light a match until she was about twelve or thirteen; before that time, she could not be brought to take one in her hand.—Now I'm all out of associations again. Shall I smoke a pipe? Is my persistent abstinence from smoking a method of retaining my infantile period? I'm much less sexually excited; rather dull and indifferent. Occasionally energetic in speech (talking myself into it) but then soon quiet. Now I am seized with a fear (the wish) that I won't dream anything to-night. Fear of Riga. The lonesomeness. The examinations. The growing power of the returning fetishism and homosexuality there.

Succinctly. Under par. No appetite, no desire to play the guitar. Talking gets on my nerves. Dull tension.

I would like also to mention that the right hand in his last dream is also a symbolization of his sister. He has been fixated to her and must now be separated from his fixation. He reacts to my attempts in this direction with the development of hatred. He doesn't want to give up his phantasies. He is in a state of deep dejection and is trying to analyze himself. He is told to stop this mulling around in his own ideas. I recommended diversions to him (theatre, lectures, work, etc.).

The following dreams are variations on older themes.

I remember the following from a series of dreams:

. . . I was with my father for some time. I am finally plunged into despair that nothing but quarreling and irritation come of our being together; that he simply cannot and will not understand me. Finally I say to him: "Do you know that I had a dream last night, that I bled profusely, and that . . ." (the memory of the dream breaks off); then I went out.

And met T—— P—— in my parents' bedroom. A large girl of about twenty-five (in reality a friend of my aunt). In reality she is also very pale. She lies down upon the sofa and I rub her forehead with Eau de Cologne; she complains that it burns her. I dip a towel in some water and place it on her forehead. She feels better.

Our last nursemaid stands near by throughout the proceeding and grins idiotically with her mouth agape from one ear to the other. Then I went into the next room again. H—— came in and asked me what my diagnosis was. I said: "Maybe hysteria, epileptoid or organic in nature." He answered: "But she was a kleptomaniac."

Then H—— appeared clean shaven and became more and more intimate. We are in the Academy of Medicine (i.e., the company of doctors). Suddenly he seizes me about the middle and begins to wrestle with me. I find the game rather out of place and the bystanders are also surprised. Then he stopped. We spoke of the patient. He said that she was quite well organically, with the exception of a small swelling on her back which permitted of the palpation of a small lymph gland. I said: "That doesn't mean anything because then I would have a sarcoma of the jaw; I've always had glands under my jaw which were described in surgery as symptoms of just that." I tried to push the glands out over the edge of the mandible. H—— palpated them quickly and said: "Yes, but that's in the text-book of surgery."

Again I see the woman in a bluish linen dress. I think she was pregnant. But Benno said she couldn't possibly be pregnant any more.

Otherwise, I might add that I'm still as sick as can be from that pipe I smoked yesterday. It's up to my neck.[8] I haven't any associations, except that grinning nursemaid is always before my mind. My grandmother has awakened my interest. I consider what relations I might have had to her bedroom. Also remember that whenever we visited her we children used to sleep there of an afternoon. This derives from the Eau de Cologne which always stood on grandmother's dresser. It always attracted me. My grandmother also had saved one of Uncle Carl's teeth, a canine, in a little wooden box. To her great astonishment, although it was quite a healthy tooth, it had been extracted long ago. It had the same long roots as my own little pocket penis.

After the extraction of my own tooth, I recalled this tooth of Uncle Carl's. Dr. Stekel's opinion that this dream is a screen memory of my coitus experiences with my sister provokes renewed resistances in me. I'm always thinking of other things. I'm especially vehement about my departure. The thought that Dr. Stekel will transfer me after Pentecost hurts me very much. A visit to the torture chamber of the Museum of Lower Austria relieved me somewhat; also the dentist who has tormented me a little. Otherwise frequent feelings of lassitude and an implacable appetite and thirst. I drink a seidel of beer; that makes me feel better than many glasses of water taken before. But even that's not just what I wanted.

To-day the dentist talked for hours, it seemed, with the patients ahead of me. With me only a couple of words. Of course, he probably is irritated by the fact that he is treating me for less money than the others. Why doesn't he talk with me? I have also begun to be jealous of the little oby who comes after me. He's a newcomer at the dentist's. In other words, a nice bouquet of resistances again. Transferences. I had a desire to be parental and fatherly to that little boy. I can't make up my mind to see that girl again, either. Since I see in her my sister, i.e., want to cohabit with her, my position, in view of my present inhibitions, is very unenviable. And since I may not busy myself too much with the analysis (it's easy enough for Dr. Stekel to say so), I'll leave the dream interpretations to him.

The patient is stuck in a morass of resistances. Last night he had a dream, but he recalls only a short bit.

Dr. Stekel plays my guitar. . . .

The dream shows that he has not given up his original wish that I play with him (guitar—genital). As the dreams of the night before show, he conceives the analysis as a sort of wrestling match. I dare not conquer him. He will not give me the satisfaction of having triumphed over him, cured him. His emotions are transferred from his father to me. He bleeds for this affection. (See dream 1.)

Dream 2 is a variation on the theme of his sister experiences. But no new material is produced. Nor can he say anything further about castration. He sees the approach of Pentecost with a sort of fear because he knows that we shall have two holidays then and there will be no analyses. What shall he do? Shall he go out with that little girl again? He is afraid to make a fool of himself. He fears coitus. It appears that he insulted her, too. He said: "I'll call you up when I haven't anything else to do." Then he was angry with himself when she refused to meet him again. But he received a friendly letter from her afterwards and now he is again faced with the necessity of a decision. Should he give up his old attitude? The moment he takes the girl, an old phantasy will crash in ruins.

He has a fixed idea: As long as I remain abstinent, my sisters will remain abstinent. As soon as he should become intimate with his girl, he will have to give up his sisters, his harem. But that's what he doesn't want. He cannot give up his past and his fantastic plans.

The resistances have become so great that the analysis doesn't budge. He tries all kinds of tricks. Yesterday he said to himself: "You will cohabit with the girl just to revenge yourself on your father." He visited her and they were alone in the room. He played with her, got an erection, but it subsided again. He constructed divers inhibitions and began to depreciate her in his own mind. It was easy for him to discover that she had a bad breath. He had seen another girl in the street car who would have appealed to him had she not also had a bad breath. He then tried to change the disgust to desire. He tries to make the odor a sort of stimulant. It had once been possible in the case of a soldier who had sweaty feet. After he had overcome his disgust, the odor had provoked him. As a soldier, he had loved the miasma of the company; the mixture of sweat, filth and other bodily odors. He was sorry to become an officer because that meant that he had a room to himself. He would then return to the soldiers' quarters with the excuse that he wanted to make a tour of inspection, but the truth was that he wanted to enjoy the odor of the place again. He recalled his mother's odor in the morning; it was a peculiar one indeed. His uncle termed it: the sour morning odor. That sour morning odor was also a stimulus to him.

His little girl couldn't kiss very well yesterday, he said, because her lips were too thin and he could feel her teeth. He also complained that she couldn't find a comfortable position. In short, he finds all kinds of rationalizations because it is one of his neurotic conditions not to have intercourse. The condition is: As long as I remain chaste, my sisters shall also remain chaste.

In order not to make the analysis an endless repetition, I shall pass over most of the other dreams. The patient opens the session with a declaration of war to the hilt. Yesterday he visited his girl again and thought of all the possibilities involved in intimacies, including a possible pregnancy. He concluded: "Only unscrupulous people can be healthy. Ergo. Become unscrupulous."—But that was easier said than done. In a dream, he had a duel with his second ego, his Christian ideal. The Christian ideal is ascetic, but the Semite enjoys life unscrupulously. The Christian has a sense of responsibility, but the Semite is egoistic and asocial.

Finally, he began to think about his conditions anent cohabitation and the honor of his sisters. He realized that his father had given him instructions to be a sort of watchdog of their virginity. Were he not to remain chaste himself, he should never be able to demand satisfaction from any other man who might dishonor the chastity of his sisters. He is the *custos virginitatis sororum.*

His bandage symbolizes the loin cloth of chastity and his object is an ascetic. We know that the first bandage was intended as a covering for his penis and that it simultaneously was to prevent any activity on his part.

It is probable that he thought his abstinence would also make him stronger and conduce to greater mental productivity on his part.

Yesterday he indulged in plain coitus phantasies with his eldest sister. His mother had corroborated the suspicion that she had been born with the aid of the forceps. It had been a difficult birth; the umbilicus was wound about her neck and she was nearly asphyxiated. They had talked about this birth for some time at home, for he recalls having heard much about it when he was a little boy. This gives us a new determination for his fear of the dentist's forceps; and the same holds true for neckties. He had also made several attempts to hang himself. He seems to have overheard several conversations when he was a child and it was this period of his life which gave rise to his anxiety.

The patient requested that he be permitted to continue the description of his analysis himself. He has finally displayed his virility.

"The description of my first night of love." [9]

Having resolved to practice coitus interruptus, I undertook the trip with her and we were lucky in being able to get a room with one bed at some peasant's house. She was quite excited and tense with anticipation, but she was determined "to make me happy." The painful part of the business was quickly dispatched. Instead of love, which seemed to fly further away the closer I came—I was like a stick; no erection at all. I touched her heart by relating to her my lamentable position and my inexperience.

Thereupon we got into bed and there began a 6 hour stretch of exercise. She was very impassioned, but I was very cold, though determined. We began with protracted preparatory exercises of the simplest sort. She wanted to be accepted as my mistress under all circumstances, but I protected myself with all kinds of emotional bulwarks. Then I decided to go at the business with determination. Couldn't find the entrance. She helped me, however, and I tried to preserve my erection. I was quite without feeling and worked only automatically. Every time I entered, she constricted her muscles in pain and begged me to be careful because it hurt terribly. After considerable effort, the impulse faded. The second attempt was somewhat better. I had rejected the aid of phantasies the first time and the second time they were present only temporarily but with effect. The erection was better, too. Some feeling, also. But I thought only of myself.

Then we just lay there together like two children. Rest and

peace. She thought that was nice, too. But I was somewhat depressed. Feeling her touch my perineum and genitals, I became greatly impassioned and, after a protracted and powerful erection the softening of which I overcame both physically and mentally, I tried a third time and achieved a moderate orgasm but a tremendous ejaculation. She was constantly worried about whether I would pull it out in time, and as a result I withdrew four times, each time, too early. Every time I put it in again, she expressed considerable pain. Occasionally she produced movements, too, but then I would lose the rhythm.

Final result: I achieved ejaculation, was rather depleted but satisfied. Glad that it was over; felt a little tired the next morning and was susceptible to relapses.

Second night:

Since we had exerted ourselves greatly during the day as well as the night—she too was dog-tired—we decided to go to bed early that night. She in the bed and I on the floor. I thought to myself: "I hope she doesn't start up again." But I was determined to collect all my strength and show her a good time. I had even told her as much during the day. She had claimed that I didn't love her enough, but I refuted that by telling her that she was too hard to satisfy and that she had fabricated some reason or other for not getting an orgasm. I myself was desirous of giving her one good dose in order that this would satisfy her for a while and keep her from wanting to pet and hug all the time. So I gathered strength and even felt a thrill, a desire for coitus; wanted to demonstrate my virility. About half-past ten I crawled into bed with her and we slept together until about five in the morning without getting into any affectionate scenes. Then we began again and I found that her ticklish parts began just below the mons veneris and passed all the way into her vagina, especially if she pressed her legs together. She tickled my genitals, but I soon told her to stop that because I felt that it was childish. I had a continuously strong erection. Worked around cautiously and kept tickling her clitoris which she seemed to like very much. That continued for a long time. A few times I thought I heard her say something about pains and that it was all useless.

Although I tried hard to satisfy her, it began to get on my nerves and I finally completed the act with great gratification for myself. Then we washed and put the bed in order, only to get in it again and repeat the process. I tried again and had a great erection which was aided by her touching my genitals and tickling me in the perineum. Finally, after the interruption and ejaculation, I remained upon her for a time. But we didn't move because she feared that she would be contaminated by the semen.

At about 8 o'clock I went into the Danube and had a swim. When I returned, I wanted to do it again, but, unfortunately, the best I could do were what I called gynecological manipulations. Influenced by the thought that she would be dissatisfied the whole day long, I executed just the movements she wanted "very lightly, slowly and deeply." Then she got a terrific orgasm and I desisted from cohabiting with her a third time. She even asked me to, but I suppose it was foolish of me.

I would like to add to the report of the first night by saying that I tried the supine position, but had no erection whatever. I would have liked to try the side position, but it didn't work.

As we rode back in the evening, I felt very happy, but the Viennese atmosphere and her sharp-eyed landlady somehow depressed her and we parted without saying much to each other.

I must mention in addition that (true to my principles in analysis) I did not advise him to test his virility in heterosexual heroics. The decision to try heterosexual intercourse was his own, and he came by it only after the conquest of considerable resistances. The girl wanted him to say that he loved her, but he refused to say this. He avoided every manifestation of spiritual contact and satisfied himself with the purely physical relationship. His fixation to his sister was too great for him to say such a thing. His conclusion (unconsciously) was: "If I have capitulated physically to this girl, I can at least retain my spiritual love for my sister and consider that part of me hers."

His description cannot possibly convey the greatness of his sacrifice and the ravages of his mental conflicts. He drags the whole thing into the ridiculous and assumes a cynical tone which is far from the truth of the actual situation. I might add that I have edited the actual report somewhat. He then continued his description of the analysis and brought another dream.

1. . . . I am with Prof. B—— in some place or other. At the right there was a window through which one could look into

something like a scientific closet.  He asks me if I have already seen the new collection.  The door is closed, but next to it there hangs a box with all kinds of shimmering butterflies' wings and beetles.

He said that somebody must be in the place and then we went around to a second window.  There, too, was a mounting with all kinds of colorful biological preparations.  Ergelett came out, but we didn't go in.

2. Instead, we stood out in the open and I noticed that I had on a tie.  One of the men, large and virile, looked me over with a curious glance.  I began to joke with one of the assistants and cudgled him in the ribs with my fists or elbows; as if he were a drum.  He seemed to find fun in it, too, but I soon ceased, especially because of that other man who seemed very much surprised.

3. Then I was in my grandmother's dining room.  My aunt was behind me.  On the buffet lay some new, violet-colored silk stockings which belonged to my grandmother.  I wanted to tie one around my neck like a tie.  I heard my aunt behind me saying: "Don't you dare to take one of grandmother's stockings." But I took it anyhow and then went through the hall to my grandmother's bedroom.  There I found a sock on a chair.  It also belonged to grandmother.  It had small black and white checks. But I didn't tie that on.

When I had returned to the others, I suddenly noticed that I already had on a black tie; it was under the other one, only I hadn't thought of it.  So, I can present myself to my father after all.

Associations: It is certainly strange that my grandmother's bedroom, the violet color and my aunt appear together again—the aunt as the threatening governess.  Also that the dream recalls me to my grandmother's room which, as I have already repeated, exerted a great attraction upon me.  I used to sit on the foot rest and doubtless observed grandmother's feet and calves.  My grandmother was quite heavy (my distaste for obese women).

Even later, I used to put on and take off her shoes for her occasionally.  I was a regular cavalier whenever I visited there, and the old lady didn't have to bend herself.  She had an abdominal hernia.  It's curious that I haven't remembered that she has worn a truss as long as I can recall.  She also wears a corset and I know that I used to watch her lace it together.  My mother also wears a corset, but my sisters never have taken to that.  I now remember that one of my greatest disappointments was the feel of a corset stay on the body of one of my first loves.

Dr. Stekel is "delighted" [10] and claims that the truss must be the origin of the whole fetishism. I must have observed the application of the truss because as early as 8 years of age I used to rummage around in her room, especially in the night table, after something, and wasn't quite clear in my own mind what it was that I was looking for. When, after the war, I saw the truss again for the first time with any degree of consciousness, I was disgusted. My disgust with the odor of old people's bodies is and always has been considerable.

Dr. Stekel believes that behind this memory must be hidden some birth phantasy, e.g., that the belly bursts when the child comes out, and that that is the reason my mother and grandmother have to wear corsets and lace themselves together.

The infantile appreciation of these observations then must have led to the fear that I could also get a child and that that could be prevented by lacing and corsets. This then could have led to the later lacing impulse and the fetishism. But the truss has been totally repressed and never appeared in my phantasies. The corset had to be long and very stiff before I could exploit it in my phantasies and then it would be applied particularly to boys and young men reared as girls.

Dr. Stekel also sees the tie as a fetishistic symbol. It is the compulsion executed upon the neck. One ties it on oneself.

Aside from an actual experience of the sort displayed in the dream (a hawker in the market who used a woman's stocking as a tie about his neck) I also recall having made use of odorous and worn stockings in the early period of my masturbatory practices. I would tie them about my neck, over my eyes, or stuff them in my mouth. They were my own stockings, however.

I can't seem to place the violet color of the stockings, but I do recall that mother, grandmother and aunt had at some time worn some violet-colored article of clothing. I can't get any further on this track, however.

The feeling of inferiority or weakness may be explained by the fact that my grandmother's great size must have oppressed me, little child that I was.

I can't remember whether or not I may have been surprised by my aunt at some time while I was digging and searching around in my grandmother's things. It is possible that she also used the expression mentioned in the dream. But I do remember another scene from later. My aunt substituted for my parents at times. I had stolen some chocolate and when she asked me whether it had been I or not, I answered no, although I had my mouth full of it. She handed me a box on the ear.

Dream:
First a vague recollection of noisy halls in some hotel and then at home. Much good food, but I didn't come to the table. Then I was standing on the balcony of our house, the second floor, looking down on the street where I saw Lena Kreidler with some one else. She carried a large bag on her left arm which weighed a half (pound? stone? kilogram?). She was to leave that with us. I went directly from the balcony to the street and took the sugar from her, but she had to leave promptly.

Then I notice a rough crowd coming around the corner. I was afraid that they would come into our house, but they stopped in front of the house and I went across the street because I was very much afraid. Then I saw the policeman. He was on a horse and had a beard. The crowd annoyed him, but he said nothing and rode off. I went around the corner to the left and the policeman, like a fool, came after me with the crowd following him. Then there was a little boy there, dragging a hand-cart after him loaded with empty boxes. The boy began to pull the horse's tail with all his might, but instead of the policeman defending himself, he stretched out full on the horse's neck and the mob began to throw snowballs at him until both he and the horse were all white. But then he mustered some energy and turned upon the boy. I thought: there'll be some shooting now; but at that moment two uniformed men sprang between him and the mob. I knew that that was the neutral committee. They jumped about excitedly and whenever the policeman wanted to shoot, they yelled: "Hey! Wait! It's not your turn yet!" I wanted to say: "Gentlemen! All Germany is astounded at your injustice!" But I reconsidered, thought that that might be of evil consequence for me and said instead: "True neutrality is expected of you." The rest was hazy. I awoke.

One of the neutral commission reminds me of a Frenchman who sat across from me in the car yesterday. He had on a Greek uniform and his movements reminded me of the funny motions of a motion picture constable.

Lena K. is a girl I know in Riga. That reminds me of my

friends Rolf B. and Kurt M. It was said once that the latter was engaged to her.

Dr. Stekel thinks she represents my sister, but I take more stock in her homosexual significance (because of the associations). I always missed my friends at home, and the two I mentioned were especially dear to me.

Functionally, therefore, it would mean that all the women and pleasures (the rooms and good food) I seek at home are not enjoyable at all. I prefer to keep to my homosexuality which, on the other hand, gives me only half an anchorage and also exposes me to the attacks of my instincts (the mob). The policeman (Stekel's presiding conscience) and my asceticism are mobilized against my impulses, but they retreat before the latter and are afraid. That means that this protection is no longer sufficient, the fetish is depreciated. The policeman doesn't control the infantile playfulness and pranks with sufficient energy. The little one makes a fool of him.

But let us go a little more deeply into this dream. The patient had frequently had dreams of restaurants and hotels. He comes into a restaurant and sees many people eating there, but he doesn't get a chance to fill himself. He cannot remember a single dream in which he had satiated himself. He stands before the enjoyments and opportunities of life and hasn't sufficient courage or power to partake of them. On the other hand, the dream also indicates clear-cut relations to his mother complex. Mother is the first restaurant we experience in life. He then produces a mass of memories in reference to his childhood eating habits, and finally we arrive at the significant fact that his love object represents the nursling. Every fetishist expresses the compulsions of being bound and swaddled in diapers and cloths by the symbolic method of a representative but coerced ideal object. He also remembers his baby chair in which he was frequently tied down. It appears that he has not forgotten his earliest years. He often watched his mother nurse the younger sisters and the business of pressing the breast from out the blouse or corset was particularly provocative. His phantasies reproduce something similar.

He seems to have suffered the period of weaning greatly. For a long time afterwards, he remained a thumb sucker; they smeared his thumb with mustard, but that only produced the opposite effect: he became an impassioned lover of mustard. But purée of peas, which he often received as a baby, has ever since been a disgusting dish for him.

His sucking bag and the mother's breast were forcibly torn from him. It is possible that that also aided in the determination of his dentist phobia. That is: I sha'n't let them tear anything more out of my mouth. His objects represent the well-diapered nursling, the symbol of his happiest days. He follows these men and thinks of his childhood. He is following his past.

Dream:
We are on parade and await the kaiser and the empress. I am with the Elizabeths. I am a captain, but somewhat embarrassed because I don't just know whether my position and stance are correct or not. Then we were arranged in groups and the empress Auguste Viktoria and Kaiser Wilhelm approached. The Empress promptly addressed me. The first of all. I do her the honors, but instead of keeping my helmet on my head, I held it before my face and looked at her through a hole about the size of a quarter. Suddenly I realize the error I have made and take my helmet in my right hand. The kaiser looks gloomily at me. I can hardly hold on to the helmet, it is so crooked, the edge so thick and the point so unsuitable for a hold. I can hardly stand any more, I feel dizzy, although I felt something supporting me from behind and leaned back upon it. The empress inquired if our garden were now in better condition and I answered: "That I cannot say, Your Majesty." She asked me again whether the dirt and truck had been removed, and I answered again that I didn't know. Then a hungry little Austrian whom we had taken into the garden with us out of sympathy was sitting there. The kaiser told him to remove himself. Meanwhile, place cards had been passed among all the soldiers; so that I had no place among the Elizabeths any more. I return to the Nines, my old regiment and have a soldier (Harry) show me one of the cards. It was a ready-written picture post-card.
. . . I'm running down a steep hill with my little girl. I have a belt in my hand. She is very fearful and soon begins to cry about not getting to school on time. There is another fellow behind me and I'm afraid that he's a gossip. The road is on

the left, and we are on the meadow to the right with a garden bed of about a yard and a half breadth between us and the road. I jump across the bed and land clear, but the girl jumped onto the bed.

I tell her: "If anybody should ask you, you just tell them that it was my fault. I'll take the blame." She bawls lustily, but then she dried her tears away and we saw that school hadn't begun yet. The teachers weren't there yet, either. They were supposed to hold a lecture for parents and adults, with lantern slides, and I wanted to be present. The preparations had not yet been completed, however. I saw an almost endless number of small girls (school girls) in the hall, and there was also a group of teachers in a corner.

Then I left.

Associations: The kaiser and the empress stand for father and mother. Strange, because the Empress Auguste Viktoria is dead. Death wishes against my mother? I look through the helmet: mother's breast. In other words, I look at my mother from the point of view of my infantile state. As I am about to do my virile honors, I get dizzy and can hardly stand. The helmet has become a vulva. I can hardly hold it properly. Lately, I played with my little girl's vulva. My mother dare not learn of that. Or is it that, having laid aside my helmet—my fetishism—I cannot face my mother? She must see that I had my hands in someone's vulva. I also had a dagger in my hand. Am I bisexual? I have both the penis and the vagina in my hand. Does that peeking through a hole indicate infantile peeping habits? I used to like crawling under the table, my father's writing desk included, and would then play bow-wow. I used to get great fun out of peeking through holes in curtains, portières and blankets. The garden in the dream is doubtless my own soul. I once had to dig up a small garden plot at home for my mother, but I kept putting it off. At the same time, however, I helped a friend of mine dig up potatoes in their garden. My mother reproached me and I felt the sting of it. But I can't answer the question about how I know that, either. After all, I haven't been home for a long time. But I know very well what she means. I cannot tell her that I am healthy and cured; I doubt it; I have the desire to leave all the dirt and truck in the old garden because it is appealing to me in its original and overgrown state. I'm afraid of the question: "Are you cured?"

The Austrian is Dr. Stekel. He is humiliated and I feel elevated for having accepted him out of sympathy. My father tells him to go, i.e., I tell him. And now comes the dilemma. I was with the Elizabeths or the Frances regiment, i.e., with the Austrians. I had gained a contact (the little girl), and then I sacrificed my infantile habits for homosexuality again. And now I can't return to her. Ergo, I return to my old sexual habits, my old regiment, the Nines. The post-cards remind me of the caricature post-cards of confirmation with the facsimile hand-writing on them.

The soldier who showed me the post-card is Alfred Kor, an Alsatian, who died during the war from pneumonia. He is doubtless a symbol of his friend Marly who was my aide for some time and with whom I cultivated rather intimate physical relations. I also loved him very much. Ergo: return to homosexual practices. Depreciation and derogatory attitude towards heterosexuality. I evidently didn't feel very sure of myself in this heterosexual rôle because I didn't feel very much a part of that Elizabeth company.

The little girl in dream two reminds me of Frieda G., a friend of my sister's. We played bride and bridegroom on the sandpiles and hooked arms. I suppose we also played doctor together, but all I can recall is games with dolls. I must reiterate my fun in crawling under the tables.

I was very much interested in dolls; what they had inside their bellies and why their eyes could clack so. On occasion I used to make a thorough examination of this situation, with the well-known results.

The girdle in my hand: a penis symbol.

Dr. Stekel asked me whether playing school, hitting or being beaten were memorable to me or not. I'm sure that we played school, but I can't recall any free hitting parties. The doll-children surely received whippings and beatings, however.

Is there an infantile experience behind these memories? Anxiety that something may be found out?

Dream:
I am lying with my head in Dr. Stekel's lap or rather on his left thigh. I feel very happy and get the warmth of his body. Rolf Riemer, whom I had sought for a long time, came in and said he had heard from Dr. Stekel. He said: "I was such a happy fellow before. I'd like very much to have a friend to

love again." Dr. Stekel said something to him. . . . He seems also to have been very happy. I now wish that Dr. Stekel had laid his hands on my head in the dream.

That must have been the end of a protracted, excited, searching series of dreams.

His relations to his father crop up more and more clearly in the analysis. He is transferring all his affect in this respect to me. He still expects me to change my attitude at the last minute. He wants to spend an evening with me and become more closely acquainted with me. He realizes how much time and energy I have sacrificed for his sake, but he wants more. In the last dream, he has his wish fulfilled. He lies in the lap of Abraham. R. R. is a representative of himself. His sexual relationships are quite normal. He is a very potent fellow with all his girl friends and can gratify them all with a good orgasm because he knows how to prolong the act. Otto's teeth are all in order now and the missing ones have been replaced by bridges. He is now prepared to continue with his important scientific paper which he had neglected for the past two weeks.

Otto continues his report.
Dream (the associations in parentheses).
I am at the main depot which seems to mingle with the city through all its great entrances and stairways, a complex of houses and courtyards (like my neurosis); behind a fence (barracks) I see a fellow who, I know, is learning how to ride and is being tormented and tortured in the process (I see only the trunk and head over the fence). (Before the war they used to tie a bucket filled with water to each leg of a soldier and make him gallop that way). I go below and the picture is gone. Then I went up into the depot again and saw the entrance to the barracks. A fellow was being led in by two men. He is bound and wears a singular sort of strait-jacket (reminds me of the Chinese Kang). His eyes are blindfolded and there is a gag in his mouth. He is driven into the gate. (I think the other fellow who was on horse was also fixed up in some manner; with blinders, I think.) I try to get a closer view of the scene but get lost in the maze of streets and houses.

Then I am on the railway platform. My train is about to leave. It is already made up, and the cars are full (nothing but rich foreigners). An extra-fare train. I see the diner. Then there is a barber there and a clothing store. That can't be my train, I think, and then, to be sure, I see the sign on the train: "Switzerland" (in the hills there is liberty). I have to take the next train. That carries a sign: "Berlin." But that one is filled to the top, too. I looked for a seat in every coupé and finally found one in the last car. There we sit, as if we were on the poop of a ship. Outside the protecting decks. It rains, but I don't get wet. I begin to speak with a man and the train starts backwards. The cars in front of us have open platforms and they seem to disappear in the water as we move, but they remained with us nevertheless. We sailed around the end of the breakwater and I thought that was marvelous. Then we made fast on the other side of the mole. Then I missed my baggage. I opened one door after the other. Full of young fellows, lots of people (Wandervögel, Boy Scouts and pathfinders). They lay in piles; all asleep. Whenever I bumped against one of them I was afraid he would awaken. Then I came into a room where there were only two women. The room seems light enough, but in the middle of it there was a pile of dirt (Soviet Russia, Bolshevism). The woman at the left had her blonde baby at her breast. She herself was blond. The one at the right is dark (later I imagined that the dark-haired one had put her child on the pot. She is Anna, my eldest sister).

The next door opened on a bath tub in which was sleeping some fellow with his clothes on and rolled in blankets. The tub was full of water. His face turned into the face of a Catholic sister, my eldest sister (she is dead. She is in her coffin. She is compressed within the uterus; swims in the amniotic fluid). I am afraid to awaken him. Keep on searching for my luggage. It's not in the depot, either. My family must have it with them in the train, they're all in there, too. I run back, meet a picket-fence, and climb over it. Just as I had jumped over it, I saw the train pull out.

Hang it! Now you're left! But, I say to myself, your baggage must have been put in the baggage car. You'll just follow with the next train. All you've lost is a day.

My mother asks me: "Is it true that you have had intercourse with Anna (my eldest sister)?" I said: "Yes, and there was an adult there when I did it." My mother: "That must have been that maid." I was afraid the presence of the adult might mortify my mother (before that my father seems to have been there and we discussed my condition quite peacefully with each other).

Otto, whose reports and associations had been getting more and more sparse, didn't take the trouble to analyze this last dream. The dream indicates clearly enough the patient's tendency to drop out of the analysis. He goes home and leaves Vienna. His parapathia is portrayed as a maze of houses and streets. He is the poor fellow who is learning how to ride. But he describes it as if I were teaching him how to perform homosexual intercourse. His sexual adventure is also represented as the tormenting of his parapathic (ascetic) ego. The compulsiveness of the parapathia is replaced by the coercion of the normal man and the analyst. He is gagged and put in a strait-jacket.

He can't ride very easily, i.e., he doesn't know very well how life will treat him. He tries to penetrate the darkness of the future; he's as free as a bird and doesn't even carry luggage. His sister is married and has a child which creates envy in him.

But still he would not like to give up his sister and his paraphilia (his luggage). He has himself and his sister die, but only in order that they may be resurrected. The dream leads him back into his fetal state where he begins life anew. His sister, too, is reborn. That gives them an opportunity to avoid any sinful acts.

He misses the train and has to remain another day in Vienna. He must wait and that gives him a chance to return to me. He has saved himself the necessity of confessing anything at home. His mother knows everything. He has nothing more to confess. He can converse quietly and sensibly with father. So why be afraid to go home? Everything that bore down on his soul at home has been taken care of in the dream. He can look father full in the eye.

The analysis is finished. Otto cannot remain any longer in Vienna. The practical result is an excellent one. The dentist phobia has been overcome, he can perform heterosexual intercourse and his objects have lost their effect on him.

Time alone will tell how permanent the result is. But we achieved a great deal in two and a half months. Theoretically, a further analysis would doubtless be of great interest. But have we physicians the right to demand that?

This case is an excellent corroboration of every one of the theses I have expressed in the foregoing chapters. Let us collect the chief features of the case in a résumé.[11]

We have here a man who attempts to repress his sexuality and live the life of an ascetic. He retreats from heterosexuality and considers himself a homosexual. Indeed, he even brought a boy home and confessed to his mother that he had had intercourse with him. His father learned of it through the mother, and that was doubtless the purpose of the confession. He revenges himself on his family, in other words, for refusing him the gratification which he desires. The nucleus of the patient's condition is his love for his father to whom he is homosexually fixated. This affection seems to have been transformed to hate and that is the thought which is most deeply repressed. Nor was he conscious of his fixations to his mother, sisters and grandmother before the analysis.

Two traumatic situations may be considered as the source of his condition. One is the death of his youngest sister. He felt guilty of this death because he had wished her dead, he had thus been the one to kill her. This is the source of his inferiority feelings and his tendencies towards expiation and atonement. His burning ambitions are well checked by these feelings of inferiority. He dare not achieve anything in life because he doesn't deserve it. He must reject all the enjoyments of life (his ascetic tendencies expressed in his avoidance of women, tobacco, alcohol, his self-denial and his poor clothing, etc.). He hopes to weaken the wrath of God by this ascetic tendency and to achieve the status of one of the saints (his Christ neurosis). The other serious trauma was his intercourse with his sister when he was a child. His very earliest dreams indicate this trauma. This analysis should be read twice. Only then does one get an idea how frequently the early dreams announce the knowledge which we achieved only later. The determining influences in the specific form of his fetishism were several infantile impressions. 1—His first suspenders. 2—The rescuing umbilical dressing. 3—Grandmother's truss. 4—Mother's badges. 5—His memory of his happy infant state. 6—Christ's loin cloth.[12]

His fetishistic objects are a condensation of the divers components of his parapathia.

The object represents:

1. Himself. He is crippled and protected by the bandages.

2. His sister and her skull bandage.

3. Some spirit, his dead brother, his dead sister.

4. Christ.

5. A victim of castration.

6. A swaddled baby.

7. Œdipus and the patricide.

8. Poor Lazarus. The eternal warning (be happy that you have your healthy limbs!).

His other diverse impressions were also of importance. The boy he saw in the hospital when his sister died. The picture of poor Lazarus. The bandage on his mother's toe when his sister was born. The gag as a memory of his sucking bag and the forceps. The splints his sister wore. His mother's corset. His identification with the horses (the curb-bits). The phimosis and the anal compulsion.

The most significant impression was probably the picture of poor Lazarus. He is Lazarus himself and, as such, will some day lay his head in the lap of Abraham.

The therapeutic effect in this case proves what I have always stated: The fact that these conditions are independent of anything that has to do with the internal secretions and that homosexuality and genuine fetishism are curable.

# XVI

## ANALYSIS OF A CASE OF TRANSVESTITISM

### By EMIL GUTHEIL [1]

Case 70.

Introductory remarks: This patient agreed to an analysis under one condition: that under no circumstances should we destroy her particular sexual strivings. She was only desirous of enlisting our aid in gaining permission from the police to wear men's clothing.

Elsa B., thirty-four years old, government clerk.

Physical status: Slender stature, sloping shoulders, asthenic thorax, pale skin, female larynx. Primary and secondary sexual characteristics of normal appearance. Menses regular, onset about thirteen years of age. Claims to be able to undertake the hardest of work even during her period. Self-possessed appearance, male type of walk with long steps. Hesitates to give her correct age and blushes when she speaks of her sexual history. Alto voice. She claims that she had a tenor voice but that it became lower during puberty. She urinates in a standing position. No special signs of degeneration. The following are her physical measurements in centimeters. [2]

The patient is of average intelligence, shows good grasp of mental content, and some artistic interests (plays the violin). [3]

The introductory letter to Dr. Stekel:

"Dear Doctor: When I last visited you, you asked me to write you a description of my character. Although I cannot consider myself an accomplished writer, I shall nevertheless try to give you as clear a picture of myself as I am able.

"I had a distinct dislike of girls' toys as far back as I can recall. I played only with boys' things, e.g., sabers, guns, soldiers, etc. My favorite toy was a large rocking horse. A doll which I received for Christmas once was destined to destruction at my hands, and a box of knitting goods was thrown into the fire. My desire to ride an animal, which I indulged one summer during a vacation in M. on the back of a St. Bernard dog, was made memorable by a scar which I still have. I also recall a winter coat of dark blue cloth which I once had. It had ties instead of buttons and I cherished it very much. It is possible that the resemblance between this coat and the uniform coats of the hussars was what influenced my taste; to such an extent, indeed, that I insisted on wearing the coat even in the spring and summer.

"As I grew older, my dislike of girls' toys increased. But, since my destructive tendencies earned me severe punishment, I learned to rid myself of them simply by hiding them in the darkest corners of the house where they would be left to their fate. I was actually ashamed to have anything to do with them.

"I cannot recall having had any girl friends or playmates during the time I went to school. I had no desire to confide in them, nor were their games at all to my taste. And since, in the course of time, my favorite playthings were taken away from me, allegedly because they did not suit a girl like me, I began to cast about for other forms of amusement. From that time on my best friends were not people, but books.

"As the years passed, the question of clothing became a serious dilemma. To go out dressed in airy skirts and hats with ribbons and lace made me feel like a dressed-up monkey. Following promenades or visits in such clothing, I would be overcome with a deep depression and was glad when I reached home again and could tear the stuff from my body. Even then I felt just as dissatisfied with such clothing as I do to-day. Every new dress was the signal for a bitter struggle, and if I did submit to the necessity of putting it on, I felt rather like hiding myself away in a corner than being seen among people in it.

"Naturally enough, these differences finally led to an increasing estrangement between my family and myself and in the course of time this break was not to be bridged any more. My relatives could not understand my peculiarity and I myself was not yet clear as to the foundations of my feelings.

"For these many years now I have been living alone and am dependent upon that which I myself can earn. But I am still forced to wear clothes which make me just as unhappy as ever and frequently lead to the most embarrassing experiences on the street. During the war, I was often stopped on the street because I was taken for a man, but even to-day, it is unpleasant enough for me to walk in public. I can often not avoid walking with my fellow workers, both men and women; and I need not describe to you how painful it is for me when people stop and gossip so that even my friends can hear.

"But this occurs in the street car and the trains as well as on the street.[4] The frequently insulting remarks to which I am exposed in public have made me circumscribe my movements to the very most necessary errands. Thus, for example, I have now got to the point where I go only to my work and back again. For the sake of avoiding unpleasant occurrences, I have given up walks and outings entirely. Just what the effect of all this on my mental and physical state may be, you yourself may best be able to judge.

"But please do not believe that I have over-stated anything in these declarations. I would be only too glad if you would check this matter by consulting with a person who has been a witness to these things only too often.[5]

"And now I would beg you, dear doctor, to help me gain permission to wear men's clothing and thus enable me to live a more human and happy life. I am sure that I shall not infringe upon the rights of anyone thereby, and I can assure you that I should forever be thankful for your generous aid."

## I. Anamnesis and Dream Analyses

First Session. Memory from third to fourth year [see introductory letter].[6] It is said that I was a seven months' baby. Was weak and had all the children's diseases. When I was two, father died at seventy of paresis. He was a teacher in a normal school. He had married mother at thirty-eight when she was seventeen, and this difference in their ages later often led to quarrels because she was full of life and liked clothes, whereas he was a serious-minded and settled man. Looking for a good time at every opportunity, mother naturally had little time or interest in my care. The result was that I had to be brought up by my grandparents. But grandfather (an ethnologist) and grandmother also paid little attention to me, the result being that I grew up more or less by myself. Four years after the death of my father, mother married again. With the development of my present habits, the relationship between my grandparents and myself, which had been bearable until then, was broken up, and I left home to start life on my own. Luck was with me; I was able to get a position in a government bureau, and for the past ten years I have been living on my own earnings apart from my family. When I was twenty-five, my grandfather died, and two years later my grandmother.

I do not suffer because of my make-up (*). Usually played

with boys as a child and disliked the company of girls. Had no girl friends until I was fifteen or sixteen and my first friendly relations consisted of playing musical instruments together (*). The only woman towards whom I feel any friendship is Mrs. Justine, who is my landlady. She is sixty-four years old and I love her like a mother (I also call her "mother").

My relations to men are strictly those of a comrade or companion. No erotic background. On the contrary, the thought of intimacy provokes disgust in me [in answer to my question] even if the man wears female clothing. Sexual enlightenment came late, about eighteen or nineteen (*) and at about the same time my sexual instincts appeared (*), although I had no actual sex experiences (*). My sex interest is directed towards women, but I always conceive the love relationship as something ideally Platonic and abhor the thought of physical union (*).

As regards clothing, I may say that simply putting on men's clothing gives me pleasure. The whole procedure is comparable to that of tense anticipation of pleasure which subsides in relief and gratification as soon as the transvestiture is complete. I even experience lustful satisfaction in dreams of this act.

Dream one: I walk about freely dressed in men's clothing and accompanied by my "mother" (Mrs. Justine).

[In answer to my question] I feel so well and comfortable in my men's dress that I haven't any desire to look in a mirror and as far as I am concerned I wouldn't worry if there were no mirrors (*). I have, however, had myself photographed in men's clothing. People tell me that in this photo, I look very much like my father.

[Does that make you happy?]

Yes!

I have a great desire to have a family, but I would want to be the provider. In my phantasies, I often see myself as the father of a family, caring for a wife and children. That is also our present relationship between Mrs. Justine and myself. I provide for our mutual existence; she cooks, sews and tends to the other details of a wife's duties.

Second Session. I consider my condition as doubtless constitutional and perhaps abnormal, but not in the least pathological. Nor have I ever had any nervous complaints (*). In my thirteenth or fourteenth year [in the last session it was the fifteenth or sixteenth year] I had my first affair with a girl named Marie.

Between twelve and sixteen we went to a convent school together. There were kisses, hugs and embraces—but no more. I think the girl had just as passionate feelings as I did [(*) Cf. the statements of the last session on this point].

My stepfather often bought me dolls, but I broke them and destroyed them and demanded boys' playthings. I was always hurt by the fact that I did not know my father, and envied the children I saw in the company of their mothers and fathers. My own company was usually that of my grandmother. The first experience of a transvestitic character was the winter coat I mentioned in the letter (*). I can't recall any more, from whom I received it. When they tried it on me I got a distinct feeling of pleasure.

Mother married again when I was six or seven. I couldn't stand my stepfather and later suffered many unpleasant experiences as a result of this situation.

A maid offered me sexually enlightening information when I was about eleven or twelve. [Cf. with the last session in which she stated that the enlightenment occurred when she was eighteen or nineteen. Her sexuality is being gradually dated back.]

Third Session. Dream two [the first in the analysis and for that reason of considerable importance]. I ride home in a train from a concert or a church. Some people come into the coupé who are hawking pictures (artist's photos with autographs). A picture was offered to me and I asked the price. It was twenty-two thousand crowns. Since the price was too high for me, I refused.

[The associations refuse to rise. Resistance. The dream could therefore be interpreted only later. It has two determinants. The first concerns the resistance and means: We—Dr. Stekel and I—offer her pictures of her future in payment of which she will divulge to us the secret of her twenty-two years; but the price is too high (the zeros in the figure twenty-two thousand can be neglected. At twenty-two she broke with her femininity, bobbed her hair and began to wear men's clothes; see below). The second determinant contains the reproduction of a traumatic experience. The patient's resistance prevented the full and final resolution of the dream which became possible only later.]

It appears that the relations between my father and mother were not of the best for after he died she spoke in derogatory terms of him. During the last several years of his life, they lived quite apart from each other.   My mother is supposed to have "worn the pants" at home.

With the passing of years, I seemed to become more and more antipathetic to mother, probably because I reminded her of her deceased husband.

By her second marriage, mother had two sons.   The first, Edward, was eight years younger than I, and the second, Otto, ten years younger.   I liked them both and we often played together.   When I was about twenty-three or twenty-four, mother had her ovaries removed and I thought: Aha!   That's the consequence of love!   [There follow irrelevant details which bring the patient off the track.   In order to bring her back to the discussion and association of her sexual themes, I ask her what disappointments she may have had with men.]   None whatever.   I have had no sexual experiences with them.   The most memorable sexual experience was with Marie (thirteen or fourteen) (*).

Fourth Session.   My position at home became more and more acute in the course of time.   At the outbreak of the war, August 1914, my insurmountable difficulties drove me out of the house and I rented a room with a single woman.   Meanwhile, my stepfather tried to take me to court because he wanted to place me under tutelage.   Fate then had it that I was suspected of being a Serbian spy because of my striking attire, and the result was that I was once severely beaten by people on the street.   That was then the first time that I begged the police for permission to wear men's clothing.   The request was answered by a notice for me to visit the police officials.   There the police surgeon turned me over to the psychiatric clinic for observation.   But they found no basis for placing me under guardianship and released me after six days with the statement: condition improved!   There followed considerable financial privation for me.

The patient brought another dream:

Dream three.   I am married and have a wife.   I am having intercourse with her and am happy at the size of my penis and the male form of my chest.   Then ejaculation and following that an orgasm which lasted for minutes.

[This is a distinct wish dream; the large phallus of which she dreams can also be nothing else than a wish phantasy.   The striking point of the dream is the fact that the orgasm *follows* the ejaculation.   Now, we know that this succession is not to be found in either man or woman.   It is possible with women that the orgasm last longer than the ejaculation, but the latter is always to be found at the parabolic height of the former. The patient evidently desires to experience a "male" orgasm in the dream, and we learn that she believes that a man first has the ejaculation and then the orgasm. This affords us a very instructive example of the dependence of the orgasm upon the specific images concerning the same. For further discussion see Stekel, *Impotence in the Male*].

When I was eight or nine years old, I noticed on my brother that he had other genitals than myself and I envied him because of this difference. I also had dreams at the time which showed me in possession of a penis [these statements are incomplete. She is hiding an important and significant complex]. I recall getting beaten (by mother?) during some outing when I ten or eleven years old. An unknown teacher who was with a group of her children near by felt sorry for me and lay her arm protectingly about my neck. That gave me a thrill, a lustful pleasure which was like an electric shock. I didn't know why that was at the time, but later, when I was eighteen or nineteen, it became the basis of onanistic phantasies. My masturbatory activity used to be performed by my lying prone on my abdomen and making the movements of a male in coitus. I have never suffered any physical ill health from my onanistic practices and consider it quite a natural expedient for me. [We also see through this statement that it was not the sexual enlightenment which occurred at eighteen or nineteen, but the onanism. Cf. also the first session: "There were no sexual experiences."]

Fifth Session. [No dreams. Resistance. Probable beginning of the transference. All her data are beside the point.]

Sixth Session. Since I had a great desire for tenderness and affection in childhood, but never got satisfaction from any of my relatives in this respect, I used to phantasy another mother to myself who, I was sure, would not refuse children this necessary attachment. For example, I would imagine such a woman lovingly slipping her hands down about my head and face, or over my cheeks; or she would press me close to her, etc. As I grew older, I came to feel these phantasies so intensively that I could almost sense them physically and a shudder of delight would run through me. [Mother and sexual object appear here to have been condensed to one parapathic person.]

After many years, I wrote letter after letter to mother, but I never received an answer. That was then the end of my attempts to make up with her. At the time, and even to-day, I suffered greatly because of this indifference. Many times when I am walking on the street, I think to myself: How would you act if you should meet your mother now? I don't even know what happened to my brothers in the war; whether they fell or whether they simply broke with me.

I am not religious, but on the holidays I go to church. I got this habit from my grandparents, but my parents were very pious.

Seventh Session. [Out of a series of several dreams, I choose one which is a transference dream and shows a trace of her castration complex.]

Dream four. I am at the dentist's and find myself in his operating room. He begs me to wait in the waiting room. But since that was a little too boring for me, I decided to leave and return later. I left and then noticed on the way that I was carrying a long sort of object in my left hand. I cannot recognize what this object might possibly be, but I said to myself that it must belong to the doctor. I therefore promptly turned about to go back and return the article before its loss should be noticed; for the thought began to trouble me that the doctor might easily believe that I wanted to steal it from him.

[As we shall see later on, the castration complex is the most important sign of the patient's erotic attitude towards the opposite sex. My own person thus easily enters into the scope of her strivings, and it is just this fact which turned out to be rather productive in this case. As we have already mentioned, the patient hadn't the slightest desire to become cured and, on the other hand, we could not make any use of the usual methods to provoke the aid of the patient in the progress of the analysis. It is alone on the basis of this transference that we were able to exploit the deeper levels of her unconscious.—I must call attention to the erotic charge of the mouth in the case of the dreamer. I appear to her as a dentist, i.e., the scope of my activity also includes the buccal cavity.]

I cannot imagine my condition being curable. If anyone came along now and told me that he could make me feel like a woman, I would reject his offer.

[To what extent can you call your transvestitism erotic?]

It affords me downright sexual pleasure. Simply putting on my suit can provoke an orgasm.

[I can very well believe that your homosexual tendencies make the wearing of this apparel preferable. But is it not rather the pleasure of forbidden fruit which makes this clothing so delightful?]

Not at all. The question of clothes is a very special one with me. It has nothing to do with my character. The transvestiture has a far greater pleasure-value in my eyes than any intercourse, and I could easily forgo the latter in favor of the former.

I long ago thought to myself that it would be hard to make acquaintances for the sake of homosexual intercourse, and seducing a heterosexual woman would have had the direst consequences for my own state of mind for I should have thought that my act would determine the subsequent course of her love life. That is then why I was satisfied to indulge my striving in the transvestitic habits and my autoerotism.

That reminds me that when I was about eight or nine years old my fifteen-year-old cousin told me that he wanted to marry me when I grew up. I thought of such a future condition and found the phantasy quite satisfying. When I was between five and seven, we children played "father and mother." I often played the part of the mother (+), and dolls and playmates were my children. I also had a "husband" who went to "work" while I stayed home and cooked. In my phantasies I had identified myself with my mother, and even tried to fix my hair in the same way that she wore it [Cf. second session].

In my childhood, I had to suffer very much from my feelings of inferiority. No one paid me any attention at home and I was afraid of the present and the future. I didn't understand why I should be so disregarded by everybody. Nor did the derogatory remarks about my father, which I usually heard from my stepfather, help me any. I thought to myself that I was borne by my mother just as well as his children. I often harbored death wishes against him.

Eighth Session. [A dream gives us a clue to the fact that the patient has not yet achieved the strictest uprightness. She still feels annoyed by the fact the "strangers" want "to peek" behind the scenes of her soul.]

Dream five. It seems to be morning. There is a bed in the

room I'm in and a woman is lying in it. I myself am up and dressed, but I have on only a shirt and vest, but no skirt. Dressed in this fashion, I was sitting on the edge of her bed and covering her breast, neck and cheeks with my kisses. As I was about to get up from the bed, I looked behind me and noticed with some degree of painful surprise that there was no wall there, but that I could look without hindrance into the open. There I saw strangers looking up at us. The thought of having been observed is very unpleasant.

[No very complicated analytical technique is necessary in order to recognize the woman in bed as the "mother" from a similar phantasy (Cf. sixth session). The dream is an expression of a mother fixation. The male attire of the patient in the dream reflects exactly the attire she wears by day, with exception of the fact that the skirt was left off; but this is precisely what completes the effect of the male in the dream. The next dream is produced under similar emotions. Other dreams of this series were unimportant.]

Dream six. I go on an outing with my mother (Justine). We had just arrived in a fair-sized village and, because we were both hungry, I went into a delicatessen store, where I bought long rolls, salami and a package of ginger-bread. I paid the bill, put the package away in a brief case I had with me, and stepped out of the store to resume our walk. We stopped across the way from a church and many people filled the market place. We decided to await developments. It did not take long (mother had meanwhile disappeared) before I noticed that this was a singular procession which was passing before my eyes. The line consisted of men in red costumes who were carrying flags. Then suddenly I was back in my office, bending over some figures at my desk. After a while, I took the brief case into my hands to search for something inside, and found the untouched food there. I became irritated that I hadn't eaten it with mother.

[This dream is equally as important as dream two. As in that dream, we have here the motif of watching and the costumed men. Also, as in the case of the other dream, her persistent resistance expressing itself in the form of halting associations prevented me from arriving at a definite solution. But the dream did contain the following: the outing with the mother is a correction of reality, for she had never gone on an outing (Mrs. Justine is but a screen object). She buys long rolls, salami and ginger-bread cakes: all phallic symbols which, like the delicatessen store and the brief case (vagina) into which she puts the things, clearly reveal the sexual basis of the first part of the dream. The dreamer is then a witness to a singular procession. Men in red costumes march by her carrying flags (again the phallic symbols). This part is to be conceived as follows: The patient's soul is torn between two tendencies. She vacillates between the inn (oral erotism; note the choice of phallic symbols: rolls, salami and ginger-bread cakes) and the church (religion) ; between sensuality and asceticism. The men in red costumes are men in general, the dangers of the street [7] from which she is protected by her male attire. But why does she protect herself against men?—The church in the dream is a condensed symbol of the religious tendencies in her soul. The answer to the above question is: she dare not—for reasons which become clear later on—come in contact with men. That is why we see her back in the office again after the scene at the inn and the church (she is an official). The symbolic meaning of the office is that of duty; in a more general way that of compulsion in the wider sense of the word. We shall speak of this again.—The third part of the dream reproduces an onanistic act ("I took the brief case in my hand"). It also indicates the sexualized oral zone (the food and the brief case) and expresses her dissatisfaction at not having shared the phallic symbols with her mother.—This session as well as the ninth and tenth did not produce anything essentially new.]

[Following upon obstinate resistances, the patient relates this strange memory:]

When I was about ten or eleven our maid told me the following tale with the purpose of sexual enlightenment [Cf. the first session where she said that the enlightenment occurred rather late, i.e., "between eighteen and nineteen].

A father sleeps with his daughter in order to protect her from violation of her chastity (!). But one night she crept out of bed and ran into the courtyard where her lover was awaiting her. There, leaning against a wagon, they performed the act (detailed description of the same). But the shaking of the wagon caused a scythe which was lying there to fall down between the two of them in such a way that it lopped off the boy's penis (!). The daughter fled with the bleeding phallus still in her vagina, and crawled back into bed over the sleeping form of her father. But as she crept over him, the penis dropped out of her vagina and straight into her father's mouth (!!!).

This tale impressed me terrifically and continued to pursue me
for some years afterwards.

[Don't you find this scythe, this deus-ex-machina, sort of
strange?]

Indeed, but I never considered the logic of the story; I only
had an indefinable feeling about the matter: sheer anxiety.

[In answer to my further questioning] I imagine now that the
contact between the penis in the girl's vagina and her father's
mouth may not have been such an accidental one. It is possible
that it was a form of sexual intercourse.

[This tale indicates a castration complex and a fellatio phantasy. If we are to believe the patient, then we must assume that
the maid—who was doubtless a psychopath—incited the paraphilia
of the castration and fellatio complex in the child or at least aggravated the paraphilic tendencies already present. At any rate, we
later find the patient afflicted with both these complexes, although
they doubtless derive from a much earlier period. For that reason
we are inclined to consider the story a fabrication, an hysterical
wish-phantasy, despite the fact that this could not be directly got
out of the patient.]

Twelfth Session.  In the first few years of my life my mother
often showered me with tenderness, and even as a little older
child I yearned for her kisses and hugs. But, unfortunately,
after my third or fourth year, they had fled forever.

Dream seven.  I am just coming out of a railway station. At
that moment a carriage which had been standing before the depot
began to move. Two of my girl friends were in it and one of
them called to me that I would have to go on foot because I had
tarried so long. And, despite the arguments of both the coachman and the other girl, they proceeded. So I began my long
walk and, since a young fellow was just passing by me, I took
the opportunity to ask him the way. He gave me directions and
even accompanied me for a short distance on the road which led
through the place. Arrived in the town, he said good-bye and I
continued alone. A steep road lay before me. On the right there
is a forest and the meadows lie on the left. The road becomes
steeper and stonier and I proceed with difficulty. The carriage
which had disappeared from view before now reappeared before
me. The coachman happened to turn around and saw me; he then
turned towards the girls as if to ask them whether they wouldn't
have me ride with them. But by that time I had approached the

carriage and before my friend could answer the coachman's question, I refused the courtesy with thanks. I thought to myself: I won't presume upon your company; you let me walk alone and now I will continue alone; the more so since I find it much more satisfying alone than otherwise. After a rather hard climb, I finally landed in a little mountain village. It seemed as if I had wandered far from home for the people and their customs were foreign to me. The villagers seemed to be celebrating some holiday for they were all crowded on the market place and dressed in their gay peasant costumes. I stopped and watched their ceremony. They had formed a large circle, leaving a free space in the center, and most of them carried two small, square, red vessels which they then threw to the ground. As the vessels crashed on the earth, out sprang a red-costumed figure; alternately a male and a female. Their costumes were about those of Satan and Satanella. And then these little pairs, which were about ten inches high, began a funny battle to the delight of all the onlookers. I watched the proceedings for a short time and then removed myself, shaking my head at such a queer custom.

[It is not difficult to see that the dream is a symbolic reproduction of her own family situation. The young fellow who shows her the way is her analyst and the "steep road" is her own parapathic life. Her obstinate attitude is easily gleaned from the words she used in the dream. The second part of the dream is also quite important. Two vessels are thrown to the earth from which a little man and a little woman spring. These then begin a "funny struggle" with each other. This the conflict between the male and female trends in her own soul. The word holiday, however, also means a creative holiday from which both men and women spring. The dreamer is both together, a psychic hermaphrodite, a kind of Lingam (Stekel). It appears that the psychic hermaphroditism is the basis of her transvestitism.]

Thirteenth Session. My step-father had early strived to educate me to the task of helping in the household duties and becoming a good housewife. That always made me angry. He purposely bought me girls' playthings and knitting goods and hoped in this way to excite my love for such things. But I hated everything that came from him. My mother always reproached me for not being friendlier to my stepfather, and I know that such an attitude would have spared me many a conflict. But I just couldn't do otherwise. Moreover, I recall that both my grandfather and my stepfather had a low opinion of household duties. I always looked upon a housewife as an unpaid working woman. [Other material irrelevant.]

Fourteenth Session. When mother engaged herself a second time (I was six or seven), I learned that she had never wanted to have a daughter, that my being born disappointed her, as it were. She said that it was her dearest wish to have boys, at least in her second marriage. Now, don't you think that a mother's wish has some influence on the constitution of her children?

[That I can hardly answer you. But it seems plausible to me that a child who realizes that to be the parents' wish, and strives to attract its parents' affections, may, under certain circumstances, be very much influenced in its character formation by such a wish alone.]

Until I was about twelve or thirteen, I wore earrings and girls' clothes. It was at about that time that my desire for men's clothes first appeared. But both my stepfather and my mother looked upon such an idea with the greatest disapproval. And that was why I first bobbed my hair and occasionally put on men's clothing in my room only after I was twenty-two, i.e., after I had lived apart from my parents at my grandmother's for about seven years. Meanwhile, i.e., between twelve and twenty-two, I succeeded only in wearing my hair trimmed, and putting on starched collars, ties and cuffs; it cost me considerable effort to keep my girls' clothing on, however. [Cf. the information in the first session and the introductory letter, in which the impression is given that her transvestitism began with the blue winter coat. It will be necessary to examine the notion of the transvestiture a little more closely.]

[Will you please try to give me as clear a conception of your feeling while wearing the winter coat as possible.]

Oh, yes! Now I remember that I would look in the mirror. Cf. her remarks about the mirror in the first session and when I put on that coat and was very well pleased with myself.

[Did you get the impression at that time that it was similar to a hussar's coat?]

No. That is my present notion. At that time, I was only satisfied; I was proud of my handsomeness. Everybody who looked at me then, praised my looks.

[Could you tell me whether that was the reason why you always wanted to wear that article of apparel?]

I can't recall that, but the idea seems very plausible to me. It was an extraordinary gift, and a bit of clothing which quite elevated me above the other children. I thought myself very superior, doubtless for the first time in my life.

Fifteenth Session. From my earliest childhood I had heard frequently enough that my mother had been irritated by the fact that she had not borne a son. I felt sorry for her, and later I thought that this must be the reason why she neglected me. If I had been a boy, everything would have been different.

[You said the last session that it was your vanity which provoked you to the constant wearing of that winter coat. Didn't you have an opportunity to indulge your vanity with any of your other clothes?]

I hardly think so. No article of apparel, no manner of fixing my hair seems to have suited my person. My hair often plunged me into such fits of rage that I wanted to cut it off on the spot. I later found that having it bobbed fitted me much better than having it long.

Dream eight. I am at home in my room and look by chance at my bird only to find that he's lying on the bottom of his cage in the sand, his eyes closed as if something's happened to him. I call mother (Justine) in, open the cage-door and pull the bird out. Meanwhile, mother has brought some water. I dipped a sponge into the water and began washing the bird. As soon as I noticed that he began to move, and opened his eyes, I put him back in the cage again. At this move, the animal soiled my arm, and I also had the feeling as if my mouth were full of feces, too. The feeling of disgust awakened me.

[The dream is determined by a plurality of motives. The beginning of it indicates masturbation ("I wash my bird"). It is a characteristic of the homosexual trend of the patient's thoughts that the genital symbol is bisexually exploited: the bird is usually a phallic symbol.—But the onanistic phantasy is controlled by her mother fixation.—Finally, the dream corroborates our supposition that her mouth represents an erogenous zone. This part is a manifest fellatio phantasy.—As later information shows, this phantasy is expressed in both the negative or phobic form (disgust and revulsion) and the positive form. The second interpretation leads via bird—blue bird—the romantic, to her parapathia. The patient here prevents the death of her parapathia. "I have feces in my mouth" expresses her disgust at having to speak of such "vile" things in the analysis. In this sense, the dream is a resistance dream.—Koprophilic tendencies need not be considered. The dream may also be interpreted as meaning that her apparently dead sex life awakens during the analysis, but she locks the cage again as soon as she notices this.

Finally, there is another problem to be considered. The dreamer waking her "birdie" means: she revives her phallus which has remained undeveloped (dead); it is easy to see how this must be one of the most important phantasies in the infantile life of this girl. The notion of the mother ("mother fetched some water") appears significantly related to the revival of the phallus.]

Dream nine. I am walking on the street and soon go into a large house. I climbed up the stairs and then stopped before a closed door, as if I had to buy something and were waiting. As my eyes glide down over my clothes, I notice that I have a man's suit on. Since I had intended to go to the office after my purchase, I now had to remove myself because I feared that someone from the office might come and see me in this dress. I decided to take the street car home in order to change my clothes. On the street, however, I was pleased to note that I felt quite free in these clothes; I was not annoyed by anyone; and I was happy to see how much better I looked. I climbed aboard a car and rode home.

[Here again we meet with the problem of the street. As the associations showed, the purchase concerned love; in a more specific sense, the male genitals. The patient's attitude towards the male attire in the dream betrays a mechanism which we already know. I consider that part about not being annoyed on the street as the most important. It means that the male attire protects her against the onslaughts of daily life, i.e., against men in particular. The word "free" explains the complex suggested in dream six. Assuming male clothing dispels a compulsion: the necessity of being a woman. She feels free; she revolts against the destiny of being a female and constructs a fixed idea, the compulsion to be a man.

The mechanism of this case reveals significant relationships with that of a case of compulsion neurosis. The narcissistic background of the parapathia is also clear.]

Sixteenth Session. Dream ten. I am taking a walk along with a number of other people. We turn into an old house; first into the courtyard and then up a flight of stairs. The persons accompanying me persist in teasing me. As we are going up the stairs,

I look into a window off the hall and seem to see a tailor's shop in there. I walk in and a woman approaches me to ask what my wish may be. I ask her if this is a tailor's shop, and she answered that it was. Then I asked whether it were a ladies' or men's tailor. At that moment a young fellow of about twenty years, pale and sickly, came into the room. She pointed to this fellow and said that her son was primarily a men's tailor but that the slack season had forced him to take on work for ladies, too. I then asked how much a suit would cost and left. I went downstairs and out into the courtyard. Some of my friends were standing on the open porches of the halls above and began throwing leaves, stones, waste-paper, etc., down at me.

[The dream contains a womb phantasy (the trip through the old house). But the meaning of the whole is that the patient has herself tailored over (tailor—clothes—sexuality). The sickly son is the patient herself. Formerly, she used to take on "work for men" (i.e., she was heterosexual in her childhood), but now that the season is slack, she must take on work for ladies (i.e., become homosexual). And again we meet with the question of what the price will be.—The persons who throw all kinds of waste and stones down upon her, primarily express her guilt consciousness, but they are also the plastic symbolization of the derogation of her femininity. The scene also affords us an indication of her Christ identification which we shall discuss later.—What is the meaning of the womb phantasy? Giving up her utopic dreams of happiness, turning back the wheels of time, going home, returning to "the old house" in order to start life anew in a manner more suited to her. The feeling of having failed to make use of the days of her life is expressed in a poem she wrote during her puberty:

> They are not empty, hollow words
> You hear in my sad song.
> One cannot know the yearnings
> Into my heart did throng.
>    Nor know the many tortures
> I voicelessly did bury;
> And all the ugly vultures
> About my soul did tarry.
>    I yearned for love and tenderness,
> But plucked the flowers of pain.
> Whilst the brightest days of youthfulness
> Untouched, unused did wane.

Oh! That I should find the heart
That beats for me alone.
That on my soul the sun's rays dart
Before I'm dead and gone!

The son of the woman in the dream is also the patient's brother
with whom she seems to identify herself in her parapathia.]

Seventeenth Session. [I pass over an unimportant dream.] At
times I have the deepest dislike of sausages. Between ten and
twelve I couldn't touch them. I couldn't stand the fat in them
and threatened to vomit the sausage if I ate it. It is possible
that a case of ptomaine poisoning which I had as a child may
have had something to do with that. But, curiously enough, I
also feel a similar disgust of fat men.

[What has caused you the most violent disgust in your life?]

That makes me think of a really revolting experience. I was
about fifteen or sixteen at the time and was riding home in the
car one day. The car was empty with exception of an older
man who was sitting across from me. Suddenly the car went
through a little tunnel and he stood up, exhibited his genitals and
masturbated right there before me. [Cf. the third session in
which she denied having had a traumatic experience with a man.]
The suddenness of the act paralyzed me with fright at first, but
then I became sick with disgust and left the car. I think it is this
coarseness which did much to cultivate my dislike of men.

[What did you think of the moment you saw the man's
phallus?]

I can't recall. I was simply weak with fright.

[Perhaps you will think a moment. Such questions cannot be
answered immediately.]

Ah, yes. But it was quite a banal thought. I had the idea:
Cut it off with your scissors! This is just what you want! Seize
it! My disgust was so great because the size of the penis seemed
so unusual to me. Don't you find it rather queer that I should
have been so disgusted and at the same time so desirous of
having it?

[She persists in distracting my attention from the castration
complex. For which reason I ask her directly:

Did you have the thought of cutting off a penis in any other
situation?]

Yes. When I was about eight or nine, I remember having

seen my brother's penis. I promptly realized that that was what made the difference between myself and boys. That was what mother wanted to see on me. And then: You're stronger than he. Cut it off and take it for yourself. But these thoughts were as transient as lightning. They disappeared immediately. I thought: Well, you've been ill and you're still smaller and sicklier than the others of your age. Your penis will grow yet. But when I began to menstruate, I realized that all was in vain, and then I was depressed for the longest time.

I can also remember that up to the time I was eight or nine, I differentiated between the sexes only according to the difference in clothing. In my mind it was only the clothing that made the difference between boys and girls.

[This information contains important details. The interpretation of dreams two and five becomes more clear; the "watching" and the "red-costumed men" become more understandable in their significance. Dream two is a symbolic reproduction of the traumatic experience she has just described. The costumed figures as well as the flag-bearing red-costumed men are all phalluses which she has observed. Red-costumed men also mean those who are sensually desirous or simply men. The word autograph indicates her autoerotic habits: the onanism and also a trait which she has as yet failed to mention. The "price is too high" refers to the great size of the phallus and the taboo character of the castration thought.—The dream, in short, indicates the patient's sexual attitude towards the opposite sex: the picture of disgust, and anxiety of her own criminality.—Dream five is also transparent from this point of view.—I also wish to call special attention to the expression which indicates the patient's infantile notion of sex differences.]

Eighteenth Session. Did I say yesterday that the sight of genitals disgusts me? Well, I must correct that statement. Only male genitals excite revulsion in me. If I had a woman whom I loved, I should even be able to perform cunnilingus. [(+) Cf. second session.] I must even add that such things have happened, too. The woman with whom I lived after I left home was a former actress and a confirmed morphine addict. She was absolutely unreliable as to mood and one day she suddenly suggested that we perform mutual cunnilingus. I was agreeable and from that day on we satisfied ourselves frequently in this manner. She also received many male visitors. But the very thought of those men coming into the house sickened me. And since this disgust robbed me of my pleasure in the cunnilingus in the course of time, we satisfied ourselves simply by mutual masturbation (in lying position). It was at this time that I realized that I was totally anæsthetic in the vagina.—That which attracts me most about women is the breasts, particularly the nipples which I like to kiss and suck during intercourse. The sucking is one of my most deeply gratifying practices.

Nineteenth Session. It is not just any kind of male clothing, but only the European type of male attire which interests me. In any other part of the world I would feel comfortable only as a European. [Other details irrelevant.]

Dream eleven. I am walking with another woman on the street. We come to a large building on a corner and it gave the impression of being in the oriental style. I thought it was a mosque. We go inside and it looks like the interior of a shrine. We kneel in short prayer and then I wanted to see the image of the Holy Virgin. But since I did not know where it might be found, I asked my friend. She pointed to a great staircase where many people were going up and down. She said I should go up those stairs; at the top I would find a novitiate nun to whom I should mention my pass-word. Then she would show me the way that led to the image of the Holy Virgin. I complied with this direction and started up the stairs where I met a woman to whom I made my wish known. I also greeted her by taking off my hat. She asked me for my pass-word which I told her, and then she began to lead the way for me. The path led us through halls and halls, in one of which there stood a number of beds. She stepped up to one of the beds and I noticed that papers were lying on it. She searched for something among these papers, but we soon continued on our way. Finally, we arrived at the image. It looked like a madonna, and I heard it crying. Then I pulled out a pouch and scooped up some tobacco with a little vessel within the bag and placed it in a vessel standing just before the image. Then I removed myself in search of the woman who had brought me there.

[Two other dreams were of no special importance.—But the above dream is one of the most significant in the whole analysis. It reveals her mother complex and her religious tendencies in a single condensation: the cult of the madonna. In her phantasies the dreamer makes a pilgrimage to her mother in order to beg for her blessing. Grace for her rebellious actions during childhood and grace as an expression of love. The patient now suddenly realizes that her ideal type of woman is a madonna. The nursing mother of God had always passed before her mind's eye as a most rapturous phantasy. And it is quite clear that she herself is the nursing child.[8] In other words, we have here another case of the Christ neurosis (Cf. dream twelve). She bears the cross of her parapathia upon her back and has also remained chaste as Christ himself. Her parapathia protects her from inchastity, i.e., from any contact with men. Gradually she also develops grandiose ideas about earning a great deal of money, giving to charity, building hospitals and schools, etc. Marie, her first homosexual love, was just such a madonna type. She remained in a convent, however (the novitiate[9]). Associating on the pass-word, she thinks of the word Laurentius. She had made use of the first name of the violin maker Storioni as a pass-word for the postal savings bank books which she kept. The associations then pass to Stradivarius and then to her father who was also a violinist. When I told her that the pass-word in the dream, which had been repressed, was probably "father," she suddenly recalled a part of the dream which she had forgotten: "In the name of the Father, the Son, and the Holy Ghost!"

The fact that she then greets a woman on the stairs by taking off her hat (as the men do it) rhymes well according to this information with the interpretation of the dream as her act of gaining admittance to her mother "in the name of the Father." The woman who leads her to the image is probably her phantasy, i.e., her parapathia in the stricter sense of the word. On the way to the mother of God, she passes through several halls where there are beds with papers on them. According to Stekel, the halls are memories. The beds indicate onanistic acts which were performed with the mother as the phantasy-content (beds on the way to mother; the masturbation performed in bed). It is probable that the letters unanswered by the mother were also of symbolical effect.—The madonna cries, i.e., the mother cries regretfully at her daughter's unhappiness; she is ready for forgiveness.—The final scene represents a sacrifice with a sexual motif. The spilling of tobacco into the little urn is also an expression of her maleness.]

Twentieth Session. Because of my condition, i.e., because of the discrepancy between my physical make-up and my spiritual trends, I have often suffered deeply. [(+) Cf. with the information in the first session.] And curiously enough, it was always at such periods of stress and depression that the thoughts of cutting off a penis would appear more frequently, usually in the form of delightful and grandiose phantasies. I have also phantasied myself slitting open the bellies of snakes and the like. In general, I must say that I cannot stand the sight of a penis; the castration idea is promptly provoked thereby. Ever since that scene with my brother I have reacted in this manner.

[This information gives us insight into the deepest foundations of the patient's homosexual parapathia.]

Twenty-first Session. My stepfather used to tell me as long as I knew him that I was ugly. I heard it so often that I finally believed it myself and was very much hurt. At eleven or twelve I had myself photographed, but I looked so badly in the picture that I burned it. I believe that my vanity plays a large part in my life (+). That was especially prominent when I bobbed my hair.

[How do you feel as a man?]

I believe myself to be a rather handsome male. When I was twelve or thirteen, my grandfather was once away from home and I secretly put on his suit. I looked at myself in the mirror and noticed that it quite fitted me and made me look much better than in female attire. Then I desired to have such clothes. The same thing happened one New Year's Eve when I tried on a suit of my brother's (about fifteen or sixteen). I found myself rather attractive in that suit. It seems that the impression of my stepfather's words must have been very great, especially since I began myself to believe that I was the apotheosis of ugliness. This feeling has no basis in fact. But in men's attire I do not feel so; a great oppression leaves me and instead of feelings of inferiority, I feel free and easy.

[We have just focussed another source of her parapathia: her narcissism. Later on we shall have further opportunity of examining this factor in the etiology of transvestitism somewhat critically.]

Twenty-second Session. An interesting dream. N. twelve. I go to a celebration along with several colleagues of mine. After a while we arrive at some village where there is a large inn on the market place. We walk in and sit down in a hall which is very large and filled with many people sitting at tables. We can see the market place through the windows of the room. We ordered something to eat and drink, and in a little while the crowd seemed to become happier; began to sing and laugh. The market place, too, seemed to have become lively; someone was making a speech, there was a crowd out there, an orchestra played and then a choir sang some songs. Just as the people had dispersed and the market place became free again, a sacristan appeared carrying a cross which must have been very heavy because he was plainly having great difficulty in carrying it. He strode across the market place and then disappeared from view.

[After what we have learned in the interpretation of the other dreams, the interpretation of this one need not be difficult. Again we see the contrast between inn and church. While indulging her sensual pleasures, she sees the "sacristan with the cross" through the windows of her parapathia: that is the reflection of her own spirit.[10] Her striking attire brings down the jeers and the enmity of the crowd and every road through the city becomes the road to Golgotha.[11] She is a martyr in the cause of her parapathia. She has actually bled for her passions (see session four).]

Twenty-third Session. At twenty-five or twenty-six I bought a man's suit with my own earnings and that led to an open break with my family. I knew that that meant a decision on my part as to whether I would remain with them or capitulate to my instincts. I decided in favor of the latter. I tried both in my external appearance and in my character to identify myself with my father as far as I had any recollection of him. My mother's second marriage went against my grain for I considered my stepfather a robber who had taken my mother.

[How do you feel about your mother to-day?]

I hate her. But in my phantasy, I created a situation in which I did not feel her faults so much.

Twenty-fourth Session. As soon as my secondary sex characters began to develop, I was forced to bury my original hope that my phallus would yet grow. It was at this time (about twelve years) that I began to strive to develop the male character of my clothing. I seemed to have the desire not to be a woman if I could not be a man. My yearning for my father became distressing, and I often thought that if he were only alive, things would not be so bad for me. Nor did I want the usual cut-and-dried education and that was why I turned to the study of music and history. In respect of the latter studies, I might say that I was interested in the various cultural epochs, particularly, however, that of antiquity. [Even here, parapathic motives were definitive. Father had been a good violinist and that was one of the reasons why the patient took over this characteristic in her identification with him. This trend was also a manifestation of obstinacy towards the educative efforts of her stepfather. The distress of the present as well as the riddle of her father's person caused her to seek relief in a search through antiquity.]

For a long time I was subject to serious depression, but in the course of time, the whole question of sexuality was revolving about the matter of the dress, until to-day the dress forms the external appearance of my maleness which, together with my feeling of being spiritually male, also, enables me to forget the actual constitution of my person.

Twenty-fifth, twenty-sixth and twenty-seventh Sessions [brought nothing of importance].

Twenty-eighth Session. I often thought of why I needed a stepfather at all. I was frequently very jealous and whenever mother would do me some injustice I thought that my stepfather was the one who had stolen her affections away from me.

After her marriage to him, mother and he went to the station to begin a honeymoon trip to S. I cried when I saw her go off with a strange man and felt very angry that she had left me behind (at six or seven).

I now remember a habit I had when I was about fifteen or sixteen. I collected autographs of famous artists and had already brought together quite a number from the hands of the most famous of them. I did it by sending the individuals their own photographs and begging for their autograph. It was really nothing but vanity. I was proud to have come in contact with such personalities. I also collected the post-cards of the famous paintings of famous artists. Among my most prized possessions was a series of madonna paintings.

[This gives an important aid in the interpretation of dream two. In that dream she is offered pictures with autographs, but their price is too high for her. In Stekel's *Peculiarities of Behavior* there is an exhaustive description of this collecting mania, and he there indicates the sexual background of such tendencies.

We know that in addition to the vanity the patient mentioned, this case also discloses erotic phantasies as a basis for the mania; her "contact" with the artists thus became much more "intimate." The price for the male sexual object is too high for her (for twenty-two years she was a woman externally, and after that she took on the appearance of a man). This means: You must remain a woman.—Her collecting mania is also an attempt to sublimate her incestuous erotism.—I would also like to call attention to the fact that this habit of the patient's is quite typical of the harem cult of fetishists.]

Twenty-ninth Session.
Dream thirteen. Went with my older brother into a hiding place to see whether everything were all right or not. Arrived there, we opened the door and stepped in. We looked to see if everything was still there (coal, and materials for burning), but discovered that divers things were missing. We were just on the point of leaving when we noticed that someone was hidden there. Since we took the person to be a thief, we stepped out and locked the door behind us. I told my brother to stand there and see that the thief didn't get away, but that I had to run off to the office.
[As we might well expect, the dream brings us a corroboration of her sexual fixation to her brother. She betrays to us the fact that she desires to "lock up" her brother, the thief of her burning coals (real love). Let us hear her associations.]
My first recollection of Edward is from my second or third year. He had run a nail into his foot and the whole house was in a turmoil of excitement. I also remember that when he was about five, a gander wanted to pick at him while we were playing in a meadow and I was very anxious on his account. When he was six they had to operate on him for some nasal polyps. Whenever I thought of the operation and its pains and tortures, I felt sick and feared he would die. When he was eleven and I nineteen, I accidentally saw his genitals as he lay sick in bed. I envied him.

Thirtieth Session. I believe that I was already distinctive in my clothing at the time I was going to the convent school with Marie. The men, of course, paid me very little attention because I was not very attractive to them. The beginning of my transvestitism also occurred at this time (between fourteen and fifteen), and I experienced my first orgasm in a suit belonging to my brother Edward. We had all put on costumes for a ball, and when I looked at myself in the mirror, I found that I resembled my father remarkably.

Thirty-first Session. I was greatly impressed by the opera "Madame Butterfly." The woman who played the rôle of Madame Butterfly exerted a great sexual attraction upon me. During and after the performance, I developed the most vivid phantasies in which I was either being coddled by her or wooing her myself as an officer. Any woman with a pathetic strain in her character quite captivates me.

These sessions ended our anamnestic examination of the woman. The thirty-second and thirty-third sessions were dedicated solely to general considerations.[12]

## II. Analysis of the Parapathia

The dominant feature of this woman's sexual make-up is the electra complex which is parapathically expressed in her identification with her father. Her relation to her brother Edward is simply another edition of the earlier incestuous orientation, which contained the most curious and deeply psychological determinations. As a rule, this identification, this "introjection of the object into the ego," occurs at the time in which the electra-attachment is to be given up (Freud).

When, now, the individual cannot find an extra-familial substitute for her incestuous object because of one reason or another, two possibilities arise: Either the infantile attitude is preserved in sublimated form, the result being any kind of a parapathia, or an identification with the object to be given up is effected, the result being that (a) the dissolution of the incestuous attachment is frustrated and (b) the basis for a homosexual parapathia is laid.

Because of certain other circumstances which we shall discuss below, the result in this case was the last one mentioned above. Indeed, it even took place at a much earlier period of her life than is usual, and this because of the early death of her father and the singular circumstances which characterized the patient's youth.

Her mother turned away from her in her earliest infancy, neglected to satisfy her need for affections and soon gave her to understand that she was not wanted because a boy had been desired. But what was the difference in the girl's eyes? Her first answer was: the clothes. But, regardless of what the real difference may have been, she did not want to be a girl. When, later, her stepfather kept telling her she was ugly, she resisted the humiliation doggedly, long before she even realized what may have been the basis for it. She simply wanted to be pretty.

That the girl's final sexual striving derived solely from her psychic make-up is shown by the fact that as a girl she had occasionally also accepted the rôle of the female (the mother); had cooked, played with children and thought of marriage (seventh session). But the feeling of femininity and the sense of personal ugliness soon injured her infantile narcissism to such an extent that her healthy psychic orientation was repressed.

One day she recognized the real basis of sex differences and then it first dawned upon her why she could not achieve her mother's love. Her infantile mind was then convinced that the only attribute which attracted a mother's love was the possession of certain physical adnexa.

If, as has been assumed, a depression is the consequence of the frustration of a secret wish (N.B.: Freud's super-ego) (Stekel), then we should expect that a depression would have set in at this point. The foundation for it would have been the hopelessness ever of achieving her mother's affection. But the infantile make-up cannot suffer such conditions as a rule and that is why in this case there occurred an almost reflex exacerbation of the castration thought ("That's what you want. Cut it off!"). It served to compensate for the thing she lacked (seventeenth session).

Her memories of her brother Edward (twenty-ninth session) are almost solely under the influence of the castration thought; there is not a single association in respect of him which does not touch upon this complex (the nail in his foot—the wound —the gander snapping at him—cutting off the penis—nasal operation—nose for phallus, etc.). All these associations also contain dangerous situations for the brother and are derived from manifest death wishes against him. These death wishes expression jealousy on the one hand, but on the other they are the expressions of the polarity of her fixation to him. The impossibility of this persistent sadistic situation was the cause of its repression.

Instead of the repressed castration complex, then, there appeared the consoling feeling that the phallus was only rudimentarily developed as a consequence of ill health and that it would develop in the course of time. With the onset of menstruation and the development of secondary sex characteristics, however, this conception had to be given up. It is at this point that the depression which should have appeared in infancy turns up, but it is now further loaded by marked feelings of guilt. It is at this point, too, that the crisis in her psychosexual orientation took place. She was finally forced to forgo the last glimmer of hope of becoming a boy by natural means.

But even the depression was gradually effaced by the positive tendencies of youth. Her actual ineffectiveness in the face of destiny disappeared in the developing fiction of her own maleness; the feeling of maleness which served to express all the elevating notions of handsomeness, similarity to brother and father and, not least of all, her being different.

With the aid of her parapathia, this woman transformed the depths of despair and mental anguish into the heights of self-possession, pleasurable state of mind, comparative euphoria.[13]

Like all children who express the parental matrimonial state in their parapathia, this girl, too, manifested a double attitude towards father and mother in her fetishism. The transvestiture affords her the sexual contact with her father (orgasm in putting on the clothing) and impels her in her male attire to seek a mother substitute as an object. There is, however, still another psychological motive involved. It is of the greatest importance to us that, after several transvestitic trials, her orgasm first came when she put on the suit of her brother. This scene manifests all the characteristics of fetishism and portrays the phantasy that she has finally achieved equality with her brother and may now aspire to her mother's true affections. She had seen clearly enough that her mother preferred and favored her brother. Thus, the object of her identification and sexuality is at once the condensation of both her ideals: father and brother (Cf. Madame Butterfly in the thirty-first session). From here there are many threads which lead to her religious complex and to the phantasy that she is the son of the Holy Virgin Mary and simultaneously her lover.

This fixation is patent in many of the patient's dreams and day-dreams. She calls her landlady "mother," but their relationship is more like that of a man and his wife or a mother and her son.[14]

The patient's hatred of her stepfather is easily traceable from her earliest childhood. She protested inwardly against her mother's second marriage for the simple reason that she herself wanted to play the rôle of the husband.[15]

Looking at the problem from this point of view, we see that the transvestitism is an anchorage of the patient's heterosexuality, the difference being that instead of the forbidden incestuous object she has fixed upon a symbol: the clothing.

The basis of the homosexuality lay in her total identification with the object of the opposite sex; the further development of this sex deviation was then enhanced by factors we shall discuss somewhat further on. This woman was a manifest homosexual, but other cases (see below) show us that it frequently appears in latent form, with expressions of heterosexuality being interspersed.

Stekel states that homosexuality is a flight from the opposite sex promoted by paraphilic and sadistic attitudes. This case is a neat corroboration of his point of view, the chief cause of the flight being an active castration complex expressed in a manifestly sadistic phantasy. We understand the sources of the castration complex with considerable clarity, but its significance and, particularly, its place in the homosexual parapathia will become plainer to us when we realize that this girl could not suffer the sight of the membrum virile at all; that the castration phantasy became immediately associated with the sight of it (twentieth session).

Under such circumstances any direct contact with a phallus

was unthinkable. Her anxiety of her own criminal thoughts and the guilt feelings which resulted from them were certainly contributory to the repression of her heterosexuality.

I must stress particularly the fact that a passive castration complex was not discoverable in the analysis. It was not possible to elicit the fact that the patient had imagined herself once in the possession of a phallus and thought that she had somehow—either *in utero* or in early life—lost it; and this although she had womb phantasies. We were, however, well able to elicit the fact that an active castration complex was of the greatest etiological importance in her flight from the other sex.

It is not out of place to recall the fact that even the homogeneous flow of sexuality in one direction is subject to inhibitions; so that we may well speak of such a state as a diminished copulatory desire. But to say that this were due to the fact that sexual attraction is conditioned by clothing would be superficial. Nor is it in point to speak of somatic distaste in this respect for it is not with a defection of sexuality that we deal, but with a displacement of the libido to another object. The analysis shows that this displacement is an expression of the flight from the opposite sex, and the motives of this retreat are the deepest psychological problems involved in the case.

The cardinal motive among these is the religious, the ascetic complex. The solution of dream eleven gave us great insight into just this problem. The transvestiture is in fact effected "in the name of the Father, the Son, and the Holy Ghost." The "father" is the primary infantile ideal, "the son" (brother Edward) the actual object fixated, and the "Holy Ghost" is the great miracle which the patient awaits; the miracle of her sexual metamorphosis which is parapathically realized in her transvestiture. Outwardly she appears to be a freethinking nature, but inwardly she is deeply religious. We begin to realize that the terrific polar tension between instinct and inhibition must have had a dire effect upon the mental mechanisms of the girl. We gain a deeper perspective of the frequent coincidence of public places and churches in her dreams: In the name of the Father, the Son and the Holy Ghost, she dare not permit herself any erotic relations with the other sex.

And now let us consider two other, somewhat accidental and

androphobic impulses which were not unimportant in the development of her parapathia.   They were also helpful in the successful repression of her heterosexual strivings.   These are the forces which derived their strength from the fellatio phantasy and that experience with the exhibitionist when she was about fifteen or sixteen.   The first one was expressed in her divers eating phobias (seventeenth session), in her sexual enlightenment (eleventh session), and the pleasurable habits performed on women's nipples (eighteenth session), not to mention her identification with the suckling child Jesus (nineteenth session).   In this category belong also her acts of cunnilingus (directed towards the female membrum) and the contents of dream seven.   We must suppose that the sight of the male member not only provoked associations of active castration, but also associations of fellatio; indeed, the latter may have been the primary ones.   But this association, too, is calculated to augment her anxiety of the male member, to increase the distance between herself and the opposite sex, and thus to have a pathological effect.

The effect of the traumatic experience with the exhibitionist is sufficiently described in the seventeenth session itself.

Hirschfeld's biological theory of transvestitism has already been refuted by psychoanalysts (Stekel, *Frigidity in Woman,* an analysis of a transvestite).   Nor could this case serve as a basis for Hirschfeld's theory.   On the contrary, we were able to find a psycho-sexual foundation for the genesis of this instinctual tendency and also defined the divers relationships.

The patient's claim that the transvestitism originated in the attachment to the winter coat (in her third year) must be conceived as false memory.   This notion was a development of her feelings of ugliness.

The first real thought of transvestitism appeared between thirteen and fourteen (see fourteenth session) following her depression at the realization of her lack of a phallus.

The normal road to the male was blocked for this girl by tremendous feelings of anxiety and disgust.   Her self-assurance was greatly undermined by criminal thoughts, coarse mistakes in upbringing and alleged hatred of her person.   But her injured narcissism found a way to pleasure and beauty.   At the age of three, she first tasted the full feeling of beauty and vanity when she donned the winter coat. It was not the imputed similarity between this coat and a hussar's jacket which caused her to wear it so persistently (fourteenth session), but the naïve fact that she conceived herself to be beautiful in it. The connection between "handsome" and "virile" dawned upon her only later. She had once noticed that she was a handsome man. The resemblance with her father was a welcome impulse towards the complete metamorphosis, deriving from her electra attachment. If we did not know this and clung to the impression that the clothing were but an expression of a special constitution in these cases, of a sort of intermediate type (Hirschfeld), we would not be able to understand the orgasm which takes place upon the change of clothing. The incestual sex-pleasure as well as the vain feeling of beauty were represented in the clothes; the infantile narcissistic ideal had been recaptured. To be a man, or at least to give the appearance of being one; but to be so in the face of destiny, to the glory of God, and after the manner of the beloved father (brother) : that was the deepest motive behind this girl's transvestitism.

III. Critique of Hirschfeld's book *Die Transvestiten* [16] and our conception of transvestitism

Hirschfeld was the first to give us an exhaustive series of cases on transvestitism with an attempt to analyze them critically. But he overlooks the manifestations of latent homosexuality in his analyses and treats of this aberration as an intermediate sexual constitution. In his book on *Onanism and Homosexuality,* Stekel refuted this approach. The reason why such a capable scientist as Hirschfeld could have overlooked this important trait of transvestitism in his voluminous and exhaustive studies is to be found in the fact that he dispensed with the technique of deep psychological analysis. Some of his patients affectedly denied homosexuality (cases I, III, and VIII) ; or they dream (nearly all) of sexual embraces with individuals of their own sex, e.g., cases II, III, IV, VII, and others; or (nearly all of them) they claimed that they could cohabit only *in actu succumbentes* (I, III, V, XIII and others); or, finally, they were manifest homosexuals such as cases VII, XII, and XV. We know [17] that so-called heterosexual transvestites have only masked their homosexuality.

In our case, we found only a slight tendency towards copulation, and when we examine Hirschfeld's series we find precisely the same conditions prevailing there.[18] Case I performed his first coitus at twenty-four and then lived in abstinence for four more years; II cohabited only after he was twenty; III never cultivated intimacies with women until after he was thirty-five; IV "didn't even dream" of having intercourse with his mistress during the six years he knew her. And all the rest of his seventeen cases cultivated intercourse just as infrequently. We have already pointed out that these traits are primarily derived from the patients' religious or ascetic tendencies and from their narcissism.

In Hirschfeld's descriptions of cases, we also find frequent mention of masochistic tendencies, which, as we know, are reversals of the true state of the patients' mind and revolve about the asceticism of the individual.

According to the law of the bipolarity of all psychic phenomena (Stekel), we cannot consider masochism as a separate and indivisible entity as Hirschfeld does when he assigns a special rôle to this factor in its relation to transvestitism. Masochism is a *pendant* to sadism, a parapathic, ethically determined reversal (the hatred which is turned upon the individual's own ego). It is, after all, the inner conflict with the sadistic trends which drives the patient's sexuality, openly or latently, into the arms of homosexuality; this is what constitutes the most important factor in transvestitism. Hirschfeld speaks of manifest masochism, i.e., the attitude overtly expressed to the partner. But we know, on the contrary, that these patients are very active and that they occasionally manifest sadistic tendencies. The masochism Hirschfeld describes is a specific trait of male transvestites, and it seems to me that this particular expression on the part of the individuals is a portrayal of their passivity, of their femininity.[19] But a deeper driving psychological analysis will always elicit the sadism which is casually con-

nected with the latent or manifest homosexuality of the transvestites.

Hirschfeld's treatise also gives us a good picture of the importance of imitation in these cases; the rôle of identification
with the objects of the opposite sex; and how influential is the
effect of the infantile narcissism in the development of the
parapathia. But he has unfortunately left the problem of incestuous attachments untouched, although many of his patients
spoke a rather unambiguous and clear-cut language.

Thus, for example, case I:[20] "My mother and sister did a
good deal of sewing and knitting and I manifested a great interest in these activities. I even learned to knit myself and made
some rather fine pieces in wool and yarn . . ." Also:" . . . I
can also whistle well, but in that I am just my mother's son,
for she could whistle excellently. . . ."

Case II reported that his sisters' aprons cast an irresistible
spell upon him. Case IV had his first experience when he
secretly put on his mother's cream-colored satin dress. Case V
had tried to put on his sister's dress when he was four and persisted even in later years in the same habits. Cases VI, VII,
XI, XII, XIII, XVI, and XVII reported similarly. The argument that the patients had had no other opportunity to develop
the transvestitic habits except during such experiences in childhood is quite correct; just as the argument that one desires to
acquire the characteristics of the other sex only when one possesses a psychic predisposition. But, as our own case distinctly showed, and as Hirschfeld's cases would certainly disclose if their analyses were in the least deepened, the basic and
driving motive behind the metamorphosis is an incestuous attachment. This is what constitutes the psychic predisposition.
To what extent the wish can affect the subjective feelings of
the individual may be illustrated by the report of a transvestitic
Hungarian physician to Krafft-Ebing:[21] ". . . Every four
weeks when the moon is full, I have all the physical and mental
*molimina* of a woman, except that I don't bleed. But within
me I have the distinct feeling that fluid is being lost, that my
genitals are swollen as well as my belly. A fine time. . . ." (!)

In many a case, we learn that the patient had acquired a thin,
high voice by practice, or that exercise had enabled him to walk

in the best feminine manner, swaying the hips and imitating the walk (case V). But even the dreams express the wish fulfillment of the patients; thus, for example, case VII: "I was a high-born damsel in a large, medieval German room. I was dressed in a light blue girlish bodice and had a child at the breast, while a clumsy girl played with a doll at my feet. From the wooden balcony I could look far over forests, hills and dales. I laid the baby in its crib and sat down at the spinning wheel. The little girl grasped my skirt and said: *"Mama!"* [22] I kissed her on the forehead. Then a flourish of trumpets resounded and my conquering hero, my husband, came in and *embraced me in his strong, manly arms."* [22]—This dream is so unambiguous in meaning that it hardly needs an analysis.

The expressions of Hirschfeld's case VII are particularly instructive however:

"There developed in the little boy a special attraction to his sister who was but a few years older. He was particularly attached to her throat or the low cut of her dress and *all her clothing.*[22] He actually experienced this attachment as erotic for he soon kept it as a dark secret. 'When my sister came home from school and sat down to lunch, I would climb up on her chair from behind and cover her neck with kisses . . .' "

Furthermore:[23] ". . . But he also had the 'pleasure' of seeing the *daughter of the school principal*[24] occasionally enter his class. On the way home afterwards, he would follow her at a distance, and the wish awakened within him *to be a girl like that 'in a fragrant, deeply cut dress.'* "

". . . When he was nine, dreams and phantasies[25] set in. 'I had the illusion as if a whole row of the *most beautiful women were standing before me in deeply cut-out dresses, and that I would kiss and lick their necks and breasts to my heart's content.'* "[26]

". . . At ten he once was overcome with great excitement at the sight of a 'very décolleté little girl of six or seven.'[27] This impression was still vivid enough to enable him to mention all the details of the dress in his description. 'I was sorry that I, too, was not dressed so airily about the neck, that my hair was not permitted to grow so long, etc."[28]

Further:[29] ". . . In the summer of the same year I could no longer resist the temptation: I sneaked up to the hamper when no one was about and pulled forth one of my sister's soiled dresses or chemises in order to dress myself in it. It had such a fine odor of perspiration. My heart seemed to be bursting, shivers ran through my body and I trembled like an aspen leaf. I was so thrilled that I bit into the hem of the chemise and beat happily on my breast, shoulders and arms.' " [30]

It is not hard to trace in these excerpts the transition of the incest motive to fetishism and then to transvestitism. Another passage from the report of case VI is also interesting:

". . . But finally I became bolder and complained that my shoes hurt me when skating; so that mother was moved to lend hers. This did not attract special attention. I was so impassioned in those days that I could have attacked any girl whose shoes appealed to me. I could have robbed them of their boots. . . ." [31]

The mirror and the habit of looking at oneself in it also play a special part in the cases of transvestitism, and on occasion we even note marked acts of exhibitionism (a deeper driving psychoanalysis would probably disclose a vanity or beauty complex in these cases). Hirschfeld's case III says: ". . . Whenever I . . . stand before the mirror and see so much femininity in myself, I become perfectly composed . . . ; it is like a refreshing rest after much exertion, the feeling of being completely at home in the rôle of the female." And case XII: ". . . I have spent whole nights sitting before the mirror and making a woman out of myself by means of my mother's dresses." Case VII stated: ". . . I had a flush of pleasure in my breasts then and would often open my shirt and feel them and stroke them." [32]

The author writes in respect of the same case: "On warm summer days, he would wander about the paths of the vicinity without a vest on. Soon he would put roses or daisies in his hat and put his collar, tie and cuffs in the pocket of his jacket which would carry on his arm. Now his shirt was a blouse and he would make his 'swan's neck' still more appealing to chance passers-by, by tying a black velvet ribbon and a golden medallion of some kind about his neck."

And now we must consider the question as to whether transvestitism may be conceived as a form of clothes fetishism or as something distinct. Hirschfeld denies that it is a form of fetishism [33] by stressing the fact that "the object of (the transvestite's) striving is, first of all, connected with a second person; in some more pathological cases even separated from that person and loved for itself alone (e.g., a cut-off lock of hair or a stolen handkerchief). But the object is never a part of the individual himself." He also declares that "the marked striving" in his cases, "to acquire the form of the beloved object, to identify oneself with it," is not present in cases of fetishism.

Separating transvestitism and fetishism in this manner, Hirschfeld necessarily touches only the surface of the problem. The true foundations of the difference lie much deeper.

### CONCLUSIONS

Dr. Stekel and I have arrived at the following conclusions in this question.

In transvestitism, we do not find the systemization, nor the marked condensation of the symbol in the service of a certain trend characteristic of fetishism. The clothing is the expression of a very deep desire, a controlling idea: I want to be a man (woman).

Whereas fetishism is really a religion exploited for the purpose of avoiding the dangers of sexuality and active sexual indulgence, in these cases, the dress is used for the purpose of avoiding the complex of appearance and ugliness by flight to the opposite sex (by identification). It is certainly possible to find different mechanisms in different cases. But Dr. Stekel has been able in almost every case to reveal the nucleus of the condition to be the beauty or ugliness complex, e.g., in the case of an otherwise heterosexual actor who would dress himself in female attire in order to see whether he were lovely enough thus also to attract attention. This appears to be due to a feeling of rivalry with the other sex which, as it were, is beaten upon its own field.

The marked impulsiveness of fetishistic conduct is softened in these cases to a simple desire to be dressed in the attire of the opposite sex.   In such transformation, the transvestite feels himself a sort of bisexual creature; fulfills an old, infantile ideal (the "lingam principle").

The impelling infantile motive here—in other cases similar principles seem to be present—is an incestuous attitude; in our own case, the wish to replace the man as the partner of her mother.   It is this primary basis which transvestitism shares with fetishism; also the concentric reduction in the scope of erotic activity, and in many cases also the ascetic tendency, i.e., the striving to avoid the true expression of one's sexual make-up.   We also find in the cases of transvestitism a certain trend to become a martyr (to suffer for one's ideas), that curiously libinal expression of parapathic religion which we found in our cases of fetishism.   The fixed idea is common to both forms of parapathia.

Despite its striking inner resemblance with fetishism, we cannot consider transvestitism as a form of genuine fetishism. It is a special form of a compulsion neurosis in which the patient's desire for the genital of the other sex is displaced to the clothing.

The transvestite satisfies himself with the appearance of belonging to the opposite sex; he makes use of the clothing in order to possess some rudiment of reality in the fictitious transformation which he has accomplished.   Whereas the fetishist reconstructs an infantile scene and becomes a child again in order to experience something definite, the transvestite projects his wish into the future and anticipates the great miracle, the miracle of his sexual metamorphosis.

Fetishism is thus retrospective and transvestitism prospective in purpose.

# XVII

## RETROSPECT AND PROSPECT

Ein Narreng'wand wird immer besser 'zahlt als ein ver-
nünftiger Anzug.

NESTROY.

Fetishism is a curious combination of synthesis and antithesis. The singular fact that the parapathic does not understand himself is due to the splitting of his personality. Every
fetishist goes through a period in which we can observe his
parapathic ego and his moral self in a bitter struggle, and the
total personality sometimes takes the part of one side and sometimes the part of the other. The final outcome is a compromise, a synthesis of both tendencies. In order to understand
this synthesis we must dig down into the psychogenesis of the
moral ego of the individual. Every human possesses some
kind of moral imperative. It is both congenital and acquired,
consists of inherent and adapted material. Much of the external influence (upbringing, precept, religion, law) is assimi-
lated mentally and made one's own. This moral imperative
then demands realization. It builds an ideal-ego (Freud) in
our mind the goal of which often reaches up into the heavens.
Divinity is the projection of this ideal-ego into infinity. Op-
posed to this ideal-ego or divine-ego, there stands the animal-
ego or primitive self. The animal and the ideal-ego, instinct
and moral imperative, are always in a state of struggle.

The ideal-ego demands submission to ethical law, the sacrifice
of instinctual conduct, in favor of social habit; but it also impels to elevation of the individual above the usual and average.

The striving for independence which resides in every one,
manifests itself in two ways. 1—Independence of the pressure of the external world (outward freedom). 2—Independence of the instincts (inner freedom).

In the first case, the individual confronts the demands of the world with an attitude of resistance. The moral imperatives of society are countered by amoral imperatives which raise the instincts to a divine position and tend to a full expression of the self.

On the other hand, every man strives to overcome his own impulses, to achieve mastery of his own ego: inner freedom. Everyone lives in hope of outward and inner freedom, but the moral and amoral imperatives acquire in the process the rôle of the enemy and tyrant.

The fetishist stands between these two powers. His soul is torn by both the moral and the amoral imperatives. He finally arrives at a compromise which achieves the impossible: he satisfies both demands at once. He founds himself a new religion. He smelts his animal ideal and his divine ideal into a new concept. His fetish becomes a god to him just as it does to primitive man. But it is really a caricature of a god. The analyst, however, can retrace the divine features underneath the grotesque lines of the caricature. It is precisely this amalgamation of the religious and the ideal which makes the fetishism almost indissoluble. Thus, we arrive at a formula which at first sight may appear paradoxical: the fetish represents the divine ideal as well as the animal ideal. The synthesis between God and Satan has succeeded. Both rule over the individual, but the division of power is the one guarantee that neither the one nor the other may achieve complete tyranny. Love and religion have been molten into a single, mystical union. If love means nothing more than the discovery of one's god, then the fetishist has found his lost love-ideal, which his conscience as the representative of the moral imperative wanted to tear from him, and has reunited it with God. In his love-ideal, he has found his god, and in his god, his ideal love. He has fused heaven and hell to a new intermediate realm which has access neither to heaven nor hell.

But there is a wonderful fusion of two other bipolar tendencies in fetishism: the impulse to public activity and the desire to keep the paraphilia a secret. It seems as if every secret contains a latent urge to be transformed into public knowledge. This impulse drives the fetishist into public. Finally, he either masturbates publicly or he commits some

breach of orderly conduct which betrays his secret (the fer-
menting forces of secrecy). This impulse also corresponds
to the counter-impulse to be rid of the compulsion. Following
court action or analyses, we often observe improvement in the
patient's condition which is due largely to the fact that the
secret has finally become an open one. The fetishist lives in
a state of terrible social isolation. He is proud of it and also
suffers thereby. His yearning for the normal battles with his
pride in being extraordinary, unusual, eccentric.

The secret guilt consciousness, without which there is no
true fetishism, drives the fetishist into situations in which he
must suffer for his paraphilia. We have already seen how
strong is the primary sadism in all these cases, but we have
also noted how it turns upon the ego itself and thus becomes
a masochism which enhances the fictitiousness of the martyrdom.

All our cases manifested a circumscription of the erotic
horizon, a pathological faithfulness to the object. This reduction of erotic interest also leads to a diminution of the total
mental interests of the individual. In this we find a corroboration of an old truth that our erotism feeds and fires all our
affectivity, i.e., that interest and erotism are intimately bound
together. Ever and again we can see that sexuality deter-
mines all our thinking and feeling, our lives and our social
adjustments. The fetishist is controlled by a cardinal idea
(idée fixe), and such an attitude is determined by a fixation
of affectivity. Behind this emotional tone there lies a certain
wish. The fetishist is a parapathic who cannot and will not
give up his infantile ideal. His trend is retrospective. He
strives to achieve the impossible: the revival of the past in the
present. This tendency separates him from reality and forces
him to construct for himself a fiction. The primary experience
seems to be of paramount significance in this fictitious scheme,
but it is a question whether or not this primary experience is
a screen memory in Freud's sense and thus covers a much more
important attitude. It is in his day-dreams that the fetishist
re-lives his past, and that is perhaps the reason why the dreams
of these individuals so seldom correspond to their system. One
would imagine that the fetishist would always dream of his

fetish and there experience the realization of his wishes, but our analyses have disclosed the opposite to us. The dreams are only rarely an expression of the basic system. On the contrary, they usually manifest the hidden ascetic tendencies; they are a warning, a threat, a vain attempt to overcome the paraphilia. They are usually prospective in scope. This is the contrast between the nightly dreams and the day-dreams which forms one of the cardinal characteristics of the genuine fetishist.

But how can we conceive the genesis of a case of fetishism?

One of the never failing bases is the incest wish. This incestuous striving is directed at some article of clothing or some object which, because of the displacement of affect, has become the representative of the wish. The wish itself is unattainable and impossible of realization because of the resistance of religion and the ethical feeling. Man is always filled with unattainable desires. The hope of realizing these wishes is then transferred from the world of reality to the realm of phantasies. There is developed a fictitious life in which the fetish assumes the rôle of the desired person. The repression deflects the original wish from the object and transfers it to the fetish. The impulse is displaced. As a consequence of the resistive attitude towards God and destiny, the following formula is evolved: If I cannot attain the desired object (mother, sister or some substitute), I shall also reject any other partner.[1] The transient obstinacy shown towards God, the blasphemous period of life, the depravity, all are repressed; the guilt feelings are increased; the ascetic tendencies stressed; and the fictitious scheme takes on a religious character. Religion itself is replaced, just as the incest wish was replaced following the repression. The marked affectivity of the situation leads necessarily to a diminution of the scope of consciousness and all of life is expressed within the narrow circle of the fictitious set-up. As a result of the repression, the displacement and the condensation, the fetish assumes the part of a symbol and thus increases the appearance of reality. The original incestuous nucleus is surrounded by a constantly growing number of layers; for all the paraphilic impulses and feelings are gradually adjusted to the scheme. Such a fictitious and schematic form of life finally leads to a splitting of the personality; the affective value of reality grows constantly smaller and the compensation is found in a world of dreams. As a result of the poverty of emotional tone, the real things of life lose their interest and the repetition compulsion behind the fictitiousness of conduct leads to such a consolidation of the fiction that it acquires the character, the appearance of reality, and the individual begins to believe in it. He has, like a poet, evolved a new form of life for himself out of phantasies.

In every man's breast there lurks a poet who expresses himself in dreams. Our unconscious speaks its own language in our dreams. The riddles of dreams may be interpreted only when we understand the archaic and symbolic language of the soul, the mechanisms of transformation, reversal, displacement and condensation which Freud has taught us with such outstanding mastery. We have had surprising evidence of how the fetishist exploits the same mechanisms. The specific value of the fetish lies in its symbolism, and it is in the displacement, the condensation and conversion that the symbol achieves its invaluable quality. The fetishist builds his system just as if he were constructing a dream.

The close study of fetishism has netted us a by-product whose value or appearance we had not originally considered. We have come to understand the prime importance of symbolism, and it may well be our hope to achieve an understanding of normal symbolical usage through a study of pathological symbolism. We must not forget that the "parapathic symbol" and the concept of a "normal symbolism" are to be strictly separated.

A parapathia is a tyranny of the symbol. That is an old dictum of mine. But fetishism is that form of parapathia which manifests this tyranny in its crassest expression. The normal individual is also subject to the power of the symbol. Indeed the world is full of symbolical acts and habits. But it is only when symbolical conduct over-runs our adjustment to reality that we have the right to speak of "parapathic symbolism."

It will be well for us to consider the essential nature of the symbol for much is spoken of as symbolical which is not truly characteristic of symbolism at all. What is a symbol, after all?

The concept of "symbol" is somewhat indefinite. Some have given it a broader, some a stricter, meaning. The change of meaning which words usually undergo in the course of time, almost invariably leads in a degrading, downward direction; they sink to their lowest possible meaning.

The word symbol is an infrequent contrast to this fate. Originally, it was quite common in a rather banal sense as meaning sign, seal, contract, pass, or tax receipt. But, in the course of time, it lost this low significance and developed the finer and more spiritual qualities of the philosophical or religious (which vacillated between the meaning of omen, sign and revelation) until the word—aside from its purely ecclesiastical meaning of "symbolum" or "symbolon" or this or that church—took on that many-sided and fashionable, but often protested, meaning of æsthetics which we know to-day. To say that is the meaning we "know" to-day, is stating a great deal in view of its frequently uncertain connotation. But it is not difficult to see that since its earliest development, the concept has gradually achieved definite characteristics which we may consider as distinctive. Before we attempt to define these characteristics in a few words, it will be well to hear the conclusions of some authors who have been identified with the more recent development or definition of this concept. In this summary, we shall be greatly aided by the excellent treatise of Max Schlesinger, *Geschichte des Symbols* (A History of the Symbol), Berlin, 1912.

Of inestimable service in the revival and clarification of the concept of symbolism was the work of Friedrich Creuzer, that romanticist and mythologist who has been so well mentioned in the psychoanalytical papers of Herbert Silberer. Creuzer summarized the development of the symbol in his own gifted and extravagant manner, but he also added several new points of view to what was already known. He was particularly interested in the symbol as a vehicle of the transmission or conveyance of knowledge. ". . . It (the symbol) contains in its meaning the relationship between the gods and men which is not susceptible of explanation, but only of interpretation. The

oldest form of the Christian church took it from the still more
primitive forms of mystical service for the expression of special, elevated mind-pictures, formulæ and signals; the visible
signs and indications of the invisible salvation.   Still another
basic conceptual meaning was given to it by our physical language or mimicry, the essence of which is brevity; it served
the purpose of immediate plasticity. . . .  Since, in earliest
times, the physical was not yet separated from the spiritual and
the intuitively perceptual and pictorial were not willful but absolutely necessary, it is clear that the pictorial character of
thought, the symbolical nature of it, was inevitable. . . .  The
elements of the symbol disclose its dual origin in the world
of ideas and the realm of the senses and that is the cause of
its volatile, vacillating meaning; such shall always be its fate
because of the plentitude of meaning as compared with the
brevity of expression. . . . *Only the most important things
should be clothed in the honor of the symbol.*   That which
makes us suspect and fear, which gives us great thought, which
occupies our whole soul, reminds us of the secret mystery of
existence and fills and motivates life . . . love and hate . . .
those are the things which demand the use of the symbol. . . .
In art and religion it (the symbol) must swell to the proportions of the infinite and boundless. . . . *It either assumes a
mystical character or it becomes . . . the symbol of God.*   It
speaks everything which is characteristic of this category: *the
immediate, the totality of the thing, the necessity of it, the inexplicable. . . . This one word indicates the appearance of
the divine and the clarification of the mortal. . . . In the symbol, the concept (i.e., the idea represented therein) somehow
passes into the realm of the physical."*
    Creuzer was especially noted for his masterly treatise on the
symbolical elements in mythology (Cf. his work *Symbolik und
Mythologie der alten Völker*—Symbolism and Mythology of
Ancient Peoples.   In its mythological aspects this work has
naturally been outmoded by more recent developments, but in
its conceptual foundations it has remained unshaken).   Just
prior to Creuzer, Dupuis also emphasized the natural symbolism of the myths, but he had a political end in view and
manifested considerable demagogic verve.   In his writings, the

symbol was also recognized as a developing form of knowledge of pre-conceptual material, but his attitude is somewhat different than Creuzer's. Dupuis also thought of the pictorial basis as consciously developed rather than natural in man's nature, a point of view which is certainly incorrect.[2]

According to Hegel, the voluntary connections between the expression and the idea, which is sufficient for the development of a "sign" is contrary to the purpose of the symbol; for example, the colors of a flag. These colors are later, of course, given certain thoughts and feelings, but they were originally not present. The symbol, he says, is a sign whose very externals contain the content of the idea which caused it to appear. The form of the symbol need not always carry the same meaning. (In other words, the symbol possesses a plurality of meanings. As Silberer put it, it is "pregnant with meanings.")

That great æsthetic philosopher Friedrich Theodor Vischer calls the concept of symbolism "difficult, a plastically changing proteus." He considers it the function of the symbol: to infuse the physical world with spirit and the spiritual world with substance. . . . The symbol derives from our desire to fuse the spirit and substance of the world, despite their apparent divergence of character. It serves the purpose of unifying the universe before our mind and phantasy.

Usener derives symbolism from the two "elemental" or "unconscious" processes of imagery: inspiration and pictorialization.

Jodl states that "all activity of thought and poesy strives towards materialization by means of symbols (in the widest sense) because these alone permit of conveying the idea to others and because their use helps to fix the transitory structures of our tertiary consciousness.

René Ghil (in his *Traité du Verbe*) called symbolization a synthetic form which creates pictures for the purpose of linking the objects to be considered in thought. Verlaine also stressed the synthetic quality of the symbol.

Höffding states that all forms of symbolization make use of images derived from circumscribed but perceptual states for the expression of relations or states which are not directly expressible because of their grandeur or ideal nature.

The historian Lamprecht stressed the dynamic element in symbols. "The symbolical instinct invariably created symbolical conduct. . . . The symbol is the mental picture of the act, closely connected with the peak of conduct."

Joseph Hillebrand speaks of a symbolism of the senses, imagery, or thought. It is especially in point wherever conceptual expression fails to fulfill the need; wherever feeling has not yet developed into thought; or where the deepest and most puzzling questions apropos of origin, existence and death, of pre-historical time or the future, have not yet been answered.

Friedrich Albert Lange sees in the symbol "that complement to reality with which man cannot dispense."

Together with Creuzer, Silberer [3] stresses the fact that we can achieve an understanding of some of the main features of symbols if we compare it with the allegory. At least in its simplest emblematic forms, the allegory is a sort of symbol and can be solved with a simple equation as its formula; e.g., "that woman with the wall-like crown is that or that city." The symbol, however, despite its modesty of form, is of almost inexhaustible content. It is never emptied by the indication of but one example. Silberer mentions Goethe who, in his *"Sprüchen in Prosa"* (Proverbs in Prose) says: "The allegory transforms the appearance to a concept, the concept to a picture, but in such a manner that the concept within the picture is still intact and well defined and can always be expressed.—Symbolism changes the appearance to an idea and the idea to a picture, but in such a manner that the idea within the picture remains infinitely effective and unattainable; expressed in all languages and yet ineffable." According to Silberer the allegory possesses a more static, the symbol a more dynamic, character. He also finds that the symbol acutely or intensively unites all the feelings which strive towards it. It manifests a certain quality of necessity as distinct from the accidental conventionality of the sign. He also treats of the symbol from the point of view of a temporary (surmising) form of knowledge (mythological knowledge); he thus naturally considers the symbol as present in all those forms of thought or knowledge which have sunk to a relatively low capacity (dream, exhaustion states, etc.). On the basis of his experiences with hypnagogic pictures, he then proceeds upon paths indicated both by the mythologists and the Freudian and Zürich schools of analysis.

With this step we have arrived at the psychoanalytical study of symbolism. Freud, in his *Interpretation of Dreams* stresses the primitive feature of symbolical expression. He was the first to recognize the sexual background of dream symbols. But he still conceives them in their material aspect and fails to see their functional significance. Nevertheless, he was the one who first opened our eyes and taught us to read the hieroglyphics of this language. But, now that we have learned the principles of this gifted method, we can dig even deeper. Freud compares symbolism with an ancient tongue which has almost died out, leaving stray remnants of its former fullness here and there.

Psychoanalysis became especially interested in the connections between the symbol and the unconscious or the repressed. Riklin ( *Wunscherfüllung und Symbolik in Märchen*—Wish fulfillment and symbolism in fables—Vienna, 1908) was doubtless the first of the analysts who undertook to augment the material collected by Freud himself. He "shows that the human mind quits universally produces a form of symbolism which is based upon unconscious material and expressed in the primitive poesy of fables, dreams and psychopathological conduct." Not only he, but also Abraham, Rank, and, in a somewhat different manner, Jung describe the effects of the repressed material in the symbol (in addition to the strongly emphasized over-determination and condensation). Silberer also believes that the symbol is ultimately connected with the repressed material as a part of the unconscious system, but he considers that that is not the most essential quality of the symbol. He does not agree that "only that is symbolical which expresses repressed material" as many psychoanalysts, of whom we shall speak presently, state.

In their paper on "The Significance of Psychoanalysis for the Mental Sciences" (Wiesbaden, 1913), Rank and Sachs attempted to summarize the value of psychoanalysis for the study of symbolism. It is practically called "a form of expression for the unconscious." The characteristics of "true" symbols are, "according to the points of view presented in the lectures

of Professor Freud," "The representation of unconscious
material, the constant and never changing significance, their
independence of individual conditions (?), their phylogenetic
basis, their speech relations, and their parallels in phylogenesis
(mythology, cults, religion, etc.)."

As we have already seen, this alleged independence of individual conditions does not meet the facts. Nevertheless, we
must stress the fact that Rank and Sachs have come very close
to creating an accurate picture of the symbol when they say:
"By symbol we understand a special kind of indirect expression which is distinctly separated by virtue of certain peculiarities from any other similar forms such as the simile, the metaphor, the allegory, the allusion and other types of pictorial expression or thought. In a way, the symbol seems to be an
ideal union of all these other forms of expression: It is a representative, perceptual, substitutive expression for something
hidden with which it is related either by means of noticeable
characteristics or by association. Its essence lies in its plurality
of meaning, just as it has itself sprung from a condensation or
union of several discrete elements. Its tendency from the conceptual towards the pictorial gives it a primitive character, and
it is as such that symbolical thought belongs essentially to the
unconscious. As a compromise between divers tendencies,
however, it nevertheless does not dispense with the conscious
determinant which varyingly influences both the formation and
the understanding of the symbol."

A rather more exhaustive and excellent summary of this
problem, with a touch of the critical, has been written by Ernest
Jones ("The Theory of Symbolism," *Brit. Journ. of Psychol.,*
Vol. IX, Part 2, Oct., 1918). Jones comes to the following
conclusions: "All of our psychoanalytical experience goes to
show that the only experiences which can be susceptible of
symbolical treatment are our most original and primitive ones,
i.e., those experiences which relate to the body itself, our relations to our family, birth, death and love. These experiences
persist in unconsciousness throughout our lives and it is from
them that the more secondary interest of conscious life derive.
Since all energy flows from them and never towards them, and
since, also, they represent the most deeply repressed portion of

our mental life, it becomes understandable that symbolism can be created only in one direction. Only that which is repressed can be symbolically expressed, and whatever has been repressed cannot be expressed except by symbolization. This conclusion is the keystone of the psychoanalytical theory of symbolism."

In a rather detailed critique of this paper (*Psyche und Eros,* Vol. I, No. 1, p. 53 and Vol. II, No. 4, p. 249) Silberer shows that the statement that only repressed material is symbolically expressed is correct only when the symbol is previously defined as the expression of repressed material, and when the proofs are chosen on the basis of the *petitio principii*. Nor need it be proclaimed that the repressed material is the meaning of the symbol simply because some repressed strivings may often be found to be in the shadow of the symbol.

Jones writes: "Symbols serve to represent the individual's own ego blood relatives or the phenomena of birth, love and death. In other words they express the most primitive of ideas. But their actual number is much greater than one would expect on the basis of this summary. They probably number about 100. . . . The ego represents the whole of our body or any of its parts, but not our psychic life (?). . . . The field of sexual symbolism is surprisingly rich, the great majority of symbols belonging in this group. There are probably more symbols for the phallus alone than all the other symbols together (?) . . ."

Silberer justifiably criticizes the declarations noted above by our question marks. The first statement to the effect that our psychic life is not an object of genuine symbolization may be summarily discarded. In respect of the other questionable statement, Silberer points out that it is a characteristic of symbols to express abstract notions in concrete form. The male member as such (or any other part of the body) is not abstract; for which reason it is not permissible, strictly speaking, to talk of its being symbolized. There are, indeed, phallic symbols, but no symbols of the phallus, unless, of course, the phallus itself is considered as the representative of a whole complex of un-perceptual ideas, feelings, etc. But that would bring us back again to the field of psychic life.

An important category of symbolism which Silberer has defined is that class of symbols which express the life of thoughts themselves and the processes of the soul (the unconscious ones included), and not thought content.

Jones did not overlook this well-founded class of symbols which is so contrary to his theory; indeed, he corroborated its presence. But he sought to dispose of it by separating this type from the field of genuine symbols and adding them to the class of metaphors, a step which is simple for him because of his original definition of symbols.

For Jones, and perhaps for most psychoanalysts of the Freudian school, the power behind the formation of a symbol derives from repressed affective thoughts and images. Silberer stresses the more general condition of "apperceptive insufficiency" (Jones correctly adds the less important factor of insufficiency of expressibility) and thus makes it possible to consider this insufficiency as due to repressed affect (or affect altogether) *or* to a relative deficiency in the capacity for understanding. Both create an expression of the (difficult or resistive) real in the form of the unreal (which is more easily understood, portrayed or digested).

Another very fruitful conclusion of Silberer's is that many symbols represent, in addition to the psychoanalytically approachable, "titanic" content, a corresponding "anagogic" tendency: a striving upwards, towards the metaphysical goals of mankind, as it were. Thus it is that many symbols (of myths, dreams, poetic creations, etc.) possess not only an analytical meaning, but also an ethical or religious meaning, and it is only from that point of view that their human significance may be achieved.

Finally, we must mention that several analysts, notably Jung, are of the opinion that symbols may be acquired directly from heredity. They conceive the symbol as a sort of archaic form of thought. Symbols are the language of a lost period of our lives; a point of view which corresponds in many respects with that of Freud.

To summarize: The symbol of the normal human and that of the parapathic are two entirely different concepts. The parapathic exploits the symbols of the normally adjusted human, but he fills them with new meaning. There, also, general and individual symbols. We have already observed that erotic symbolism and fetishism pay no attention to the general significance of their objects or to their original symbolical value. These trends create their own primitive and original symbols, e.g., the apron fetishist whose case we discussed. The apron is a symbol of femininity, but in his system it is exploited in a myriad of ways.

Every symbol is created by three different factors: Repression, condensation and displacement. The authors mentioned above have not even mentioned the factor of displacement, and have only suggested the rôle of condensation. A parapathic symbol manifests the attributes of a genuine symbol in magnified form.

1. It trades plurality for unity (condensation). That is true of very many symbols (the flag represents a whole regiment, the cross the whole *ecclesia militans*). In the fetishistic symbol, all the separate bundles of a ray of light are focussed as by a magnifying glass. The same is true of the cross, for example. It represents all of Christianity, but it also stands for the suffering of Christ himself.

2. The fetishistic symbol is derived from a displacement of affect. One could also say repression. For it is only an unpleasant, i.e., affectively loaded thought which is repressed. Even the symbols of normal humans must represent the presence of some secret if they are to be more than similes. The affect is deflected from some forbidden or taboo object and attached to the symbol. The mother is symbolized by the apron whenever the thought turns upon painful incestuous strivings which must be veiled before our consciousness. But it is displacement which first creates such a mechanism. We have spoken of innumerable examples of how articles of clothing achieved a sexual significance through the mechanism of displacement.

3. The symbol expresses a wish fulfillment. The repressed wish is realized in the symbol.

4. The fetishistic symbol acquires its first affective value as a screen memory. It represents a long lost scene from the individual's past.

5. The anagogic tendency of the fetishistic symbol is expressed in its religious meaning. We have sufficiently discussed

the high ideals of fetish lovers.   They rival Christ and even
identify themselves with the Savior.   The symbol is an expression of the religious component.

6.   The symbol is characterized by something mystical.   It
is the sign of the fetishist's secret.   But, in order that the mystical element may not be destroyed by the criticism of reality,
the original symbol is transformed to a greater or less degree.
It is distorted by degenerative changes and then reconstructed
by a new type of regeneration.   By means of circumscription
and augmentation, displacement to a small part or to a great
whole, by the mechanism of estrangement and approach, the
symbol is so continuously changed that it is finally a riddle to
the fetish lover himself; the fetishist himself finally fails to
understand its meaning.

7.   The symbol represents something alive and pulsating.
It has been elevated to the level of a living thing by animistic
tendencies.

8.   The fetishist identifies himself with his symbol, and
through the mechanisms of identification or differentiation, the
symbol is either a reflection or a caricature of the individual's
ego.

9.   The symbol is exploited for the service of functional
symbolism.   It represents a condition, a state of the soul and
that, as I wish to stress with Silberer in contradistinction to
Jones, is perhaps its most important function.

10.   The symbol is primarily exploited in hyponoic states
(the apperceptive insufficiency of Silberer).   The fetish lover
is a dreamer and that is why the symbolism of dreams is so
closely related to that of fetishism.

11.   The symbol becomes the sign of a "pathological faithfulness."   Many examples of cases have shown us how difficult
it is for the fetish lover to separate himself from his symbol.
The plurality of his collection serves to replace the one and
only for him.   The cult of the harem is but the mask of an
obstinate erotic monotheism.

The fetish becomes the symbol of all his feeling.   It represents the man's faithfulness to the objects of childhood.   Since,
however, resolutions are often hidden behind these fixations,
the fetish can also represent these resolutions.   In that case,

every onanistic act would be a repetition of the resolve to preserve this faithfulness throughout life. ("I'll remain true,
even if all others betray you.")   The fetishistic symbol is thus
the eternal element in the stream of life.

12.  The significance of the symbol in the parapathic system
of the individual finally leads to the breach of reality by the
symbolical values.   The question as to what the fetish represents to its possessor is clearly answered by Sadger (l.c., p.
328): "The real and original fetish which is always sought
and seen, whatever may be the external form of the object, is
the naked genital of the mother or the mother imago."   Now,
we have come to understand the complex significance of the
fetish, but we have not observed one single case in which the
fetish represented the genital directly.   If Sadger had said:
The fetish is a substitute for the mother, his declaration would
have had some basis in fact.   But is it really possible that the
shoe, the handkerchief, or the glove can replace the genital?
Certainly, the fetish substitutes for the whole person of an
object, represents the possession of the beloved; and the complete possession of an object for the purpose of pleasure doubtless includes the genitals, too.   We must realize that the child
often expresses its fetishistic tendencies at a time when it has
not yet achieved any clear understanding of the significance of
the genitals.—At such a time of life, the "erogenous zones"
are still in the ascendency.   Freud relegates the primacy of the
genitals to the pubertal period.   He writes: "With the onset
of puberty, those changes occur which have the purpose of
transforming the infantile sexual life of the individual to its
final and normal character.   Up until then, the sex instinct was
primarily autoerotic; but at that time it is transferred to its
sexual object.   Up to this period of life, the sex instinct expressed itself in individual instincts which derived from separate erogenous zones affording independent pleasure as independent sex goals.   But now a new sexual goal is conceived,
and its achievement depends upon the combined activity of all
the partial instincts together.   The separate erogenous zones
are subsumed under the primacy of the genital zone."—Freud
states quite unambiguously that the child seeks only a certain
pleasure which it can gain from the different erogenous zones.

It is a well-known law of sexual life that we seek our pleasures in those zones of our partner which have been a source of pleasure in our own bodies. That would show that the child only seldom seeks the possession of the genital before puberty. In most instances, it is satisfied with the gratification of the olfactory or visual instincts (osphresiolagnia and scoptolagnia), with pleasure in defecation or micturition, in short with one of the forms of infantile gratification such as I have described exhaustively in *Infantile Psycho-Sexuality*. Freud seems actually to consider fetishism as the preservation of one of the original partial instincts, as, e.g., Abraham bases his case of foot fetishism on a repressed olfactory instinct. That, of course, is something quite different from the conception of a fetish as a genital. Sadger has confounded two concepts which must be strictly separated. The fetish lover genitalizes his fetish, i.e., the fetish supplants the genital which otherwise is the object of love and the source of pleasure for an adult. But genitalization is nothing else than an expression and means to say that the fetish lover finds his gratification in the fetish *instead of* in the genital. At the time when the fetishism is being developed, the genital is not as yet a sex goal. We have already heard of the importance of the odors of soiled or old clothes. They smell because they are soaked with the odors of the wearer's body. They replace the odor of the wearer, they create the illusion that the possessor is being smelled. This is the phenomenon of displacement. But that Sadger hasn't the faintest notion of the significance of the symbol is sufficiently revealed by his writings.

The essential importance of our newer knowledge lies in our emphasis upon the affective value of the symbol. All previous students of symbolism have completely neglected this point of view. The symbol is distinguished from the emblem, the allegory, the metaphor, the simile (all of which are only comparative in form and indicate one thing by another) by virtue of the affective moment and the mechanism of displacement. The relationships of the symbol are not determined by its content, but only by the emotional trends. The emotional qualities being repressed, however, the content of the symbol is not readily appreciable by the recipient.

Certain banal symbols, such as the flag, also contain some degree of emotional tone; they reveal the phenomenon of *pretium affectionis*. But such feelings are worn on the sleeve. We know that the flag represents the regiment and thus also the homeland; that the honor of the regiment, for example, is crystallized in the flag.

But the parapathic symbol derives its affectivity from the unconscious. It is the fetish lover's support for his fictitious scheme of life. He conducts himself as if the symbol were the living object which it really represents. It is this "as if" which explains the animism directed at the fetishistic symbol.

It is only in a fictitious world of dreams that the symbol could develop to such proportions. Adler has correctly stressed the significance of fictions in the life of the parapathic, but he has made the great mistake of conceiving the patient's sexual attitudes as a fiction, too. The parapathic acts "as if" he were desiring his mother, but that is a great distortion of the facts. He loves his mother and forms his dreamy plan in order to act as if he did not love her.

It is the incest complex especially which drives the parapathic to the construction of a fictitious principle of life. Sexuality as such is no "as if." The fetishism is developed in order to create an "as if" of sexuality.

In fetishism, the parapathic's tendency towards the formation of a fictitious form of life is raised to the nth degree. He becomes a fetish lover, represses his religious piety and acts as if he were a parapathic. The tendency towards the fanciful and phantastic derives from infantile habits.

Hans Vaihinger, to whom Adler expressly refers, has recognized the origins of fictions in the play of children. In a popular paper, he discussed the "As-If in Daily Life."

"It is a preconception to say that the philosophy of the As-If is a hyper-modern discovery of mine. I have frequently shown that fictitious forms of thought and conduct, i.e., consciously false attitudes, have often played a leading rôle in the history of man from the earliest times. It is thus also a biassed attitude to say that the as-if point of view is a matter of abstract philosophy. On the contrary, it plays a tremendous part in our daily life.

"I purposely choose some banal examples. Whoever rejects an unpleasant visitor by having the maid tell him that he is not at home or whoever hangs out a sign 'Not In,' although he may be at home, is not expressing untrue facts, committing fraud or telling lies. On the contrary, the individual exploits a well-known, recognized and much used conventional fiction. It may be that he has someone else in the house with whom he desires to be alone; or he may be preparing a lecture which he has to give in another hour; or he may be writing a letter upon the immediate dispatch of which the most serious consequences hang; or he may be physically or mentally exhausted without actually saying that he is ill. In short, there are a thousand and one reasons which need not interest the other party, but they give us the right and even the duty to reject the visitor. Nevertheless, to be rejected when the person is home and not ill is a most painful and insulting experience. That is the reason why society agrees upon the convention or fiction that one is 'not at home.' The recipient of the visit acts 'as if' he were not at home.

"Another example from an entirely different field. Aunt Frieda has a charming little niece whom she would gladly see at the altar. To this end, she arranges a tea to which she invites a young man whom she met recently during a trip and who, at present, has just looked her up during a short stay in this city which is far from his home. She is convinced that both of them are quite suited to each other and even tells each of them so before they meet. And surely enough, after about a half year, the threads of affection have been spun between them. Amor has bound both hearts in the deepest of love. The engagement is to take place at Easter. 'We are both destined to have met each other from time immemorial. It is not chance, but some eternal fate which has brought us together,' etc., etc. This is the feeling of both the two young people and it can even become a religious belief with some. But it can also be a conscious form of self-deception, a purposeful auto-suggestion, a conscious fiction which pleases both parties.

"Ten years later. They have a little daughter who plays with her dolls. The eight-year-old child knows very well that the doll is made of leather, porcelain, saw-dust or some other filler. But, for the playing girl, the doll is something alive. The child speaks with the toy as if it were alive and had movements and sensations. All the play of children, e.g., the 'robber games' of boys, is based upon such fictions. It would be a gross mistake of education and upbringing to stand upon the form of adult logic and tear these children out of their 'conscious self-deception,' their clearly recognized day-dreams. Only a coarse pedant could ever commit such an error upon the temple of youth. The children would drive such a person away with the greatest of resentment.

"The couple of whom we speak also have a son. Another ten years later and he has entered the political arena. What does he find there? Our political life is based upon parties whose programs are biassed and one-sided structures. But despite this one-sidedness, they are necessary in just this form and must be so preserved at least for a time. The spiritual leaders of the divers parties often recognize this fact themselves, but they may nevertheless stand for such a platform as if they fully believed in its present form; and they may treat the program as if it were still full of its original meaning. It is also a fiction when each political party declares that it 'speaks the will of the people.' The will of the people is also a fiction which does not become more real by receiving the fashionable name of 'la volonté-général.' But this is nevertheless a necessary fiction in the affairs of state. Our lives are pervaded by such political fictions of more or less bad character. The most potent fiction of this kind in modern times is the notorious section of the Versailles Treaty which conceives Germany as the sole instigator of the war. A portentous fiction, indeed.

"One of the strangest fictions of our times in this respect is the so-called imprisonment of the pope. Everybody knows that the pope may and can leave the Vatican at any time that he chooses; that no one would hinder him from walking, riding or going wherever he pleased in the world. But the Roman church supports the fiction as if he were a prisoner. He may not leave the Vatican, i.e., the gardens of the Vatican, even in the hottest months of the year; nor may he visit the cool and pleasant palaces of former popes in the hills. The entire Catholic world lays down its life for this fiction.

"Like everything else in life, the fictions may also be abused, but this is covered by the old proverb: *abusus non tollit usum:* misuse is no ground for rejection of a usage.

"A justifiable use of fictitious attitudes is universally common to religion. The language of our religions and our clerics is full of pictorial allusions the greater or lesser accuracy of which is more or less conscious in the minds of those who exploit them. In France, there once developed, on the basis of Kant, the Protestant sect of 'Simbolo-Fideis.' That was a school founded by Sabatier which made use of symbolical or pictorial elements in their belief. The same is true of the 'modernistic' element of the Catholic church founded by Le Roy, who was preceded to a great extent by Renan. They all openly acclaimed these fictitious usages and thus recognized the mystical element in religion."

What a wonderful example was here chosen in the child playing with the doll! The fetishist first conceives his fetish as a sexual plaything. He creates the fiction and then plays with it so long that he no longer is able to recognize the fetish as a toy. He is an actor who stages a comedy for himself. It is thus really erroneous to speak of fetishism as "erotic symbolism." It is just a simple form of symbolism. It is an "erotic fiction" in which logic is misapplied to further the fiction. Logic becomes the slave of passion. The irrational commits a rape upon the rational. The fetishist rationalizes his fiction until he has made it compatible with logic. He even knows how to think up motives which are far removed from reality simply because he will not see the true motives at hand. We are concerned in these cases with a state of not wanting to see, and it would be a gross mistake to assume that these patients cannot see.

The fetishist achieves this "apperceptive insufficiency" because he is able to work himself into a sort of trance. The ecstasy of this state is achieved by virtue of a stasis of affect which is then suddenly released. In the early stages of the fetishism, the fetish lover doubtless lived in two separate worlds. He was able to differentiate between the world of dreams and the realm of reality. But as soon as the phantasies began to over-run the world of reality, the dreamily playing child is transformed into a full-blown fetishist. The fetish lover is an eternal child; he holds fast to his infancy and preserves the dream-world of childhood. The psycho-sexual infantilism of the fetishist represents the dream world of the normal child.

Indeed, all these cases of fetishism can be understood only if we remember that the fetish lover lives in a world of phantasy in which the borders between reality and the dream have become very hazy. They are all day-dreamers. The little of their system which they permit to trickle into consciousness is but an infinitesimal part of their constructions. Their phantasies stand in abrupt contrast to their waking life. But that is precisely the great danger which besets them. It incapacitates them for the burdens of the real world, they are incapable of real work, they withdraw all interest and attention from their business and sink more and more into the morass of their dreams. Their system is to be compared with a neoplasm; at first unseeming and small, it spreads and grows until it has supplanted healthy tissues and endangered the life of the organism. The comparison goes even further: we have been able to show that in this case, too, we are dealing with "embryonal cells," the infantile cells of the mind—infantile strivings which displace the individuals from the present. The impulse to revive the old is what drives these people to their impulsive acts.

All children manifest rudimentary forms of fetishism and a tendency to systematized structures of the mind. The fictions are their very own inventions and they cling to them obstinately against all outside influences. The system is a secret which loses all its piquancy once it is revealed. The child symbolizes and lives in a fictitious world of phantasy. The child still possesses the wonderful capacity of drinking from the primitive fountain of poesy. It is a poet blessed by God. The fetishist, too, has preserved a part of his childhood and has retained as an adult the system he formed in childhood.

The uninitiated can hardly conceive the efforts which go into the formation of such a system. A most intense creative energy is necessary to the construction of such systems; a wealth of phantasy is needed to live in such a world and still influence the unbending nature of reality. But that is possible only by means of a persistent annulment. The fiction can be preserved only at the cost of a complete destruction of the forces of reality. That is why this parapathic constantly transforms the meaning of all values; he simply rejects or annuls everything which does not fit into his system. He effaces time and space, refuses to recognize the majesty of death or the limits of the possible. Everything is possible and even the death of a beloved object does not hinder him from exploiting the experience in the interests of his system. It is not improbable that every fetishist is a lost poet. If he had but the gift of sublimation and the outward projection of his conflicts, he could save himself from the bonds of his paraphilia. But he does not project; on the contrary, he introjects, as Ferenczi acutely put it. He exploits the outside world in augmenting his system, whereas the poet or creative writer uses his system for the enrichment of the world. With every piece of creative effort, the poet rids himself of one more complex, whereas the fetishist makes use of every external impression to increase the extent or scope of his psychic structure.

But a creative spirit is necessary even in the construction of a fetishism. I believe that this is one of the reasons why there are so few women among fetishists. They do not manifest this phantastic and intuitive constitution. In his own way, the fetishist is a symbolistic genius. I have not personally analyzed a case of female fetishism and the case which Binswanger so exhaustively studied is an exception. It is possible that the reasons may be found in the fact that women lack the rich creative capacity of men. But there is, of course, another circumstance to be considered. For a long time I was struck by the fact that, with one exception, all the fetishists whom I studied were Christians. My material otherwise regularly shows about thirty to thirty-five percent Jews who make up a large proportion of parapathics. The only fetishistic Jew whom I analyzed was not circumcised and manifested a distinct tendency towards the Christian religion. These facts may well be related to the presence of the Christ neurosis in these cases. We have already observed the importance of the patient's identification with Christ in the psychopathology of fetishism. Women and Jews achieve such an identification only with difficulty. But there is even another factor to be considered: the identification of the parapathic with his phallus.

Strangely enough, most of my patients suffered from a more or less marked phimosis and every one of them had been an enuretic. Hitschmann has already called attention to the relationship between urine erotism and compulsion neurosis.[4] The circumscription of the penis by the tightened prepuce and, furthermore, the compulsive attitude which these enuretics had to take towards their bladders, may well have been the bases for the development of the fetishistic compulsion itself.

It seems to me that the compulsions which the child exerts upon the rectum, with its sources of pleasure in the retention of feces, are also a predisposing factor in the development of fetishism. These cases reveal a curious form of conversion: the organ sensations are translated into psychic mechanisms. It is just the reverse of the conversions which Freud first described. The conversion of mental mechanisms in organic symptoms leads to an organic form of expression of the soul which is already well known to us. They were especially treated in Volume I of this series. But in fetishism we meet with a transposition of organ sensations and compulsions into the language of psychic compulsions and obsessions; a phenomenon which I choose to term the "phenomenon of psychic superstructure."

An excellent example is to be found in the case of the phimosis. The child must certainly feel the tightening of the penis as a result of the phimosis as a pleasurable sensation. The rubbing of the foreskin over the sulcus coronarius wakens sensations and creates irritation which demand repetition. In addition to this, we must not forget that most men identify themselves with their genitals. There must also be added the factor of memories of the blessed time when one was well swaddled in diapers. In dreams, the genital is symbolized as a child. The phallus (the little one) represents infancy. Other thoughts and images are then grouped about this nucleus. The compulsions which are exerted by the organs on the bladder and the rectum become the symbol of upbringing and obsessions altogether. In earliest infancy, the child doubtless capitulated to the impulse and released the pleasure of retention by defecating or micturating. But our analyses show us that these functions were originally very pleasurable. It is only under the stress of education and punishment that the child can be brought to control itself and defecate or urinate only at certain times. Education begins with the first compulsion in this direction, the first demand to control the eliminative functions. It is the first compulsive influence from without. The psychic compulsions which the fetishist then develops are reflections of these organic ones. For immediately following the struggle over the child's unbridled indulgence in the eliminations and excretions, the battle over its sexuality begins. The parents note that the child strives to gratify itself in onanistic (autoerotic) manipulations, and they strive to repress them. The first struggle against onanism usually ends with a victory for the parents or educators. But we have seen that all true fetishists are true onanists. They revenge themselves for this first violation by a later persistence in their earlier habits.

The question now arises as to whether the individual feels his sexual instinct as a compulsion or not. We must answer it in the affirmative. This obsession then allies itself with the others, and is not the least important. We have observed how bitterly the fetishist struggles against his own sexuality. His system is a compromise, the net result of this very struggle. His basic tendency is an autoerotic one. He thus becomes progressively asocial, retreats more and more from his partner, experiences his sexual orgies in his distorted phantasy and becomes increasingly more introverted. His asceticism is manifested in his flight from the partner. To the male fetishist, the woman is a symbol of sin and depravity, whereas onanism is stubbornly preserved as a form of atonement and expiation, but also as a means of self-punishment and pleasure. Nearly all of these patients believe in the deleterious effects of onanism and yet they persist in the practice, perhaps just for this reason. They place themselves consciously under the influence of a compulsion which insures, however, that they must avoid coitus. The system is then extended as an expression of resistance to society. It is the patient's own creation which triumphs over society.

Even religion is conceived as something foreign, obsessive, coercive. That is why they throw the conventional religions overboard and create a religion of their own which gives their own sexual expression plenty of elbow room. But the antitheses rub against each other here just as in every other form of compromise. But these are closely bound and unified. That is why we must not be astonished to find the paraphilia and religion occupying the same mind, being expressed in a single symptom. Fetishism unites heaven and hell, the high and the low, the past and the future, but it also indicates the regression and the progression, the final tendency of asceticism and the neglect of the present as well as all teleological trends.

In this sense, the fetishism is a curative tendency. Indeed, for the patient it signifies a protection against their own sadistic trends. It is pleasure and pain in one. They all feel themselves to be the martyrs of their own instincts. They seem to sacrifice as much as they enjoy. The symbol of their martyrdom is Christ who saved the souls of men through his own death. I am, however, convinced that still other identifications with the martyrs occur in such cases. That shows us how potent the guilt feelings of these patients are. We have already emphasized the relations between sadism and fetishism in this book. The cruelty which was originally projected outwards is later turned upon the individual's own personality.

The recognition of this aggressiveness, the introspective knowledge of his own inimical attitudes towards society, the fact of his asocial-autistic tendency leads the parapathic to the formation of his guilt consciousness as the most biting expression of his conscience. Primitive man had no conscience. He knew no other guilt but that towards himself. It was only after the formation of social units that conscience arose as a measure of social protection. Conscience was originally anti-conscience—a knowledge of the imperatives of the external world which are directed against our striving for pleasure. The guardians of the law which protect society against the individual were originally individuals. The king or chief was also the judge and executioner. Since, however, the chief could not have a knowledge of all transgressions, he had to have help in his name. The law is directed against all asocial tendencies. A second, a higher judge, was erected: divinity. God is omnipotent and all-seeing. There is no hiding and no fleeing from His justice. The fact that asocial creatures might easily delight in the oversight of their transgressions, necessarily led to the concept of an even-handed justice in the Beyond. This heavenly justice could then punish the earthly transgressions which had led to pleasure and had been overlooked.

The fetish lover fears the punishment of God and bends himself in humiliation before His commands. But he himself becomes a god. He punishes himself and thus saves his soul. He creates a hell on earth for himself in order that he may be sure of a place in heaven. He creates his own heaven of pleasure by suffering the tortures of hell while alive.

The conflicts of the fetishist represent the conflicts of every civilized man; the difference being that they are very much magnified, caricatured and distorted by condensation and displacement. His religiousness is infantile in character. It is anchored in his feelings, hammered in by the impressions of early childhood and indestructibly fixed for life. Intellectually, the fetishist lives beyond the pale of his own faith. He cannot understand his beliefs; he can only feel them. His intellect is ashamed of them, and he is thus forced to hide them from himself and play the part of the freethinker. He acts towards God as towards his own father. Most of these patients seem to have overcome the influence of their fathers, but they nevertheless cling to them. Our case 69 was an instructive example. Behind the hatred of the father, or the indifference towards him or the depreciation and derogation of the father, there lurks the infantile over-estimation of the man, the pride in him, the rivalry with him, the envy of him which the Freudian school has so well delineated for us. Father, teacher, God, the higher-ups and society all run together in one single complex: the complex of authority. The fetishist is an anarchist and yet a slave of society and social custom. As I have repeatedly emphasized, there is room for all antitheses in his system.

The fetishist is thus a distorted reflection of our ailing times which vacillate between faith and faithlessness, between the past and the future. He is the sacrificial lamb of education which creates religious foundations in our youth that only live to be destroyed. The education to a fear of God leads to this most curious of all the masks of religion.

We have placed our hand upon a festering wound. Long ago the friends of man recognized that we sorely need a reformation of our religious education; and they attempted to solve this problem by the introduction of free schools. But the question is: shall we educate our children without any religious teaching whatever or shall we rather inculcate in them a general religious background which supplants the fear of God by the love of God?

The chief feature of our education to-day is that it is an education under anxiety. Fetishism is a self-protective measure against this anxiety. As long as the fiction of a hell and a punishment in the Beyond of an almighty judge in heaven are supported, we can hardly hope for a general alleviation of these paraphilias. The world does not yet seem to be ready for a replacement of the religion of fear by the religion of love. That is, to love the good because of a pleasure in the good and not because of a business arrangement whereby one receives a special reward in heaven. If we could educate our young to the religion of Ethos, we would certainly be able to prevent the development of most fetishistic cases. But such an education to-day is an utopia. Agreed that we had a whole mass of free schools, what does their number mean in the face of the power of the church which shall undoubtedly preserve its mighty power for a long, long time? I believe that the sudden recall of the religion of fear would lead to a catastrophe in which the aboriginal and primitive animal nature of man would go wilder than during the World War of unhappy memory. It will be many thousands of years before the bulwarks of anxiety have been replaced by the solid pillars of human affection. It is even questionable whether mankind will ever achieve this goal, despite the fact that it strives to attain it by means of all kinds of roundabout routes.

The prophylaxis of fetishism can be carried out only within the family. In the previous volumes of this series we have sufficiently outlined how such a free upbringing may be executed. In this book, I wish only to stress the fact that the chief duty of all educators is to plant the love of Ethos in the hearts of all children, but without enslaving the young by feelings of anxiety. I have sufficiently shown how the false notion of sexual intercourse as an hereditary sin may be one of the motives in the development of a fetishism. Sexuality must again be enthroned as a natural, human event in the realm of biology. That can be ensured only by an open and properly gauged enlightenment of the child, but even more by an avoidance of gross mistakes in upbringing. But the road from our present moral hypocrisy to the rehabilitation of normal sex life is a long and winding one.

Looking over the panorama of our present day social conditions, we must confess that we are witnessing a struggle between Clericalism and Socialism, the sharpness of which was hardly suggested before the war. The two parties often barely hold each other at bay and then again they may alternate in their leadership. But which party will become the final conqueror?

The metaphysical needs of the individual and the broad masses are considerably under-estimated. We have not yet witnessed the creation of a religion of Socialism. Perhaps every religion begins as a religion of Socialism and ends by serving Conservatism and Capitalism. Christianity began in this way. There was a time when it was preached that a camel could sooner pass through the eye of a needle than that a wealthy man might enter heaven. Has this axiom prevented men from seeking wealth and becoming rich? And does not the church rest upon the broad backs of the poor to-day as well as upon the arms of the rich? And does it not protect the wealthy against the suspicions of the poor? It is easy to see why Communism looks upon Socialism with a suspicious eye and considers it as an even more insidious enemy than the bourgeois himself. And yet Christian teaching, like its Hebrew forerunner, was originally a Communistic one. Shall we witness a repetition of history and the actual decline of the West?

Fetishism is a social disease. But since the struggle between the freethinkers and the faithful believers will doubtless become more acute with the passing years, it is probable that the number of fetishists will increase generally. Every man is free to build a little chapel at home for his prayers if he feels that he will be scoffed at or scorned on the way to church. Fetishists are seekers of God. They approach God by dark

and devious routes.  As in a dream, they wander among the
depths and the depravities of life.  But, for themselves, they
have found God.  He also gives them the love which they
desire.  In its bipolar tendencies every one of their onanistic
acts is at once a sacrilege and a prayer.  They possess the faith
of primitives and children, the belief which permits them to
beat their God when he scorns their wishes.

Cure can be effected in two ways.  The fetishist recognizes
the deeply religious foundations of his condition and replaces
this mock-religion by a more instinctive and adjusted one.  He
forms a compromise between his infantile faith and his present
philosophy of life.  Or, he may try to overcome the infantile
religion and arrive at agnosticism or atheism.  But I openly
confess that I have never been able to observe a fetishist take
the latter path, although an agnostic, reserved, observing attitude often takes place.

In all these cases we have been able to note the presence of
a tremendous ambition, a pathological will to power which
found its cardinal expression in their Christ neurosis.  But
always, we were able to disclose the presence of infantile, sexual
roots; in a word, the Freudian mechanisms.  The cure of the
fetishist demands his inner separation from his family, the conquest of his psycho-sexual infantilism and the rejection of the
fixed idea which may be expressed in the formula: "If I may
not achieve my secret sexual goal, I refuse to be satisfied with
any other form of sexuality."  By this I mean the satisfaction
gained in the object.  The dangers of masturbation may be
read in this obstinate retention of the fixed notion, the original
phantasy.  The physical detriments of masturbation are about
zero.  But the psychic detriments in these cases are very extensive.  Every onanistic act re-opens the old wound, the
primal scene of Freud.  It is the nail which fixes the man to
the cross of his paraphilia.  If the fetishist has been able to
give up his autoerotic habits and has taken to alloerotic gratification, then we can speak of a practical cure.  But I have
seen many cases which manifested another type of conduct.
The fetishist may marry and indulge in alloerotic gratification
and yet persist in his onanistic habits with the aid of the fetish.
These are the men who are in danger of a relapse at any time.

Especially if the marriage becomes incompatible, a situation which is easily constructed in view of the man's incomplete cure. Psychoanalysis alone is in a position to break up the infantile fixations of the patient, his distorted sexual guiding principles; it alone can help him to return to the habits of normal gratification.

But the patient answers the physician's attempts in this direction with obstinate resistances. He does not want to give up his infantile sources of pleasure. He has, after all, built up his system in open resistance to all authority, especially against his father. It is the eternal admonition that his educators intruded upon his sex life and either made his pleasures hard or bitter for him.

This hate now turns against the analyst whom he begs for cure although he fears it. The analyst becomes a representative of the father who intruded upon the patient's secret sex life. It takes considerable technical skill to steer through the rapids of this torrent of emotion. The patient must be told again and again that he is resisting the accomplishment of his cure, that he scoffs at and scorns the physician and wants to triumph over him just as he triumphed over every other authority with his system. The patient must learn just how he has made himself socially impossible. He must learn the meaning of that simple but, to him, inexplicable truth: *Tua res agitur.*

The physician has a great aid in the fact that the communication of the fetishist's phantasies promptly deflates their value. Ridiculous situations or ridicule itself kills. And all these fetishistic nuances have something ridiculous about them. If the patient has come to criticize his own phantasies during the ventilation of them; if he not only understands, but also feels the foolishness of his phantasies, then he is able to withstand the power of the emotional deluge created by his fetishistic phantasies.

We must not overlook the forensic side of this question. In many cases in the text, we have shown how the neglected act leads to substitutive conduct. These men are subject to the power of irresistible impulses. They easily become kleptomaniacs or exhibitionists, and the question of punishment or exculpation is not easy to decide. If we should demand acquittal for all these men on the grounds of transient loss of responsible knowledge or the presence of an irresistible impulse, without afterwards considering the patient's condition further, the number of such transgressions would certainly increase. The fear of punishment keeps many of them from capitulating to their impulses.

But we can demand this: Every one of these men should be turned over to an analyst for treatment after a preliminary examination. If the analysis reveals the presence of a genuine fetishism, then, instead of having the man spend time in a cell or an asylum at the expense of the state, let him be treated at the expense of the state. Case 59 by Petersen shows that such patients can be cured without an analysis if the shock of legal proceedings is strong enough to mobilize all the defense mechanism of the personality. But how much more potent would it be to have the man undergo an analysis which would reveal many other more important motives and fixations behind the so-called primal experience—motives which resist cure until they become conscious.

The forensic psychiatrist of the future will be a psychiatrist and analyst in one. Indeed, the time is not far off when psychoanalysis will be an integral part of psychiatry. That is why I close all my works with the one demand: Sexology and psychoanalysis must become an integral feature of the curriculum in every medical school; or, at least, it must become a distinct part of the obligatory post-graduate courses for all physicians.

# NOTES TO VOLUME TWO

## CHAPTER XII

¹ Note the contradiction. He had said at first that he began at fourteen. Many parapathics disclose this tendency to falsify their anamnesis.

² He calls his aunt's husband his brother-in-law.

³ See my paper on the neurotic as actor, l.c.

⁴ Later we shall find another motive for this attitude: he also wanted to be a brother-in-law.

⁵ Cf. *Impotence in the Male,* the chapter on "Ejaculatio Præcox."

⁶ This statement was found at the end of the analysis to be false.

⁷ These occurrences are, unfortunately, not so seldom among our lower classes and even in the "best circles" I have been able to find such misdeeds on the part of mothers.

⁸ I often see little children in picture galleries. I once saw an English father explaining the horrors of the infanticide of Bethlehem to his three-year-old son. Other children like to satisfy their peeping instincts there. The sadistic elements are also stilled.

⁹ See *Die Träume der Dichter* (The Dreams of the Poets); Chapter I on "Der tiefe Brunnen" (the deep well).

¹⁰ *Drei Abhandlungen zur Sexualtheorie,* p. 21, footnote, 4 ed.

¹¹ " Ein Kind wird geschlagen," in the *Sammlung kleiner Schriften z. Neurosenlehre.* Five series, p. 198.

## CHAPTER XIII

¹ *Jahrbuch f. psychoanalytische und psychopathologische Forschungen,* Vol. III, 1911.

² The direct excerpts from the analysis will be found hereafter in small print.

³ Later, Gerda said: "When I think of a birth, I get weaker down below, as if my bottom didn't belong to me."

⁴ "When the foot is lifted, one sees the *crack* (between the sole and the loose heel). It doesn't bother me while standing, but when the person walks, it's unbearable. Lifting the foot is the worst part, then one can see that something is wrong. It's all open." In short, she is not only afraid of heels, she is impelled to look at them.

⁵ Cf., the heel phobia.

⁶ The only other factors which indicate her original delight in defecation, etc., are the statement that she liked especially to sit on father's large pot, and a dream in which she was suddenly surprised by her father while she was defecating. The patient manifests a marked exhibitionistic instinct, whereas her peeping instinct is very much repressed. The latter reappears, however, in her impulse always to look at people's heels and feet.

⁷ I can warmly recommend Binswanger's original paper to every analyst.

⁸ Cf., later the transformation of her mother complex.

⁹ She had once dirtied the bed at night.

¹⁰ We recall that Gerda had another younger brother, Albert. She was two when he was born. Just how much she still remembered of that birth and then reactivated at the time Max was born is hard to say. It seemed as

if he had always been here, the inseparable and always preferred escort of his sister.

[11] Another time she used the expression "take in."

[12] Her usual expression for navel.

[13] It must be stated that Gerda wanted to appear as slender as possible, clothed herself tightly, etc. She liked to feel her intestines full only at times; then she would feel: "Now it'll go through, it'll push its way out." She would then eat with an appetite inexplicable to herself.

[14] As small as a "little doll."

[15] Patent onanistic phantasy with strikingly "male" tendency.

[16] Gerda had often begged her mother to present her with twins, and when this wish was not fulfilled, she blamed only her mother's unwillingness and was angry with her.

[17] The heel and the shoe as infanticidal instruments.

[18] When Gerda realized that this was the point, she felt much freer, "felt joy in her soul," as she put it, and cried out: "Now we have it!"

[19] This is doubtless an expression of "female" shoe symbolism.

[20] As we have already learned, Gerda had once fainted in a strange shoe shop. She explained that at that time she felt as if she had renounced something, committed an injustice. We must also remember that Gerda had fainted just as the salesgirl was opening the shoe and widening it, so that Gerda might more comfortably step into it.

[21] This expression recalls the cutting of a shoe into swollen feet (see above), and the experience in which the skate clamp cut into the heel.

[22] The symbolic use of shoe for something old is illustrative.

[23] I.e., birth.

[24] This expression shows that we were not dealing with newly created material, but that the patient was divulging infantile material which had never really been forgotten. It was nevertheless necessary to go to the pains described in the monograph in order to bring all that to light. Once this has occurred, the patients believe they "have known it all the time," and seem to depreciate the value and effects of the analysis.

[25] The constipation which she still has must be looked upon as a consequence of this long-standing habit.

[26] Nor shall I go into the means by which we achieved this knowledge (operations, pregnancy, her own pregnancy, etc.).

[27] Freud, Analyse Eines 5 Jährigen Knaben; and Jung, Ueber Konflikte der Kindlichen Seele. Jahrb. f. psychoanalyt. und. psychopathol. Forsch, Vol. II, p. 33 ff.

[28] Dr. Binswanger communicated the following to me regarding her further destiny: "I have not seen Gerda since the analysis and have heard but seldom from her directly. In the beginning, I corresponded with her husband, who sent me good reports. Then I didn't hear about her for a long time until I learned indirectly that she had had a relapse. I learned the reasons only later. Her husband disappointed her severely, squandered her money, and appears to have turned out to be a very inferior person. They were divorced after about four or five years of married life. Both the children and the mother are again living with Gerda's mother. I can't say whether she desisted from writing me because of unanalyzed inhibitions (her entire attitude towards the male sex remained, unfortunately, unanalyzed) or because of her pride which prevented her from communicating to me her disappointment and unhappiness. Both reasons are probably valid."

## CHAPTER XIV

[1] Incorrect. Patient is greatly stigmatized in the direct maternal line. He also states now that he was born in 1889 whereas before he said 1890.

## CHAPTER XV

[1] By bodily contact the patient means the simple contact of the two naked bodies. That was the limit of his sexual activity and beyond that he never attempted to pass.

[2] I confess that I wrote on some old and poor quality paper which carried the letter head of my American monthly "Psyche and Eros."

[3] This is incorrect, as we shall see later on. Formerly he used to include various female pictures in his collections.

[4] This change is important and shows us that on occasion the boys may also represent girls.

[5] Such a prophecy is a good means of preventing the patient from leaving. They remain out of obstinacy. Some patients even arrange to run out of money and then want to borrow from the analyst.

[6] One can frequently observe that people find difficulty in parting with parts of their own body. I know patients who have looked longingly at their excised appendix and then wanted to keep it (Cf., also the bottling of gall stones). This is an expression of narcissistic love of one's own body. Pertinent remarks on this subject may be found in Schilder, "Ueber eine Psychose nach Staroperation (Psychosis following cataract operation), Int. Zeitschr. f. Psychoanalyse, Vol. VIII, No. 1, 1922. Leonhard Frank's book, *Der Mensch ist gut* (Man is good) also describes in moving terms how difficult it is for wounded soldiers to part with their amputated limbs.

[7] The bipolar tendency of these rescue phantasies (rescuing and killing) is discussed in the Int. Zeitschr. f. Psychoanalyse, Vol. VIII, 1922, by Abraham: "Vaterrettung und Vatermord in den neurotischen Phantasiegebilden" (Father rescue and patricide in neurotic phantasy).

[8] He had tried to smoke a pipe which I had given him. Fellatio phantasy!

[9] This whole scene took place on an outing into the Wachau (the valley of the Danube above Vienna.—Trans.).

[10] There was no talk of this in reality. I always avoid such demonstrations of emotion. But the patient thus expresses the wish to have satisfied the analyst by these disclosures.

[11] Otto was too much under the influence of the analysis to be a reliable guide for prognosis.

[12] Dr. Missriegler suspects this to be a memory of a menstrual cloth, but there was no relevant material. One might consider the bandage as a *custos virginitatis*, however.

## CHAPTER XVI

[1] This analysis was carried out under my direction and with my aid. I would like to emphasize, however, that my aid consisted only in helping to deepen the dream analyses and in formulating the conclusions.—Dr. Stekel.

[2] The measurements were done according to the system of Dr. Arthur Weil. Geschlechtstrieb und Körperform (Sexuality and Physique). Supplement to Vol. VIII, No. 5, 1921, of the Zeitschr. f. Sexualwissenschaft, edited by Dr. Max Marcuse. Verlag A. Marcus and E. Webers, Berlin and Bonn.

### TABLE I

| Shoulder breadth [1] | Hip breadth [2] | Pelvic breadth [3] | Height [4] | Arm length [5] | Trunk length [6] | Limb length [7] |
|---|---|---|---|---|---|---|
| 36 | 40 | 37 | 162 | 69 | 77 | 85 |

# SEXUAL ABERRATIONS

## TABLE II

| Sexual Proportions | | | Asexual Proportion |
|---|---|---|---|
| Shoulder: Pelvis | Shoulder: Hips | Trunk: Limbs | Height: Arm Length |
| 103 (94, 97) [8] | 111 (82, 86) | 110.4 (106, 91) | 42.5 (44, 44) |

[1] Distance between both processus coracoidei.
[2] Distance between both trochanters.
[3] Distance between both spinæ iliacæ anteriores superiores.
[4] Distance from vertex to the floor.
[5] Distance between proc. coracoideus and the tip of the middle finger.
[6] Distance from vertex to the coccyx.
[7] Distance from the coccyx to the floor.
[8] The figures in parentheses are taken from Dr. Weil's paper (l.c.). The first of his figures refers to homosexual women of his observation and the second to the heterosexual women. As can be seen from the above figures in our case, the relationship between shoulder-pelvis and shoulder-hips is markedly displaced towards the pelvis-hip side of the comparison which denotes a distinct heterosexual trend. The woman's asthenic thorax is, of course, considerably at fault for these figures. But the proportion between trunk-limbs and the asexual proportions are almost typical in this respect.

[3] The following pages contain an abridged statement of the patient's own information as collected in the succeeding sessions. This will give the reader an idea of what may be expected of the information received from parapathics before the transference has been fully established. Those who are not analysts usually fall into the traps laid in the initial information of patients. The statements followed by an asterisk (*) in the text are not true in fact and were later corrected by the patient herself. Those declarations followed by a cross (+) are correct. The former are due to the patient's usually unconscious tendency to distort (gain through illness). This circumstance alone gives one an indication of the difficulties met with in analysis. And this despite the fact that the patient had no desire to be cured. The material, also, was collected by sessions; and although this necessitates a lack of unity, it gives us the advantage of plasticity.

[4] The patient's appearance is, indeed, striking. Upon a bobbed head with parted hair there sits a man's soft felt hat. A raincoat reaches nearly to the ankles and makes it questionable as to whether trousers or a skirt may be found beneath it. But she wears a skirt, the only female attribute on her person. Over a blouse or shirt, she wears a man's vest, a starched collar, tie and starched cuffs. All the rest is men's clothing: shoes, pocket-knife, cigarette lighter, cigarette case, etc.

[5] She means Mrs. Justine (see first session).

[6] My remarks are in brackets, hers in parentheses.

[7] Her associations on "red" are interesting: blood—operation—surgeon—steer—bull fight—toreador.

[8] Origin of the fellatio phantasy.

[9] Cf., also: Holy Mary.

[10] She is a faithful sacristan of *her* own church.

[11] Cf., dream 10. The patient's willingness to give us her photos is doubtless also due to her desire to show the world and posterity (especially her mother) her martyrdom.

[12] While this book was in the press, we received information from the patient to the effect that her request of the police department had been satisfactorily passed upon and that she was already indulging her transvestitism to the full.

[13] My assistant found these mechanisms without knowledge of Adler's theory.

[14] The patient was said to have resembled the deceased son of Mrs. Justine very much; so that the relationship seems to have been sexually determined from that side as well.

[15] It is of interest to learn that she wore a marriage ring on her hand. She claimed that she had bought it because it had appealed to her.

[16] Die Transvestiten, eine Untersuchung über den erotischen Verkleidungstrieb. Verlag Max Spohr, Leipzig. Here are explained Hirschfeld's four stages of intermediate sex: Hermaphrodites (I degree); Androgynes (II degree); Uranians (III degree); Transvestites (IV degree).

[17] Stekel, Vol. II.

[18] l.c., p. 167.

[19] According to Krafft-Ebing, sadism is "an increase in male psycho-sexual characteristics" (cited after Hirschfeld, l.c.).

[20] l.c., p. 7.

[21] Cited after Hirschfeld, l.c., p. 246.

[22] Italics mine.

[23] l.c., p. 59.

[24] Sister imago. Italics mine. Principal for father.

[25] Day-dreams, the typical symptom of parapathia and split-personality.

[26] Italics mine. We can see in this a harem-like construction. Plurality takes the place of the forbidden unity.

[27] Manifest sister imago.

[28] Italics mine. Identification with the unattainable sexual object.

[29] l.c., p. 61.

[30] A narcissistic feature. The breast, shoulders and arms have a partialistic significance for him. Cf., above the chapter on partialism. Note also the sado-masochistic significance of the transvestiture in this case.

[31] l.c., p. 55.

[32] l.c., p. 67.

[33] l.c., p. 203.

## CHAPTER XVII

[1] And the affect intended for these persons is also transferred to the object.

[2] Cf., also Schopenhauer, Vol. I, pp. 316 and 321.

[3] See *Die Zeichen des Tempels* (The Signs of the Temple). His other papers striving towards a deeper psychological understanding of the symbol are: *Probleme der Mystik und Ihrer Symbolik* (Problems of Mysticism and Its Symbols). *Durch Tod zum Leben* (Through Death to Life), Leipsic, 1915. The essay entitled *Phantasie und Mythos* (Phantasy and Mythology) and the studies on symbol formation which have been continued in the Freud-Bleuler Jahrbuch für Psychoanalyse.

[4] "Urethralerotik und Zwangsneurose," *Int. Zeitschr. f. Psychoanalyse*, Vol. VI, p. 263, 1920. Hitschmann postulates an "urethral character" whose chief features are "burning ambition" and a preference for work dealing with water. The burning ambition may be looked upon as a trait of every parapathic, whereas dealing with water is doubtless present in enuretics but is rather a sign of psychosexual infantilism. Hitschmann's paper only points out the coincidence of compulsion neurosis and anal as well as urethral erotism.